**Applied Mathematical
Demography**

Applied Mathematical Demography

NATHAN KEYFITZ
Andelot Professor
of Sociology and Demography
Harvard University

A WILEY-INTERSCIENCE PUBLICATION

JOHN WILEY & SONS, New York ● London ● Sydney ● Toronto

Copyright © 1977 by John Wiley & Sons, Inc.

All rights reserved. Published simultaneously in Canada.

No part of this book may be reproduced by any means, nor transmitted, nor translated into a machine language without the written permission of the publisher.

Library of Congress Cataloging in Publication Data:

Keyfitz, Nathan, 1913-

    Applied mathematical demography.
    "A Wiley-Interscience publication."
    Bibliography: p.
    Includes index.
    1. Demography. 1. Title.
HB881.K473   301.32′01′51   77-1360
ISBN 0-471-47350-2

Printed in the United States of America

10 9 8 7 6 5 4 3 2 1

To the students at Chicago, Berkeley, and Harvard
who are responsible for any merit this book may have

PREFACE

This book is concerned with commonsense questions about, for instance, the effect of a lowered death rate on the proportion of old people or the effect of abortions on the birth rate. The answers that it reaches are not always commonsense, and we will meet instances in which intuition has to be adjusted to accord with what the mathematics shows to be the case. Even when the intuitive answer gives the right direction of an effect, technical analysis is still needed to estimate its amount. We may see intuitively that the drop from an increasing to a stationary population will slow the promotion for the average person in a factory or office, but nothing short of an integral equation can show that each drop of 1 percent in the rate of increase will delay promotion to middle-level positions by 2.3 years.

The aim has been to find answers that will be serviceable to those working on population and related matters, whether or not they care to go deeply into the mathematics behind the answers. My earlier book, *Introduction to the Mathematics of Population*, had the opposite purpose of developing the theory, and mentioned applications mostly to illuminate the theory. Because of their different objectives there is virtually no overlap between the two books.

Population theory has developed at a sufficiently fast rate and in enough directions that no book of reasonable size can include all of its applications. A full development of theory ought to recognize not only age-specific rates of birth and death but also two sexes and two or more species. Age-specific rates can vary through time, and the theory can be stochastic in allowing to each individual member of the population his own separate risk, or deterministic in supposing that whatever probability applies to each individual is also the fraction of the population that succumbs to the risk. Thus population theory can be classified into the 16 categories shown in the accompanying table. By far the largest part of what is taken up in this book falls into the upper left category: it deals with one sex, usually female, and one species, man; it takes the age-specific rates of birth and death as fixed through time; it is deterministic rather than stochastic. This upper left-hand cell is conceptually the simplest of the 16, and it is mathematically the most tractable. But are these decisive arguments for its emphasis, given that real populations include two sexes; human populations interact with other species; birth and death rates change through time; and all life is stochastic?

Classification of population theory

	Fixed rate		Changing rate	
	Deterministic	Stochastic	Deterministic	Stochastic
One sex				
One species	*			
Two or more species				
Two sexes				
One species				
Two or more species				

The art of theory construction is to start with simple assumptions and then to introduce greater realism, which means more complexity, as required. On the path from simplicity to realism one must stop at a compromise point. My taste may not always be that of my readers; they may often say that a particular model I use is too simple, that they need to take into account factors that I neglect. This line of criticism is welcome, even though it leads to further and more difficult mathematics.

During 10 or more years of work on this book I have incurred more obligations than I can acknowledge or even remember. Students pointed out errors and obscurities; they helped in some cases by conspicuously failing to understand what I was saying and compelling me to think the matter through afresh. Colleagues looked at drafts and were generous with comments. Editors and referees of journals were helpful, especially Paul Demeny. No one is responsible for errors that remain but me.

Among these colleagues, students and correspondents who have been a source of ideas and a means of correcting errors, I recall especially William Alonso, Barbara Anderson, Brian Arthur, John C. Barrett, Ansley J. Coale, William Cochrane, Joel E. Cohen, Prithwis Das Gupta, Paul Demeny, Lloyd Demetrius, James Dobbins, Barry Edmonston, Jamie Eng, Thomas Espenshade, Nora Federici, Griffith Feeney, Gustav Feichtinger, Jair

Fereira-Santos, James Frauenthal, A. G. Fredrickson, Robert Gardiner, Campbell Gibson, Noreen Goldman, Antonio Golini, David Goodman, Leo A. Goodman, Louis Henry, Jan Hoem, Barbara Keyfitz, S. Krishnamoorthy, Paul Kwong, Juan Carlos Lerda, John Lew, Gary Littman, Robert Lundy, James G. March, Robert Mare, George Masnick, John McDonald, David McFarland, Geoffrey McNicoll, Paul Meier, Jane Menken, Walter Meyer, George C. Myers, Frank Oechsli, Beresford Parlett, James Pick, Robert G. Potter, Jr., Samuel H. Preston, Thomas Pullum, Robert Retherford, Roger Revelle, Andrei Rogers, Norman Ryder, Paul Samuelson, Robert Sembiring, David P. Smith, Leroy O. Stone, Richard Stone, Michael Stoto, Michael Teitelbaum, Harold A. Thomas, Robert Traxler, James Trussell, Etienne Van de Walle, Kenneth Wachter, Frans Willekens and Harrison White, every one of whom has had some effect on the book. To be singled out especially for their help in the final stages are Noreen Goldman, David P. Smith, Gary Littman, S. Krishnamoorthy, and Michael Stoto, who read much of the manuscript and all of the page proof.

The most important acknowledgment is to my wife, who edited and typed the manuscript, some parts of it many times.

NATHAN KEYFITZ

Cambridge, Massachusetts
February 1977

NOTE. Conventions in the printing of this book include parentheses around references to equations when these are used independently of any descriptive term—"We see from (1.1.1) that..."—and omission of parentheses when the number is in apposition to such words as "equation," and "expression"—"Expression 1.1.1 is...."

ACKNOWLEDGMENTS

An early version of Section 1.3 appeared as "How many people have lived on the earth?" *Demography* **3**: 581–582 (1966).

Section 1.9 was published as "A general condition for stability in demographic processes," *Canadian Studies in Population* **1**: 29–35 (1974).

The life table method of Chapter 2 first appeared as "An improved life table method," *Biometrics* **31**: 889–899 (1975) (with James Frauenthal).

Much of Chapter 3 was included in "Mortality comparisons: The male-female ratio," *Genus* **31**: 1–34 (1975) (with Antonio Golini).

Section 4.8 is a condensed version of "Individual mobility in a stationary population," *Population Studies* **27**: 335–352 (1973).

Some of Section 6.5 appeared in "Migration as a means of population control," *Population Studies* **25**: 63–72 (1971).

Section 6.6 is an abridged version of "On the momentum of population growth," *Demography* **8**: 71–80 (1971).

Parts of Section 7.3 were published as "Age distribution and the stable equivalent," *demography* **6**: 261–269 (1969).

Some parts of Chapter 8, as well as Section 9.3, were included in "On future population," *Journal of the American Statistical Association* **67**: 347–363 (1972).

Section 9.5 is an abridged version of "Backward population projection by a generalized inverse," *Theoretical Population Biology* **6**: 135–142 (1974) (with T. N. E. Greville).

The substance of Sections 9.10 and 9.11 was included in "Population waves," in *Population Dynamics* (edited by T. N. E. Greville), Academic Press, 1972, pp. 1–38.

Parts of Chapter 10 are from "Family formation and the frequency of various kinship relationships," *Theoretical Population Biology* **5**: 1–27 (1974) (with Leo A. Goodman and Thomas W. Pullum), and "Addendum: Family formation and the frequency of various kinship relationships,"

Theoretical Population Biology **8**: 376–381 (1975) (with Leo A. Goodman and Thomas W. Pullum).

An early statement of Section 11.1 appeared as "How birth control affects births," *Social Biology* **18**: 109–121 (1971).

Chapter 12 is reprinted with some modifications from "How do we know the facts of demography?" *Population and Development Review* **1**: 267–288 (1975).

CONTENTS

Applied Mathematical
Demography

Chapter One

INTRODUCTION: POPULATION WITHOUT AGE

Age is the characteristic variable of population analysis; much of the theory of this volume will be concerned with the effect of age distribution, either fixed or changing. Abstraction is necessary in demographic as in other theory; is it possible to abstract even from age and still obtain results of value?

To represent a population as a number varying in time, and in disregard even of its age composition, is like treating the earth as a point in space—though too abstract for most purposes, it is useful for some. Partly as an introduction to the subsequent two-thirds of the book, the nine sections of this chapter take up questions to which answers can be obtained without reference to age.

These topics vary in depth and subtlety. The first deals only with the use of logarithms to base 2, that is, the number of doublings to go from one total to a larger total. Such logarithms show dramatically how close birth rates must have been to death rates throughout human history. Next comes an aspect of bisexual reproduction, and some of the difficulty it causes; consideration of one sex at a time is a powerful simplifying device for understanding demographic mechanisms. Another question concerns a population made up of a number of subpopulations, each increasing at a *fixed* rate; we will see at what *increasing* rate the total population is expanding. Attention will be given also to the migration problem, from which the one-sex population recognizing age will emerge as a special case; that a proposition concerning age follows directly from one on migration illustrates the advantage of a formal treatment.

1

Definitions of Rate of Increase

Population change is expressed in terms of *rate of increase*, a notion different in an important respect from the rate of speed of a physical object like an automobile. If a country stands at 1 million population at the beginning of the year, and at 1,020,000 at the end of the year, then by analogy with the automobile its rate would be 20,000 persons per year. To become a demographic rate this has to be divided by the population, say at the start of the year; the population is growing at a rate of 20,000/1,000,000 or 0.02 per year. More commonly it is said to be growing at 2 percent per year, or 20 per thousand initial population per year.

The two kinds of rate are readily distinguished in symbols. The analogue of the physical rate x' in terms of population at times t and $t+1$, P_t and P_{t+1}, is

$$x' = P_{t+1} - P_t \quad \text{or} \quad P_{t+1} = P_t + x',$$

while the demographic rate x is

$$x = \frac{P_{t+1} - P_t}{P_t} \quad \text{or} \quad P_{t+1} = P_t(1 + x).$$

Just as x' is similar to a rate of velocity, so x is similar to a rate of compound interest on a loan. Both are conveniently expressed in terms of a short time period, rather than 1 year, and in the limit as the time period goes to zero they become derivatives:

$$x' = \frac{dP(t)}{dt} \quad \text{and} \quad x = \frac{1}{P(t)} \frac{dP(t)}{dt}.$$

When population is thought of as a discrete function of time, it will be written as P_t; when a continuous function, as $P(t)$. Such a distinction is not always clear cut, but an attempt will be made to recognize it throughout.

The rates x' and x give very different results if projected into the future. A population continuing to grow by 20,000 persons per year would have grown by 40,000 persons at the end of 2 years, and by 60,000 persons at the end of 3 years. One increasing at a rate of 0.02 would be in the ratio 1.02 at the end of 1 year, in the ratio 1.02^2 at the end of 2 years, and so on. The latter is called *geometric increase*, while the fixed increment is called *arithmetic increase*.

Thus the very notion of a rate of increase, as it is defined in the study of population, seems to imply geometric increase. In fact, it implies nothing for the future, being merely descriptive of the present and the past; rates need not be positive and can be zero or negative. Moreover, being positive today does not preclude being negative next year: ups and downs are the most familiar feature of the population record.

The future enters demographic work in a special way—as a means of understanding the present. To say that the population is increasing at 2 percent per year is to say that, if the rate continued, the total would amount to $1.02^{10} = 1.219$ times the present population in 10 years, and $1.02^{1000} = 398{,}000{,}000$ times the present population in 1000 years. If this tells anything, it says that the rate cannot continue, a statement about the future of a kind that will be studied in Chapter 8.

Still, the conditional growth rate whose hypothetical continuance is helping us to understand the present can be defined in many ways. In particular, in the example above, it could be an increase of 20,000 persons per year just as well as of 0.02 per year. Arithmetical and geometrical projections are equally easy to make; why should the latter be preferred?

The reason for preferring the model of geometric increase is simple: constancy of the elements of growth translates into geometric increase. If successive groups of women coming to maturity have children at the same ages, and if deaths likewise take place at the same ages, and if in- and out-migration patterns do not change, then the population will increase (or decrease) geometrically. Any fixed set of rates that continues over time, whether defined in terms of individuals, families, or age groups, ultimately results in increase at a constant ratio. That any fixed pattern of childbearing, along with a fixed age schedule of mortality, implies long-run geometric increase is what makes this kind of increase central in demography. (The stationary population and geometric decrease can be seen as special cases, in which the ratios are unity and less than unity, respectively.)

1.1   DOUBLING TIME AND HALF-LIFE

The expression for geometric increase gives as the projection to time t

$$P_t = P_0 (1 + x)^t, \tag{1.1.1}$$

where x is now the fraction of increase per unit of time. The unit of time may be a month, a year, or a decade, so long as x and t are expressed in the same unit. Any one of P_0, P_t, x, or t may be ascertained if the other three are given. When the quantity x is negative, the population is decreasing; and when t is negative, the formula projects backward in time. If x is the increase per year as a decimal fraction, then $100x$ is the increase as percentage and $1000x$ the increase per thousand population.

We are told that the population of a certain country is increasing at $100x$ percent per year, and would like to determine by mental arithmetic the population to which this rate of increase would lead if it persisted over a long interval. Translating the rate into doubling time is a convenience in grasping it demographically as well as arithmetically.

Since annual compounding looks easier to handle than compounding by any other period, we will try it first. We will see that it leads to an unnecessarily involved expression, whose complication we will then seek to remove.

If at the end of 1 year the population is $1 + x$ times as great as it was at the beginning of the year, at the end of 2 years $(1 + x)^2, \ldots$, and at the end of n years $(1 + x)^n$ times, then the doubling time is the value of n that satisfies the relation

$$(1 + x)^n = 2. \tag{1.1.2}$$

To solve for n we take natural logarithms and divide both sides by $\ln(1 + x)$:

$$n = \frac{\ln 2}{\ln(1 + x)} = \frac{0.693}{\ln(1 + x)}. \tag{1.1.3}$$

The Taylor series for the natural logarithm $\ln(1 + x)$ is

$$\ln(1 + x) = x - \frac{x^2}{2} + \frac{x^3}{3} - \ldots. \tag{1.1.4}$$

Entering the series for $\ln(1 + x)$ in (1.1.3) gives for doubling time

$$n = \frac{0.693}{\ln(1 + x)} = \frac{0.693}{x - (x^2/2) + (x^3/3) - \ldots}. \tag{1.1.5}$$

The right-hand expression can be simplified by disregarding terms beyond the first in the denominator. We could write $n = 0.693/x$, but for values of x between 0 and 0.04, which include the great majority of human populations, arithmetic experiment with (1.1.5) when x is compounded annually shows that it is, on the whole, slightly more precise to write $n = 0.70/x$ or, in terms of x expressed as a percentage (i.e., $100x$), to write $n = 70/100x$.

The expression

$$n = \frac{70}{100x} \tag{1.1.6}$$

is a simple and accurate approximation to (1.1.3). It tells us that a population increasing at 1 percent doubles in 70 years, and so forth. For Ecuador in 1965, $100x$ was estimated at 3.2 percent, so doubling time would be $n = 70/3.2 = 22$ years. The 1965 population was 5,109,000, and if it doubled in 22 years the 1987 population would be 10,218,000; this compares well with the more exact $(5,109,000)(1.032)^{22} = 10,216,000$. Similarly a further doubling in the next 22 years would give a population in the year 2009 of 20,436,000, as compared with $(5,109,000)(1.032)^{44} = 20,429,000$. The formula $n = 70/100x$ is plainly good enough for such hypothetical calculations.

The Period of Compounding. All this is based on a definition of x by which the ratio of the population at the end of the year to that at the beginning of the year is $1 + x$. Interest calculations are said to be compounded annually on such a definition. A different definition of rate of increase simplifies this problem and others and without any approximation gets rid of the awkward series in the denominator of (1.1.5).

Suppose that x is compounded j times per year; then at the end of 1 year the population will have grown in the ratio $(1 + x/j)^j$. Is there a value j more "natural" than 1? There is: infinity. When the rate x is compounded instantaneously, we will call it r. We then have

$$\lim_{j \to \infty} \left(1 + \frac{r}{j}\right)^j = e^r,$$

where e is the base of natural logarithms and equals 2.71828. [To see how fast this converges try $(1 + r/100,000)^{100,000}$ for $r = 1$ and show that the results agree with e to five significant figures. To how many does $(1 + r/1,000,000)^{1,000,000}$ agree?]

Our calculations from this point will suppose such instantaneous compounding of population, unless otherwise stated; we will take it that a population increasing at rate r will equal e^r at the end of 1 year and e^{nr} at the end of n years. Thus, instead of saying that a population is increasing at 3.20 percent per year compounded annually, we will make the equivalent statement that it is increasing at 3.15 percent per year compounded continuously. Most formulas are thereby made simpler.

This device would equally simplify financial calculations. Tradition has caused these to be made on the basis of a variety of compounding periods —semiannually, quarterly, monthly, daily. If the rate compounded annually is 3.2 percent, the equivalent rates (percents) for other compounding periods are as follows:

Semiannually	3.1748
Quarterly	3.1623
Monthly	3.1540
Weekly	3.1508
Daily	3.1500
Continuously	3.1499

[Show that in general the rate compounded n times per year equivalent to the rate x compounded annually is

$$x_n = n\left[(1+x)^{1/n} - 1\right],$$

and verify the above numbers.] To quote interest rates, like rates of population increase, continuously avoids a good deal of unnecessary complication.

With r defined as an annual rate compounded continuously, the equation for the doubling time n becomes $e^{nr} = 2$, whose solution is just $n = 0.693/r$ or $69.3/100r$. For Mexico the rate of population increase is about 3.5 percent per year compounded momently. The population therefore doubles in $69.3/3.5 = 20$ years, quadruples in 40 years,..., and multiplies by $32 = 2^5$ in 100 years (strictly, 99.02 years).

For decreasing populations the same applies except that now we want halving time, and so we equate e^{nr} to 0.5, and obtain $n = -0.693/r$. If $r = -0.01$, the $n = -0.693/(-0.01) = 69$ years, and this is the half-life. At the level of abstraction of the present section the continuous model of population is identical with that of radioactive substances.

The expressions are equally usable to find r, given n; if we know that a population has doubled in $n = 100$ years, its annual rate of increase compounded momently must be $r = 0.693/100 = 0.00693$. In general, $r = 0.693/n$.

Application to Human History

The simple apparatus of (1.1.6), or else doubling time $= 0.693/r$, can be applied to show how nearly equal birth rates have been to death rates for most of human history. Our race must have started with a sizable group; and even if there had been periodic censuses at the time, questions of definition would have made their interpretation controversial. Suppose for this example that one human couple living a million years ago has multiplied to equal the present human total of about 4 billions, and that it has grown uniformly by geometric increase over the entire period. Since $2^{10} = 1024$, multiplication by 1000 is about 10 doublings, multiplication by 1 billion is 30 doublings, and by 2 billion is 31 doublings. If just 31 doublings have occurred over the last million years, then each must have taken $1,000,000/31$ or just over 32,000 years on the average.

But we saw that a population that takes n years to double is increasing at $r = 0.693/n$ per year. If the doubling time n is 32,000 years, the annual rate of increase is $0.693/32,000 = 0.000022$. In a population closed to migration (which the earth as a whole must be) the rate of increase must equal the birth rate (say b) less the death rate d: $r = b - d$, or $b = r + d$. Thus, with a doubling time of 32,000 years, if death rates were 40.000 per thousand population, then birth rates must have been 40.022 per thousand. Over the million years birth and death rates must on the average have been this close.

It is fanciful to average over a million years; consider now the shorter period from the time of Augustus, with a world population of about 250 million, to the mid-seventeenth century with 545 million people, a ratio of 2.18, or an average rate of increase of $\ln 2.18/1650 = 0.00047$. If death rates were 40.00 per thousand, then birth rates must have been 40.47 per thousand on the average; again simple arithmetic gives an idea of how close, on the whole, birth and death rates have been over historical time.

To show further how exceptional is the situation in which death rates in many places have dropped to 20 per thousand while births stay at 40, let us see how short a time it would have taken to arrive at the world's present 4 billion population with birth rates that are 20 per thousand higher than death rates. Doubling would take 35 years, so 31 doublings would take $31 \times 35 = 1085$ years. A single couple starting two centuries before William the Conqueror would have produced more than the present world population.

Lest anyone think that this argument is original with me, I quote from Boldrini's *Demografia*, published in Milan in 1956. Given, he says, one couple and the rate of increase in population in the first half of the twentieth century of $r = 0.0082$, how long would it take to attain the world population of 2438 million? He finds 2567 years, or about the elapsed time from the founding of Rome (Boldrini, 1956, p. 46). [Show that the numbers given work out to 2551 years if the rate 0.0082 is compounded continuously, or to 2562 years if it is compounded annually. Minor errors of this kind are easy to detect with a modern hand calculator.] Boldrini then goes on to give other variants of the same thought.

Long before Boldrini, Bortkiewicz (1911, pp. 75, 76) showed the usefulness of (1.1.2) and the following expressions for doubling time, and he in turn had precursors. Süssmilch (1788, pp. 291ff) was interested in doubling time and asked his contemporary, Leonhard Euler, about reproduction under some extreme circumstances. Euler provided an account that comes close to modern stable theory.

Logarithms to Various Bases

The use of doubling time or half-life in such calculations is arbitrary; we might prefer to do the arithmetic by means of tripling time or one-third-life. Tripling time is equal to $n = (\ln 3)/r = 1.099/r$. Instead of using 2 or 3 for the base of calculation, we might use 10; the time for tenfold increase is $n = (\ln 10)/r = 2.303/r$. A population increasing at 3.5 percent per year will multiply by 10 in $n = 2.303/0.035 = 66$ years, by 100 in 132 years, and so on.

The number of doublings that correspond to a specified ratio of a final to an initial population is called the *logarithm of that ratio to base 2*; thus the logarithm of 1000 to base 2 is the power to which 2 has to be raised to equal 1000. Since $2^{10} = 1024$, we can say approximately that the logarithm of 1000 to base 2 is 10; multiplication by 1000 is about equivalent to 10 doublings (more exactly, to 9.97 doublings). Then multiplication by a million is equivalent to 20 doublings, and by a billion to 30 doublings, so the logarithms of these numbers to base 2 are 20 and 30, respectively. For thinking about a steadily increasing population, doubling time is a more convenient unit than years or centuries, and logarithms to base 2 are correspondingly valuable.

To translate from number of doublings to number of triplings is to translate from logarithms to base 2 to logarithms to base 3. If x is the number of doublings and y the number of triplings, then

$$2^x = 3^y.$$

We take natural logarithms of both sides to obtain

$$x \ln 2 = y \ln 3,$$

which is the same as

$$y = \frac{\ln 2}{\ln 3} x = \frac{0.693}{1.099} x = 0.63x. \tag{1.1.7}$$

If x doublings constitute an increase in any given ratio R, then $0.63x$ triplings constitute the same increase. We found that to go from 2 persons to 4 billion persons requires 31 doublings. This is equivalent to $31 \times 0.63 = 20$ triplings.

In general, if x is the log of R to base a, and y is the log of R to base b, so that

$$a^x = b^y,$$

then taking logarithms to an arbitrary base gives

$$x \log a = y \log b,$$

whatever the base. If the base is b, then, since we know (from the fact that $b^1 = b$) that $\log_b b = 1$, we have

$$y = x \log_b a. \tag{1.1.8}$$

This says that to go from $\log_a$ to $\log_b$ we need merely multiply by $\log_b a$.

As a particular case of $y = x \log_b a$, we put $b = e$, and obtain

$$\log_a R = \frac{\log_e R}{\log_e a} \equiv \frac{\ln R}{\ln a}.$$

For purposes of calculation one usually starts with logarithms to base e, designated as ln, and this formula changes to an arbitrary base a. For example,

$$\log_2 7 = \frac{\ln 7}{\ln 2} = \frac{1.946}{0.693} = 2.807.$$

It is convenient also to know that $\log_b a$ is the reciprocal of $\log_a b$. [Prove this.]

Prospective Possible Doublings

Doubling times provide a quick perspective on future limitations as well as on past history. We saw that of the 31 doublings from the hypothetical primeval couple about 4 have occurred since the time of Augustus. Filling all of the land surface of the planet Earth to the density of Manhattan would take us to only 10 more doublings from where we are. Spreading with equal density over the bottoms of the oceans as well would permit about 2 additional doublings. More realistic considerations suggest that the 31 doublings so far vouchsafed to man, with at most one or two more, are all he will ever have. The number 31, plus or minus one or two, may be thought of as a constant of nature.

1.2   ONE-SEX VERSUS TWO-SEX MODELS: DESCENDANTS OF THE PILGRIM FATHERS

Bisexual reproduction means that each of us has two parents, four grandparents, and eight great-grandparents, in general, 2^i great^{i-2}-grandparents. These are outside numbers; there must have been some inbreeding during the last 30 generations, since 2^{30} is 10^9 or 1 billion, and this has to be compared with the number of people on earth 30 generations ago. The number then living would not have sufficed to provide each of us with 2^{30} distinct great^{28}-grandparents, for going back 30 generations takes us to about the year A.D. 1200, when the world population was barely half a billion. Notwithstanding the ultimate unity of the human race, moreover, the ancestors of each of us since A.D. 1200 must have been a subgroup of humanity.

From this viewpoint ancestry is simpler to deal with than progeny, for each of us can have zero, one, two, or more children, but each of us must have had exactly two parents. Thought of as a branching process, each step backward in time is a simple bifurcation; forward in time each step can involve up to 10 or more forkings. But this simplicity of the backward process is more than offset by intermarriage.

Demography must transcend the detail of family trees, just as macroeconomics must aggregate the detail of individual transactions. The various sections of this book can be thought of as different ways of summarizing genealogies for the purpose of drawing conclusions on populations. A useful summarizing device is to consider only one sex at a time.

A large part of our work will treat only the female side of the population, or only the male side. This is not to imply that the other sex is not necessary, but rather to suppose that it exists in whatever numbers are required to produce the growth in the sex being followed. The present section is intended to show how this device gives clear answers to questions otherwise indeterminate. We will use the number of descendants of the Pilgrim fathers—not in itself an important demographic issue—as an extreme example of the uncertainty introduced when both sexes are considered simultaneously.

We saw that an increase of $100x$ percent per year implies a doubling time of about $70/100x$. Evidence from the total population of the United States and that of French Canada suggests that 2 percent per year, or a doubling in 35 years, is about right for an American group over the three and one-half centuries since the landing of the Pilgrims in 1620.

The population of the United States increased from 3,929,000 in 1790 to 204 million in 1970, or 51.9 times. This is 5.7 doublings, or say 6, and implies about $180/6 = 30$ years per doubling. The increase does include immigration, however, and 30 years is therefore too short a time for the doubling of a native group.

A self-contained population that probably had birth rates somewhat higher than those of the Pilgrims is the French Canadians, including the Franco-Americans. There were fewer than 10,000 original newcomers, say of average time of arrival 1700. By 1970 there were about 5,500,000 French Canadians; over the course of 270 years they had multiplied by 550, which is 9 doublings and hence also about 30 years per doubling. Their growth was almost entirely due to excess of births over deaths, with immigration making only a trifling contribution, but their birth rates continued to be high long after those of the Pilgrims' descendants had fallen.

This broadly supports a figure of about 35 years per doubling for the Pilgrims, which also happens to be convenient for the arithmetic of our example. Following the male line for each Pilgrim (except that for the few women Pilgrims we follow the female line) would give 10 doublings in the 350 years from 1620 to 1970. (The male line is sons of sons of sons, etc.; the female line, daughters of daughters of daughters. In this way of reckoning, the son of a daughter of Elder Brewster is not taken as a descendant.)

About half the Pilgrims are said to have died during the first hard winter; let us consider only the survivors, say 50 in number. Then each Pilgrim would have $2^{10} = 1024$ descendants through the line for his own sex, and all of them together would have 50×1024 or somewhat over 50,000 male descendants of male Pilgrims and female descendants of female Pilgrims. This would also approximate the present total if the Pilgrims had been a nuptially isolated group, which is to say their descendants were separated from the rest of the population and were always able to find spouses from their own numbers. This would have required an equal number of each sex from the beginning (or the appointment of a number of honorary female Pilgrims in the first generation).

More difficult is the question of descendants in view of the fact that they actually were not isolated. At the other extreme, if they could always have married spouses who were not descended from Pilgrims, and we count all their children rather than the line for one sex, the expansion of the Pilgrim-descended population would be at twice the rate of the preceding paragraph. Now each would have four descendants in the time supposed for two above, which is to say that time for doubling would average just one-half of 35 years. Thus each would have 2^{20} or over 1 million descendants in the 350 years to 1970, and the 50 Pilgrims surviving through the first winter would together have over 50 million descendants.

The number of persons now alive who can claim descent from the Pilgrims is thus at least 50,000 (if they were an isolated subpopulation, and the fact that numbers of the two sexes were not equal at the beginning is disregarded) and at most 50,000,000 (if they completely avoided marrying one another). Without data on the extent of intermarriage we have no way of narrowing the range between 50,000 and 50,000,000 descendants. [What are some of the difficulties of collecting data on intermarriage?]

The purpose of this account being merely to illustrate the indeterminacy of a two-sex model, I have simplified the data. A more realistic analysis would start with the fact that just 23 of the Pilgrims founded continuing families, and would use historical records to ascertain with more precision just what their family sizes were in successive generations. Apparently the Mayflower Descendants Society counts about 15,000 members, all of whom have proved their descent, but this number is far short of the actual total of descendants.

That the one-sex problem gives the simple and unique answer of 50,000 on our assumptions, whereas the corresponding two-sex problem leaves us in the range of 50,000 to 50 million, is only one aspect of the difficulty. Another is the effect on marriages and births of adding a number of males to a population, as against the (presumably greater) effect of adding the same number of females. Hunting female rabbits affects reproduction more than hunting male rabbits—how much more depends on how actively the remaining males get around. Satisfactory answers to such questions are not easily found. They cannot be obtained without facts or assumptions regarding individual behavior of a more detailed kind than demography ordinarily introduces.

In most of the following chapters the population will be assumed closed to migration and will usually appear to consist only of females or only of males. We will not care how many individuals can trace their ancestry back to a given origin, but we will want to know how fast a closed population is increasing, and what determines its age distribution and other features. For that purpose we will consider the two sexes separately and avoid examining the availability of mates, a question whose difficulties it is the purpose of the present section to suggest.

The fact that the one-sex model gives simple answers to difficult questions, and that under a considerable range of circumstances these answers are realistic, makes it a positive achievement.

1.3   HOW MANY PEOPLE HAVE LIVED ON THE EARTH?

The number of people who have lived on the earth can be estimated by the births at two or more points in time and supposing uniform increase between these points. First we find the rate of increase r when births are given.

If in year t_1 the births were n_1, and in year t_2 (later than t_1) were n_2, the ratio of increase was n_2/n_1. In terms of r, the average annual rate of growth compounded momently, this same ratio of increase must be $e^{r(t_2-t_1)}$. Equating these two expressions,

$$\frac{n_2}{n_1} = e^{r(t_2-t_1)},$$

and taking logarithms of both sides and solving for r gives

$$r = \frac{\ln n_2 - \ln n_1}{t_2 - t_1}. \tag{1.3.1}$$

Now we have to find the total births over a long interval of time. If during the interval from t_1 to t_2 the rate of increase was at all times exactly r, in any intermediate year t the births were $n_1 e^{r(t-t_1)}$, and integrating this gives the total births as

$$\int_{t_1}^{t_2} n_1 e^{r(t-t_1)}\,dt = \frac{n_1}{r}\left[e^{r(t_2-t_1)}-1\right] = \frac{n_2-n_1}{r}, \qquad (1.3.2)$$

using the fact that $e^{r(t_2-t_1)}=n_2/n_1$.

We want to express the births over the interval in a way that does not require explicit knowledge of r. To do so we substitute the value of r from (1.3.1) in (1.3.2) and so obtain for the births that occurred in the interval, which is the same as the total persons who lived, the simple result

$$\text{Persons who lived} = \frac{(n_2-n_1)(t_2-t_1)}{\ln n_2 - \ln n_1}. \qquad (1.3.3)$$

A widely quoted article of the Population Reference Bureau (Cook, 1962) estimated annual births at four points in the history of mankind as follows:

t	n
600,000 B.C.	1
6000 B.C.	250,000
A.D. 1650	25,000,000
A.D. 1962	110,000,000

For the first of the three intervals between these four points, that between 600,000 B.C. and 6000 B.C., the expression on the right of (1.3.3) gives persons who lived as

$$\frac{(n_2-n_1)(t_2-t_1)}{\ln n_2 - \ln n_1} = \frac{(250{,}000-1)(600{,}000-6000)}{12.4292-0} = 11.9\times10^9,$$

and for the other two intervals we have similarly 41.1×10^9 and 17.9×10^9, respectively. Adding the three intervals gives $11.9+41.1+17.9=70.9$ billion (not 77 billion, as the Population Reference Bureau calculated).

If we had more points at which population could be reasonably assessed, the estimate would turn out to be different. Assuming a longer stretch of time than 600,000 years would raise the number, and supposing arithmetic rather than geometric increase would raise it greatly. With the high mortality prevailing in most times and places, only about half of those born lived to maturity, so the number of *adults* who have ever lived is far less than the number of persons.

Deevey (1950) has looked into the past and present populations of the planet in more detail, and makes estimates for 12 points of time from 1 million years ago to the year 2000. He is not satisfied with the exponential curve, but applies three successive logarithmic curves, one for each of the three main phases of human evolution—toolmaking, agriculture, and scientific–industrial. He concludes that 110 billion will be the world total over all time to the year 2000.

Taking these and other (e.g., Winkler, 1959; Fuchs, 1951) calculations together suggests that the nearly 4 billion persons now alive constitute between 4 and 6 percent of those who have ever lived, a proportion that would be somewhat smaller if we moved human origins back in time. The corresponding fraction for adults is greater, and the fraction of those with specific modern occupations who have ever lived, for instance engineers, much greater.

We now drop the homogeneity and suppose subpopulations having different rates of increase.

1.4 A MIXTURE OF POPULATIONS HAVING DIFFERENT RATES OF INCREASE

A population of initial size Q growing at rate r numbers Qe^{rt} at time t, r being taken as fixed and the population as homogeneous. Now suppose heterogeneity–a number of subpopulations, of which the ith is initially Q_i growing at rate r_i, so that at time t the total number is $P(t) = \sum_i Q_i e^{r_i t}$. We will show that the total never stabilizes, that its rate of increase forever increases, and that the composition constantly changes.

The definition of rate of increase over a finite time δ may be written as

$$\frac{1}{P(t)} \cdot \frac{P(t+\delta) - P(t)}{\delta},$$

and in the limit as δ tends to zero this becomes

$$\frac{1}{P(t)} \cdot \frac{dP(t)}{dt}. \tag{1.4.1}$$

Thus at time t the derivative of the total population, $dP(t)/dt$, when divided by $P(t)$, provides us with the rate of increase, which for our mixture of populations can be written as $\bar{r}(t)$. The derivative of $P(t) = \sum_i Q_i e^{r_i t}$ is $dP(t)/dt = \sum_i Q_i r_i e^{r_i t}$. Hence the rate of increase must be

$$\bar{r}(t) = \frac{1}{P(t)} \frac{dP(t)}{dt} = \frac{\sum_i Q_i r_i e^{r_i t}}{\sum_i Q_i e^{r_i t}},$$

which is the arithmetic mean of the r_i, each weighted by its population at time t.

The change in this mean rate of change, by the rule for the derivative of a ratio of two functions $u(t)$ and $v(t)$,

$$\frac{d(u/v)}{dt} = \frac{1}{v}\frac{du}{dt} - \frac{u}{v^2}\frac{dv}{dt},$$

is obtained from

$$\frac{du}{dt} = \sum_i Q_i r_i^2 e^{r_i t} \quad \text{and} \quad \frac{dv}{dt} = \sum_i Q_i r_i e^{r_i t}$$

as

$$\frac{d\bar{r}(t)}{dt} = \frac{\sum_i Q_i r_i^2 e^{r_i t}}{\sum_i Q_i e^{r_i t}} - \left(\frac{\sum_i Q_i r_i e^{r_i t}}{\sum_i Q_i e^{r_i t}}\right)^2. \tag{1.4.2}$$

Equation (1.4.2) informs us that the increase in the mean rate of increase at time t is equal to the difference between the mean square and the square of the mean of the rates weighted by the number of people at that time.

Variance is ordinarily defined as the mean square deviation from the mean: if a variable x takes values $x_1, x_2, \ldots, x_N$, then

$$\bar{x} = \sum x_i / N \quad \text{and} \quad \sigma^2 = \sum (x_i - \bar{x})^2 / N.$$

But

$$\frac{\sum (x_i - \bar{x})^2}{N} = \frac{\sum \left[(x_i - \bar{x})(x_i - \bar{x}) \right]}{N}$$

$$= \frac{\sum \left[x_i (x_i - \bar{x}) \right] - \sum \left[\bar{x}(x_i - \bar{x}) \right]}{N},$$

and the second summation vanishes to leave

$$\sigma^2 = \frac{\sum x_i^2}{N} - \bar{x}^2,$$

because $\sum (x_i - \bar{x}) = 0$ and $\sum x_i \bar{x} / N = \bar{x}^2$. The argument applies equally well if the x_i are weighted, and in particular it applies to our r_i weighted at any moment by their respective populations.

Hence (1.4.2) is the same as the variance among subpopulation rates of increase:

$$\frac{d\bar{r}(t)}{dt} = \sigma^2(t), \tag{1.4.3}$$

where $\sigma^2(t)$ is the variance among the r_i, each weighted according to its current subpopulation $Q_i e^{r_i t}$.

The nonnegative derivative of $\bar{r}(t)$ in (1.4.3) proves that $\bar{r}(t)$ is always increasing, unless the r_i are all the same, in which case the variance is zero, the derivative of $\bar{r}(t)$ is zero, and $\bar{r}(t)$ is constant. But, though it keeps increasing when the rates of increase of the component subpopulations are not all the same, $\bar{r}(t)$ is bounded above; being an average of the several r_i, it can never be larger than the largest r_i. It will approach as close as we please, however, to the largest r_i; to prove this, note that with a finite number of subpopulations the one that is increasing fastest will come to have as high a ratio as we please to the one increasing second fastest, and indeed to the sum of all the other subpopulations. This example of instability contrasts with the stability described in Section 1.9, where the operation of fixed rates in homogeneous populations leads to fixed ratios among ages, regions, and other subgroups of the population.

The foregoing argument is more than adequate to prove that the sum of the several projections will be greater than the projection of the sum at the average rate of increase existing at the outset. An alternative proof requiring no calculus consists in reducing the proposition to the known fact that the arithmetic mean of distinct positive quantities, say $a > 0$ and $b > 0$, $a \neq b$, is greater than their geometric mean; in symbols, $(a + b)/2 > \sqrt{ab}$. The separate projection of two subpopulations amounts to $Q_1 e^{r_1 t} + Q_2 e^{r_2 t}$; the combined projection is

$$(Q_1 + Q_2) \exp\left[\left(\frac{Q_1 r_1 + Q_2 r_2}{Q_1 + Q_2} \right) t \right].$$

The sum of the separate projections is greater if

$$\frac{Q_1 e^{r_1 t} + Q_2 e^{r_2 t}}{Q_1 + Q_2} > \exp\left[\left(\frac{Q_1 r_1 + Q_2 r_2}{Q_1 + Q_2} \right) t \right].$$

But the first is the arithmetic mean of $e^{r_1 t}$ and $e^{r_2 t}$, weighted with Q_1 and Q_2, respectively, and the second is the corresponding geometric mean.

The general proof that an arithmetic mean is greater than a geometric mean can be developed in several ways, and Beckenbach and Bellman (1961) devote much of Chapter 4 of their book to it. That the inequality must hold for $Q_1 = Q_2 = 1$ we can see at the level of high school algebra. Plainly

$$\left(e^{r_1 t/2} - e^{r_2 t/2} \right)^2 > 0, \qquad r_1 \neq r_2,$$

and expanding the square gives

$$\frac{e^{r_1 t} + e^{r_2 t}}{2} > \exp\left[\left(\frac{r_1 + r_2}{2} \right) t \right].$$

The argument can be extended to n subpopulations by induction; if Q_i of the n are increasing at r_i, and so on, the proof then applies to integral weights Q_i; from there it can be carried to real weights Q_i. To present this in detail would carry us too far from demography, which is concerned only with the result that separate projection of each of the various elements of a heterogeneous population gives a total greater than is obtained by projection of the whole population at its average rate.

An Arithmetic Example for Two Subpopulations

To use round numbers for an example of how (1.4.3) operates, we take the United States population to be 200 million in 1970, increasing at 0.75 percent, and that of Mexico to be 50 million, increasing at 3.5 percent. The average rate is $[(200\times0.75)+(50\times3.5)]/250=1.3$ percent, and 250 million increasing at 1.3 percent for 50 years equals 478,885,000.

Let us now work out the sum of the two trajectories, using for each of the United States and Mexico, considered subpopulations, its own exponential (Table 1.1). After 50 years at these rates the populations would be $200,000,000\times e^{50\times0.0075}=290,998,000$ for the United States and $50,000,000\times e^{50\times0.035}=287,730,000$ for Mexico. The total is 578,728,000, or 100 million more than we had in the single calculation. The combined rate of increase now would be over 2.1 percent and rising, as column 6 of Table 1.1 shows. By 2020 the increase in the increase, $d\bar{r}(t)/dt$, would be $(0.021267-0.021076)=0.000191$, as given in column 7.

According to (1.4.3), this ought to be the same as the weighted variance of the rates in 2020. The mean rate is $[(291)(0.0075)+(288)(0.035)]/(291+288)=0.02118$, the weights being the entries in columns 1 and 2 for 2020.

Table 1.1   Calculation of rate of increase in combined population of the United States and Mexico if each continues at its own fixed rate (thousands of persons)

Year	United States increasing at $100r=0.75$ (1)	Mexico increasing at $100r=3.5$ (2)	Total (3)=(1)+(2)	Annual increase (4)	Mean population [average of successive years in (3)] (5)	Rate of increase (6)=(4)/(5)	Increase in increase [difference from (6)] (7)
1970	200,000	50,000	250,000				
2019	288,824	277,834	566,658				
				12,070	572,693	0.021076	
2020	290,998	287,730	578,728				0.000191
				12,440	584,948	0.021267	
2021	293,189	297,979	591,168				0.000188
				12,821	597,578	0.021455	
2022	295,396	308,593	603,989				

The variance is $[291(0.0075 - 0.02118)^2 + 288(0.035 - 0.02118)^2]/579 = 0.000189$, identical except for rounding with the entry in column 7 previously calculated.

In summary, we have calculated the rate of increase of the combined population by differencing successive years, showing the rate to increase from 0.021076 in 2019–20 to 0.021267 in 2020–21, an annual increase of 0.000191 in the rate of increase. The separately calculated weighted variance between the two component rates in 2020 is 0.00189, or virtually complete agreement.

1.5   RATE OF INCREASE CHANGING OVER TIME

We started with a homogeneous population having a fixed rate of increase r and went on to a heterogeneous population composed of subpopulations each having a fixed rate of increase. The present section reverts to homogeneity, in which there is only one r at any given moment, but now the increase is time dependent, and to remind ourselves of this we call it $r(t)$. Our purpose is to determine the population after T years resulting from the variable increase $r(t)$.

If we divide time into short intervals dt, and for the first short interval suppose $r(t)$ to be fixed at r_0, and if at the start the population numbers P_0, after time dt it will number $P_0 e^{r_0 dt}$, for we saw in Section 1.1 that the ratio of increase over a finite time at rate r compounded momently is equal to the exponential of the rate times the time. This can be applied to each of the short intervals dt into which, for this purpose, we divide the scale of time. Let the rate of increase be approximated by $r_0, r_1, r_2, \ldots$, in those successive time intervals, each of length dt. Then we have an exponential for the ratio of increase over each interval, and the population at time T will be the product of these exponentials:

$$P(T) = P_0 e^{r_0 dt} e^{r_1 dt} e^{r_2 dt} \cdots$$

$$= P_0 e^{r_0 dt + r_1 dt + r_2 dt + \cdots},$$

so that in the limit, as dt tends to zero, the exponent tends to the integral of $r(t)$:

$$P(T) = P_0 \exp\left[\int_0^T r(t)\, dt \right]. \tag{1.5.1}$$

The above derivation of (1.5.1) proves *ab initio* a proposition of the integral calculus. Let us avoid this by starting with the definition of the rate of increase $r(t)$ as given in (1.4.1):

$$r(t) = \frac{1}{P(t)} \cdot \frac{dP(t)}{dt}. \tag{1.5.2}$$

The demographic definition can be treated as a differential equation. Its solution is obtained by separating the variables and integrating both sides of

$$r(t)\,dt = \frac{dP(t)}{P(t)}.$$

This gives

$$\int_0^T r(t)\,dt = \ln P(t)\big|_0^T,$$

or, on taking exponentials,

$$P(T) = P_0 \exp\left[\int_0^T r(t)\,dt\right],$$

as before.

The result can be checked by calculating $r(t)$ from the trajectory of population $P(T)$. Taking logarithms of both sides of (1.5.1) yields

$$\ln P(T) = \ln P_0 + \int_0^T r(t)\,dt,$$

and then, differentiating with respect to T, we have

$$\frac{1}{P(T)} \cdot \frac{dP(T)}{dT} = r(T), \qquad\qquad (1.5.3)$$

which brings us back to the definition of $r(t)$ in (1.4.1) and (1.5.2).

A convenient way of writing (1.5.1) is in terms of $\bar{r}$, the arithmetic mean rate over the interval from zero to T:

$$P(T) = P_0 e^{\bar{r}T}, \qquad \text{where} \qquad \bar{r} = \frac{\displaystyle\int_0^T r(t)\,dt}{T}.$$

In words, the numerical effect on the population total of a varying rate of growth is the same as though the arithmetic average rate applied at each moment over the time in question.

Special Cases of Changing Rates.   We may try various special functions for $r(t)$. If $r(t)$ is a constant, say r, then (1.5.1) reduces to $P(T) = P_0 e^{rT}$. If $r(t)$ is equal to k/t and we start at time 1, then

$$P(T) = P_1 \exp\left(\int_1^T \frac{k}{t}\,dt\right) = P_1 \exp(k \ln T)$$

$$= P_1 T^k.$$

With $k = 1$ this declining rate of increase would give us a linearly rising population.

As a numerical application of (1.5.1) suppose that the rate of increase starts at ρ in 1970 and declines to $\rho/2$ during the 30 years from 1970 to 2000, and that the decline is in a straight line. Then in any intermediate year t we will have

$$r(t) = \frac{\rho}{60}(2030 - t), \qquad 1970 \leqslant t \leqslant 2000. \tag{1.5.4}$$

The proof that this $r(t)$ is the one specified is (a) it is linear in t; (b) for $t = 1970$ it equals ρ; (c) for $t = 2000$ it equals $\rho/2$. Entering (1.5.4) in (1.5.1) gives for the population in year n, where $1970 \leqslant n \leqslant 2000$,

$$P_n = P_{1970} \exp\left[\frac{\rho}{60} \int_{1970}^{n} (2030 - t)\, dt \right],$$

and for $n = 2000$ this is equal to

$$P_{2000} = P_{1970} e^{22.5\rho}.$$

As a further example, suppose that a population in successive years increases at the rates 2, 3, 2.5, 2.7, and 2.3 percent. The arithmetic average of these rates is

$$\frac{2.0 + 3.0 + 2.5 + 2.7 + 2.3}{5} = 2.5 \text{ percent.}$$

Hence the population at the end of 5 years is

$$P_5 = P_0 e^{(5)(0.025)} = P_0 e^{0.125} = 1.133 P_0.$$

This is the same outcome as is obtained by calculating the population year by year with the given rates (all assumed to be compounded continuously):

$$P_1 = P_0 e^{0.02}, \qquad P_2 = P_1 e^{0.03}, \qquad \ldots,$$

and substituting successively,

$$P_5 = P_0 e^{0.02} e^{0.03} e^{0.025} e^{0.027} e^{0.023} = P_0 e^{0.125}.$$

Equation 1.5.1 is worth this extended study because of its important applications. In particular, when $r(t)$ is interpreted as $-\mu(a)$, $\mu(a)$ being mortality at age a, the result carries over to cohorts; a cohort is defined as a number of individuals born at a particular time and followed through life. Such a cohort is a peculiar population, in that it never receives new members after the initial moment, and its initial births die off during the 100 or so years of the cohort's duration. Equation 1.5.1 tells us that the survivors to age x, $l(x)$, of a cohort numbering l_0 at birth, are equal to

$$l(x) = l_0 \exp\left[-\int_0^x \mu(a)\, da \right]. \tag{1.5.5}$$

This expression is useful in discussion of the life table. The decrement $\mu(a)$ may represent death at age a, death from a particular cause, failing the ath grade at school, break-up of a marriage in its ath year. Whatever the nature of the decrement, (1.5.5) translates the several hurdles into a probability of surviving the course to the xth hurdle.

1.6   LOGISTIC INCREASE AND EXPLOSION

Verhulst (1838) and Pearl and Reed (1920) modified the exponential law of increase by supposing a fixed ceiling to population, set by nature or by the combined limits of nature and human techniques. Fixed growth, represented by the equation $dP(t)/dt = rP(t)$, of which the solution is $P(t) = P_0 e^{rt}$, can be modified by writing a further factor, say $1 - [P(t)/a]$, on the right-hand side to define the logistic function

$$\frac{dP(t)}{dt} = rP(t)\left[1 - \frac{P(t)}{a}\right].$$

The right-hand side equals zero when $P(t) = a$, so that must be where growth stops on the logistic curve. When the factors involving $P(t)$ are collected and then decomposed into partial fractions, we have

$$\left[\frac{1}{P(t)} + \frac{1}{a - P(t)}\right] dP(t) = r\,dt,$$

which can be readily integrated as $\ln\{P(t)/[a - P(t)]\} = rt + c$, where c is a constant. Taking exponentials and then solving for $P(t)$, and changing the constant to $t_0 = -c/r$ in order to locate the midpoint of the curve at t_0, we obtain

$$P(t) = \frac{a}{1 + e^{-r(t - t_0)}}. \tag{1.6.1}$$

Pearl and others thought that fitting such a curve to a population time series would provide realistic short-term forecasts as well as estimates of the ultimate stationary population a. They were greatly encouraged by predicting the 1930 U.S. Census count with an error that was probably less than the error of the census itself. But the 1940 Census was a disappointment—it fell far below the curve, and the logistic was dropped amid a barrage of criticism no less intense than the earlier enthusiasm. The fall in the birth rate over most of the last 20 years, however, makes the logistic look much better, and this, along with visible difficulties in the environment, has brought the logistic back into fashion in some circles. The fit to the United States population from 1800 to 1960 shows $a = 256.41$ million persons, a ceiling not sharply contradicted by current tendencies.

As Pearl expected, the logistic is hardly invariant with respect to the period over which it is fitted. He saw population as moving toward a ceiling at any given moment, but from time to time technical advance would create a new and higher ceiling, so that progress would take the form of breaking into the higher logistic before the course of the earlier one was completed.

No detailed fitting is required merely to find the ceiling a. [If the population is p_1, p_2, and p_3 at times t_1, t_2, and $2t_2 - t_1$, respectively (i.e., at times that are equidistant), prove that the asymptote will be

$$a = \frac{1/p_1 + 1/p_3 - 2/p_2}{1/p_1 p_3 - 1/p_2^2},$$ (1.6.2)

and using as data the United States resident population for

1870	40 million,
1920	106 million,
1970	203 million,

verify that the ultimate population will be 324 million.] The logistic to the censuses from 1800 to 1910 inclusive shows an upper asymptote of 197 millions; if one accepts the theory behind the logistic, one would say that the conditions of life and technology had changed during the course of the twentieth century in such a way as to raise the population ceiling of the United States by 127 millions. Although this could be true, one would need considerable confidence in the appropriateness of the logistic to accept such a conclusion without more evidence.

Even more important than the selection of the time interval over which a fit is made is the nature of the curve chosen. Consider the United States population from 1870 to 1970, and fit to it the hyperbola (von Foerster et al., 1960)

$$P(t) = \frac{\alpha}{t_e - t}.$$

The hyperbola contains two constants, of which t_e is the time of population explosion, when $P(t_e) = \infty$. The time t_e is easily calculated from observations at two dates, t_1 and t_2, where the population is known to be p_1 at time t_1 and p_2 at time t_2; the reader may show that

$$t_e = \frac{p_2 t_2 - p_1 t_1}{p_2 - p_1}.$$ (1.6.3)

The 1870 resident population of the United States was 40 million and the 1970 population 203 million, and from (1.6.3) t_e works out to 1995.

Thus, based on the United States population from 1870 to 1970, the logistic shows that an upper asymptote of 324 millions would be approached (about the twenty-first century), whereas the hyperbola shows an explosion to infinity by 1995. Such experimenting suggests the hazards and perplexities of forecasting by the fitting of curves. [Show that no one need fear the explosion in hyperbolic form, for it would require toward the end an infinite birth rate.]

Can one discriminate among curves on the basis of their fits to past data? Winsor (1932) showed that the logistic is a better fit than the cumulated normal,

$$\frac{1}{\sigma\sqrt{2\pi}} \int_{-\infty}^{t} \exp\left(-\frac{(x-\mu)^2}{2\sigma^2}\right) dx,$$

where μ and σ are constants to be determined by data from censuses. Either the logistic or the cumulated normal does better than the arc tangent curve, which has some resemblance to them. But in general past data are not very helpful in selecting from the considerable number of s-shaped curves that can be devised.

As a means for population forecasting, the logistic has become something of a museum piece. Any such overall approach, disregarding births, deaths, migration, and age distribution, is useful only in circumstances where resources decisively determine population. When, on the other hand, births, migration, and even deaths are socially determined, we are better off to attempt their separate forecasting, however uncertain this has been shown to be. That is why the logistic appears in ecological models, and the components approach in demographic ones, though for neither type do knowledgeable writers claim much forecasting capability.

1.7 THE STALLED DEMOGRAPHIC TRANSITION

In a famous article Notestein (1945) wrote about "the stage of transitional growth ... in which the decline of both fertility and mortality is well established but in which the decline of mortality precedes that of fertility and produces rapid growth." His demographic transition refers to the uniformity of change from high to low birth and death rates among the countries of Europe and those overseas that had developed industrially. They showed first a decline in death rates, starting at the beginning of the nineteenth century or earlier, followed after a longer or shorter interval by a decline in birth rates. In France the fall in births was nearly simultaneous with that in deaths, whereas in England births did not begin to decline until about 1870, but all countries resembled one another to some degree

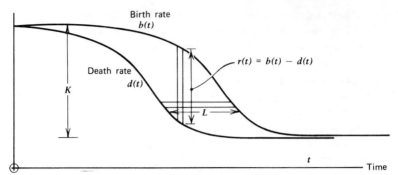

Fig. 1.1 Stylized form of transition from high to low birth and death rates.

(Flieger, 1967). Our first question concerns the difference to the ultimate population of a given delay in the fall of the birth curve, a question of concern to the countries of Asia and Latin America whose deaths have now fallen but whose births remain high.

Suppose the deaths of a population go through a descending curve $d(t)$ and its births through $b(t)$, as in Fig. 1.1. The initial and final conditions are both of zero increase, that is, the curves coincide at beginning and end. We seek the ratio of increase in the population between its initial and final stationary conditions.

Whatever the shape of the two descending curves of Fig. 1.1, if they begin and end together the exponential of the area between them is the total increase over the time in question. For $\int_0^T [b(t) - d(t)] dt = \int_0^T r(t) dt = A$, say; according to (1.5.1) the ratio of increase in the population must be $\exp[\int_0^T r(t) dt]$, or simply e^A. This applies for any pair of monotonically descending curves that start at the same level and end at the same level.

In the special case where the birth and death curves of Fig. 1.1 have the same shape as well, with $b(t)$ lagging L behind $d(t)$, and both dropping K over the transition, the area A equals KL, that is, the common difference between initial and final height, multiplied by the time by which the birth curve lags behind the death curve. For by dividing the interval between them into horizontal strips, equal in length to the lag L, it is plain that the same strips can be arranged as a rectangle of length L and height K. The ratio of increase in the population of a country, $e^A = e^{KL}$, is a constant e^K taken to the power of the lag in the fall of birth rates.

If K, the common decline of births and deaths, is 0.02, and births follow deaths downward but with a lag L of 30 years, the population will increase in the ratio $e^{KL} = e^{(0.02)(30)} = 1.82$ before constancy is reestablished. If the lag is 60 years, the ratio will be the *square* of this, or 3.32; if 90 years, the cube, or 6.05. Note that this takes no account of a momentum effect due to

Table 1.2   Ratio of increase during the course of demographic transition as a function of the lag in fall of birth rate after fall of death rate

Lag (years) L	e^{KL} ($K = 0.02$)	e^{KL} ($K = 0.03$)
15	1.35	1.57
30	1.82	2.46
45	2.46	3.86
60	3.32	6.05
75	4.48	9.49

age, which, as we will see in Section 6.6, can by itself add 60 percent or more to the ultimate population. The need for haste in lowering the birth rate in less developed countries is illustrated in Table 1.2, showing the effect of lag on the ultimate population, given $K = 0.02$ and $K = 0.03$.

This section has covered the general case of curves $b(t)$ and $d(t)$, similar to one another but with $b(t)$ lagging behind $d(t)$. We now proceed from longitudinal to cross-sectional observations, and consider differential fertility insofar as it is a phenomenon of the demographic transition.

1.8   DIFFERENTIAL FERTILITY DUE TO THE DEMOGRAPHIC TRANSITION

Books on population treat the demographic transition in one chapter and in a quite different chapter deal with the differentials of fertility between social classes, educational groups, and religious denominations. The transition is thought of as applying to whole countries, and differential fertility as applying to groups within a country, in which, *grosso modo*, the better off, better educated, and urban have the fewest children. There may well be uncertainty as to how far these classical differentials are permanent, applying to all societies at all times, and how far they occur in a particular historical conjuncture, that in which all birth rates are falling but with different timing. Some observations show a positive relation—the richer the group, the higher its birth rate—both before the transition and after it has been passed and birth control techniques made effectively available to all strata. Much of the economic theory of fertility, summarized by Leibenstein (1974), Becker (1960), T. W. Schultz (1974), and T. P. Schultz (1974), has a bearing on this issue. The present section will examine a simple aspect of the problem: to what degree the different times of entry

into the transition can account for the different levels of fertility among
social classes at any one moment.

We will approximate the birth rate $b(t)$ by a straight line going from
upper left to lower right in the range of interest; the slope or derivative
$db(t)/dt$ is taken as negative. We suppose also that the slope is the same
for all social groups, and that these are distinguished from one another
only by their degree of horizontal displacement.

The sloping line on the right in Fig. 1.2 is displaced from the population
mean by Δt, say. It represents a social group whose fall in fertility takes
place later by Δt than the average of all groups in the country in question.
Suppose that because of its lag this group has fertility Δb higher than the
average at the time when the country as a whole is passing through the
midpoint of its drop from high to low rates. Then the derivative $db(t)/dt$
common to all the sloping lines serves to relate for the given subgroup of
the population the departure of the birth rate from the mean at a given
moment and the lag in time:

$$\Delta b = \frac{db(t)}{dt} \Delta t. \qquad (1.8.1)$$

Now suppose many sloping lines, representing the several groups in the
country, and square and average over these lines on both sides of (1.8.1) to
find

$$\sigma_b^2 = \left[\frac{db(t)}{dt} \right]^2 \sigma_t^2, \qquad (1.8.2)$$

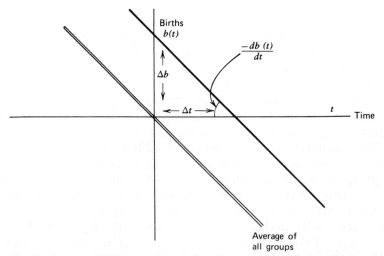

Fig. 1.2 Simplified explanation of differential fertility in terms of demographic transition.

where σ_b^2 is the variance of birth rates at the time when the population average goes through the halfway point of decline, and σ_t^2 is the variance of the times at which the several groups go through this point. Take square roots of (1.8.2) to find

$$\sigma_b = \frac{db(t)}{dt}\sigma_t. \tag{1.8.3}$$

In this stylized version each statistically identifiable subpopulation has its own demographic transition and falls according to its own straight line, but with all the straight lines having the same slope. The result (1.8.3) relates differential fertility σ_b to variation in time of undergoing the transition σ_t.

1.9 MATRICES AND GRAPHS IN DEMOGRAPHY

A Two-Subgroup Model

Within a population in which there exist statistically recognizable subpopulations—regions of a country, social classes, educational levels—we consider now not changes within, but transfers among, such groupings. Given the rate of growth in each subpopulation and the rates of transfer among subpopulations, it is possible to describe a trajectory by a set of differential or difference equations. For a simple special case, suppose two subpopulations of sizes p_t and q_t at time t. If growth of the subpopulations is accompanied by migration in both directions, change in the system can be described in terms of constants r_{ij}, $i = 1, 2, j = 1, 2$:

$$p_{t+1} = r_{11}p_t + r_{12}q_t,$$
$$q_{t+1} = r_{21}p_t + r_{22}q_t. \tag{1.9.1}$$

Equations 1.9.1 are identical to the matrix equation

$$\begin{bmatrix} p_{t+1} \\ q_{t+1} \end{bmatrix} = \begin{bmatrix} r_{11} & r_{12} \\ r_{21} & r_{22} \end{bmatrix} \begin{bmatrix} p_t \\ q_t \end{bmatrix}, \tag{1.9.2}$$

which can be written compactly as

$$\mathbf{P}_{t+1} = \mathbf{R}\mathbf{P}_t, \tag{1.9.3}$$

where $\mathbf{P}_t$ is the population vector at time t, and $\mathbf{R}$ is the matrix of growth and transfer rates, referred to indifferently as a transition or a projection matrix. If the rates r_{11}, r_{21}, r_{12}, and r_{22} are fixed over time, (1.9.3) recurrently determines the population at any arbitrary time subsequent to

t. The population at time $t + n$ equals that at time t successively operated on n times by $\mathbf{R}$:

$$\mathbf{P}_{t+n} = \mathbf{R}\big(\ldots (\mathbf{R}(\mathbf{RP}_t) \ldots) \big) = \mathbf{R}^n \mathbf{P}_t. \tag{1.9.4}$$

If $r_{12} = r_{21} = 0$, and $r_{11} \neq r_{22}$, the argument of Section 1.4 applies; the two subpopulations never come into a finite, nonzero ratio to one another, and the subgroup with the higher rate keeps growing relative to the one with the lower rate. But if r_{12} and r_{21} are positive, then, no matter how different r_{11} and r_{22} may be, the two subpopulations will ultimately tend to increase at the same rate. This stability of the ratio of one population to the other will of course occur more quickly if r_{12} and r_{21} are large in relation to the difference between r_{11} and r_{22}.

The aspect of stability referred to above is that in which the ratio of the sizes of the subpopulations ultimately ceases to depend on time. When this occurs, it follows that each of the subgroups will increase at a rate not depending on time, that is to say, in geometric progression. For when population q is c times as large as population p, for all times, then, from the first member of (1.9.1),

$$p_{t+1} = r_{11}p_t + r_{12}q_t = (r_{11} + cr_{12})p_t,$$

which proves that p_{t+1} is a constant multiple of p_t. This applies to any number of subgroups, and shows for the linear model of (1.9.1) that, if the ratio of the sizes of the subgroups to one another is constant, each is increasing geometrically. It can then be shown that all the groups are increasing at the same rate. Conversely, if the subgroups are increasing geometrically and at the same rate, they are in fixed ratios to one another.

When the process of which (1.9.1) is an example attains stability, not only are all its subpopulations increasing at the same rate and in fixed ratios to one another, but also those ratios are not in any way influenced by the starting ratios. It could be that p_0 is 1 million times as large as q_0, or that q_0 is 1 million times as large as p_0; the two cases will have the same ultimate ratio of p_t to q_t. This property of the process, forgetting its past, is a third aspect of stability.

There is no moment when stability is suddenly attained. Stability is a limiting property by which a time can be found when the several subpopulations increase at rates that are arbitrarily close to one another.

Problems arise involving scores, even thousands, of subgroups within a population; the matrices become very large and the conditions for stability very complex, so that it is convenient to have a way of ascertaining without explicit calculations whether the system, if continued, would lead to stability. Fortunately two general rules suffice to determine which projection matrices will result in stability, rules expressed in terms of *graphs*.

A graph consists of *vertices*, corresponding in our problem to the states or subgroups of a population, and *edges*, representing transitions among states, regions, and so on. (Formally the vertices and edges are not defined except as points and the lines joining them.) In our work the edges will always be *directed*, the direction indicated by an arrow, and the graphs will be the special kind known as *digraphs*.

An exact correspondence can be drawn between a digraph and a matrix containing zeros and ones. Consider the 3×3 matrix **A** and an initial population vector **P**:

$$\mathbf{A} = \begin{bmatrix} 1 & 0 & 1 \\ 1 & 0 & 0 \\ 0 & 1 & 0 \end{bmatrix} \quad \text{and} \quad \mathbf{P} = \begin{bmatrix} p_1 \\ p_2 \\ p_3 \end{bmatrix}.$$

The matrix provides for transitions wherever it has nonzero elements. For example, in the matrix multiplication **AP** the positive entry unity in position 1, 3 represents a transition from state 3 in the initial vector to state 1 in the final vector. The matrix **A** provides for transitions from state 1 to itself, from 3 to 1, from 1 to 2, and from 2 to 3. In general, a positive entry a_{ij} (row i, column j) represents a transition from state j to state i; if $i = j$, it represents a transition from state i to itself. A zero entry in a_{ij} means that no transition is permitted from state j to state i. With states denoted by vertices and possible transitions by arrows, the matrix **A** is equivalent to the digraph of Fig. 1.3.

Irreducibility or Connectivity

A necessary condition for ultimate stability is that the projection matrix be *irreducible*; the corresponding digraph is called *strongly connected*. A graph is strongly connected if passage is possible from any vertex to any other

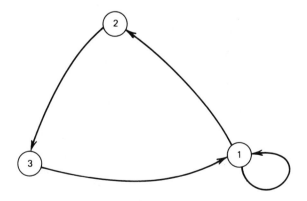

Fig. 1.3 Digraph corresponding to matrix **A**.

vertex, with or without going through additional vertices on the way; a matrix whose graph does not satisfy this condition is *reducible*. Thus the graph in Fig. 1.3 is strongly connected. A matrix is reducible, for instance, if its graph divides into separate noncommunicating blocks, as in Fig. 1.4*a*, or if it has even one point out of which no passage is provided, as vertex 4 in Fig. 1.4*b*. Anyone who prefers can replace the word "irreducible" by the corresponding "strongly connected," the former being more often used in reference to matrices, the latter in reference to digraphs.

Irreducibility of a matrix is a necessary but not sufficient condition for stability to occur at high powers of the matrix. What is further required is that the matrix fill up with positive elements, so that it contains no zeros, as it goes to high powers. Consider the matrix

$$\mathbf{B} = \begin{bmatrix} 0 & 0 & 1 \\ 1 & 0 & 0 \\ 0 & 1 & 0 \end{bmatrix}$$

and the corresponding irreducible digraph in Fig. 1.5: the cube $\mathbf{B}^3$ is the identity matrix, as may be verified by multiplication, and thus $\mathbf{B}^4$ is the

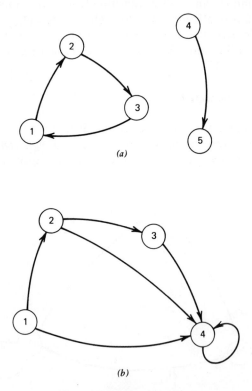

(a)

(b)

Fig. 1.4   Reducible digraphs.

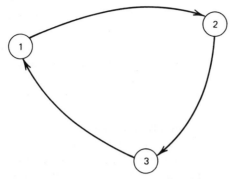

Fig. 1.5   A cyclic digraph corresponding to matrix **B**.

same as **B**. Though each cell becomes unity at one time or another, the matrix at no time fills up with positive numbers; instead it goes through endless cycles. Repeated multiplication of a population vector by **B** will never produce stable ratios.

Primitivity

By permitting one element of **B** to communicate with itself, we can destroy the cyclic character of **B**. For example, matrix **A** given above is not cyclic. In particular, $\mathbf{A}^8$ contains only positive numbers, and this special type of irreducible matrix is called *primitive*. An arbitrary matrix **D**, is primitive if some power of it, say $\mathbf{D}^N$, has only positive elements. For the corresponding graph primitivity implies that a number N can be found such that one can go from any vertex of the graph to any other vertex in exactly N moves.

Irreducibility requires only that every point be reachable from every other point, not necessarily in the same number of moves; in the irreducible graph B of Fig. 1.5 one can go from 1 to 2 in one move but not in two, and from 2 to 1 in two moves but not in one. The number of moves is called the *length* of a route. Primitivity, defined only for an irreducible matrix, requires the existence of a number N such that a route of length N on the graph can be found between any two points, a special case of irreducibility. We will accept without proof the fact that primitivity of a nonnegative irreducible matrix is a sufficient condition for stability (Perron, 1907; Frobenius, 1912; Parlett, 1970).

A fundamental theorem permits the primitivity of a matrix to be recognized from its digraph. A *circuit* of a digraph is a unidirectional closed subset of vertices and directed edges whose length is equal to the number of edges of the subset. Thus, if vertex 1 connects with itself, it forms a circuit of length 1, whereas the circuit drawn in Fig. 1.5 is of length 3. The theorem expresses primitivity in terms of the lengths of circuits in a digraph: an irreducible matrix is primitive *if and only if its digraph has at least two circuits whose lengths* l_1 *and* l_2 *are relatively prime.* (Two numbers are relatively prime if they have no common divisor greater than 1.)

This theorem has essentially the same content as a proposition in number theory: given integers l_1 and l_2, which are relatively prime, there exists a positive number beyond which every greater integer can be written in the form $al_1 + bl_2$, where a and b are nonnegative integers.

Application to Birth and Death

Consider the above theorem in terms of the survival and aging process. Aging corresponds to a digraph that goes from the first to the second, to the third, to the fourth, ... age groups (Fig. 1.6). The matrix corresponding to this digraph is neither irreducible nor primitive; everyone drifts to the end of life. Suppose a provision for birth in the sixth age group, and hence one circuit (Fig. 1.7). Since the seventh and eighth age groups lead purely to extinction and generate no further population, we drop these ages, and the digraph up to age group 6 becomes irreducible. However, since it has only one circuit, the digraph is not yet primitive. To obtain primitivity we

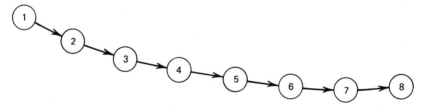

Fig. 1.6   Aging process.

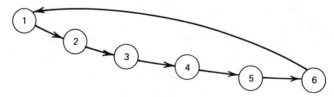

Fig. 1.7   Aging with one age of childbearing.

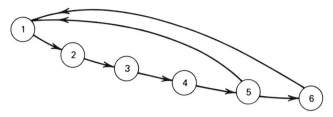

Fig. 1.8 Aging with two consecutive ages of childbearing.

need at least two age groups of childbearing, and we must be careful to choose these age groups relatively prime; for example, the third and sixth ages would not serve. Providing for fertility in the fifth and sixth ages gives Fig. 1.8, and now the digraph is strongly connected and the corresponding matrix is primitive (Demetrius, 1971).

To summarize, an irreducible matrix that is also primitive makes any population vector that it is repeatedly premultiplying come to a fixed set of ratios, which do not depend on the original composition of the population. This ergodic property, the tendency of a vector or population to forget its past, has been illustrated above by examples in which the same matrix is applied repeatedly. An analogous property of a series of different matrices was conjectured by Coale: that two different vectors become similar to one another when they are acted on by the same series of matrices. This important theorem was proved by Lopez (1961).

The results of the present section apply whenever we seek to understand a current movement by asking what would happen if it continued indefinitely into the future. Any linear projection with fixed transitions, recognizing ages, regions, occupations, school grades, and so on, may be treated in the same way. Using the methods of this section, we might study, for example, migration between California and the rest of the United States over a decade, as did Rogers (1968), and ask what would be the stable condition if both in-migration and out-migration continued indefinitely; we might study movement through the educational system (Stone, 1972), through the occupational structure (Tabah, 1968), and through many other networks. In all such cases the transitions can be represented as a matrix, and the stability properties of the matrix studied by means of a graph.

Chapter 4 considers in much detail one case of stability—a population developing under fixed mortality and rate of increase. To prepare for it we need to transform raw mortality data into a life table, and this is the subject of Chapter 2.

Chapter Two

THE LIFE TABLE

The main part of this book starts where demography itself started, with the life table. The life table is couched in terms of probabilities for individuals, but for populations it is a deterministic model of mortality and survivorship. That it presents expected values and disregards random variation is contrary to the way nature works and, in particular, oversimplifies demographic mechanisms, yet a rich variety of useful results is based on it. A method is valuable in direct proportion to the substantive conclusions to which it leads, and in inverse proportion to its complexity.

The life table is mathematically simple and has large substantive payoff. First, it answers questions concerning individuals: what is the probability that a man aged 30 will survive until he retires at 65, or that he will outlive his wife, aged 27? But it also answers questions concerning cohorts, groups of individuals born at the same time: what fraction of the births of this year will still be alive in the year 2000, or how many of them will live to the age of retirement? Third, it answers population questions: if births were constant from year to year in a closed population of constant mortality, what fraction of the population would be 65 and over?

2.1 DEFINITION OF LIFE TABLE FUNCTIONS

The probability of surviving from birth to age x is designated as $l(x)$ for a continuous function of x and as l_x for discrete x. Life tables usually present the probability multiplied by 100,000, which is to say, on a *radix*, l_0, equal to 100,000. If l_x is a probability, then, strictly speaking, what life tables show is $100,000 l_x$, but it would be pedantic to repeat the 100,000 each time the l_x column is referred to. When l_x is interpreted as surviving members of a cohort, the radix is arbitrary; and setting $l_0 = 100,000$ enables one more easily to think of the column as numbers of persons reaching the given age.

The difference in number of survivors for successive ages, $l_x - l_{x+1}$, is designated as d_x; and, more generally, the difference for ages n years apart, $l_x - l_{x+n}$, is $_n d_x$. This divided by l_x is the probability of dying during the next n years for a person who has reached age x:

$$_n q_x = \frac{l_x - l_{x+n}}{l_x} = \frac{_n d_x}{l_x}.$$

The total number of years lived during the next n years by those who have attained age x is

$$_n L_x = \int_x^{x+n} l(a) \, da,$$

which is also the number of persons aged exactly x to $x+n$ (or x to $x+n-1$ at last birthday) in the *stationary* population. Setting n equal to infinity or (indifferently) to $\omega - x$, where ω is the highest age to which anyone lives, gives

$$_\infty L_x = T_x = \int_x^{\omega} l(a) \, da.$$

The quantity T_x is the total number of years remaining to the cohort, when it reaches age x, until the last member dies at age ω. Dividing by l_x gives the average share in this total per person reaching age x:

$$\overset{o}{e}_x = \frac{T_x}{l_x} = \frac{\int_x^{\omega} l(a) \, da}{l_x}.$$

In terms of probabilities $\overset{o}{e}_x$ is the mean of the distribution of years to death for persons of age x and is called the *expectation of life*.

The age-specific death rate in the life table population is $_n m_x = {_n d_x}/{_n L_x}$. This may be compared with the probability $_n q_x = {_n d_x}/{l_x}$, and one can think of $_n q_x$ as something less than n times $_n m_x$. It is distinct from $_n M_x$, the observed death rate in a real population; $_n M_x < {_n m_x}$ for increasing populations at ages beyond about 10.

Theoretical statements on mortality are often expressed most simply in terms of the age-specific death rate in a narrow age interval dx, designated as $\mu(x)$:

$$\mu(x) = \lim_{n \to 0} \frac{l_x - l_{x+n}}{\int_x^{x+n} l(a) \, da} = \frac{-1}{l(x)} \frac{dl(x)}{dx}.$$

[Show that the solution of this gives (1.5.5).] The age-specific death rate could also be written as

$$\mu(x) = \lim_{n \to 0} {}_n m_x = \lim_{n \to 0} \frac{{}_n d_x}{{}_n L_x},$$

if the mixing of continuous and discrete notation can be excused.

Mortality the Same for All Ages. A mathematical form that has often been used for short intervals of age, is one in which the force of mortality is constant. If $\mu(x) = \mu$, solving the differential equation that defines μ,

$$\mu = \frac{-1}{l(x)} \cdot \frac{dl(x)}{dx},$$

gives

$$l(x) = e^{-\mu x}.$$

The probability of living at least an additional n years after one has attained age x is

$$\frac{l_{x+n}}{l_x} = \frac{e^{-\mu(x+n)}}{e^{-\mu x}} = e^{-\mu n}.$$

The expectation of life is

$$\overset{o}{e}_x = \frac{1}{l(x)} \int_0^\infty l(x+t)\,dt$$

$$= \frac{1}{e^{-\mu x}} \int_0^\infty e^{-\mu(x+t)}\,dt = \frac{1}{\mu}.$$

Both the probability of living an additional n years beyond age x and the expectation of life at age x are constants independent of x. The prospect ahead of any living person is the same, no matter how old he is, on this peculiar table. All the columns of the life table are in general derivable from any one column, and if any column is age-independent all the others referring to a person's prospects must be also.

Application of these definitions to other mathematically specified forms of $\mu(x)$ requires more difficult integration to find $l(x)$ and $\overset{o}{e}_x$. The function $\mu(a) = \mu_0/(\omega - a)$ is applied in Section 3.3. Here we proceed to methods for constructing a life table from empirical data.

2.2 LIFE TABLES BASED ON DATA

We read that for the United States during the year 1967 122,672 men aged 65 to 69 years of age at last birthday died, and that the number of men of these ages alive on July 1, 1967, was 2,958,000. These may be called observations. We can divide the first figure by the second and find that the age-specific death rate for males 65 to 69, denoted as $_5M_{65}$, was 0.04147, again straightforward enough to be called an observation. How do these observations tell us the probability, $1 - (l_{70}/l_{65})$, that a man chosen at random from those aged exactly 65 will die before reaching age 70? This is the same as asking what fraction of a cohort of men aged 65 would be expected to die before reaching age 70, and its complement, l_{70}/l_{65}, the fraction of those aged 65 who survive to age 70. From time period data we want to know something about a cohort, men moving from age 65 to 70. This cohort is necessarily hypothetical, for with only one period of observation the best we can manage is to suppose mortality to be unchanging through time. No real cohort is likely to exhibit the regime that will be inferred from 1967 data.

The observations of a given period, the calendar year 1967, are, moreover, ambiguous because we know nothing about the distribution of exposure within each 5-year age interval, affected as it is by all the accidents of the birth curve and of migration.

Assuming Constant Probability of Dying within the Age Interval

If, in addition to supposing that the probability of dying is invariant with respect to time, we suppose it to be invariant with respect to age within the 5-year group, the probability l_x can be inferred from the rate $_5M_x$ in a straightforward manner. We saw in Section 1.5 that a population initially of size P_0 and increasing at constant rate r reaches a total $P_0 e^{rt}$ after t years. If it is decreasing at constant rate μ, as will be the case if it is closed and subject to a constant death rate μ, and it numbers l_x at the start, then at the end of 5 years it will be $l_{x+5} = l_x e^{-5\mu}$, as in the preceding section. Identifying $_5M_x$ with μ gives

$$\frac{l_{x+5}}{l_x} = e^{-5 {_5M_x}} \tag{2.2.1}$$

as a first approximation to the desired ratio l_{x+5}/l_x. For our data on the United States in 1967, (2.2.1) is

$$\frac{l_{70}}{l_{65}} = e^{-5 {_5M_{65}}} = e^{-5(0.04147)} = 0.81274.$$

This would be exact if either (a) the death rate were constant through the 5-year age interval, or (b) the population exposed to risk were constant through the 5-year age interval. Neither of these, however, applies in practice; in general, beyond age 10 the death rate is increasing through the interval and the population is diminishing.

The Basic Equation and a Conventional Solution

Suppose that the exposed population follows the curve $p(a)$ within the age interval x to $x+5$, and that at exact age a the age-specific death rate is $\mu(a)$. Then the observed rate $_5M_x$ can be identified with a ratio of integrals:

$$_5M_x = \frac{\int_x^{x+5} p(a)\,\mu(a)\,da}{\int_x^{x+5} p(a)\,da}. \qquad (2.2.2)$$

Making a life table is a matter of inferring l_{x+5}/l_x from (2.2.2). This is equivalent to inferring the unweighted $\int_x^{x+5}\mu(a)da$ from the weighted average of the $\mu(a)$ in (2.2.2), for from (1.5.5) we know that $\int_x^{x+5}\mu(a)da = -\ln(l_{x+5}/l_x)$, so the unweighted average of the $\mu(a)$ gives the $l(x)$ column (Weck, 1947).

Basic equation 2.2.2 reminds us that the interpretation of the observed $_5M_x$ depends on the (unknown) distribution of population within the age interval x to $x+n$. We must somehow extract $\int_x^{x+5}\mu(a)da$ from (2.2.2), a task that appears hopeless when nothing is known but $_5M_x$. Yet every life table based on empirical data in 5-year groups implicitly infers $\int_x^{x+5}\mu(a)da$ from (2.2.2); this is achieved by making assumptions that somehow restrict $p(a)$.

One common solution of (2.2.2) is to assume $p(a) = l(a)$, and also to suppose that $l(x)$ is a straight line. The integral under the straight line is

$$\int_x^{x+5} l(a)\,da = \tfrac{5}{2}(l_x + l_{x+5}). \qquad (2.2.3)$$

Since $\int_x^{x+5} l(a)\,\mu(a)\,da = l_x - l_{x+5}$, (2.2.2) may be written as

$$_5M_x = \frac{l_x - l_{x+5}}{\tfrac{5}{2}(l_x + l_{x+5})}, \qquad (2.2.4)$$

from which the value of l_{x+5}/l_x may be obtained by dividing numerator and denominator on the right by l_x, and then solving a linear equation for l_{x+5}/l_x to find

$$\frac{l_{x+5}}{l_x} = \frac{1 - 5\,_5M_x/2}{1 + 5\,_5M_x/2}. \qquad (2.2.5)$$

For United States males aged 65 to 69 this is 0.81213, obtained from $_5M_{65} = 0.04147$. This is closer to the corrected value than the 0.81274 of

(2.2.1). From (2.2.5) the probability of dying is

$$_5q_x = 1 - \frac{l_{x+5}}{l_x} = \frac{5 \, _5M_x}{1 + 5 \, _5M_x/2} \, . \qquad (2.2.6)$$

A Precise Life Table without Iteration or Graduation

To improve on (2.2.5) or the exponential (2.2.1), we go a step farther in extracting from (2.2.2) the quantity $\int_x^{x+5} \mu(a) \, da$. We would expect the answer to emerge as $\int_x^{x+5} \mu(a) \, da = 5(_5M_x + C)$, where it will turn out that C is a correction easily obtained on the assumption that both the population $p(a)$ and the death rate $\mu(a)$ change linearly within the interval.

We calculate the correction to $_nM_x$ for a general interval of n years, starting at age x. First we change variables by writing $a = x + (n/2) + t$; (2.2.2) with n in place of 5 becomes

$$_nM_x = \frac{\displaystyle\int_{-n/2}^{+n/2} p\left[x + (n/2) + t\right] \mu\left[x + (n/2) + t\right] dt}{\displaystyle\int_x^{x+n} p(a) \, da} \, . \qquad (2.2.7)$$

Expanding each of the fractions in the numerator by Taylor's series to the term linear in t gives

$$_nM_x = \frac{\displaystyle\int_{-n/2}^{+n/2} \left[p(x+n/2) + tp'(x+n/2)\right]\left[\mu(x+n/2) + t\mu'(x+n/2)\right] dt}{\displaystyle\int_x^{x+n} p(a) \, da}$$

$$= \frac{\left[tp(x+n/2)\mu(x+n/2) + \dfrac{t^3}{3} p'(x+n/2)\mu'(x+n/2)\right]_{-n/2}^{+n/2}}{\displaystyle\int_x^{x+n} p(a) \, da}$$

$$= \frac{np(x+n/2)\mu(x+n/2) + (n^3/12)p'(x+n/2)\mu'(x+n/2)}{\displaystyle\int_x^{x+n} p(a) \, da} \, . \qquad (2.2.8)$$

But this can be translated into known quantities as follows:

1. If $p(a)$ is a straight line in the interval between x and $x+n$, then $np(x+n/2)$ is the same as $\int_x^{x+n} p(a) \, da$ and cancels with the denominator.

2. If $\mu(a)$ is a straight line between x and $x+n$, then the midvalue $\mu(x+n/2)$ is $1/n$ of the integral we seek, i.e., is $(1/n) \int_x^{x+n} \mu(a) \, da$.

3. The integral $\int_x^{x+n} p(a) \, da$ is the observed population in the age interval, $_nP_x$.

Thus (2.2.8) becomes

$$_nM_x = \frac{1}{n}\int_x^{x+n}\mu(a)\,da + \frac{n^3}{12\,_nP_x}p'\left(x+\frac{n}{2}\right)\mu'\left(x+\frac{n}{2}\right), \qquad (2.2.9)$$

which after transposing provides the desired $\int_x^{x+n}\mu(a)\,da$ as

$$\int_x^{x+n}\mu(a)\,da = n\,_nM_x - \frac{n^4}{12\,_nP_x}p'\left(x+\frac{n}{2}\right)\mu'\left(x+\frac{n}{2}\right). \qquad (2.2.10)$$

All that remains for the application is to express the first derivatives on the right of (2.2.10) in terms of known quantities. One might make the natural assumption that the slope within the interval x to $x+n$ is given by the difference between neighboring intervals:

$$p'\left(x+\frac{n}{2}\right) = -\frac{_nP_{x-n} - \,_nP_{x+n}}{2n^2},$$

$$\mu'\left(x+\frac{n}{2}\right) = \frac{_nM_{x+n} - \,_nM_{x-n}}{2n}, \qquad\qquad (2.2.11)$$

and so the calculable value of l_{x+n}/l_x is

$$\frac{l_{x+n}}{l_x} = \exp\left(-\int_x^{x+n}\mu(a)\,da\right)$$

$$= \exp\left[-n\,_nM_x - \frac{n}{48\,_nP_x}(_nP_{x-n} - \,_nP_{x+n})(_nM_{x+n} - \,_nM_{x-n})\right]$$

$$= \exp\left[-n(_nM_x + C)\right]. \qquad\qquad (2.2.12)$$

[I am grateful to James Frauenthal for correcting my original approximation to $p'(x+n/2)$ in (2.2.11), which had n rather than n^2 in the denominator.]

The expression for l_{x+n}/l_x in (2.2.12) is the outcome of the search for a life table that would accord with the data in the sense of having the same underlying $\mu(x)$ as the observations, yet be calculable in one simple step. It is equivalent to using the simple exponential $l_{x+n}/l_x = e^{-n\,_nM_x}$, but first raising $_nM_x$ by the quantity $C = (_nP_{x-n} - \,_nP_{x+n})(_nM_{x+n} - \,_nM_{x-n})/48\,_nP_x$, a product that is positive wherever the population is declining with age and the death rate is rising.

The accuracy of (2.2.12) has been impressive in the tests so far done. Applying it to Swedish males, 1965, at ages 20 to 65, for example, we found that l_{65}/l_{20} differed by 0.00001 from the value obtained by interpolating to fifths of a year separately for deaths and population, constructing the life table in fifths of a year, and then reassembling into 5-year age groups. It also differed by about 0.00001 from the more elaborate iterative life table (Keyfitz, 1968, Chapter 1).

In an age of computers ease of calculation is less important than it once was, but nonetheless Table 2.1 is introduced to show the extreme simplicity of the arithmetic.

Table 2.1   Example of life table calculation without iteration or graduation, United States males, 1972

$$\frac{l_{x+5}}{l_x} = \exp[-5_5M_x - \frac{5}{48_5P_x}(_5P_{x-5} - _5P_{x+5})(_5M_{x+5} - _5M_{x-5})]$$

$$= \exp[-5(_5M_x + C)]$$

Age	$\dfrac{_5P_x}{1000}$	1000_5M_x	Correction to $_5M_x$; $C =$ $\dfrac{(_5P_{x-5} - _5P_{x+5})(_5M_{x+5} - _5M_{x-5})}{48_5P_x}$	$\dfrac{l_{x+5}}{l_x} =$ $e^{-5(_5M_x + C)}$	$_5q_x =$ $1 - \dfrac{l_{x+5}}{l_x}$
x	(1)	(2)	(3)	(4)	(5)
35	5458	3.017			
40	5720	4.623	− 0.0000058	0.97718	0.02282
45	5814	7.483	0.0000025	0.96326	0.03674
50	5616	11.367	0.0000388	0.94457	0.05543
55	4828	18.092	0.0000990	0.91306	0.08694
60	4192	27.483	0.0001667	0.87088	0.12912
65	3294	39.958	0.0003802	0.81735	0.18265
70	2330	59.770			

The present method can be adapted to the ages at the beginning and end of life. However, these ages involve data problems as well as rapidly changing mortality rates. The reader is referred to Shryock and Siegel (1971, Chapter 15), Wolfenden (1954), Keyfitz (1968, Chapter 1), or other source for ages under 10 and over 80.

A further point due to Kenneth Wachter and Thomas Greville is that the derivative $\mu'(x + n/2)$ cannot strictly be estimated by $(_nM_{x+n} - _nM_{x-n})/2n$, for the M's are *weighted* averages of the μ's and in a growing population will always be too low. We can escape the difficulty by a second iteration. When an approximate value has been found for the l_x, we in effect have an approximation to the unweighted $\int_{x-n}^{x}\mu(a)\,da = -\ln(l_x/l_{x-n})$, and can enter this divided by n in place of the $_nM_{x-n}$. In short, we would substitute for $_nM_{x+n} - _nM_{x-n}$ the quantity $(1/n)\ln(l_x l_{x+n}/l_{x-n}l_{x+2n})$ obtained on the first iteration.

The numerical effect can be judged from the following values obtained from Table 2.1:

Age	$_nM_{x+n} - {}_nM_{x-n}$	$\frac{1}{n}\ln(\frac{l_x l_{x+n}}{l_{x-n} l_{x+2n}})$
45	0.00674	0.00679
50	0.01061	0.01070
55	0.01612	0.01625
60	0.02187	0.02215

The differences $_nM_{x+n} - {}_nM_{x-n}$ are in all cases too low, but the largest discrepancy is about 1.25 percent. This means that our correction, itself of the order of 1 percent of $_nM_x$, would be raised by about 1 percent on the iteration. Few users will regard this correction of the correction as numerically important.

Greville and Reed–Merrell Methods Derived as Special Cases

The generality of (2.2.10) can be demonstrated by applying it to derive a well-known expression due to Greville (1943):

$$\int_0^n \mu(x+t)\,dt = n_n m_x + \frac{n^3}{12}{}_n m_x^2 (\ln {}_n m_x)', \qquad (2.2.13)$$

in terms of $_n m_x$, the life table death rate defined as $_n d_x / {}_n L_x$, where the prime again signifies a derivative.

The demonstration starts by writing $l(x)$ for $p(x)$ in (2.2.10) and noting that $l'(x+n/2) = -l(x+n/2)\mu(x+n/2)$. Thus, when $_nM_x$ is replaced with $_n m_x$ and $_nP_x$ with $_n L_x$ (as though the data came from a stationary rather than an increasing population), (2.2.10) becomes

$$\int_0^n \mu(x+t)\,dt = n_n m_x + \frac{n^4}{12_n L_x} l\left(x+\frac{n}{2}\right)\mu\left(x+\frac{n}{2}\right)\mu'\left(x+\frac{n}{2}\right)$$

$$\doteq n_n m_x + \frac{n^3}{12}{}_n m_x {}_n m_x',$$

if we approximate $l(x+n/2)/{}_n L_x$ by $1/n$ and $\mu(x+n/2)$ by $_n m_x$. Multiplying and dividing the correction term on the right of the last expression by $_n m_x$, and then using the fact that $_n m_x'/{}_n m_x = (\ln {}_n m_x)'$, provides Greville's result (2.2.13).

Greville expressed his result as (2.2.13) to make use of the virtual constancy of $(\ln {}_n m_x)'$ through most ages and for most life tables. If this is taken as $(\ln {}_n m_x)' = 0.096$, then (2.2.10) becomes

$$\int_0^n \mu(x+t)\,dt = n_n m_x + 0.008 n^3 {}_n m_x^2,$$

so that the survival probability is

$$\frac{l_{x+n}}{l_x} = \exp\left[-\int_0^n \mu(x+t)\,dt\right] = \exp\left(-n_n m_x - 0.008 n^3 {}_n m_x^2\right), \quad (2.2.14)$$

which is the expression derived empirically by Reed and Merrell (1939). The tabulation of (2.2.14) included in the Reed–Merrell paper has been used more extensively than any other system for making a life table. It was indeed convenient in the days before computers were available, but it rests on two gross assumptions: (1) that the observed population provides the stationary age-specific rates of the life table; and (2) that the same form, $0.008 n^3 {}_n m_x^2$, serves to correct the ${}_n m_x$ for all ages and for any life table. The simple expression 2.2.12 avoids both these restrictions.

Bounds on Error

All of the above discussion would be superfluous if there were some *correct* way to make a life table. Unfortunately ignorance of the distribution of population and deaths within each 5-year age interval has to be compensated for by more or less arbitrary assumptions. For most populations single years are sought from the respondent, but the information is published only in 5-year intervals, a wise policy on the part of the statistical authorities in view of the inaccuracy of individual reporting. Whether the age intervals 5 to 9, 10 to 14, and so on, are the best is another matter; concentration on multiples of 5 causes these to understate the mean age in comparison with 3 to 7, 8 to 12, and so on.

The deaths and population can of course be interpolated so finely that the outcome is unique whatever the interpolation formula. Whole years or fifths of a year are sufficiently fine since the uncertainty of converting ${}_n M_x$ into ${}_n q_x$ decreases with the cube of the interval n. To be convinced of this, compare two formulas generalized from (2.2.1) and (2.2.6), respectively:

$$_n q_x = 1 - e^{-n_n M_x} \quad \text{and} \quad _n q_x = \frac{n_n M_x}{1 + (n/2)({}_n M_x)}.$$

Expanding these in powers of n gives

$$1 - e^{-n_n M_x} = n_n M_x - \frac{n^2 {}_n M_x^2}{2!} + \frac{n^3 {}_n M_x^3}{3!} - \cdots.$$

and

$$\frac{n_n M_x}{1 + (n/2)(_n M_x)} = _n M_x - \frac{n^2 {_n M_x^2}}{2} + \frac{n^3 {_n M_x^3}}{4} - \cdots .$$

The two agree up to the term in n^2; then the exponential is lower by the difference $n^3 {_n M_x^3}/12$, disregarding higher-order terms. Thus the difference in single years is approximately $1/125$ of the difference in 5-year age groups.

But interpolation cannot provide a uniquely correct table, since it depends on a choice of formula that is inevitably arbitrary. Iterative methods also make various assumptions; one such method (Keyfitz, 1968, p. 19) supposes local stability—that the observed population has been increasing uniformly within 5-year age intervals. The method of the present chapter avoids both interpolation and iteration; its arbitrariness involves the derivatives for the correction to $l_{x+n}/l_x = e^{-_n M_x}$ in (2.2.12), calculated by stretching a straight line between the age intervals below and above the one of interest, and experimenting has shown that different ways of calculating the first or higher derivatives make little difference.

Lacking knowledge of the true life table, can we at least set bounds on it? We can, establishing the higher bound by supposing the population (and corresponding deaths) within the age group x to $x+n$ to be all concentrated at the low end. This would mean that the observed death rate really refers to exact age x, so that what we call $_n M_x$ is not an average of the rates $\mu(t)$ from x to $x+n$, but is really $\mu(x)$. If, on the other hand, the population is all concentrated at the high end, what we observe as $_n M_x$ is really $\mu(x+n)$. These two opposite possibilities furnish the extreme bounds; the $_n M_x$, and hence the l_x column derived from it, could refer to a population $n/2$ years younger than stated, or to a population $n/2$ years older. No logic can demonstrate that either such freak situation is impossible, improbable though it may be in even a small population.

For the United States life table of 1967, $\overset{o}{e}_{15}$ for males was 54.22 years. On the above-mentioned argument this number could really represent anything from $\overset{o}{e}_{12\frac{1}{2}}$ to $\overset{o}{e}_{17\frac{1}{2}}$. Since at these ages $\overset{o}{e}_x$ is declining by about 4.75 years per 5 years of age, the true $\overset{o}{e}_{15}$ could lie approximately in a range from $54.22 - 4.75/2$ to $54.22 + 4.75/2$, or from 51.84 to 56.60. Such a range is too wide to be of much practical interest, and yet I see no logic by which one can narrow the possibilities. Not only is there no correct life table, but also there is not even a simple way of establishing a realistic range of error, analogous to the 0.95 confidence interval that is used where a probability model applies.

A lower bound to the error of the life table is obtained by supposing that individuals die independently at random, each with probability $_nq_x$ for his age x. The expression for this is easily derived (Keyfitz, 1968, p. 341, is a secondary source with references). But such an error seems as far below the true error as that of this section is above.

2.3   FURTHER SMALL CORRECTIONS

The method of calculating a life table expressed in (2.2.12) has proved highly satisfactory in practice, giving negligible departure from graduated life tables and from iterated tables, without requiring either graduation or iteration. However, it depends on solving basic equation 2.2.2 for the integral for $\mu(a)$, and therefore some readers may wish to look more closely at the rationale of (2.2.2).

Measure of Exposure.   A diagram, due to Lexis (1875), that displays the population by age and time will help in this. Each individual at any moment is represented by a point; the collection of points for any individual is his life line through time; the end of the line is at the moment and age of his death.

Figure 2.1 shows the beginning and end of the year 1967, for which the observations are being analyzed, as horizontal lines, and ages 65 and 70 as vertical lines. In the rectangle $ABCD$, 122,672 male lines come to an end for the United States in 1967. We do not quite know how many lines are in the rectangle, but it was estimated that 2,958,000 crossed the horizontal

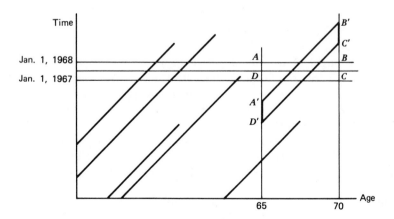

Fig. 2.1   Living and dying population displayed on plane of age and time in Lexis diagram.

line for July 1, 1967, and this number, $_5P_x$ in general, is commonly used to estimate exposure; it would be better to use person-years.

Other directions of improvement, which the reader may wish to investigate, include the use of higher derivatives in the Taylor expansion of (2.2.8), and better ways of estimating the first derivative. Differences useful in approximating to the derivatives are provided in Table 2.2. Their effect on the correction C of Table 2.1 will be found to be slight.

Table 2.2 Population and deaths, United States males, 1972, along with their first and second differences

Age x	Population $_5P_x$	$\Delta_5 P_x$	$\Delta_5^2 P_x$	Deaths $_5D_x$	$_5M_x = \dfrac{_5D_x}{_5P_x}$	$\Delta_5 M_x$	$\Delta_5^2 M_x$
50	5,616,000			63,838	0.011367		
		− 788,000				0.006725	
55	4,828,000		152,000	87,348	0.018092		0.002666
		− 636,000				0.009391	
60	4,192,000		− 262,000	115,208	0.027483		0.003083
		− 898,000				0.012474	
65	3,294,000		− 66,000	131,620	0.039957		0.007339
		− 964,000				0.019813	
70	2,330,000		218,000	139,264	0.059770		0.008784
		− 746,000				0.028597	
75	1,584,000		84,000	139,974	0.088367		0.006392
		− 662,000				0.034989	
80	922,000			113,734	0.123356		—

2.4 PERIOD AND COHORT TABLES

We have noted that, although in each age group the life table estimates how much a cohort will diminish by death, the probabilities for the several ages are chained together in a way that can represent only the period for which the data are gathered. The result describes what is sometimes referred to as a synthetic cohort.

To follow genuine cohorts we can chain together the survival probabilities of a sequence of periods. In 1919–21 the chance of survival for 5 years for a male just born was 0.87420 (Keyfitz and Flieger, 1968, p. 142); in 1924–26 the chance of survival from age 5 to age 10 was $88{,}574/89{,}600 = 0.98855$ (p. 144); in 1929–31 from age 10 to age 15 it was $88{,}814/89{,}587 = 0.99137$ (p. 145); and so on. Chaining these together gives

$$l_0 = 100{,}000, \qquad l_5 = 87{,}420, \qquad l_{10} = 86{,}419, \qquad l_{15} = 85{,}673 \quad \text{etc.,}$$

as an estimate of survivorship for a real child born about 1917. Portrayal on a Lexis diagram suggests that the result is a reasonably good approximation, provided that mortality does not change abruptly over time. Refinements of the cohort calculation are being carried out by Michael Stoto, who has improved estimates of population and deaths in the lozenge $A'B'C'D'$ of Fig. 2.1.

2.5 FINANCIAL CALCULATIONS

Demography has a part of its origin in actuarial calculations, just as probability sprang from gambling consultancies. The center of gravity of demography has shifted far from the insurance business, but at least the style of actuarial calculations is worth exhibiting here, perhaps as a small contribution toward bringing these disciplines closer together again.

Single-Payment Annuity and Insurance

The present value of a life annuity of 1 dollar per year, paid continuously starting from age x of the person, is equal to

$$\frac{1}{l_x}\int_0^{\omega-x} l(x+t)\,dt = \overset{o}{e}_x$$

dollars, if money carries no interest. It needs no mathematics to see that the expected number of dollars that a person will receive at the rate of 1 for each year of life is the same as the expected number of years he has to live. If money carries interest continuously compounded at annual rate i, a payment t years from now has a present value of e^{-it}; hence the present value of the annuity is

$$a_x = \frac{1}{l_x}\int_0^{\omega-x} e^{-it} l(x+t)\,dt \tag{2.5.1}$$

dollars. Similarly the present value of an assurance of 1 dollar on a life now aged x must be

$$A_x = \frac{1}{l_x}\int_0^{\omega-x} e^{-it} l(x+t)\,\mu(x+t)\,dt \tag{2.5.2}$$

dollars, which is the same as (2.5.1) except for the factor $\mu(x+t)$ in the integrand. [Show that, if interest is zero, $A_x = 1$, corresponding to the fact that dying is inevitable. Show also that, if $i > 0$, $A_x > \exp(-i\overset{o}{e}_x)$.]

Annual Premiums and Reserves

To find the annual premium P_x, note only that the annuity of premiums must cover the assurance, that is to say, the quantities $P_x a_x$ and A_x must be equal; hence we have for the premium $P_x = A_x/a_x$ or, written out in full,

$$P_x = \frac{\int_0^{\omega-x} e^{-it}l(x+t)\,\mu(x+t)\,dt}{\int_0^{\omega-x} e^{-it}l(x+t)\,dt}. \qquad (2.5.3)$$

In the early years of the policy, claims will be less than premiums, and a reserve will accumulate that will be drawn on in later years. After the policy has been in force for y years the present value of the claims will be A_{x+y}, and cannot be covered by the present value of the premiums $P_x a_{x+y}$, a smaller quantity for the ages at which mortality is rising; the difference $A_{x+y} - P_x a_{x+y}$, is the reserve prospectively needed.

2.6 CAUSE-DELETED TABLES AND MULTIPLE DECREMENT

If a person dies of one cause, he cannot die at some later time of another; the literature speaks of competing causes of death. Since dying of a given cause avoids exposure to other causes, if we wish to know what the mortality from these other causes would be if the given cause were deleted, we need upward adjustment to the observed rates. Over a finite interval of time or age it would be incorrect to delete a cause simply by neglecting all deaths from this cause and calculating the life table from the remaining deaths; such a procedure would give too low mortality from the remaining causes. We need an estimate of exposed population that does not include persons dead of the deleted cause. To make the estimate it is customary to assume that the several causes act independently.

Dependence of Causes of Death

Think of a watch or other machine having parts and operating only as long as all the parts are functioning. Each part has its own life table; the chance that the ith part will operate for x years is $\bar{l}^{(i)}(x)$, calculated without reference to other parts. Then the chance that the watch will still be going x years after its birth is

$$l(x) = \bar{l}^{(1)}(x) \cdot \bar{l}^{(2)}(x) \cdots \bar{l}^{(n)}(x), \qquad (2.6.1)$$

a statement true if the mortality of each of the parts is unaffected by its incorporation in the watch. Then, if

$$-\frac{1}{\bar{l}^{(i)}(x)} \frac{d\bar{l}^{(i)}(x)}{dx} = -\frac{d\ln\bar{l}^{(i)}(x)}{dx} = \mu^{(i)}(x),$$

it follows by taking logarithms and differentiating in (2.6.1) that

$$\mu(x) = \mu^{(1)}(x) + \mu^{(2)}(x) + \cdots + \mu^{(n)}(x). \tag{2.6.2}$$

The additivity of the instantaneous death rates follows from the multiplicativity of the survivorships.

We can think of many ways in which these conditions would not be fulfilled. The watch might keep going with one part defective but break down when two are defective. Or else the weakening of one part might put a strain on other parts; the watch would become "sick," and its death might ultimately be attributed to one of the parts that was so subjected to strain rather than to the part that became weak in the first place. There is no limit to the number of ways in which independence could be lost.

The parts of the watch might be said to resemble the parts of a person, and these would be independent if it could be said that he dies if his liver fails, or if his heart fails, and so on, and these were unrelated. The probability of each organ continuing to function might be thought of as the $\bar{l}^{(i)}(x)$ given in life tables showing the net probabilities of survival for the several causes. Unfortunately for this argument, human parts depend on one another more than do watch parts; separate life tables for the various organs, as though they were interchangeable, are to this degree artificial.

In addition to interrelations of parts, selection operates: the persons who die in skiing accidents are probably healthier on the average than the general population; therefore, if precautions that reduced the number of fatal accidents were introduced at ski resorts, the death rate from other causes would also be lowered. The nature of such dependencies is extremely difficult to establish. As long as we know only that A died of heart disease, B of kidney failure, and so on, nothing can be said about what would happen if one of the causes was reduced or eliminated. Faced with no evidence on the nature of dependencies, it is conventional to treat each cause as independent of the others. If parts (of a person or a watch) looked weak or had other clear symptoms before they failed altogether and brought the machine to a stop, and if such signs were present exactly y years before they would prove fatal, then something better could be done regarding dependencies. But even the most conscientious medical tests pre- and postmortem hardly provide such information.

It looks as though the analysis of interdependencies of the several organs will have to await further data. One kind of relevant data will become available when parts are commonly and safely replaced or interchanged among individuals. At present, however, such a possibility belongs to science fiction rather than to demography.

Method of Calculation

If all causes but the ith were removed, what would be the probability of surviving? To answer this without further data we suppose that the several causes act independently of one another, that is to say, that their forces of mortality are additive:

$$\mu_x^{(i)} + \mu_x^{(-i)} = \mu_x, \qquad (2.6.3)$$

where $\mu^{(i)}$ is the mortality due to the ith cause, and $\mu^{(-i)}$ that due to all other causes. If the survival probability with only the ith cause acting is $\bar{l}_x^{(i)}$, we have from (1.5.5) and the additivity of the $\mu_x^{(i)}$, as a converse of the argument leading to (2.6.2),

$$l_x = \bar{l}_x^{(i)} \bar{l}_x^{(-i)}.$$

Thus essentially the same argument can start with the additivity of the $\mu_x^{(i)}$ and infer the multiplicativity of the $\bar{l}_x^{(i)}$, or else start with the latter as we did in (2.6.1).

Now expression 1.5.5 applies to the $\bar{l}_x^{(i)}$ just as it does to the l_x; hence, as pointed out by Jordan (1952, p. 258) and Chiang (1968, p. 246), we have

$$-\ln \frac{\bar{l}_{x+n}^{(i)}}{\bar{l}_x^{(i)}} = \int_0^n \mu^{(i)}(x+t)\,dt$$

$$= \left[\frac{\displaystyle\int_0^n \mu^{(i)}(x+t)\,dt}{\displaystyle\int_0^n \mu(x+t)\,dt} \right] \int_0^n \mu(x+t)\,dt$$

$$= R \int_0^n \mu(x+t)\,dt, \qquad \text{say,}$$

and, on multiplying by -1 and taking exponentials of both sides,

$$\frac{\bar{l}_{x+n}^{(i)}}{\bar{l}_x^{(i)}} = \left(\frac{l_{x+n}}{l_x} \right)^R. \qquad (2.6.4)$$

Once the ordinary life table from all causes together is available, all we need do is raise its survivorships to the powers represented by the R's; each is the ratio for an age group of the integral of the force of mortality for the ith cause to the corresponding integral for all causes.

Chiang (1968) takes R to be simply the ratio of the age-specific rates for the interval:

$$R = \frac{{}_nM_x^{(i)}}{{}_nM_x}. \qquad (2.6.5)$$

We will use the technique of Section 2.2 to make a slight improvement on this. By expanding the $\mu^{(i)}(x+t)$ and $\mu(x+t)$ in a Taylor series about the midpoint of the n-year interval and then carrying through the integration, we find

$$
R = \frac{\displaystyle\int_0^n \mu^{(i)}(x+t)\,dt}{\displaystyle\int_0^n \mu(x+t)\,dt} = \frac{\mu^{(i)}(x+n/2) + (n^2/24)\,\mu^{(i)\prime\prime}(x+n/2)}{\mu(x+n/2) + (n^2/24)\,\mu''(x+n/2)} \qquad (2.6.6)
$$

to second derivatives. Replacing the midperiod forces of mortality by the age-specific rates, using a symmetric estimate of the second derivatives, and then simplifying gives

$$
R = \frac{{}_nM_x^{(i)}}{{}_nM_x}\left[1 + \frac{1}{24}\left(\frac{{}_nM_{x+n}^{(i)} + {}_nM_{x-n}^{(i)}}{{}_nM_x^{(i)}} - \frac{{}_nM_{x+n} + {}_nM_{x-n}}{{}_nM_x}\right)\right]. \qquad (2.6.7)
$$

The result would still hold with all M's replaced by D's, where ${}_nD_x^{(i)}$ is the number of deaths observed from the ith cause between exact ages x and $x+n$.

In the way such calculations are used, the life table of interest is that in which one cause is deleted. For instance, on data for United States females in 1964, the complete expectation of life for females is $\overset{o}{e}_0 = 73.78$ years; if heart disease (CVR) is deleted, the $\overset{o}{e}_0^{(-\text{CVR})} = 90.85$ years (Preston, Keyfitz, and Schoen, 1972, p. 771). Deletion of cancer gives $\overset{o}{e}_0^{(-\text{cancer})} = 76.34$ years. The gain by eradicating heart disease is 17.07 years; by eradicating cancer, 2.56 years.

Multiple Decrement

The probability that a person will die of a certain cause in the presence of other causes is presented in a multiple-decrement table. If the observed number dying of the given cause is ${}_nD_x^{(i)}$ and the life table number dying of that cause is ${}_nd_x^{(i)}$, we want to find how the life table deaths ${}_nd_x$ are distributed among the several causes, given the observed distribution among causes; given ${}_nd_x$, ${}_nD_x$, and ${}_nD_x^{(i)}$, we seek ${}_nd_x^{(i)}$. One way (Spiegelman, 1968, p. 137) to make the calculation is

$$
{}_nd_x^{(i)} = \frac{{}_nD_x^{(i)}}{{}_nD_x}\cdot {}_nd_x, \qquad (2.6.8)
$$

but, as before, we try going one step in the refinement of this.

We have by definition

$$\frac{_nD_x^{(i)}}{_nD_x} = \frac{\int_0^n p(x+t)\,\mu^{(i)}(x+t)\,dt}{\int_0^n p(x+t)\,\mu(x+t)\,dt}$$

and applying the Taylor expansion used earlier results in

$$_nd_x^{(i)} = {_nd_x}\frac{_nD_x^{(i)}}{_nD_x}\left\{1 + \frac{1}{48}\left(\frac{_nP_{x+n} - {_nP_{x-n}}}{_nP_x} + 2n_nM_x\right)\right.$$

$$\left. \times\left[\frac{_nM_{x+n} - {_nM_{x-n}}}{_nM_x} - \frac{_nM_{x+n}^{(i)} - {_nM_{x-n}^{(i)}}}{_nM_x^{(i)}}\right]\right\}. \qquad (2.6.9)$$

Table 2.3   Part of multiple decrement table applying to cardiovascular disease, comparing (2.6.9) with iterative and uncorrected methods, United States females, 1964

Age	$_nd_x^{(i)}$	$_nd_x^{(i)}$	$_nd_x^{(i)} = {_nd_x}\dfrac{_nD_x^{(i)}}{_nD_x}$
x	Iterative	From (2.6.9)	From (2.6.8)
25	65	64.80	64.71
50	1,067	1,067.56	1,066.41
75	10,173	10,175.53	10,165.27

Table 2.3 shows that the correction in (2.6.9), as compared with using the simple $_nd_x^{(i)} = {_nd_x}[_nD_x^{(i)}/_nD_x]$, is trifling. We seem to have reached a point at which it is usually immaterial whether the correction is made or not. Nonetheless cases will arise where within an age group one cause is declining and the others rising, and then correction 2.6.9 will bring improvement.

2.7   THE LIFE TABLE AS A UNIFYING TECHNIQUE IN DEMOGRAPHY

The painstaking development of a method for inferring probabilities from observed rates is justified by the fact that the same problem arises in many fields. The ordinary life table, for which the data consist of the number of deaths and the exposed population, both by age, is only the best-known example. Figure 2.2 shows some other applications.

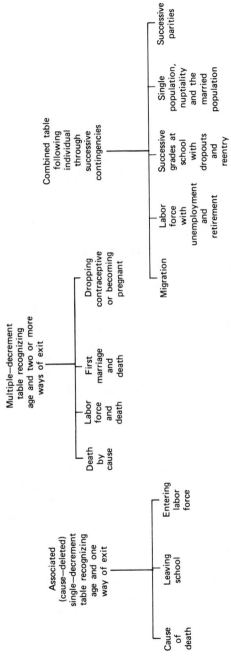

Fig. 2.2 Some extensions of the life table.

Chapter Three

MORTALITY COMPARISONS; THE MALE-FEMALE RATIO

The United States in 1975 showed an expectation of life at birth for males of 68.5 years and for females of 76.4 years, a difference of 11.5 percent. But male death rates at most ages are at least 50 percent higher than female rates. The ratio of male to female rates, simply averaged over the ages, may show males 80 percent higher; the average with living population as weights may show males 70 percent higher; with deaths as weights males may be 50 percent higher. Our question is whether male mortality is 10, 50, 80, or 70 percent higher than female. The issue is raised in Sheps (1959) and Golini (1967).

The same difficulty arises when we compare two countries—the United States and Italy, or the United States and India—or two parts of the same country—South and North in Italy, or city and countryside. It arises also in comparisons through time: has mortality been improving in Europe and America during recent years, and if so by how much? Essentially the same issue can be expressed in terms of the conditional future: *if* mortality is reduced on an average of 5 percent at each age, what difference will this make to the expectation of life? The question is of special interest with respect to cause of death: if deaths from cancer are reduced by 10 percent on the average of the several ages, what will be the effect on expectation of life, provided that all other causes are unchanged? A more sophisticated form of the question is to suppose that deaths from cancer are reduced by 10 percent and to note the effect if cancer mortality is positively correlated to a given degree with other causes, that is, if those subject to cancer are somehow more susceptible also to other causes, but this is out of our scope.

In the simplest aspect of the problem a person saved from death through one cause at a particular time is rescued only to be exposed to the same cause and others in the subsequent period. To avoid death from heart disease at an age typical of the ages at which heart disease occurs can offer only a brief respite, since overall death rates increase rapidly in later life. Lower mortality of young and middle-aged females allows them to survive into ages at which mortality is very high for everyone. That the curve of death rates by age is concave upward and that populations are heterogeneous in risk are what give rise to the questions with which the present chapter deals.

Variation by Age in the Sex Ratio of Mortality

To bring the theory into contact with concrete data we show the ratios of male to female age-specific death rates for four countries in Table 3.1. The tendency is toward a characteristic pattern, with peaks around 0, 20, and 60, and troughs around 1, 35, and 85, the pattern being shown clearly by the United States and less clearly by Mexico.

3.1   THE MULTIPLICITY OF INDEX NUMBERS

The most familiar comparison of mortality is by direct standardization: how many deaths would occur in a given population if it had the age distribution of the (standard) population with which it is being compared, and what is the ratio of this number to the deaths in the standard population? Kitagawa (1964) widened the perspective by assimilating the issues to those of price index numbers. Her formulas can be applied readily to the excess mortality of males. If the male population is p_x^m, the female population p_x^f, the male death rate μ_x^m, and the female death rate μ_x^f, the relative mortality at age x is μ_x^m/μ_x^f, and the index in which such relatives are weighted by *male population* is

$$I_p^m = \frac{\Sigma_x p_x^m \left(\mu_x^m / \mu_x^f \right)}{\Sigma_x p_x^m},$$ (3.1.1)

and by *female population* is

$$I_p^f = \frac{\Sigma_x p_x^f \left(\mu_x^m / \mu_x^f \right)}{\Sigma_x p_x^f}.$$ (3.1.2)

Table 3.1   Ratio of male to female age-specific death rates for four countries

Age	United States, 1967	France, 1967	Greece, 1968	Mexico, 1966
−1	1.30	1.31	1.11	1.20
1–4	1.25	1.21	1.10	0.95
5–9	1.38	1.50	1.37	1.06
10–14	1.72	1.63	1.55	1.17
15–19	2.51	2.14	1.92	1.25
20–24	2.80	2.31	2.10	1.31
25–29	2.26	2.08	1.78	1.31
30–34	1.81	1.95	1.56	1.40
35–39	1.68	1.89	1.34	1.41
40–44	1.72	2.02	1.51	1.56
45–49	1.79	2.07	1.59	1.50
50–54	1.95	2.09	1.73	1.45
55–59	2.07	2.37	1.69	1.41
60–64	2.10	2.35	1.68	1.21
65–69	1.91	2.19	1.62	1.23
70–74	1.82	1.80	1.32	1.12
75–79	1.56	1.59	1.17	1.08
80–84	1.33	1.41	1.06	0.88
85 +	1.08	1.24	1.15	0.75

Source: Based on Keyfitz and Flieger (1971).

The index weighted by *male deaths* is

$$I_d^m = \frac{\sum_x p_x^m \mu_x^m \left(\mu_x^m / \mu_x^f \right)}{\sum_x p_x^m \mu_x^m}, \tag{3.1.3}$$

and by *female deaths* is

$$I_d^f = \frac{\sum_x p_x^f \mu_x^f \left(\mu_x^m / \mu_x^f \right)}{\sum_x p_x^f \mu_x^f} = \frac{\sum_x p_x^f \mu_x^m}{\sum_x p_x^f \mu_x^f}. \tag{3.1.4}$$

The one of these four indices preferred in demography is I_d^f, the directly standardized rate (3.1.4). In economics I_d^f is called an aggregative index, in which the μ_x might be prices and the p_x quantities; f might be the base period and m the current period in a time comparison.

In addition to the four index numbers of (3.1.1) to (3.1.4) we can obtain four further numbers by using the harmonic means. For the male-population-weighted harmonic mean H_p^m we have

$$H_p^m = \frac{\Sigma p_x^m}{\Sigma p_x^m / (\mu_x^m / \mu_x^f)} ,$$

and similarly for the other three indices obtained by weighting by females and by deaths.

One might have thought that taking the male death rates as the denominator and then inverting the result would give additional indices. However, this merely reproduces in a different order the eight indices described above.

Geometric averaging does give different results (Schoen, 1970). The male-population-weighted index would be

$$G_p^m = \left(\prod (\mu_x^m / \mu_x^f)^{p_x^m} \right)^{1/\Sigma p_x^m}$$

and similarly for G_p^f and others.

A further variant is the exponential of the harmonic mean of the logarithms of the ratios,

$$HL_p^m = \exp \left[\frac{\Sigma p_x^m}{\Sigma p_x^m / \ln(\mu_x^m / \mu_x^f)} \right],$$

which gives another four ways of expressing the relation of the given population to the standard.

We could obtain additional indices by cross-weighting and averaging. One instance is $I = \sqrt{(I_d^f)(I_d^m)}$, which may well give about as refined a comparison as any. England and Wales show considerably higher death rates than the United States at older ages and lower rates at younger ages. To find how the two countries stand on the whole we can first standardize on the United States 1960 census age distribution taking both sexes together, and calculate the intercountry value of (3.1.4), which turns out to be 1.218. Using the same formula but standardizing on the 1961 census of England and Wales, we find 1.231. The geometric mean of these quantities is 1.224.

Other compromises between the given and the standard age distributions are possible, as well as other kinds of averages. However, the conceptual points raised later in this section will lead to some scepticism about the usefulness of extreme refinement.

Weighted Index of Male to Female Mortality

The ratios of Table 3.1 (but to more decimal places) were combined in the four ways designated above as I_p^m, I_p^f, I_d^m, I_d^f, that is, weighting by male population, female population, male deaths, and female deaths, as in expressions 3.1.1 to 3.1.4. They were also combined to give the harmonic mean H, the geometric mean G, and the harmonic mean of the logarithm HL. The results are shown in Table 3.2 for six countries. Especially for low-mortality countries weighting by population gives a much higher excess mortality of males than weighting by deaths. The reason is that deaths are relatively heavier than population at the oldest ages, where the age-specific rates of females approach those of males.

Table 3.2   Ratio of male to female mortality, United States, 1967, and five other countries

Index	United States, 1967	Austria, 1966–68	France, 1967	West Germany, 1967	Greece, 1968	Mexico, 1966
I_p^m	1.871	2.035	1.918	1.879	1.578	1.211
I_p^f	1.874	1.997	1.912	1.855	1.573	1.218
I_d^m	1.732	1.706	1.863	1.649	1.363	1.176
I_d^f	1.614	1.560	1.669	1.546	1.297	1.144
H_p^m	1.774	1.890	1.847	1.780	1.530	1.186
H_p^f	1.779	1.866	1.840	1.781	1.526	1.192
H_d^m	1.654	1.620	1.775	1.580	1.317	1.142
H_d^f	1.530	1.487	1.589	1.485	1.260	1.105
G_p^m	1.821	1.961	1.884	1.839	1.555	1.198
G_p^f	1.825	1.930	1.878	1.818	1.550	1.205
G_d^m	1.694	1.663	1.820	1.614	1.339	1.160
G_d^f	1.572	1.522	1.628	1.514	1.278	1.125
HL_p^m	1.630	1.697	1.703	1.687	1.371	1.374
HL_p^f	1.629	1.675	1.699	1.673	1.371	1.375
HL_d^m	1.407	1.444	1.631	1.445	1.185	1.960
HL_d^f	1.286	1.334	1.470	1.370	1.158	1.359
$\dfrac{e_0^f}{e_0^m}$	1.108	1.102	1.109	1.091	1.052	1.056

Note that the arithmetic ratios are higher than the geometric, which in turn are higher than the harmonic. Moreover, the geometric ratios are equal to the means of the corresponding arithmetic and harmonic ratios:

$$G = \sqrt{(I)(H)} \ .$$

For the male-population-weighted case for the United States of 1967

(Table 3.2)

$$I_p^m = 1.871, \qquad H_p^m = 1.774,$$

of which means the geometric mean is 1.822, the same as G_p^m except for rounding.

The index numbers for the countries of low mortality in Table 3.2 typically show males to have 50 percent higher mortality than females. On the other hand, the expectation of life for females is nowhere much more than 10 percent higher than that for males. The ratio of the female to male $\overset{o}{e}_0$, that is, $\overset{o}{e}_0^f / \overset{o}{e}_0^m$, may be thought of as the ratio of male to female death rates in the respective stationary populations, and why it is so much lower than the other indices is investigated in Section 3.3.

Aggregative Indices versus Averages of Relatives

Suppose one set up the criterion that an index ought to be affected in about the same amount by a change of one death at one age as at another. At least, it can be argued, the effect of an added death at one age ought not to be 100 times as great as the effect at another age. The addition of a single death to males at age x raises the death rate by $1/p_x^m$ and thus raises the numerator of the aggregative index I_d^f of (3.1.4) by p_x^f/p_x^m. Insofar as the ratio of males to females does not vary greatly in absolute numbers among age groups, the weight given to an extra male death in I_d^f is approximately invariant with age.

The same point can be made more generally by considering the effect of a small change $\Delta\mu_x^m$ in a male death rate on I_d^f; taking a small finite difference, we obtain

$$\Delta I_d^f = \frac{p_x^f \Delta\mu_x^m}{\sum_a p_a^f \mu_a^f}.$$

The denominator of this expression is the same regardless of the age x at which the change occurs; the numerator $p_x^f \Delta\mu_x^m$ is of the order of magnitude of the additional absolute number of deaths.

Quite different is the effect on the weighted relatives I_p^m of (3.1.1), where the effect of an increment $\Delta\mu_x^m$ in the male death rate is

$$\Delta I_p^m = \frac{p_x^m \left(\Delta\mu_x^m / \mu_x^f \right)}{\sum_a p_a^m},$$

which depends on the reciprocal of the female death rate at the age in question. Now the numerator contains $p_x^m (\Delta\mu_x^m)$, which is the number of additional male deaths, but it also contains the reciprocal of μ_x^f, which can be anywhere from $1/0.001$ to $1/0.1$ or even fall outside this range. That a small change in male deaths can have an effect on the comparison 100 times as great at age 20 as at age 70 argues against the index I_p^m.

3.2   SHOULD WE INDEX DEATH RATES OR SURVIVORSHIPS?

Superimposed on the great variation in the above indices is an even greater variation arising from the choice between death rates and survival rates for the comparison. Consider the United States versus England and Wales, each about the time of the last census, and take males aged 70 to 75 as an example. The probabilities of dying are as follows:

$$\text{U.S.:} \quad {}_5q_{70} = 0.2526 \quad \text{versus} \quad \text{England and Wales:} \ {}_5q_{70} = 0.2915,$$

so that England and Wales, 1960–62, would have $0.2915/0.2526 = 1.154$ times as high a probability of dying as the United States in 1959–61. The corresponding probabilities of surviving are ${}_5p_{70} = 1 - {}_5q_{70}$ or

$$\text{U.S.:} \quad {}_5p_{70} = 0.7474 \quad \text{versus} \quad \text{England and Wales:} \ {}_5p_{70} = 0.7085,$$

so that the United States has 1.055 times the survival probability of England and Wales. We do not know from this whether to say that the United States is healthier (for the age group in question) than England and Wales by 5.5 percent, or that England and Wales are more hazardous than the United States by 15.4 percent.

Without further sharpening of the model, as Sheps (1959) insists, we must abandon the statement of a percentage excess in either direction and be satisfied with the difference. The most that can be said is that the difference in the probability of dying is $0.2915 - 0.2526 = 0.0389$, this being identical with the difference $0.7474 - 0.7085$ in the probability of surviving. To say more invites the inconsistencies of the preceding paragraph.

But suppose it were the case (presented here only for illustration) that Englishmen of this age die of all the causes Americans die of plus some causes special to them. American mortality, represented by the probability of dying within a year, is q, say, and English mortality for those who do not die of the American causes is δ. Then the English probability of dying is $q + (1 - q)\delta$, and the ratio of this to q is $1 + [(1 - q)/q]\delta$, an expression that involves q and δ intertwined in complex fashion. But the American chance of survival is $1 - q$, and the English is $(1 - q)(1 - \delta)$, so the ratio of probabilities of survival is $(1 - q)(1 - \delta)/(1 - q) = 1 - \delta$. This involves δ and omits q altogether. Its complement is simply δ, the pure additional English mortality, *obtainable easily from the ratio of survivorships but not in any direct way from the probabilities of dying.*

Insofar as we adhere to this model, we ought to make an index consisting of the weighted complements of the age-specific death rates, and then take the complement of the resultant index. But the argument depends on the Englishman's being subject to a source of extra mortality that enters only if he escapes the American sources. Sheps (1959) raises the point in regard to smokers and nonsmokers; the former do have a clear added hazard if they escape all the causes of death to which the latter are liable. It is not obvious that such a model applies to the whole of intercountry or intersex comparisons, but it could apply in part. There could be a climatic or other special hazard in England; there could be some added hazard through heart disease (or, at younger ages, accident) for males in addition to the dangers to which women are subject.

Let us take the Sheps model one stage further and suppose some limited overlap, that is to say, common causes of mortality as well as causes special to each group. Let both men and women be subject to q; and men in addition to δ_m and women in addition to δ_f, the additional causes being restricted to individuals who do not die of the common causes. These are the parts of the model assumed to underlie the observed chance of survivorship for men P_m and for women P_f. Then we have $P_m = (1 - q)(1 - \delta_m)$ and $P_f = (1 - q)(1 - \delta_f)$; the ratio of survivorships is

$$\frac{P_f}{P_m} = \frac{(1 - q)(1 - \delta_f)}{(1 - q)(1 - \delta_m)} = \frac{1 - \delta_f}{1 - \delta_m}.$$

This is not bad: the ratio of survivorships taken from the raw data gives exactly the ratio of the chances of escaping the special female and male hazards, respectively.

Compare this with the ratio of the probabilities of dying, the complements of the P's, now taken as male to female:

$$\frac{1 - P_m}{1 - P_f} = \frac{1 - (1 - q)(1 - \delta_m)}{1 - (1 - q)(1 - \delta_f)} = \frac{\delta_m + q(1 - \delta_m)}{\delta_f + q(1 - \delta_f)}.$$

The interpretation of this is straightforward only if $q = 0$, that is, if there are no common causes. If, however, there are common causes, the ratio of observed death rates does not provide the ratio δ_m / δ_f of the causes special to the sexes, but a biased estimate of this ratio. Where q may be appreciable, the terms in q in numerator and denominator obscure the δ_m / δ_f that it is natural to seek.

Uncertainty as to the overlap of causes, and hence uncertainty as to whether one ought to be comparing the chances of survival or of death, constitute a major obstacle to precise comparison of overall rates. In nonexperimental comparisons this consideration serves as a caution against excessive refinement in index numbers of the type presented as (3.1.1) to (3.1.4).

3.3   EFFECT ON $\overset{o}{e}_0$ OF CHANGE IN $\mu(x)$

The index number problem applies as much to changes through time as to comparisons across space. Given a general initial age schedule of mortality, suppose a certain kind of change in that schedule and see what the effect is on the expectation of life. We do this first with a constant increase δ in $\mu(x)$ at all ages, so that $\mu(x)$ becomes $\mu(x) + \delta$.

When the fixed quantity δ is added to mortality at every age, the probability of surviving to age x becomes $\exp\left[-\int_0^x [\mu(a) + \delta] da\right] = e^{-\delta x} l(x)$, that is, is altered in the ratio $e^{-\delta x}$; if the old probability was $l(x)$, the new one is $e^{-\delta x} l(x)$. Also, the new expectation of life (distinguished by *) is the integral of this through the whole of life:

$$\overset{o}{e}_0^* = \int_0^\omega e^{-\delta x} l(x) dx. \tag{3.3.1}$$

To find the effect on the expectation of life of the addition δ to the age-specific death rates we seek the derivative $d\overset{o}{e}_0^*/d\delta$:

$$\frac{d\overset{o}{e}_0^*}{d\delta} = -\int_0^\omega x e^{-\delta x} l(x) dx = -\bar{x}\,\overset{o}{e}_0,$$

evaluated at $\delta = 0$, if $\bar{x}$ is the mean age of the stationary population. In finite terms for δ small,

$$\Delta\overset{o}{e}_0 \doteq -\bar{x}\,\overset{o}{e}_0\delta \qquad \text{or} \qquad \frac{\Delta\overset{o}{e}_0}{\overset{o}{e}_0} \doteq -\bar{x}\delta. \tag{3.3.2}$$

The relative change in the expectation of life equals minus the change in the death rate times the mean age in the life table population. Thus, if the expectation of life is 70 years, 0.001 is subtracted from mortality $\mu(x)$ at every age, and the mean age in the life table population is 35 years, the fraction added to the expectation is approximately $(35)(0.001) = 0.035$ or, in absolute amount, $(0.035)(70) = 2.45$ years.

A Proportional Difference Uniform at all Ages

However, though the effect of a fixed difference in death rates is expressible in simple form, we are more likely to be interested in the effect of a given proportional difference. Ratios of age-specific mortality rates are hardly constant between any two groups, but for developed countries the ratio of male to female mortality ranges from about 1.10 to about 2.80 (Table 3.1); certainly the ratios are closer to constancy than the differences (not shown), which vary from about 0.002 to 0.0400. The largest ratio is 2 to 3 times the smallest; the largest difference is 200 times the smallest.

Suppose now that the death rate $\mu(x)$ is multiplied by $1 + \delta$, so that $\mu^*(x) = (1 + \delta)\mu(x)$. Then the new probability of surviving to age x becomes

$$l_x^* = \exp\left[-\int_0^x \mu^*(a)\,da \right] = \exp\left[-\int_0^x (1+\delta)\,\mu(a)\,da \right] = l_x^{1+\delta},$$

and the new expectation of life is

$$\overset{o}{e}{}^*{}_0 = \int_0^\omega l(a)^{1+\delta}\,da. \tag{3.3.3}$$

The application of this to the special function $\mu(x) = \mu_0/(\omega - x)$ is satisfactorily simple. Integrating and taking the exponential gives $l(x) = \left[1 - (x/\omega)\right]^{\mu_0}$. Integrating this in turn gives $\overset{o}{e}_x = (\omega - x)/(\mu_0 + 1)$. Then we have

$$\frac{\overset{o}{e}{}^*{}_0}{\overset{o}{e}_0} = \frac{\int_0^\omega \left[l(x)\right]^{1+\delta} dx}{\int_0^\omega l(x)\,dx} = \frac{\mu_0 + 1}{\mu_0(1+\delta) + 1}. \tag{3.3.4}$$

If mortality at all ages rises by δ, then $\overset{o}{e}{}^*{}_0$ declines but by a lesser amount, as (3.3.4) shows. For males compared with females δ might be 0.43, and μ_0 might be 0.30. Then by (3.3.4) the ratio $\overset{o}{e}_0/\overset{o}{e}{}^*{}_0$ equals $1.43/1.30 = 1.10$. Integrating the reciprocal of the expectation of life as the life table death rate, an excess of 43 percent in all age-specific death rates translates into an excess of 10 percent in the life table overall death rate, roughly consistent with Table 3.2.

But this is on a hyperbolic curve for $\mu(x)$; in general the proportionate change of $\mu(x)$ does not so easily translate into a change of $\overset{o}{e}_0$, and we need the flexible differential calculus to establish a constant useful for describing life tables. To find the effect of a small change δ on the expectation of life, we seek the derivative of the right-hand side of (3.3.3) with respect to δ and find

$$\frac{d\overset{o}{e}{}^*{}_0}{d\delta} = \int_0^\omega \left[\ln l(a)\right] l(a)^{1+\delta}\,da, \tag{3.3.5}$$

a quantity that cannot be positive, since $l(a)$ cannot be greater than unity.

In the neighborhood of $\delta = 0$ we have

$$\frac{\Delta \overset{o}{e}_0}{\overset{o}{e}_0} \doteq \frac{\int_0^\omega [\ln l(a)] l(a)\, da}{\int_0^\omega l(a)\, da} \delta = -H\delta, \quad \text{say}, \qquad (3.3.6)$$

where H is minus the mean value of $\ln l(a)$, weighted by $l(a)$. (The measure H is called entropy or information in other contexts, and has been applied in population biology by Demetrius (1976).)

The ratio of integrals in (3.3.6) is necessarily negative, so that H is positive. We can imagine H as low as zero, if all mortality were concentrated at one age. If, for instance, everyone lives until 70 and then dies, $l(a)$ will be unity for all ages up to 70, and its logarithm will be zero. At the other extreme, if mortality μ is the same at all ages, we will have $l(x) = e^{-\mu x}$, $\overset{o}{e}_x = 1/\mu$, a constant, and

$$\frac{\Delta \overset{o}{e}_0}{\overset{o}{e}_0} \doteq \frac{\int_0^\omega [\ln 1(a)] l(a)\, da}{\int_0^\omega l(a)\, da} \delta$$

$$= \frac{\int_0^\infty -\mu a e^{-\mu a}\, da}{1/\mu} \delta = -\delta.$$

In this case $H = 1$, and the proportional change in the death rates translates into the same change in the expectation of life, but of course in the opposite direction. With $H = 1$, when the death rates at all ages increase by 1 percent, the expectation of life diminishes by 1 percent. [Show that for $l(x)$ a straight line, $H = 0.5$.]

Figure 3.1 shows the $l(x)$ for the two extreme cases and for intermediate ones, with corresponding values of H. Deevey (1950) gives a number of curves for animal species that resemble the several curves of Figure 3.1, with fruit flies near $H = 0$, oysters below $H = 1$, and hydra near $H = \frac{1}{2}$.

Observed Values of the Constant H

For countries of Europe and America with expectations of life around 70 years, H is now of the order of 0.2 for males and 0.15 for females, down from the 0.3 to 0.4 of about 30 years earlier. Apparently H is a convenient summary of the degree of concavity in an $l(x)$ column; as mortality improves, a larger fraction of deaths occurs in the 60s and 70s of age, and the drop in the value of H measures this tendency; with improvement in

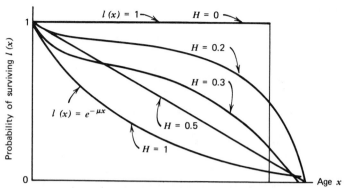

Fig. 3.1 Extreme cases of survivorship curves $l(x)$, and three intermediate cases, showing how H becomes smaller as survivorship moves toward a rectangular form.

mortality everyone dies at about the same age, and a proportional improvement in mortality at all ages makes less and less difference in the expectation of life.

When we are told that, of two countries, or two sexes, one has an expectation of life in a certain ratio to the other, we can approximate to the ratio of age-specific death rates, supposing this ratio to be $1 + \delta$, the same at all ages. Taking

$$\frac{\overset{o}{e}{}^{*}_{0}}{\overset{o}{e}_{0}} = \frac{\int_{0}^{\omega} l(x)^{1+\delta} dx}{\int_{0}^{\omega} l(x) dx}$$

as a function of δ, say $f(\delta)$, and expanding as $f(\delta) = f(0) + \delta f'(0)$, where we know that $f'(0) = -H$, gives

$$\frac{\overset{o}{e}{}^{*}_{0}}{\overset{o}{e}_{0}} \doteq 1 - \delta H.$$

If, for example, $\overset{o}{e}{}^{*}_{0} / \overset{o}{e}_{0} = 1.10$, we can say that

$$1.10 = \frac{\int_{0}^{\omega} l(x)^{1+\delta} dx}{\int_{0}^{\omega} l(x) dx} \doteq 1 - \delta H;$$

and if H is 0.20, we have the equation for δ:

$$1.10 = 1 - (\delta)(0.20),$$

or

$$\delta = \frac{1 - 1.10}{0.20} = -0.50.$$

The population with 10 percent greater expectation of life has death rates 50 percent lower. This approach can also be tried when the ratio of death rates is not uniform, and to this situation we proceed.

An Aspect of the Index Number Problem

The theory developed above seeks to find the effect on expectation of life of a uniform proportional excess in the force of mortality $\mu(x)$. What we have in practice, however, is different proportional increases at the several ages. One way of answering the question of what is the real average increase—for example, the real percentage excess of male over female mortality—is to calculate the proportional increase that, applied uniformly to all ages, will have the same effect on the expectation of life as the observed set of increases. In application to the excess mortality for the United States, 1967, which showed (Table 3.1) a ratio of 1.30 for ages under 1, 1.25 for those 1 to 4, etc., we would ask what uniform excess of male over female mortality would provide the same ratio of expectations of life as observed. Since we saw that raising $\mu(x)$ in the ratio $1 + \delta$ raises $l(x)$ to the power $1 + \delta$, we would need to solve the equation

$$\frac{\overset{o}{e}\,{}^{m}_{0}}{\overset{o}{e}\,{}^{f}_{0}} = \frac{\int_0^{\omega} l(x)^{1+\delta}\,dx}{\int_0^{\omega} l(x)\,dx} \tag{3.3.7}$$

for the unknown δ. This can be done directly by computer.

The equation can also be solved approximately in terms of our parameter H, along with other derivatives of the numerator of the right-hand side of the equation. Rewriting $l(x)^{1+\delta}$ in (3.3.7) as $l(x)\exp[\delta\ln l(x)]$ and expanding the exponential term in a Taylor series changes the equation to

$$\frac{\overset{o}{e}\,{}^{m}_{0}}{\overset{o}{e}\,{}^{f}_{0}} = 1 - H\delta + \frac{H_2\delta^2}{2!} - \frac{H_3\delta^3}{3!} + \ldots, \tag{3.3.8}$$

where

$$H_i = \frac{\int_0^{\omega} \left[-\ln l(x) \right]^i l(x)\,dx}{\int_0^{\omega} l(x)\,dx}, \qquad i = 2, 3, \ldots.$$

Approximating with the linear term only, we have for Italy, 1964, whose $\overset{o}{e}_0^f / \overset{o}{e}_0^m = 1.081$,

$$\delta = \frac{\left(\overset{o}{e}_0^m / \overset{o}{e}_0^f\right) - 1}{-H} = \frac{(1/1.081) - 1}{-(0.207 + 0.163)/2},$$

on using H from Table 3.4. (It seems best to average H for males and females.) The result is

$$\delta = \frac{0.0749}{0.185} = 0.405,$$

or $1 + \delta = 1.405$. This compares with $I_d^f = 1.441$, or an average of I_d^f and I_d^m of 1.490. [For greater accuracy the reader may wish to experiment with further terms of (3.3.8).]

Table 3.3   Values of $\overset{o}{e}_0$ and parameter $H = -\int_0^\omega [\ln l(a)] l(a) \, da / \int_0^\omega l(a) \, da$ for males and females, United States, 1919–21 to 1959–61

	Male		Female	
	$\overset{o}{e}_0$	H	$\overset{o}{e}_0$	H
1919–21	54.49	0.3804	56.41	0.3547
1924–26	56.34	0.3401	59.01	0.3113
1929–31	57.27	0.3272	60.67	0.2942
1934–36	58.53	0.3105	62.58	0.2725
1939–41	61.14	0.2747	65.58	0.2361
1944–46	62.26	0.2632	68.11	0.2087
1949–51	65.28	0.2260	70.86	0.1823
1954–56	66.45	0.2134	72.61	0.1660
1959–61	66.84	0.2083	73.40	0.1594

Source: Computed from data in Keyfitz and Flieger (1968).

Thus, given the expectations of life of two populations, along with an average H, we can say what uniform excess of mortality of one over the other accounts for the ratio of expectations. This is the converse of the way in which H was originally derived—as the ratio of expectations of life corresponding to a given uniform ratio of death rates.

For the particular hyperbolic form in which

$$\mu(a) = \frac{\mu_0}{\omega - a}, \qquad l(a) = \left(1 - \frac{a}{\omega}\right)^{\mu_0}, \qquad \overset{o}{e}_a = \frac{\omega - a}{\mu_0 + 1}, \qquad H = \frac{\mu_0}{\mu_0 + 1},$$

H tells us considerably more than is indicated by its being the first derivative. It happens also to give without approximation the value of the increase in $\overset{o}{e}_0$ (or $\overset{o}{e}_x$ for that matter) when $\mu(a)$ goes to $\mu(a)(1+\delta)$, and when δ may be large. For the ratio of expectations, we have

$$\frac{\overset{o}{e}_0^{\,m}}{\overset{o}{e}_0^{\,f}} = \frac{1}{1+\delta H},$$

under the hyperbolic mortality function assumed. In the example given, with $\overset{o}{e}_0^{\,m}/\overset{o}{e}_0^{\,f}=1/1.081$, $H=0.185$; hence the equation for δ is

$$\frac{1}{1.081} = \frac{1}{1+\delta\,(0.185)},$$

or $\delta=0.081/0.185=0.438$. Thus the fact that Italian females of 1964 have 8.1 percent longer expected life than males is the equivalent of their having 43.8 percent as high mortality.

Although this holds exactly only for the special graduation $\mu(a)=\mu_0/(\omega-a)$, it is probably an improvement when δ is substantial for any life table. Hence the rule for finding the new $\overset{o}{e}_0$ when all rates rise by δ is to divide the old $\overset{o}{e}_0$ by $1+\delta H$, rather than multiplying by $1-\delta H$ as in the first approximation to (3.3.8).

Fractional Change in Mortality Due to a Given Cause

Of at least equal interest is to find the effect, not of a change in mortality in general, but of a change due to a given cause. We might want to investigate, for example, what would happen to the expectation of life if 10 percent of the cancer deaths were eliminated at each age, and we would need for this a cause-specific analogue of the H above. If the chance of surviving against the risk of cancer deaths alone is $l^{(i)}(x)$, and that against the risk of all other deaths is $l^{(-i)}(x)$, the probability that a person will still be alive by age x, $l(x)$, under independence is the product

$$l(x)=l^{(i)}(x)l^{(-i)}(x).$$

If we let 100δ represent the percentage change in the death rate due to cancer, the new expectation of life involves $l^{(i)}(x)$ raised to the $(1+\delta)^{\text{th}}$ power:

$$\overset{o}{e}_0^{\,*} = \int_0^\omega l^*(x)\,dx = \int_0^\omega l^{(i)1+\delta}(x)l^{(-i)}(x)\,dx$$

$$= \int_0^\omega l^{(i)\delta}(x)l(x)\,dx.$$

Again resorting to the derivative, we have

$$\frac{d\overset{o}{e}_0^*}{d\delta} = \int_0^\omega \left[\ln l^{(i)}(x) \right] l^{(i)\delta}(x) l(x) \, dx.$$

At the point where $\delta = 0$ we can drop the middle factor in the integrand and have for the derivative

$$\frac{d\overset{o}{e}_0}{d\delta} = \int_0^\omega \left[\ln l^{(i)}(x) \right] l(x) \, dx. \tag{3.3.9}$$

If $H^{(i)}$ is defined as

$$H^{(i)} = \frac{-\int_0^\omega \left[\ln l^{(i)}(x) \right] l(x) \, dx}{\int_0^\omega l(x) \, dx}, \tag{3.3.10}$$

then δ small but finite gives

$$\frac{\Delta \overset{o}{e}_0}{\overset{o}{e}_0} \doteq -H^{(i)}\delta. \tag{3.3.11}$$

From (3.3.10) we see that $H^{(i)}$, like H, is minus a weighted average of logarithms, the weights being the $l(x)$ column in both cases. The logarithm of $l_x^{(i)}$ is closer to zero than the logarithm of l_x, so the linear approximation (3.3.11) is better than (3.3.6).

The several causes of death show characteristic values of $H^{(i)}$, and these values are worth studying for what they tell us about the effect on expectation of life of eradication of a small part of each cause. Table 3.4 presents $H^{(i)}$ values for 12 causes of death, for males and females, in the United States and Italy, 1930–31 and 1964. Taking, for example, cardio-vascular renal diseases (cause 4 in the list assembled by Preston, Keyfitz, and Schoen, 1972), we see that for United States males in 1964 a drop of 1 percent in CVR deaths uniformly at all ages would result in an increase of 0.0840 percent in the expectation of life, that is, about one-twelfth as much.

Note the additivity of the $H^{(i)}$, in the sense that $\Sigma_i H^{(i)} = H$. For from the fact that $l(x) = \Pi l^{(i)}(x)$, with $l_0^{(i)} = 1$, it follows that the integral for H defined in (3.3.6) must be the sum of the integrals $H^{(i)}$ defined in (3.3.10).

Table 3.4 Values of $H^{(i)}$, giving effect on $\overset{o}{e}_0$ of small fractional decrease in each of 12 causes of death, United States and Italy, 1930–31 and 1964, males and females

Cause of disease	United States				Italy			
	1930		1964		1931		1964	
	Male	Female	Male	Female	Male	Female	Male	Female
Respiratory tuberculosis	0.0194	0.0190	0.0012	0.0005	0.0266	0.0286	0.0045	0.0014
Other infectious and parasitic diseases	0.0253	0.0211	0.0018	0.0015	0.0403	0.0391	0.0033	0.0031
Neoplasms	0.0186	0.0289	0.0302	0.0308	0.0139	0.0170	0.0347	0.0300
Cardiovascular renal diseases	0.0636	0.0622	0.0840	0.0650	0.0469	0.0529	0.0612	0.0564
Influenza, pneumonia, bronchitis	0.0370	0.0308	0.0078	0.0059	0.0800	0.0715	0.0154	0.0122
Diarrheal disorders	0.0141	0.0116	0.0012	0.0011	0.0640	0.0638	0.0044	0.0040
Certain degenerative diseases	0.0252	0.0261	0.0090	0.0080	0.0167	0.0141	0.0120	0.0080
Maternal causes	0.0000	0.0089	0.0000	0.0007	0.0000	0.0049	0.0000	0.0012
Certain diseases of infancy	0.0311	0.0239	0.0170	0.0125	0.0301	0.0259	0.0250	0.0199
Motor vehicle accidents	0.0120	0.0043	0.0129	0.0049	0.0000	0.0000	0.0118	0.0025
Other violence	0.0327	0.0116	0.0192	0.0077	0.0219	0.0071	0.0109	0.0042
Other and unknown causes	0.0482	0.0448	0.0232	0.0184	0.0541	0.0478	0.0245	0.0200
Total	0.3272	0.2932	0.2073	0.1571	0.3945	0.3726	0.2075	0.1631

Source: Calculated by Dr. Damiani of the University of Rome, from data in Preston, Keyfitz, and Schoen (1972).

Comparison of $H^{(i)}$ with $\overset{o(-i)}{e_0} - \overset{o}{e}_0$

A commonly used way of ascertaining the seriousness of a cause of death is to determine by how much the expectation of life at age zero would be increased if the cause in question were eliminated: letting $\overset{o(-i)}{e_0}$ represent the expectation of life with this cause eliminated, we find that the increase in expectation of life equals $\overset{o(-i)}{e_0} - \overset{o}{e}_0$. One trouble with subtracting $\overset{o}{e}_0$ from $\overset{o(-i)}{e_0}$ is that the latter supposes the total elimination of the ith cause. What would happen with the total elimination of a cause is of less immediate interest than what would happen with the elimination of 1 percent, say, of that cause, and the latter is readily calculated from $H^{(i)}$.

Table 3.5 shows several facts about four causes of death for United States males and females, 1964. These include the years of life that would be added if the respective causes were eradicated, $\overset{o(-i)}{e_0} - \overset{o}{e}_0$. Thus eliminating neoplasms would add 2.265 years for males. Against that we have the fact that $H^{\text{(neoplasms)}}$ is 0.0302. A one percent drop in neoplasms at all ages would raise the expectation of life by $0.01 \times H^{\text{(neoplasms)}} \times \overset{o}{e}_0 = 0.01 \times 0.0302 \times 66.905 = 0.0202$ year. Since H is applicable only to small uniform percentage changes at all ages, it is not strictly proper to multiply it by $\overset{o}{e}_0$ to find the result of completely eliminating the given cause. If such a multiplication is carried out for neoplasms, the result is 2.021 years, somewhat less than the $\overset{o(-i)}{e_0} - \overset{o}{e}_0 = 2.265$ of Table 3.5. For some of the causes the agreement is closer than this. But results for cardiovascular renal diseases are much farther off, both for males and for females; the effect of eliminating 1 percent is to add far less than 1 percent of the years that would be gained by complete eradication.

The fact that $H^{(i)}$ is additive is a clear convenience—the reduction of all causes by δ would increase $\overset{o}{e}_0$ by an amount $H\delta$ equal to the sum of the effects on $\overset{o}{e}_0$ of the elimination of the several causes of death $H^{(i)}\delta$:

$$H\delta = \sum H^{(i)}\delta.$$

No such statement can be made, however, about $\overset{o(-i)}{e_0}$; the elimination of all causes would make the duration of life infinite, whereas the sum of the increases due to the elimination of 12 groups of causes would be only about 22 years for United States males in 1964. The total of $\overset{o(-i)}{e_0} - \overset{o}{e}_0$ over all causes depends on what breakdown of causes is recognized, whereas $\sum H_i$ is invariant with respect to the grouping of causes.

Table 3.5 Effects of individual causes of death, United States, 1964; two methods compared

Comparison	Neoplasms	Cardiovascular renal diseases	Certain degenerative diseases	Motor vehicle accidents
		Males: $\overset{o}{e}_0 = 66.905$		
Crude rate	0.00170	0.00572	0.00046	0.00036
Added years of life if				
eliminated: $\overset{o}{e}_0^{(-i)} - \overset{o}{e}_0$	2.265	13.299	0.627	0.874
$H^{(i)}$	0.0302	0.0840	0.0090	0.0129
$H^{(i)}\overset{o}{e}_0$	2.021	5.620	0.602	0.863
		Females: $\overset{o}{e}_0 = 73.777$		
Crude rate	0.00139	0.00448	0.00037	0.00013
Added years of life if				
eliminated: $\overset{o}{e}_0^{(-i)} - \overset{o}{e}_0$	2.558	17.068	0.637	0.366
$H^{(i)}$	0.0308	0.0650	0.0080	0.0049
$H^{(i)}\overset{o}{e}_0$	2.272	4.796	0.590	0.362

Source: Preston, Keyfitz, and Schoen (1972, pp. 768–771) for $\overset{o}{e}_0^{(-i)} - \overset{o}{e}_0$; Table 3.4 for $H^{(i)}$.

Interrelations of the Several Causes

The quantity H can be thought of as a second parameter alongside $\overset{o}{e}_0$ of the curve of survivorship. It measures the convexity of the $l(x)$ function; and though in principle it could vary independently of $\overset{o}{e}_0$, among observed human populations it seems closely related to $\overset{o}{e}_0$. Extension of life is due mostly to mortality declines at younger ages, and much less to changes beyond age 70; therefore H tends to diminish over time. A similar feature of life tables arises by a mechanism described in the following piece of fantasy.

3.4 EVERYBODY DIES PREMATURELY

A man of 65 is struck by a car while crossing the street and so deprived of the 13 years of expectation of life that he is credited with by the United States 1973 life table for males. We extend this notion, recognized in legal decisions and in common sense, and think of any death, whether from accident, heart disease, or cancer, as an "accident" that deprives the person involved of the remainder of his expectation of life. To calculate the number of years of which people are, on the average, deprived by virtue of the particular circumstances that caused their deaths, we suppose that everyone is saved from death once, but that thereafter he is unprotected and is, say, subject to the mortality shown for persons of his age in the United States 1973 (Krakowski, 1972; Cohen, 1973).

In life table notation $-dl(a)$ persons die between ages a and $a+da$ at last birthday. These are deprived of $\overset{o}{e}(a)$ years each. Hence the average deprivation is

$$\text{Dep} = -\frac{1}{l(x)} \int_x^\omega \overset{o}{e}(a)\, dl(a) = \frac{1}{l(x)} \int_x^\omega \int_a^\omega l(t)\,\mu(a)\,dt\,da. \quad (3.4.1)$$

Consider the very special life table in which the chance of dying is constant at all ages, say μ. Then $l(a) = e^{-\mu a}$, and $\overset{o}{e}(a) = 1/\mu$, a constant for all ages. In this population the average prospective deprivation for those aged x is

$$\text{Dep} = -\frac{1}{e^{-\mu x}} \int_x^\infty \frac{1}{\mu} d(e^{-\mu a}) = \frac{1}{\mu}.$$

Since $\overset{o}{e}_0$ also equals $1/\mu$, this says that in the special case of equal death rates throughout life the deprivation involves a length of time equal to one's initial expectation of life. We can therefore write $\text{Dep}/\overset{o}{e}_0 = 1$, meaning that anyone who avoids death has a completely fresh start on this peculiar schedule of mortality.

At the opposite extreme, suppose that everyone dies at exact age ω. Then the expectation of life at ω is zero, and death deprives no one of any expectation. Thus the amount of deprivation depends on the shape of l_x. If $\mu(x) = \mu$, a constant, then $\text{Dep} = 1/\mu$ and $\text{Dep}/\overset{o}{e}_0 = 1$; at the other extreme, if everyone dies at the same age, $\text{Dep}/\overset{o}{e}_0 = 0$; any real life table would seem likely to fall between these two. At the extreme values $\text{Dep}/\overset{o}{e}_0$ is identical with H but is not quite the same in general. However, $\text{Dep}/\overset{o}{e}_0$ is identical with H for the hyperbolic life table function introduced earlier:

$$\mu(a) = \frac{\mu_0}{\omega - a}, \qquad l(a) = \left(1 - \frac{a}{\omega}\right)^{\mu_0}, \qquad \overset{o}{e}_a = \frac{\omega - a}{\mu_0 + 1}.$$

[Prove that $H = \mu_0/(\mu_0 + 1) = \text{Dep}/\overset{o}{e}_0$ for this case.]

If $\mu_0 = 0.30$, as suggested above for females in a contemporary population, the deprivation is $0.30/1.30 = 0.23$ of the expectation of life at age zero. This is the fractional extra expectation if one could be excused her first death. For males it would be higher: $0.43/1.43 = 0.30$ on the same hypothetical table.

Average Expectation of Life

Similar features of the survivorship curve can be obtained from the average expectation of life in the stationary population.

$$E = \frac{\int_0^\infty l(a)\overset{o}{e}(a)\,da}{\int_0^\infty l(a)\,da}.$$

Again, with $\mu(a) = \mu$, a constant, this is equal to $\overset{o}{e}_0$; if everyone lives to age ω, it equals $\overset{o}{e}_0/2$; for intermediate degrees of convexity it varies between these numbers.

Evaluating E for the hyperbolic life table function above gives its ratio to $\overset{o}{e}_0$ as

$$\frac{E}{\overset{o}{e}_0} = \frac{\mu_0 + 1}{\mu_0 + 2}.$$

This contrasts with

$$\frac{\text{Dep}}{\overset{o}{e}_0} = H = \frac{\mu_0}{\mu_0 + 1}.$$

Thus the average expectation of life in the life table population is less sensitive to the shape of the $l(x)$ curve than is H.

The manifestations of convexity in the life table function have by no means been exhausted in the foregoing discussion. As mortality at younger ages declines in relation to that at older ages, the mean age in the stationary population rises. Additional indices could be obtained from this consideration and others. [Experiment with the joint expectation of two lives, $\int_0^\omega [l(a)]^2\,da$ as a ratio to $\overset{o}{e}_0$.]

Oldest Person in Group

Griffith Feeney presents a problem that shows another aspect of the convexity of the survivorship function. A certain tribe has the custom of making its oldest member king, and he remains king until his death. If the tribe is stationary and has B births each year, (a) what is the expected length of time that a given child just born will be king, calculated at the moment of his birth; (b) what is the probability that he will become king; and (c) what is the expected tenure at the time of appointment as king? The following solution is due to S. Krishnamoorthy and Noreen Goldman.

The probability that a given baby will become king is the same as the probability that he will be alive when all members of the tribe older than he are dead. Under the rule those younger than he can be disregarded, since none can be king while he is alive. In a stationary population with B births the number of persons aged x at any moment is $Bl(x)$, and the chance that all of these will be dead by time t is

$$\left[\frac{l(x)-l(x+t)}{l(x)} \right]^{Bl(x)}.$$

The chance for all ages x is the product of this over x, where we suppose deaths to be independent. The product can be made to mean something for the continuous case by taking its logarithm and integrating:

$$B\int_0^\omega l(x)\ln\left[\frac{l(x)-l(x+t)}{l(x)} \right]dx.$$

The exponential of the above is the probability that all are dead by time t.

(a) The chance that a given baby is still alive at time and age t is $l(t)$. Hence the expectation at birth of his tenure as oldest person is

$$E=\int_0^\omega \exp\left\{ B\int_0^\omega l(x)\ln\left[\frac{l(x)-l(x+t)}{l(x)} \right]dx \right\}l(t)\,dt.$$

(b) The probability, say P, of his attaining the post is the same with $\mu(t)$ in the outer integrand.

(c) The expected tenure once he is appointed is E/P.

To generalize the above from a stationary age distribution to an arbitrary age distribution in which $Bp(a)\,da$ persons are between ages a and $a+da$, B still being births, replace the first $l(x)$ in the expression for E by $p(x)$, and do the same for P.

Effect of a Health Improvement

Shepard and Zeckhauser (1975) emphasize that populations are heterogeneous in regard to mortality risks, and that the several causes of death are not independent. The usual ways of calculating the gain through a medical or safety improvement that disregard heterogeneity and dependence can grossly overstate the benefits to be attained. This applies whether the improvement be mobile coronary care units, prophylactic hysterectomies, seatbelts in automobiles, or the equipping of airplanes with sensing devices that warn the pilot when the plane comes too close to the ground or to an obstacle.

Professionals have long been aware that to calculate lives saved is too simple, since a young man saved from death in a motor vehicle accident has a wholly different expectation thereafter from a man of 85 with a coronary attack saved by prehospital attention. In no case can death be prevented; at most it is deferred, and the question is for how long. One way of recognizing this is to measure the effect of a particular improvement by years added. For instance (Preston, Keyfitz, and Schoen, 1972, p. 769 and Table 3.5), at rates for the United States in 1964 the elimination of cancer among males would have increased the expectation of life by 2.26 years, and of motor vehicle accidents by 0.87 year; although the number of deaths due to cancer was almost 5 times that from accidents, the years added are only in the ratio of 2.6 to 1. The values of $H^{(i)}$ are in the ratio 2.3 to 1.

Although this apparently sophisticated method takes full account of age, it can still exaggerate the benefit of a health improvement insofar as there is heterogeneity in the population in respects other than age. Populations are rarely homogeneous with regard to a risk. Some individuals are hereditarily subject to cancer; some travel more than others in airplanes. The special danger of exaggerating a benefit occurs if those subject to the risk that is diminished are subject also to greater than average risks on other accounts.

Thus allowance for age is not by itself adequate if there are other agelike differentials of mortality. Suppose that among people of a given age some are much healthier than others, and a particular improvement saves the lives of those who are in the worst general condition. Then disregard of this aspect would exaggerate the benefit of the improvement, in the same way that disregard of age would overstate for an improvement that affected old people.

Chapter Four

FIXED REGIME OF MORTALITY AND FERTILITY: THE USES OF STABLE THEORY

A stable age distribution exists when age-specific birth and death rates have been constant over a considerable past period. The stable model is an advance in realism over the stationary population of the life table representing the special case of stability in which births are equal to deaths; though the stable model is restricted, the restriction will turn out to be acceptable for a number of purposes. Stable theory tells what age distribution is implied by a given and fixed regime of age-specific rates of birth and death; conversely, it permits in some instances inferring birth and death rates from an observed age distribution. It tells the cost of old-age pensions as a function of the rate of increase in population. For a given life table and rate of increase, average time of promotion in organizations with some degree of seniority can be calculated. These and other applications of stable theory are the subject of the present chapter. Chapter 10 will show how a regime of mortality and fertility implies kinship numbers. Stable theory can be generalized in various directions by modifying the assumption of a fixed regime, as will be seen in Chapter 9.

Lotka (1939, p. 18) applied the term *Malthusian* to a population with a given life table and an arbitrary rate of increase. He used the term *stable* for the case where the rate of increase is calculated from given and fixed age-specific birth rates, and in this sense stable populations are first treated in the present book in Chapter 5. Writers subsequent to Lotka, however, have not preserved this distinction.

4.1   STABLE THEORY

Suppose that the chance of living to age x is $l(x)$, and $l(x)$ is a function of age but not of time. A population whose births number B, uniformly spread through each year, where B does not change, and which is closed to migration will contain just $Bl(x)dx$ individuals between ages x and $x+dx$ at any given time, where $l(x)$ is normed to the radix $l_0 = 1$. It will contain $B_5 L_x = B\int_0^5 l(x+t)dt$ individuals between exact ages x and $x+5$. This theory could be applied to both sexes together, using a survivorship function $l(x)$ applicable to whatever mix of men and women is taken to be present, but the usual practice is to consider one sex at a time.

The stationary population produced by this assumption of fixed annual births and a fixed life table for each sex is generalized by supposing births to follow the exponential Be^{rt}. It will turn out that even slow growth, say $r = 0.005$, affects the age distribution at any one time considerably. To recognize steady growth requires only a slight complication of the argument needed for stationarity and fits observed ages better.

Consider the female (or male) part of a large population closed to migration and subject to a fixed life table, with births increasing exponentially. These conditions are sufficient to produce a stable age distribution, in which the number of persons living in each age group, as well as the deaths in each age group and the total population, are all increasing exponentially in the same ratio.

If the probability of living to age x is $l(x)$, and the births at time t are $B_0 e^{rt}$, then, to find the expected number of individuals between ages x and $x+dx$ we have to go back in time x to $x+dx$ years, when the number of births was $B_0 e^{r(t-x)}dx$. The fraction of these births that survive to time t must be $l(x)$; therefore the absolute number of persons aged x to $x+dx$ at time t is

$$B_0 e^{r(t-x)} l(x)dx.$$

The integral of this quantity is the total population at time t, and dividing by this total gives the fraction of the population aged x to $x+dx$ at time t, say, $c(x)dx$:

$$c(x)dx = \frac{e^{-rx}l(x)dx}{\int_0^\omega e^{-rx}l(x)dx} = be^{-rx}l(x)dx, \tag{4.1.1}$$

where $B_0 e^{rt}$ has been canceled out from numerator and denominator, and b has been written for $1/\int_0^\omega e^{-rx}l(x)dx$.

The result is important enough to be worth deriving by an alternative, more intuitive means. Still supposing the fixed survivorship schedule $l(x)$, a birth rate of b per unit population existing now, and a current rate of increase r compounded each moment, it follows that the fraction of the births of x years ago that are now alive (and therefore aged x) must be $l(x)$. But if the births are increasing in the ratio e^r each year, that is, at the annual rate r compounded each moment, then, the births now being in the ratio b to the population, the births x years ago must have been be^{-rx} *as a fraction of the present population*. And of those births the fraction $l(x)$ would be expected to be still alive. Then the expected number of persons alive now and aged x to $x + dx$ must be

$$be^{-rx}l(x)\,dx,$$

still reckoned per one of the present population. This compact derivation of the stable age distribution is essentially due to Euler (1760), and it has been rediscovered many times since.

Expression 4.1.1 provides the required age distribution $c(x)\,dx = be^{-rx}l(x)\,dx$ for the fraction of the population between ages x and $x + dx$. The argument rests on the supposition that the life table $l(x)$ is fixed in time for all x, and that the births and hence the population are growing exponentially, which is equivalent to assuming that birth as well as death rates have remained the same for a long time in the past. Because $c(x)\,dx$ is the fraction of the population aged x to $x + dx$, its total $\int_0^\infty c(x)\,dx$ must be unity; hence

$$\int_0^\omega be^{-rx}l(x)\,dx = 1.$$

This may be treated as an equation in b to obtain what was given in (4.1.1) as a definition:

$$b = \frac{1}{\displaystyle\int_0^\omega e^{-rx}l(x)\,dx}. \tag{4.1.2}$$

On (4.1.1) the "radix" or norm, $c(0)$, is b. It could, if we wished, be taken as $c(0) = 1$, as is done with the life table. If $c(0)$ is taken as 1, we replace the above argument by one calculating the present population aged x *per current birth*; it will be seen to be $e^{-rx}l(x)$, or a total at all ages of $\int_0^\infty e^{-rx}l(x)\,dx$; hence the birth rate must be $1/\int_0^\infty e^{-rx}l(x)\,dx$.

The several stable age distributions produced by a given life table are shown in Table 4.1, where the Coale and Demeny model West female life table with $\overset{o}{e}_0 = 65$ is combined with $r = -0.010, 0, 0.010, 0.020, 0.030, 0.040$. As one goes from columns at the left to columns at the right, the fall

Table 4.1 Percentage age distributions 100_5C_x based on life table with $\overset{o}{e}_0$ = 65 and various values of $1000r$

Age	Values of $1000r$					
x	-10.00	0.00	10.00	20.00	30.00	40.00
0	5.01	7.26	9.98	13.11	16.49	20.02
5	5.18	7.14	9.35	11.67	13.97	16.12
10	5.42	7.10	8.84	10.50	11.95	13.12
15	5.66	7.05	8.35	9.44	10.22	10.67
20	5.89	6.98	7.87	8.46	8.71	8.65
25	6.12	6.90	7.40	7.56	7.41	7.00
30	6.34	6.80	6.94	6.74	6.28	5.65
35	6.55	6.69	6.49	6.00	5.32	4.55
40	6.75	6.55	6.04	5.32	4.48	3.65
45	6.91	6.38	5.60	4.68	3.76	2.91
50	6.99	6.15	5.13	4.08	3.12	2.29
55	6.97	5.83	4.63	3.50	2.54	1.78
60	6.76	5.38	4.06	2.92	2.02	1.34
65	6.27	4.74	3.40	2.33	1.53	0.97
70	5.37	3.87	2.64	1.72	1.08	0.65
75	4.06	2.78	1.81	1.12	0.66	0.38
80+	3.76	2.41	1.46	0.85	0.47	0.25
Total	100.00	100.00	100.00	100.00	100.00	100.00
Average age	42.20	36.96	31.97	27.46	23.54	20.25
Population $100_{30}C_{15}$	37.30	40.98	43.09	43.51	42.42	40.16
Ratio $\dfrac{_5C_0}{_{30}C_{15}}$	0.134	0.177	0.232	0.301	0.389	0.498
Ratio $\dfrac{_{10}C_5}{_\infty C_5}$	0.112	0.154	0.202	0.255	0.310	0.366
Dependency $\dfrac{_{15}C_0 + _\infty C_{65}}{_{50}C_{15}}$ 0.719	0.685	0.711	0.793	0.929	1.121

Source: Coale and Demeny 1966, p. 62.

in the proportions becomes steeper and the values at the youngest ages higher; the proportion 5 to 9 years of age, for example, is 5.18 percent for $1000r = -10$ and 16.12 percent for $1000r = 40$. The fraction 65 and over falls from 19.46 to 2.25 percent. Note that the values for ages 20 to 40 first rise and then fall, and that the percent aged 15 to 44 goes from 37.30 to a maximum of 43.51 at $1000r = 20$ and then declines to 40.16. [Find a theoretical expression for the interval at which the proportion 15 to 44 at last birthday peaks.]

A Discrete Form

Although the stable age distribution is easier to think about in the continuous version, application requires a discrete form. We need to translate $c(x)dx = be^{-rx}l(x)dx$ into 5-year age groups to match the population data as usually provided. Integrating both sides of (4.1.1) between exact ages x to $x+5$ gives for $_5C_x = \int_0^5 c(x+t)dt$

$$_5C_x = b\int_0^5 e^{-r(x+t)}l(x+t)dt$$

$$\doteq be^{-r(x+2.5)}\int_0^5 e^{-r(t-2.5)}l(x+t)dt. \qquad (4.1.3)$$

The integral here is very close to $\int_0^5 l(x+t)dt$, tabulated in presentations of the life table as $_5L_x$. To this approximation

$$_5C_x \doteq be^{-r(x+2.5)} {_5L_x}. \qquad (4.1.4)$$

[Work out an expression for the error of (4.1.4).]

Suppose that we are satisfied to integrate by putting a cubic through $l_{x-5}, l_x, l_{x+5}, l_{x+10}$, which bounds an area between x and $x+5$ equal to

$$_5L_x = \tfrac{65}{24}(l_x + l_{x+5}) - \tfrac{5}{24}(l_{x-5} + l_{x+10}). \qquad (4.1.5)$$

[Derive this expression.] In application to Mexico, 1970, females aged 60 to 64, with $l_0 = 100,000$,

$$_5L_{60} = \tfrac{65}{24}(68,745 + 62,304) - \tfrac{5}{24}(73,836 + 53,058) = 328,488.$$

Taking $r = 0.03395$ gives

$$e^{-62.5r} {_5L_{60}} = 39,355$$

as the stable number per 100,000 current births.

A more precise way to evaluate (4.1.3) is to integrate, not the function $l(x)$, but the function $e^{-rx}l(x)$. We multiply l_{60} by e^{-60r}, l_{65} by e^{-65r}, and so on. Doing this first and then integrating by the same cubic formula (4.1.5) gives the stable number 39,449, as opposed to 39,355 from (4.1.4). The difference between the two methods is usually less than 1 percent.

4.2 POPULATION GROWTH ESTIMATED FROM ONE CENSUS

Perhaps the most important fact bearing on the future of a population is its rate of natural increase, and yet for most countries of the world the obvious way of obtaining this rate—subtracting registered deaths from

registered births—does not offer acceptable precision. The task of install-
ing a modern registration system in developing countries is difficult,
because people have little use for birth certificates, which become important only under modern conditions. Proof of date of birth and of
citizenship is not required by immobile peasants, either for themselves or
for their children, so these people do not respond dependably to a law
from a distant capital requiring them to go to the town or village registrar
each time a child is born. If complete vital statistics were the only possible
source of information, the problem of rapid population increase might well
be solved before it could be measured.

   Hence indirect methods are called for. Extensive collections of possible
procedures are given in Coale and Demeny (1967) and Brass (1975). The
nature of one group of such methods is examined in this and the next four
sections.

   As in Section 2.3, each individual in the population is represented by a
line in the Lexis plane of age and time, starting at the moment of birth on
the time axis and proceeding at a 45° angle as simultaneously the person
ages and time moves forward. A census provides a count by age that
includes all life lines crossing a horizontal line at the date of the census.
Figure 4.1 shows a census taken in 1970, and marks the intervals for
individuals aged 20 and 45 at last birthday as examples. Each cohort born

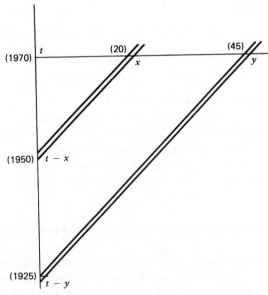

Fig. 4.1 Relation of census count at ages x and y to birth cohorts x and y years earlier.

in a particular year is a band of 1 year: measured vertically 1 calendar year, measured horizontally 1 year of age. Our problem is, for example, to make observations of the number of survivors to ages 20 and 45 in 1970 tell us how fast births were increasing between 1925 and 1950. The density at any point can be portrayed as an altitude over the age–time plane; a census gives the profile on a time section.

Expressed in more general terms, the problem is as follows: given the number of individuals P_x at age x and P_y at age y from a census taken in the year t, find the rate at which the births were increasing between years $t-y$ and $t-x$, where y is greater than x. Call the birth function for the year preceding time t $B(t)$; if the population is closed to migration, we have

$$B(t-y)L_y = P_y,$$
$$B(t-x)L_x = P_x,$$

(4.2.1)

where L_x and L_y are the fractions of each cohort that attain the census moment t in question; the equations are exact if L_x and L_y reflect the mortalities of the two cohorts, usually different.

Along with the exactitude of equations 4.2.1 goes their insolubility on the basis of the data available, which are only P_y and P_x from the census at time t. They contain two unknown survivorships, as well as the unknown function $B(t)$. To suppose that the survivorships follow the same life table, even without knowing what that table is, simplifies the problem considerably, for we can then disregard the first x years of life and be concerned only with the mortality between ages x and y. This is apparent on dividing the second member of the pair by the first, which leaves us with one equation containing only L_y/L_x:

$$\frac{B(t-y)}{B(t-x)}\left(\frac{L_y}{L_x}\right) = \frac{P_y}{P_x}.$$

(4.2.2)

But we must not forget in application that this disregard of survivorship at ages less than x is permissible only if the two cohorts have been subject to the same mortality up to that age, a point that will be reconsidered in Chapter 9.

We still have trouble; even if the life tables for the two cohorts are the same and are known, the most that (4.2.2) can do is to trace out the birth function, given P_x/L_x and P_y/L_y for the several combinations of x and y. We would like to use it to find a rate of increase—one number that holds through time. Let us take it that the birth function is an exponential, say $B(t) = B_0 e^{rt}$. This is true in the circumstance that age-specific birth and death rates have been unchanged, not only over the interval between times $t-y$ and $t-x$, but also before $t-y$. (If the births were irregular before that date, so would be the age distribution, and this would affect the birth rate between $t-y$ and $t-x$, even with a fixed regime of birth and death rates in that interval.) Equation 4.2.2 now reduces to

$$e^{(y-x)r} = \frac{P_x/L_x}{P_y/L_y} \tag{4.2.3}$$

and contains only two unknowns, r and the survivorship L_y/L_x.

If the deaths for the population are known for past times, they can be made into a life table, which ideally would be a cohort life table applicable to the common mortality of the two cohorts in question. If the deaths are known for a current period, the current life table will be applicable to the cohorts if mortality has not been changing. If even current death data are lacking, there is no recourse but to select a life table from another source that will be somehow appropriate. This could be a table for a neighboring country with presumed similar mortality, but more often one resorts to a model or reference table. Let us suppose that by some means, however arbitrary, a value of L_y/L_x has been obtained. Then (4.2.3) is an equation for r alone, which readily yields the solution

$$r = \frac{1}{y-x} \ln\left(\frac{P_x/L_x}{P_y/L_y}\right). \tag{4.2.4}$$

This is the simplest of all the ways of using a current age distribution to provide estimates of the rate of increase.

Figure 4.2, drawn for an increasing population, may help toward an intuitive understanding of (4.2.4). The life table curve is flat, and the stably increasing population less so; the formula in effect measures the relative

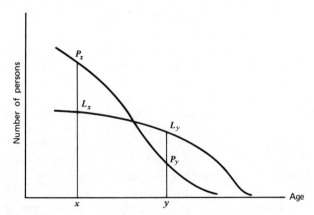

Fig. 4.2 Given and stationary populations used to measure increase.

steepness of the increasing population in terms of the steepness of the life table.

Since one value of the rate of increase r is obtained for each pair of ages, potentially thousands of values of r are available from one census. Each of these can be interpreted as an estimate of the (supposedly fixed) rate of increase, or more realistically as the rate of increase of births between the two cohorts.

The foregoing argument, whose several assertions may be followed on the Lexis diagram, has in effect been a listing of the assumptions required to bring us from the pair of equations 4.2.1, whose solution in general is hopeless, to (4.2.4), which constitutes an exact answer on the assumptions given. The data base is a census that obtained present characteristics of persons, in particular their ages. From one point of view, each person enumerated in a census is asked to report on a vital event—his own birth—that took place a long time earlier. This is a special case of retrospective information. Unfortunately, knowledge of this retrospective event can genuinely be lost, say among a people who do not celebrate birthdays or otherwise keep their ages in mind. In such an instance P_x and P_y are irrecoverable.

Effect of Choice of Model Life Table

Let us try a small experiment to find the difference that the choice of life table makes for the rate of increase in births. For Peru, 1963, the female population included $_5P_{25} = 405,179$ women aged 25 to 29 at last birthday and $_5P_{35} = 293,494$ aged 35 to 39. For several life expectancies, considerably above and below the 62.5 years surmised, (4.2.4) was applied to these data, employing the four regional model life tables constructed by Coale and Demeny (1966). For life expectancy 62.5 years Table 4.2 shows the differences across the four life tables to be satisfactorily small, with the highest rate only about 4 percent above the lowest. The variation is greater for smaller $\overset{o}{e}_0$.

Within each of the columns, however, the computed r varies considerably among life expectancies. Assuming high mortality seems to cause L_y / L_x to absorb some of the r. In the West column the value for Peru at $\overset{o}{e}_0 = 62.5$ is 0.02848; a guess of $\overset{o}{e}_0 = 52.5$ would bring this down to 0.02543, which is 11 percent lower. Life tables with $\overset{o}{e}_0$ between 52.5 and 72.5 list r as between about 0.025 and 0.031.

Data drawn from the Togo, 1961, female population, in which there were 80,746 women aged 25 to 29 at last birthday and 51,975 aged 35 to 39, were used to examine the variation for a high-mortality population.

Table 4.2   Values of r for Peru, 1963, computed for selected values of $\overset{o}{e}_0$ and the four model life tables of Coale and Demeny (1966), using $_5P_{25}$ and $_5P_{35}$ for females

$\overset{o}{e}_0$	West	North	East	South
22.5	0.01015	0.01229	0.01473	0.01482
32.5	0.01708	0.01836	0.01997	0.02028
42.5	0.02187	0.02264	0.02381	0.02415
52.5	0.02543	0.02580	0.02676	0.02721
62.5	0.02848	0.02842	0.02922	0.02958
72.5	0.03100	0.03055	0.03114	0.03125

Table 4.3 presents computations of r for each of the four regional life tables at life expectancy 40.0 years. Although rates steadily increase as one proceeds from West to South, the range of values is again small, less than 8 percent between the largest and the smallest.

More experimenting is needed to ascertain the sensitivity of the inferred r to the life table chosen.

Table 4.3   Values of r for Togo, 1961, computed for $\overset{o}{e}_0$ = 40.0 on the regional model life tables, using $_5P_{25}$ and $_5P_{35}$ for females

$\overset{o}{e}_0$	West	North	East	South
40.0	0.03259	0.03349	0.03475	0.03512

Theory for the Error Arising from Use of an Improper Life Table

Meanwhile the effect of a wrong life table can be calculated under the simplified condition that the table is wrong by a given amount, say δ, for the age-specific rates $\mu(a)$ at all ages: the true $\mu^*(a)$ equals the guessed $\mu(a)$ plus δ. If $\mu^*(a) = \mu(a) + \delta$, then $l^*(a) = l(a)e^{-\delta a}$, so that, in a slight rearrangement of (4.2.4),

$$r^* = \frac{1}{y-x}\ln\left[\frac{P_x/P_y}{L_x^*/L_y^*}\right] \doteq \frac{1}{y-x}\ln\left[\frac{P_x/P_y}{(L_x/L_y)e^{\delta(y-x)}}\right]$$

$$= \frac{1}{y-x}\left\{\ln\left[\frac{P_x/P_y}{L_x/L_y}\right] - \ln\left[e^{\delta(y-x)}\right]\right\} = r - \delta. \tag{4.2.5}$$

Thus taking a life table based on mortality rates too low by δ for both cohorts involved causes the estimate of increase to be too high by δ.

A more realistic alternative is to suppose the true $\mu^*(a) = \mu(a)(1 + \delta)$, so that $l^*(a) = l(a)^{1+\delta}$. Then for the true rate of increase r^* in terms of r we have

$$r^* = \frac{1}{y-x} \ln\left(\frac{P_x/P_y}{L_x^*/L_y^*}\right) \doteq \frac{1}{y-x} \ln\left[\frac{P_x/P_y}{(L_x/L_y)^{1+\delta}}\right]$$

$$= r - \frac{\delta \ln(L_x/L_y)}{y-x}. \tag{4.2.6}$$

Also, as was shown in Section 3.3, the effect of the same error on $\overset{o}{e}_0$ is, for δ small,

$$\overset{o}{e}_0^* = \overset{o}{e}_0(1 - H\delta),$$

where H is about 0.20 for modern populations. This gives

$$\delta = \frac{1 - \left(\overset{o}{e}_0^*/\overset{o}{e}_0\right)}{H}, \tag{4.2.7}$$

or, for $\overset{o}{e}_0^* = 65$, $\overset{o}{e}_0 = 60$ in the problem with $x = 25$, $y = 35$ of Table 4.3,

$$\delta = \frac{1 - (65/60)}{0.20} = -0.4;$$

with $\ln(L_{25}/L_{35}) = 0.03$, r^* of (4.2.6) comes out to

$$r^* = r - \frac{(-0.4)(0.03)}{10} = r + 0.0012.$$

Therefore using a life table with $\overset{o}{e}_0$ 5 years too low produces a rate of increase that is 0.0012 too low, an error of $0.0012/0.03 = 4$ percent. This is verified by doing the calculation in the West series with $\overset{o}{e}_0 = 60$ and $\overset{o}{e}_0 = 65$; the values of r obtained differ by about 0.0012.

Stable theory can be applied with two censuses, which permit more satisfactory selection of the life table to be used. It combines with and is supplemented by other devices, of which extensive selections are given in Coale and Demeny (1967) and Brass (1975). The purposes of the foregoing treatment of the simplest method were, on the one hand, to show how its assumptions can be clarified through use of the Lexis diagram and, on the other, to study in a preliminary way its degree of robustness when, as is usually the case, the assumptions do not apply.

4.3 MEAN AGE IN THE STABLE POPULATION

An increasing population must be on the average younger than a stationary population. This is due to children being born more recently

than their elders, so that with constant birth rates the increasing population must have a larger proportion of children. If the current birth rate is b,
the proportion of children under age α is from (4.1.1),

$$_\alpha C_0 = \frac{\int_0^\alpha e^{-ra} l(a)\, da}{\int_0^\omega e^{-ra} l(a)\, da}.$$

(The symbol C stands for the theoretical stable population, P for the
observed population, though the distinction is not always easy to preserve
in attempts to assimilate observations to theory.) To trace this out as a
function of r for given α and $l(x)$ we note that

$$\frac{d(_\alpha C_0)}{dr} = _\alpha C_0 (m - m_1),$$

where m is the mean age of the entire (stationary) population, and m_1 the
mean age of the part of it less than α years old. [Prove this formula.] Then
expanding $_\alpha C_0$ as a function of r about $r = 0$ gives

$$_\alpha C_0 \doteq \frac{_\alpha L_0}{\overset{o}{e}_0} \left[1 + r(m - m_1) \right],$$

$_\alpha L_0 / \overset{o}{e}_0$ being the value of $_\alpha C_0$ when $r = 0$, that is, the proportion under α
years of age in the life table. This linear first approximation is suitable for
small values of r.

By how many years is the mean age of the increasing population
younger than that of the stationary population with the same life table? We
shall see that the difference in mean ages is approximately equal to the rate
of increase of the growing population times the variance of ages of the
stationary one. Average age, as observed or as in the stable model, will be
designated by $\bar{x}$, and where $\bar{x}$ is low we will speak of the population as
young.

From (4.1.1) it follows that the average age in the stable population is

$$\bar{x} = \int_0^\omega xc(x)\, dx = \frac{\int_0^\omega xe^{-rx} l(x)\, dx}{\int_0^\omega e^{-rx} l(x)\, dx};$$

and on expanding the exponentials and integrating the separate terms in
both numerator and denominator, we find that

$$\bar{x} = \frac{L_1 - rL_2 + (r^2 L_3 / 2!) - (r^3 L_4 / 3!) + \cdots}{L_0 - rL_1 + (r^2 L_2 / 2!) - (r^3 L_3 / 3!) + \cdots}, \tag{4.3.1}$$

where $L_i = \int_0^{\omega} x^i l(x)\,dx$ is the numerator of the ith moment about zero of the stationary population of the life table. Ordinary long division on the right-hand side of (4.3.1) gives for $\bar{x}$ the series $L_1/L_0 - [L_2/L_0 - (L_1/L_0)^2]r + \cdots$, which may be written as

$$\bar{x} \doteq \frac{L_1}{L_0} - \sigma^2 r \tag{4.3.2}$$

to the term in r, where L_1/L_0 is the mean and σ^2 the variance of the age distribution in the stationary population, both necessarily positive. Hence $\bar{x}$ is less than L_1/L_0 as long as r is greater than zero, supposing that the subsequent terms are small enough not to interfere.

An exact infinite series for $\bar{x}$ would be

$$\bar{x} = \frac{L_1}{L_0} - \sigma^2 r + \frac{\kappa_3 r^2}{2!} - \frac{\kappa_4 r^3}{3!} + \cdots, \tag{4.3.3}$$

where κ_3 is the third cumulant and κ_4 the fourth cumulant of the distribution with density $l(x)/L_0$ (Lotka, 1939, p. 22). The third cumulant is the same as the third moment about the mean:

$$\kappa_3 = \mu_3 = \int_0^{\omega} \left(x - \frac{L_1}{L_0} \right)^3 \frac{l(x)\,dx}{L_0},$$

and is associated with skewness. The fourth cumulant κ_4 is the fourth moment about the mean less 3 times the square of the variance, and is a measure of kurtosis or peakedness, though its visual interpretation is not straightforward.

Let us identify the terms of (4.3.3) for Irish males of 1968, using data given in Keyfitz and Flieger (1971, p. 446). The cumulants of the life table are as follows:

$$L_1/L_0 = 36.678,$$

$$\sigma^2 = 495.59,$$

$$\kappa_3 = 2243.9,$$

$$\kappa_4 = -240{,}862,$$

$$r = 0.01889.$$

Taking four terms in (4.3.3) approximates $\bar{x}$ by

$$\bar{x} \doteq 36.678 - 9.362 + 0.400 + 0.271 = 27.987.$$

This approximation to $\bar{x}$, the mean of the stable age distribution, 27.953, is excellent. But Irish births have fluctuated considerably, and the mean of the observed age distribution is 31.806, about 4 years higher than the $\bar{x}$ calculated above.

For Colombia females of 1964 (Keyfitz and Flieger, 1968, p. 191), the first approximation (4.3.2) to the mean $\bar{x}$ of the stable age distribution is

$$\bar{x} = \frac{L_1}{L_0} - \sigma^2 r = 37.360 - (539.04)(0.0283)$$

$$= 37.36 - 15.25 = 22.11.$$

In comparison, the stable age distribution shows a mean of 24.13 and the observed female age distribution a mean of 22.32. More instances would be needed to obtain a realistic estimate of the error of (4.3.2) as an approximation to the means of the stable and the observed age distributions, respectively. Apparently the error increases with mortality and with r.

A growing population tends to be younger than the corresponding stationary population also within any particular interval of ages. An argument identical to the one above may be applied to any age interval—we did not require the limits to be 0 to ω in deriving $\bar{x} \doteq (L_1/L_0) - \sigma^2 r$. Thus children under 15 years of age are slightly younger, and people over 85 are younger, in the growing than in the corresponding stationary population. With the obvious redefinition of its constants, (4.3.2) is not restricted to the whole of life, but is applicable to any age interval.

Demographic Calculations Need Not Start at Age Zero. Various subgroups can be defined in such fashion that theory developed for whole populations applies to them. We have already dropped down to one sex and refer to the "female population," a useful abstraction but an abstraction nonetheless, since females cannot go through the process of birth and increase without males. The "population over age 15" could similarly be described as though it were self-contained. All of stable theory would apply with at most an alteration in the definitions of symbols. Now "births" would be the individuals passing through their fifteenth birthdays; survivorship would be not l_x/l_0, which we have been calling l_x, but rather l_x/l_{15}, $x > 15$; the stable fraction between x and $x + dx$ would be

$$c'(x)\,dx = b'e^{-rx}\frac{l(x)}{l_{15}}\,dx,$$

where $b' = l_{15}/\int_{15}^{\omega} e^{-rx}l(x)\,dx$, and evidently

$$c'(x)\,dx = \frac{e^{-rx}l(x)\,dx}{\int_{15}^{\omega} e^{-ra}l(a)\,da}.$$

By a further extension ages beyond 35, say, could be masked out and an expression developed for the stable population aged 15 to 34 at last birthday. It would similarly be feasible to recognize ages before birth, and even, where data on fetal mortality are available, to go back to conception.

Use of Population Mean Age

Relationship 4.3.2 may be applied in the opposite direction—to tell the rate of increase of a population when we know its mean age and the mean and variance of the life table applicable to it. This way of estimating the rate of increase of a population uses the data somewhat differently than does (4.2.4).

Transposing (4.3.2) into the equivalent

$$r \doteq \frac{(L_1/L_0) - \bar{x}}{\sigma^2} \tag{4.3.4}$$

provides an approximation to the rate of population increase r, given the life table mean age L_1/L_0, the variance of the life table age distribution σ^2, and the observed mean age $\bar{x}$. Entering the figures for Colombia, 1964, already used, we find that

$$r \doteq \frac{(L_1/L_0) - \bar{x}}{\sigma^2} = \frac{37.36 - 22.32}{539.04} = 0.0279,$$

as against the observed $r = 0.0283$.

When the additional parameters κ_3 (skewness) and κ_4 (kurtosis) are reliably enough available to be taken into account in estimating r, we can transform (4.3.3) into

$$r^* = \frac{(L_1/L_0) - \bar{x}}{\sigma^2 - (\kappa_3 r/2) + (\kappa_4 r^2/6)} . \tag{4.3.5}$$

In this iterative form we would start with an arbitrary r on the right-hand side, obtain the improved r^*, enter it on the right-hand side, obtain a further improvement, and so continue. The iteration is a way of solving the cubic equation in the unknown r represented by truncation of (4.3.3) after the term in r^3. Three or four cycles of iteration suffice for convergence to considerably more decimal places than are demographically meaningful.

Note that the method requires, not complete knowledge of the life table number-living column, but only its mean and other cumulants. In the absence of a life table we would guess the L_1/L_0 and σ^2 of (4.3.4), perhaps calculating them from a set of model tables. The less dependent the outcome on the life table chosen, the more useful is the method. We are encouraged to find that the mean ages of life table $l(x)$ vary only about one-fifth as much as their $\overset{o}{e}_0$, the expectation of life at age zero. For instance, the Coale and Demeny (1966, p. 54) model West table for females with $\overset{o}{e}_0 = 55$ shows a mean L_1/L_0 of 34.95, and that with $\overset{o}{e}_0 = 60$ has $L_1/L_0 = 35.96$.

Countries and regions lacking birth data are likely to have inaccurate censuses, and we want to rely on censuses only at their strongest points. The art of this work is to take account of what ages are well enumerated and what ones poorly enumerated, as well as to use the model with the weakest assumptions. Literally thousands of ways of using the age distribution may be devised, and ideally one should choose the method least sensitive to (a) the accuracy of enumeration of ages; (b) the appropriateness of the life table, which often has to be selected arbitrarily; (c) the assumption of stability; and (d) possible in- and out-migration. To be able to choose from among a large stock of methods is an advantage in many instances, and the following sections continue our partial inventory of this stock.

4.4 RATE OF INCREASE ESTIMATED FROM THE FRACTION UNDER AGE 25

Suppose that a population is underenumerated at ages 0 to 4 because infants are omitted, at 10 to 14 because some children of this age are entered as 5 to 9, and at 15 to 19 because young adults are mobile and the enumerator sometimes fails to find them. Suppose correspondingly that the numbers 5 to 9 and 20 to 24 are overstated (Coale and Demeny, 1967, p. 17), and that these errors offset to some degree those mentioned in the preceding sentence, so that the proportion under age 25, say α, is given correctly. We would like to use nothing but α from a census, along with a suitable life table, to estimate the rate of increase r.

Referring to the same stable age distribution (4.1.1), we can construct an equation in which both the observed α and the unknown r appear. The proportion of the population under age 25 is $\int_0^{25} be^{-ra}l(a)da$, where $\int_0^{\omega} be^{-ra}l(a)da = 1$. The ratio of the first of these integrals to the second can be equated to α and the birth rate b canceled out:

$$\alpha = \frac{\int_0^{25} e^{-ra}l(a)da}{\int_0^{\omega} e^{-ra}l(a)da}. \tag{4.4.1}$$

The problem now is to solve (4.4.1) for the unknown r, supposing the life table to be given.

One method is to leaf through a collection of model tables (e.g., Coale and Demeny, 1966, designed for such purposes) and find among those for the given mortality the one with an α that matches the given α. The r of that stable population is the solution to (4.4.1).

An alternative is an iterative formula to solve (4.4.1) for r, given $l(a)$: multiply the numerator and denominator of the expression on the right-hand side of (4.4.1) by e^{10r}, then multiply both sides of (4.4.1) by e^{-10r}/α, next take logarithms of the reciprocals of both sides, and finally divide by 10 to obtain

$$r^* = \tfrac{1}{10} \ln \left[\frac{\alpha \int_0^\omega e^{-r(a-20)} l(a)\, da}{\int_0^{25} e^{-r(a-10)} l(a)\, da} \right] \tag{4.4.2}$$

(Keyfitz and Flieger, 1971, p. 28). This equation is algebraically identical with (4.4.1) except that the r on the left has been starred to suggest its use in iteration. Starting with an arbitrary r on the right, calculating r^*, entering this on the right in place of r, and repeating, is a process that ultimately converges to $r^* = r$, and whatever r satisfies this is also bound to satisfy (4.4.1). The multiplication of (4.4.1) by e^{-10r}/α (rather than e^{-15r}/α, say) is arbitrary, and experiment shows that e^{-10r} provides fast convergence. [Use the theory of functional iteration (e.g., Scarborough, 1958, p. 209) to find the optimum multiplier in place of e^{-10r}/α.] This is an example of how knowledge of the approximate magnitude of the quantities concerned enables demographers to devise iterative procedures that are simpler than more general ones such as the Newton–Raphson method.

To apply (4.4.2) we replace the integrals by finite expressions. The usual rough but serviceable approximation is in 5-year intervals. For example, the interval from $a = 0$ to $a = 5$ contributes to the integral in the numerator of the logarithm in (4.4.2) the amount

$$\int_0^5 e^{-r(a-20)} l(a)\, da \doteq e^{-r(2.5-20)} {}_5L_0$$

$$= e^{17.5r} {}_5L_0,$$

and similarly for the other 5-year age intervals. Then the iterative formula becomes

$$r^* = \tfrac{1}{10} \ln \frac{\alpha \sum_{i=0}^{\omega-5} e^{-r(i-17.5)} {}_5L_i}{\sum_{i=0}^{20} e^{-r(i-7.5)} {}_5L_i} \tag{4.4.3}$$

in terms of the ${}_5L_i$ tabulated in published life tables (except that most life tables are on radix $l_0 = 100{,}000$; that is, in terms of the symbols here used they tabulate $10^5 {}_5L_i$). Summations in (4.4.3) are over i's that are multiples of 5. With zero as the arbitrary initial value of r, (4.4.3) converges to six decimal places in from 3 to 10 cycles in most instances.

Method 4.4.3 is easily adapted to a split in the distribution at an age other than 25, and it can be generalized beyond this to other fractions, for example, the fraction of the population between ages 10 and 30, as indicated by examples in Section 4.6.

4.5 BIRTH RATE AS WELL AS RATE OF INCREASE ESTIMATED FOR A STABLE POPULATION

We saw in (4.1.1) that in a closed population where birth and death rates have been constant for a long time the proportion of individuals between ages x and $x + dx$ is $c(x)dx = be^{-rx}l(x)dx$. Similarly the proportion of the population between ages y and $y + dy$ is $c(y)dy = be^{-ry}l(y)dy$. To adapt to 5-year age intervals we integrated each equation over 5 years to construct

$$_5C_x = be^{-r(x+2.5)}\,_5L_x,$$
$$_5C_y = be^{-r(y+2.5)}\,_5L_y. \tag{4.5.1}$$

Dividing and taking logarithms, we obtained in Section 4.1

$$r = \frac{1}{y-x}\ln\left(\frac{_5C_x/_5L_x}{_5C_y/_5L_y}\right). \tag{4.5.2}$$

Now we go on to find the value of b by eliminating r from the pair (4.5.1):

$$b = \frac{\left(\dfrac{_5C_x}{_5L_x}\right)^{(y+2.5)/(y-x)}}{\left(\dfrac{_5C_y}{_5L_y}\right)^{(x+2.5)/(y-x)}}. \tag{4.5.3}$$

We derived these formulas by defining $_5C_x$ as an integral over a range of ages in the stable population; we would apply the formulas by entering for $_5C_x$ the observed fraction, from a census or estimate, over that range.

An alternative form with 10-year intervals is

$$b = \exp\left[\frac{\dfrac{\ln(_{10}C_x/_{10}L_x)}{x+5} - \dfrac{\ln(_{10}C_y/_{10}L_y)}{y+5}}{\dfrac{1}{x+5} - \dfrac{1}{y+5}}\right].$$

Entering the numbers for Colombian females, 1965, in thousands, for ages

5 to 15 and 20 to 30 (Keyfitz and Flieger, 1971, p. 366, reproduced in Table 4.6 below) gives

$$
b = \exp\left\{ \frac{\dfrac{\ln\left[(2575/9125)/8.753\right]}{10} - \dfrac{\ln\left[(1401/9125)/8.550\right]}{25}}{\frac{1}{10} - \frac{1}{25}} \right\} = 0.0476,
$$

or 47.6 births per thousand population.

There is no need to confine the calculation to two ages (Bourgeois–Pichat, 1958). Taking logarithms in (4.5.1) provides a linear equation in r and $\ln b$ for each age:

$$
\ln b - \left(x + 2\tfrac{1}{2}\right)r = \ln\left(\frac{{}_5C_x}{{}_5L_x}\right). \tag{4.5.4}
$$

Again in application we replace the stable proportions ${}_5C_x$ by the observed proportions P. For Colombian females, 1965, the needed quantities in the six age intervals in the range 0 to 29 are shown in Table 4.4. The least square line relating $x + 2\tfrac{1}{2}$ and $\ln({}_5P_x/{}_5L_x)$ is

$$
-3.126 - \left(x + 2\tfrac{1}{2}\right)(0.0352) = \ln\left(\frac{{}_5P_x}{{}_5L_x}\right),
$$

and this identifies $\ln b$ with -3.126 and r with 0.0352; hence b is estimated at $\exp(-3.126) = 0.0439$, r at 0.0352, and d, the death rate, at the difference, 0.0087.

Table 4.4 Data for estimating b and r for Colombia, females, 1965

	Observed	Life table	
$x + 2\tfrac{1}{2}$	${}_5P_x$	${}_5L_x$	$\ln(\dfrac{{}_5P_x}{{}_5L_x})$
$2\tfrac{1}{2}$	0.1718	4.54231	-3.275
$7\tfrac{1}{2}$	0.1558	4.39360	-3.339
$12\tfrac{1}{2}$	0.1263	4.35979	-3.542
$17\tfrac{1}{2}$	0.1048	4.33516	-3.722
$22\tfrac{1}{2}$	0.0841	4.29919	-3.934
$27\tfrac{1}{2}$	0.0695	4.25043	-4.113

Source: Keyfitz and Flieger, (1971), p. 366.

The ages to be used are at our disposal; which should we choose? With only two age intervals x and y, as in (4.5.2), if x and y are equal neither (4.5.2) nor (4.5.3) tells us anything, and if they are close to one another the answers will be sensitive to random errors in the population count identified with $_5C_x$ and $_5C_y$. On the other hand, choosing x and y far apart increases the risk of straddling a substantial change in the birth rates that determine the cohort sizes, that is, a departure from stability. If the probability of a change in birth rates between x and y years ago is proportional to $y - x$, the length of the interval between them, then for given random errors in ages there will be an optimum choice of the interval $y - x$, perhaps in the neighborhood of 25 years.

Suppose a single change in birth rates in the past, at a known or suspected date D years ago. Making both x and y less than D, or both x and y greater than D, is clearly advisable. If both x and y are less than D, the more recent rate of increase will be estimated; if they are greater, the earlier rate.

If nothing is known about shifts in the past birth rate, and we want an average of all rates that have prevailed during the lifetimes of persons now alive, we might calculate all possible values of r and average them. The average would be best weighted, with a maximum weight for $y - x = 25$ years or thereabouts, and with lower weights as we moved toward $y - x = 0$ or $y - x = 50$. The population above 70 provides little information on rate of increase. Beyond 70 ages are inaccurately reported; the life table is less precisely known; the survivors have passed through a variety of mortality conditions; and their number is often too small to disregard sampling error as we have done throughout.

4.6 COMPARISON OF THE SEVERAL WAYS OF USING THE AGE DISTRIBUTION

To summarize and extend the methods described above, still supposing stability, we extract from an observed age distribution the quantity $_mP_x/_nP_y$, that is, the ratio of the observed persons x to $x + m$ years of age to those y to $y + n$. This ratio may be equated to the corresponding quantity estimated from a life table and the rate of increase, which is approximately

$$\frac{e^{-(x+m/2)r} \big/ e^{-(y+n/2)r}}{_nL_y \big/ _mL_x},$$

and the equation provides the value for r:

$$r = \frac{1}{y + (n/2) - x - (m/2)} \ln\left[\frac{_mP_x/_mL_x}{_nP_y/_nL_y}\right]. \tag{4.6.1}$$

Where m and n are more than 5 years this approximation will not serve and an iterative form is needed. Such a form was used to calculate the entries in Table 4.5 (Keyfitz and Flieger, 1971).

Table 4.5 Rate of natural increase as estimated from pairs of age ranges, Colombia, males, 1965*

x to $(x+m-1)$	All ages	y to $(y+n-1)$				
		5–ω	10–ω	0–69	5–69	10–69
0–14	0.03547	0.03486	0.03567	0.03569	0.03502	0.03589
0–24	0.03286	0.03294	0.03434	0.03290	0.03298	0.03452
0–34	0.03256	0.03278	0.03450	0.03256	0.03281	0.03473
0–44	0.03236	0.03274	0.03482	0.03230	0.03278	0.03512
5–19	0.03513	0.03439	0.03558	0.03548	0.03457	0.03587
5–29	0.03159	0.03231	0.03446	0.03135	0.03229	0.03472
5–39	0.03088	0.03245	0.03518	0.02939	0.03244	0.03563
5–49	0.03289	0.03318	0.03641	0.03270	0.03348	0.03723

*Programmed by Geoffrey McNicoll.

A special case is pairs of age intervals that approximately represent ratios of female children to mothers, where now the y group is 30 years wide. In Table 4.6, $_5P_0/_{30}P_{15}$ gives $r=0.03066$. Again the estimates are mostly in the range 3.0 to 3.5 percent, and all are greater than the 0.02814 provided by registrations. The method has been named after William R. Thompson, one of the pioneers of American demography.

Using age intervals x to $x+4$ and $x+15$ to $x+44$, so that the individuals in the first group are mostly the children of those in the second group, protects in some degree against errors due to variation in the rate of increase of the successive birth cohorts; that is, it protects against the inappropriateness of the stability assumption. To see this we note that Thompson's index,

$$\mathrm{Th} = \frac{_5P_x/_5L_x}{_{30}P_{x+15}/_{30}L_{x+15}}, \qquad (4.6.2)$$

which is in this special case the contents of the square brackets in (4.6.1), is an approximation to $e^{27.5r}$. In fact $r=(1/27.5)\ln \mathrm{Th}$ is one way of writing (4.6.1) for $m=5$, $n=30$. In terms of the 5-year age groups of the mother generation, (4.6.2) breaks down to

$$\mathrm{Th} = \frac{\dfrac{(_5P_{x+15}F_{x+15}+_5P_{x+20}F_{x+20}+\cdots)}{(_5P_{x+15}+_5P_{x+20}+\cdots)}}{\dfrac{_5L_x}{_{30}L_{x+15}}}, \qquad (4.6.3)$$

Table 4.6   Estimates of rates of increase for Colombia, 1965, females*

x	$_5P_x$	$_5L_x$
0	1,567,251	454,231
5	1,421,920	439,360
10	1,152,736	435,979
15	956,462	433,516
20	767,534	429,919
25	633,851	425,043
30	545,307	419,014
35	495,077	411,199
40	369,047	401,498
45	309,618	389,415
50	263,402	374,099
55	169,199	351,971
60	181,209	323,465
65	100,134	281,903
70	83,009	230,533
75	45,586	173,813
80	34,442	116,072
85+	28,852	106,954
Total	9,124,636	

1. Local stability (4.5.2) with 5-year age intervals

Age range		r
5–9,	15–19	0.03831
10–14,	20–24	0.03927
15–19,	25–29	0.03917
20–24,	30–34	0.03161

2. Bourgeois–Pichat regression (4.5.4) based on 30-year age intervals

Age range	b	r
0–29	0.04388	0.03520
5–34	0.04616	0.03706
10–39	0.04210	0.03255
15–44	0.04153	0.03255
20–49	0.04024	0.03185
25–54	0.03973	0.03143
30–59	0.05287	0.03848
35–64	0.04377	0.03367
40–69	0.04636	0.03535

Table 4.6 (Continued)

3. Rate of increase from Thompson's Index (4.6.2) by iterative method

Age range		r
0–4,	15–44	0.03066
5–9,	20–49	0.03451
10–14,	25–54	0.03271
15–19,	30–59	0.03147

4. Rate of increase from pairs of wide age ranges using iterated version of (4.6.1)

Age range	All ages	5+	10+	0–69	5–69	10–69
0–14	0.03415	0.03345	0.03395	0.03430	0.03351	0.03407
0–24	0.03330	0.03269	0.03346	0.03340	0.03269	0.03356
0–34	0.03378	0.03281	0.03370	0.03403	0.03284	0.03385
0–44	0.03356	0.03243	0.03362	0.03392	0.03240	0.03378
5–19	0.03615	0.03441	0.03484	0.03675	0.03462	0.03508
5–29	0.03557	0.03347	0.03431	0.03662	0.03361	0.03455
5–39	†	0.03390	0.03480	†	0.03424	0.03521
5–49	†	0.03423	0.03524	†	0.03508	0.03587
10–24	0.03190	0.03157	0.03312	0.03163	0.03136	0.03323
10–34	†	0.03164	0.03382	0.03084	0.03125	0.03414
10–44	0.03385	0.02770	0.03353	0.03349	0.02204	0.03398
10–54	0.03438	0.04228	0.03237	0.03406	0.03873	0.03243
15–29	0.04068	0.02606	0.03105	0.03883	0.02327	0.03073
15–39	0.03504	†	0.03161	0.03461	0.03994	0.03116
15–49	0.03413	0.03719	0.02928	0.03393	0.03618	0.03561
15–59	0.03411	0.03613	0.03622	0.03395	0.03555	0.03454

*Programmed by Geoffrey McNicoll.
†Indeterminate.
Source: Keyfitz and Flieger (1971) p. 366.

where F_{x+15} and so on are the age-specific rates of childbearing, in 5-year intervals, counting for this purpose only children that live to the end of the 5-year period. In effect the P's of (4.6.3) are weights on the F's. Under stability $_5P_{x+20}$ will be $e^{-5r}(_5L_{x+20}/_5L_{x+15})$ times as numerous as $_5P_{x+15}$; if it is not, the numerator and denominator of the top section of (4.6.3) are affected in the same direction.

In Table 4.6 the various methods described above are shown in application to Colombian females. No single number is trustworthy, but the collection shows a considerable degree of agreement, especially where wide intervals are involved. The agreement with results for males as given in Table 4.5 is also worth noting. [Show that (4.6.1) with the data in Table 4.6 gives 0.03042 for the first entry under Thompson, and devise an iterative form that will give the more accurate 0.03066.]

Fortunately these formulas are most applicable to populations of rapid and fairly steady increase, which happen to be just the ones least provided with usable vital statistics, though they usually have recent censuses. Further work remains to be done on robustness, however, in the face of inaccurate data and inappropriate assumptions.

Incomplete Population and Deaths

William Brass has suggested (personal communication) that one can make use of an incomplete census, along with incomplete death statistics, to ascertain r, the rate of increase of a population, provided only that the omissions at the several ages are nearly constant and the population is more or less stable. Although such assumptions may seem strong, the calculation itself checks them. Several values of r may be produced by the calculation; and if they are not in agreement, we know that the assumptions are not met and reject the method for the case in question.

The Brass suggestion requires an expression for $c(x)$, the fraction of persons at age x, in terms of the population and deaths cumulated from age x to the end of life, $_\infty P_x$ and $_\infty D_x$, respectively. An integration by parts in the expression for deaths over age x as a fraction of total population will establish the required relation. The deaths from age x to the end of life as a fraction of total population are as follows:

$$\frac{_\infty D_x}{P} = \int_x^\omega be^{-ra}l(a)\,\mu(a)\,da$$

$$= -b\int_x^\omega e^{-ra}\,dl(a)$$

$$= -b\left[e^{-ra}l(a)\big|_x^\omega + r\int_x^\omega e^{-ra}l(a)\,da\right]$$

$$= be^{-rx}l(x) - \frac{r\,_\infty P_x}{P}$$

$$= c(x) - \frac{r\,_\infty P_x}{P}.$$

Transposing gives the required relation of $c(x)$ to the cumulative population and deaths:

$$c(x) = \frac{r\,_\infty P_x}{P} + \frac{_\infty D_x}{P}. \tag{4.6.4}$$

This is interpretable as a flow equation, in which the entrants $c(x)$ into the age group x and over are equal to the net natural increase $r_\infty P_x/P$ of that age group plus the deaths $_\infty D_x/P$, all in terms of ratios to the total population.

Equation 4.6.4 may be used to calculate r, given the age distribution and the deaths, but it involves a gratuitous error insofar as the deaths suffer from more (or less) incompleteness than the population. Brass avoids this by multiplying and dividing the term on the right, $_\infty D_x/P$, by $d = D/P$, the death rate, and then treating d as unknown:

$$c(x) = \frac{r_\infty P_x}{P} + \frac{d_\infty D_x}{D}. \qquad (4.6.5)$$

Now the fact that the population and deaths are incomplete by some unknown fraction at all ages makes no difference. Any two ages, say x and y, provide a pair of equations solvable for r and d. With more than two ages one can fit by least squares, and use the magnitude of departures from the fitted r and d to check the assumptions of stability and of constant proportional completeness in population and deaths.

The logic of populations permits modification of this without further algebra—for instance, if the population and deaths under age 5 are thought to be especially uncertain; in that case one would reinterpret all the elements of (4.6.5) on the basis of the population and deaths at 5 years of age and over: $c(x)$ would be the ratio of those aged x to the population 5 and over, D would be the deaths for ages 5 and over, and P would be the population aged 5 and over. To find the rate of increase of a long past time one might consider only the part of the population 60 and over, interpret $c(x)$ as the ratio of those aged x to the number aged 60 and over, and D and P as deaths and population, respectively, over 60, and put x equal to 60 and to 70 to obtain two equations.

Taking Mexico, 1966, females as an example, we have as the equation for $x = 0$, using all ages,

$$\frac{900}{22,029} = r + d,$$

and, for $x = 60$

$$\frac{81.8}{22,029} = r\frac{1161}{22,029} + d\frac{58,923}{198,893}.$$

Solving these together gives $r = 0.0345$, $d = 0.0064$, and $b = d + r = 0.0409$.

Now suppose that we disregard the first 60 years of life, and use $x = 60$; then

$$\frac{81.8}{1161} = r + d,$$

and, for $x = 70$, still considering population 60 and over,

$$\frac{43.4}{1161} = r\frac{448}{1161} + d\frac{41,148}{58,923},$$

which solve to $r = 0.0378$ and $d = 0.0326$. In this formulation the death rate d does not have the usual meaning, since its denominator is population 60 and over, but r is an estimate of the usual rate of increase.

Estimates from Two Censuses

When two censuses, say 10 years apart, are available, much more can be done; not only can assumptions be weakened, but also increased redundancy permits a better estimate of error.

If the population is closed, and whether or not it is stable, survivorship rates can be found by comparing the number in a cohort as given by the two censuses. For instance, the chance of surviving 10 years for those aged 10 to 14 is the ratio of the number 20 to 24 at the later census to that 10 to 14 at the earlier one; if $_5P_{10}^{(t)}$ is the population aged 10 to 14 at time t, then

$$\frac{_5L_{20}}{_5L_{10}} = \frac{_5P_{20}^{(t+10)}}{_5P_{10}^{(t)}}.$$

Having a set of survivorships for pairs of ages 10 years apart, one could interpolate to construct the life table. Unfortunately the countries less developed statistically, for which reliable mortality registrations are lacking, are not likely to have accurate censuses, and inaccuracies in the census reporting of ages produce a very irregular table. Therefore we must seek a way to use the survivorships that is less sensitive to their irregularities.

One such way is to match the survivorships to model life tables. Each of the 10-year survivorships would permit picking a member of the series of life tables. With perfect data and a series of model tables appropriate to the underlying mortality of a closed population, the identical life table would be picked by the several ages. In practice, however, different life tables will be picked, and if they do not differ too greatly they can be averaged.

Once the life table is available, chosen by the observations rather than imported more or less arbitrarily as with a single census, one can use either census for estimating r by the methods outlined above. Again the degree of agreement among the several estimates of r will inform us as to how far to trust the results.

A further and obvious resource for calculating r is the intercensus increase. In some cases the accuracy of enumeration is inadequate to provide survivorships between the censuses for the several cohorts, but is sufficient to show how fast the total population is increasing; r would be obtained from the ratio of census totals as $r = \frac{1}{10}\ln[P^{(t+10)}/P^{(t)}]$. The value of r so obtained, taken in conjunction with either age distribution, can provide a life table. Arriaga (1968) used an observed age distribution along with a value of r in his study of mortality in Latin America; from (4.1.1) he obtained $l(x)$ as $e^{rx}c(x)/c(0)$.

4.7 SENSITIVITY ANALYSIS

The stable model was used in Sections 4.3 to 4.6 to estimate rates of increase of populations lacking in vital statistics. It can also provide answers to substantive questions concerned, not with data, but with the way populations—or at least their parameters—behave.

Mean Age as a Function of Rate of Increase

We have prepared the way for one example with (4.3.2), showing how the mean age of a population is related to its rate of increase:

$$\bar{x} \doteq \frac{L_1}{L_0} - \sigma^2 r.$$

Insofar as this applies, it tells what a change in r will do to the population mean age $\bar{x}$. If in our population r were higher by Δr, then $\bar{x}$ would be lower by $\sigma^2 \Delta r$, on the understanding that the life table remained unchanged. Essentially the same fact can be expressed by the derivative:

$$\frac{d\bar{x}}{dr} \doteq -\sigma^2, \tag{4.7.1}$$

and derivatives are useful in cases where the device by which (4.3.2) was established is not applicable.

For Canada, 1968, σ^2, the variance of women's ages in the life table population, was 573.7. Hence we can say from (4.7.1) that a fall of 0.010 in r would raise the mean age by 5.737 years, the life table remaining unchanged. This touches genuine causation, though it does not say what would happen in the real world, where many other changes would occur at the same time. Like any other causal law, it is capable only of telling what will happen conditionally, provided that its action is not overlaid, or reversed altogether, by other changes such as migration.

One added qualification is that the effect does not immediately follow the cause in time. In this section and others presenting sensitivity analysis it is two ultimate stable conditions that are compared, a device known in economics as *comparative statics*.

Pension Cost

Consider a pension scheme in which those over exact age 65 are paid a pension equal to salary, and salary is unity and the same for all individuals and at all ages between 20 and 65. If P is the number of persons of all ages in the population, the total payments by the fund each year will be $P \int_{65}^{\infty} be^{-rx} l(x) dx$, and the total receipts of the fund each year will be $Pg \int_{20}^{65} be^{-rx} l(x) dx$, where g is the premium as a fraction of salary. For the fund to remain in balance these two quantities must be equal, so we have for the premium

$$g = \frac{\int_{65}^{\omega} e^{-rx} l(x) dx}{\int_{20}^{65} e^{-rx} l(x) dx}, \tag{4.7.2}$$

still as a fraction of the uniform annual salary of individuals aged 20 to 65. Adapting this to salaries and pensions that vary with age, to salaries that vary at each given age, to cases where increasing numbers of persons are unable to work as they become older, and to other practical circumstances complicates the formula somewhat but entails no new principle.

A formula enables us to see how demographic conditions affect pension arrangements. For the scheme whose premium is given by (4.7.2) we might ask what difference it makes if mortality improves beyond age 65, if the age at pension is 60 rather than 65, and if the population increases more slowly or becomes stationary. The stable model permits pencil-and-paper experiments to answer such questions; let us consider the last one briefly.

To see what difference it makes if r changes we calculate dg/dr from (4.7.2). Taking logarithms and using the fact that

$$\frac{d \ln g}{dr} = \frac{1}{g} \frac{dg}{dr}$$

gives immediately, with fixed life table,

$$\frac{d \ln g}{dr} = - \frac{\int_{65}^{\omega} xe^{-rx} l(x) dx}{\int_{65}^{\omega} e^{-rx} l(x) dx} + \frac{\int_{20}^{65} xe^{-rx} l(x) dx}{\int_{20}^{65} e^{-rx} l(x) dx}.$$

The first term on the right is minus the mean age of the pensioners, say M, and the second is the mean age of the contributors, say m. Hence

$$\frac{1}{g} \frac{dg}{dr} = -(M - m). \tag{4.7.3}$$

According to (4.7.3) a small finite change Δr in r ultimately causes a relative change $\Delta g/g$ in the premium, i.e.,

$$\frac{\Delta g}{g} \doteq -(M-m)\Delta r. \tag{4.7.4}$$

In words, the fractional change in the premium equals minus the difference of mean ages in the pensioned and working groups times the absolute change in rate of increase. If the mean M is about 70 years and m about 40 years, $M-m$ is about 30, and we conclude that a decrease in r by 1 percentage point, say from 0.020 to 0.010, increases the fraction of salary to be paid as premium by $-(30)(-0.01)=0.30$. Practically without data we have found that a 30 percent increase in premiums for a contributory nonreserve pension scheme is associated with a fall in the population growth rate of 0.01. We could sharpen the 30 percent by using observed numbers for $M-m$, but 30 years is close enough to suggest how much such financial calculations depend on the rate of increase of populations. As Thomas Espenshade pointed out to me, the lower birth rate as r becomes smaller releases women into the labor force and so, if jobs are available, helps to pay the premium for the increased fraction of aged persons. With some additional data the effect of this factor and others may be calculated.

Fraction of Old People

The objective of the preceding pages can be attained more precisely by employing derivatives and then treating the Taylor expansion as a differential equation. Suppose we would like to know how the fraction of the population that is old depends on the rate of increase, and assume that death rates do not change. The fraction $f(r)$ over age 65 is

$$f(r) = \frac{\int_{65}^{\omega} e^{-ra}l(a)\,da}{\int_{0}^{\omega} e^{-ra}l(a)\,da}. \tag{4.7.5}$$

Taking logarithms and differentiating both sides gives

$$\frac{1}{f(r)}\frac{df(r)}{dr} = \kappa_1 - k_1, \tag{4.7.6}$$

where κ_1 is the mean age of the entire population and k_1 of the part of it 65 years of age and over. Integrating (4.7.6) and taking exponentials gives

$$f(r) = f_0 e^{(\kappa_1 - k_1)r},$$

where f_0 is the life table proportion 65 and over.

The result is obtainable from the term in r of the difference of two cumulant generating functions, one for the distribution of those 65 and over, the other for all ages:

$$\ln f(r) = \ln f_0 + \left(-rk_1 + \frac{r^2}{2!}k_2 - \frac{r^3}{3!}k_3 + \cdots \right)$$

$$- \left(-r\kappa_1 + \frac{r^2}{2!}\kappa_2 - \frac{r^3}{3!}\kappa_3 + \cdots \right),$$

where the k's are the cumulants of the persons 65 and over and the κ's of everyone. Taking exponentials up to the term in r^2 gives

$$f(r) = f_0 \exp\left[r(\kappa_1 - k_1) - \frac{r^2}{2!}(\kappa_2 - k_2) \right]. \tag{4.7.7}$$

Experimenting with Table 4.1, and using round numbers for the means $k_1 = 72$, $\kappa_1 = 35$, so that $\kappa_1 - k_1 = -37$, and for the variances $k_2 = 30$, $\kappa_2 = 450$, so that $\kappa_2 - k_2 = 420$, we have the fraction 65 and over as $0.138e^{-37r}$ to a first approximation, and as

$$f(r) = 0.138e^{-37r - 210r^2}$$

to a second approximation. Table 4.7 shows that the second approximation at least is very close. Such discrepancies as exist between the last column and the preceding column are due to the crude estimates of the first and second cumulants and to the omission of later cumulants.

It bears repeating that (4.7.7) gives only the ultimate difference between the original situation and the one with incremented r; it says nothing about the path by which the second is reached from the first. When the birth rate

Table 4.7   First and second approximations to the percent over 65 years of age from (4.7.7), along with the total as taken from Table 4.1

r	Approximation from (4.7.7)		As totaled from Table 4.1
	To term in r	To term in r^2	
-0.01	19.9	19.6	19.46
0	13.8	13.8	13.80
0.01	9.5	9.3	9.31
0.02	6.5	6.1	6.02
0.03	4.5	3.8	3.74
0.04	3.1	2.2	2.25

declines with unchanged $l(x)$, it requires more than one generation under the new conditions for the age distribution to stabilize. The projection techniques of Chapter 8 are capable of showing the actual path of change in a quantity such as our premium g when birth rates change in any specified manner. The results are inevitably more complicated than those of stable theory.

4.8 THE DEGREE TO WHICH PROMOTION WITHIN ORGANIZATIONS DEPENDS ON POPULATION INCREASE

In a stationary population the progress of individuals through whatever hierarchy they belong to, that is, their social and economic mobility, will on the average be slower than in an increasing population. To show the effect in its pure form we will disregard the differences in merit, luck, inheritance, and influence among individuals whereby some move up faster and others more slowly; our interest is in *average* rates of promotion. In other words, we seek the rate of promotion insofar as it is affected by one rate of population increase as opposed to another (Waugh, 1971; Bartholomew, 1967).

The concept of promotion stands out most clearly in a hierarchical organization that observes some degree of seniority in promotion, and that permits a certain fraction of its employees to be foremen and above, or colonels and above, or associate professors and above. Most organizations do not have exact ratios for the number of those above to those below these ranks, but the nature of their work and budgets is such that de facto limits exist on the numbers at higher ranks. We will take as fixed and given the ratio k of those above the given rank to those below, and we want to find the age x at which a person on the average reaches the status expressed by k; we seek x as a function of r, the rate of increase. Suppose as in (4.1.1) that the population is stable, so that the fraction of individuals between ages a and $a+da$ is $be^{-ra}l(a)da$. Then the fraction of the population above the rank in question is the integral of this from x to β, and the fraction of the population below is the integral from α to x, where α is the age of recruitment and β the age of compulsory retirement.

The condition is described by an equation in which k is identified with a ratio of integrals:

$$k = \frac{\int_x^\beta e^{-ra}l(a)\,da}{\int_\alpha^x e^{-ra}l(a)\,da}.$$

(4.8.1)

Once the life table, along with k, α, and β, is known, (4.8.1) implicitly gives the age of promotion x as a function of r.

Equation 4.8.1 cannot be solved in closed form for x, but the theory of implicit functions enables us to approximate the derivative of x with respect to r. If the ratio of integrals in (4.8.1) is called u/v, then (4.8.1) is the same as $\phi = u - kv = 0$. With a few steps of elementary calculus (details are given in Keyfitz, 1973) we find

$$\frac{dx}{dr} = -\frac{\partial\phi/\partial r}{\partial\phi/\partial x} = -\frac{1}{1+k}\left[\frac{\int_x^\beta e^{-ra}l(a)\,da}{e^{-rx}l(x)}\right](M-m), \qquad (4.8.2)$$

where M is the mean age of the group between x and β, and m of the group between α and x. Evidently dx/dr is negative; as r increases, the age of promotion declines.

To obtain an idea of how much it declines, suppose the age of recruitment α to be 20 and the age of retirement β to be 65. Then $M - m$ cannot be very different from half of the interval from 20 to 65, that is, 22.5. Consider a rank somewhat above the middle, where the person holding it has one employee above him for each two below, that is, $k = \frac{1}{2}$. With a small positive rate of increase r the expression in the square brackets of (4.8.2) will be about 15. Then

$$\frac{dx}{dr} \doteq -\frac{1}{1+\frac{1}{2}}(15)(22.5) = -225.$$

This means that, when r falls from 0.02 to stationarity, the age of promotion to a rank two-thirds of the way up the hierarchy rises by $-225 \times (-0.02) = 4.5$ years.

For a more exact result we can solve (4.8.1) numerically for x with $r = 0.02$ and $r = 0.00$. This requires interpolation in the 5-year intervals for which such data are given, including solution of a cubic equation (Keyfitz, 1973). Some of the results are shown as Table 4.8 for $l(x)$ from the United States, 1968, male life table. With $k = 0.6$ we find $x = 46.31$ for $r = 0.00$ and $x = 41.64$ for $r = 0.02$, a difference of 4.67 years, or very nearly what the derivative showed in the preceding paragraph. With $k = 1$ the difference from $r = 0.04$ to $r = 0.00$ is $40.86 - 32.71 = 8.15$ years.

The same calculation has been made on the male life table of Sweden, 1783–87, with $\overset{o}{e}_0 = 33.6$ years, representing about the highest observed mortality for which a life table is available. Such high mortality ought at least to have the advantage of speeding the promotion of the survivors, and indeed, at a given r, they show promotion to middle positions about 2 to 3 years younger than the ages in the United States, 1968, table. Thus the

Table 4.8 Age x of passing through position k for $k = 1$ up to $k = 0.2$, for $r = 0.00$ to $r = 0.04$, based on male life table for the United States, 1968

Value of	Value of r				
k	0.00	0.01	0.02	0.03	0.04
1.0	40.86	38.55	36.39	34.43	32.71
0.8	43.26	40.91	38.64	36.54	34.66
0.6	46.31	43.97	41.64	39.41	37.35
0.4	50.32	48.14	45.86	43.56	41.33
0.2	55.93	54.27	52.36	50.27	48.08

possible effect of high mortality in favoring promotion is 2 to 3 years; the possible effect of rapid population growth is 8 years. The reason for this is that the range of recorded human population growth is from $-\frac{1}{2}$ percent through stationary to 4 percent per year. The range of human mortality averaged over ages 20 to 65 is much narrower, say $\frac{1}{2}$ to 2 percent (Table 4.9) or one-third as much.

Table 4.9 Average mortality μ for males between ages 20 and 65, where $e^{-45\mu} = l_{65}/l_{20}$, compared with intrinsic rate on female-dominant model

Country	1000μ (males)	$1000r$ (females)
Austria, 1966–68	8.1	7.8
Canada, 1966–68	7.3	7.4
Ceylon, 1967	6.9	24.6
France, 1967	8.2	8.3
Malaysia (West), 1966	9.5	30.9
Mauritius, 1966	11.3	30.5
Mexico, 1966	10.1	34.6
Norway, 1967	5.7	10.4
Spain, 1967	6.5	10.1
Sweden, 1783–87	20.2	1.4
United States, 1968	9.2	5.9
Venezuela, 1965	8.8	37.6

A Simplification. The theory can be made simpler with only a small sacrifice of realism by supposing constant mortality between ages α and β (McFarland, personal communication). Mortality rises over the age interval, but we are encouraged to suppose constancy by the small effect that mortality seems to have in any case. If the death rate is fixed at μ, the probability of surviving to age a is $l(a) = e^{-\mu a}$, and the equation becomes

$$k = \frac{\displaystyle\int_x^\beta e^{-ra} e^{-\mu a}\,da}{\displaystyle\int_\alpha^x e^{-ra} e^{-\mu a}\,da}.$$

Now the right-hand side of this expression lends itself to integrations in closed form, and we have

$$k = \frac{e^{-(r+\mu)x} - e^{-(r+\mu)\beta}}{e^{-(r+\mu)\alpha} - e^{-(r+\mu)x}},$$

which may be solved for x to give

$$x = -\frac{1}{r+\mu} \ln\left[\frac{ke^{-(r+\mu)\alpha} + e^{-(r+\mu)\beta}}{k+1} \right], \tag{4.8.3}$$

an expression that is exactly the same function of μ as it is of r. Hence dx/dr is equal to $dx/d\mu$; population increase and high mortality help promotion to exactly the same degree.

The Chain Letter Principle

The analogy of the promotion process to a chain letter is easily drawn. In a chain letter (say of four names in each transmittal) the recipient (Ego) sends the person at the top of the list he has received a sum, say 1 dollar, crosses this name off the list, adds his own name at the bottom, reproduces the letter, and sends it on to four other persons. If four copies are sent on at each stage, in the short time required for five successive letters to be mailed and delivered Ego will receive $4^4 = 256$ dollars. With 10 names he will receive 10^{10} dollars. Each individual may be thought of as an ancestor of those whose names are below his on the list, and the payments are made by descendants to ancestors.

There is no fallacy in the operation of a chain letter, provided that recipients follow instructions and new people continue to be available to be brought into the scheme. Once the available population has been brought in, so that names have to be repeated, however, the scheme breaks down. And this is certain to happen long before 10^{10} names are in the process.

Payments by descendants to ancestors, say sons to great-grandfathers, in analogy to the chain letter with four names, have a very different way of cumulating than payments by ancestors to descendants, as in the ordinary passing of property from father to son. With a growing population, equal inheritance will fractionate property and give successively less to each generation. Large families and growth of population are a drawback in a regime of inherited private property, just as clearly as they are an advantage in the chain letter or promotion. Norman Ryder has emphasized this point in his lectures.

Whether the institutions of a community are such that benefits flow upward, as in promotion or the chain letter, or flow downward, as in inheritance, is crucial to attitudes on collective growth and to the size of individual families. It is arguable that the peasants' preoccupation with holding property intact in nineteenth century France was associated with low fertility; a peasant obtained security in his old age by having *few* children and thereby avoiding division of his land. In Java, on the other hand, wage labor is a main means of livelihood, and the landless laborer wants *many* children, whose combined contributions will permit him to subsist in old age. This supposes appropriate discipline in the children, just as does the chain letter.

The American pay-as-you-go social security system resembles that of Java in that the working generation supports the retired one, with the difference that in the United States the unit is no longer the family but the entire country. The U. S. system works well when there are many children to support few old people, as was the case a generation back; it runs into trouble when many old people have to be supported by few children, as will be the case early in the twenty-first century. Table 9.4 suggests the consequences for pay-as-you-go social security of the present decline in U. S. births.

It would be useful to inventory the situations in which something—money, supervisory positions, prestige—flows up from the younger generation to the older, and examine empirically corresponding attitudes on reproduction; the hypothesis of this section is that they would be found to be pronatalist. On the other hand, in situations where the flow is from the older to the younger, of which inheritance of property is the most familiar, restrictive attitudes toward reproduction would be expected.

Growth is popular in comparison to mortality: having children is preferable to dying. Moreover a given amount of growth helps as much as a given amount of mortality; and since growth varies 3 times as much as mortality among observed populations, it can accelerate promotion about 3 times as much as even the survivors can expect in a high-death community. Cessation of growth has costs and is inevitable, and the question is what generation ought to incur the cost.

Chapter Five

BIRTH AND THE INTRINSIC RATE
OF NATURAL INCREASE

The stable age distribution of Chapter 4 supposed births growing at fixed rate r and subject to probability $l(a)$ of survivorship to age a. Various conclusions were reached by noting how the stable age distribution was affected by r, treated as an arbitrarily disposable parameter. Now we regard rate r not as arbitrary but as determined by the joint action of birth and death rates.

The argument rests on birth rates $m(a)$, where $m(a)da$ is the probability that a woman who has reached age a will give birth to a girl child before age $a + da$, or alternatively that each woman will produce exactly $m(a)da$ of a child in interval da. A model in which exactly $m(a)da$ of a child is produced by each woman in any small interval of time da departs considerably from the reality of human reproduction, where children are born, not continuously, but in units of one child each, with occasional multiple births, and random variation is conspicuous. Moreover, we will deal with the female part only of the population, and disregard the contribution of males to reproduction. (Or, less often, with the male part, but not with both together.) Such fictional treatment permits some useful conclusions to be drawn and ought to be exploited to the limit before resorting to more realistic (and necessarily more complex) models. Although unusable for families and other small populations, the continuous deterministic model provides useful answers to many questions concerning mean values in large populations.

5.1   THE CHARACTERISTIC EQUATION

To find an equation for the ultimate rate of increase r by a continuation of the means developed in Chapter 4, suppose that for a long time the chance of living to age a is $l(a)$, and that births increase at fixed rate r. Then the age distribution becomes stable, a proposition proved many times (Sharpe and Lotka, 1911; Lotka, 1939; Parlett, 1970; Lopez, 1961; McFarland, 1969) and illustrated in Section 1.9. When stability has been attained, the fraction of population at ages a to $a + da$ is $be^{-ra}l(a)\,da$, as shown in the argument leading to (4.1.1). Since births are calculated by multiplying exposed population by $m(a)$, the fraction $be^{-ra}l(a)\,da$ of the population must give rise to $be^{-ra}l(a)m(a)\,da$ births per unit of total population. The integral of this last expression, from the youngest fertile age α to the highest β, is $\int_\alpha^\beta be^{-ra}l(a)m(a)\,da$, the overall birth rate.

But b is the overall birth rate in the population with age distribution $be^{-ra}l(a)\,da$, and it may therefore be equated to the integral derived in the preceding paragraph. This provides the equation

$$\int_\alpha^\beta be^{-ra}l(a)m(a)\,da = b, \qquad (5.1.1)$$

or, on dividing by b,

$$\int_\alpha^\beta e^{-ra}l(a)m(a)\,da = 1, \qquad (5.1.2)$$

obtained in more general fashion by Lotka (1939, p. 65; see Section 5.7 of the present chapter) and called the characteristic equation for the unknown r. Equation 5.1.2 tells us the ultimate rate of increase implied by $l(a)$ and $m(a)$ after they have been acting long enough for stability to be attained.

For a general net maternity function $l(a)m(a)$ (5.1.2) has an infinite number of roots, of which only the real root answers the questions treated in this chapter. The uniqueness of the real root follows from the fact that $\int_\alpha^\beta e^{-ra}l(a)m(a)\,da$, say $\psi(r)$, has a negative first derivative [prove this] and so is a monotonically decreasing function of r, which takes the value ∞ for $r = -\infty$ and the value 0 for $r = \infty$ (Fig. 5.1). Thus $\psi(r)$ can only once cross any given horizontal line in the half-plane $\psi(r) > 0$, including the line one unit above the r axis, and hence $\psi(r) = 1$ can have only one real root. The function $\psi(r)$ crosses the vertical axis at

$$\psi(0) = \int_\alpha^\beta l(a)m(a)\,da = R_0,$$

the net reproduction rate.

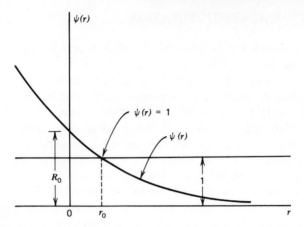

Fig. 5.1   Values of $\psi(r)$, showing $\psi(0) = R_0$, and root r_0 of $\psi(r) = 1$.

Why Stress the Female Model?

Although the argument leading to (5.1.2) is applicable to either sex, it is most often applied to females because:

1. Data on age of parent at the birth of a child are more often collected by the registration authorities for women than for men.

2. Even when the authorities present births by age of father as well as by age of mother, more cases of unstated age of father occur, especially for illegitimate births.

3. Women have their children within a narrower and more sharply defined range of ages than do men, say 15 to 50 as against 15 to 80.

4. Both the spacing and number of children are less subject to variation among women; a woman can have children only at intervals of 1 or 2 years, so she is physiologically limited to a score or so of children, whereas a man can have hundreds. Under monogamy this asymmetry of the sexes is of no consequence, but every society allows some departures from strict monogamy, even if only to permit the remarrriage of widowers.

These reasons for the emphasis on females apply over a wide range of population analysis. Both understanding and prediction must be based on whatever constancies we can find; that potential variation is less in births to women than in births to men makes the female model more useful.

On the other hand, when the age distributions and life tables for males as well as for females are available, the rate of increase can be estimated from either sex, and two estimates provide more information than one.

When only one is to be had, we must rest on the fact that usually in the short run, and always in the long run, the males and females of any population increase at nearly the same rate.

An Iterative Method for Calculating r

Means of calulating this root are given in several places (Lotka, 1939, p. 70; Coale, 1957; Keyfitz, 1968, p. 108) and need not be repeated here. But an iterative method is worth sketching because it is suggestive for other equations.

If T is an arbitrary age chosen near the mean age of childbearing, multiply both sides of (5.1.2) by e^{Tr}:

$$\int_\alpha^\beta e^{-(a-T)r}l(a)m(a)\,da = e^{Tr}, \tag{5.1.3}$$

then take logarithms of both sides, and divide by T to obtain

$$r^* = \frac{1}{T}\ln\int_\alpha^\beta e^{-(a-T)r}l(a)m(a)\,da. \tag{5.1.4}$$

The left-hand side of (5.1.4) has been marked with an asterisk to suggest the use of the equation for iteration. The unknown r enters on the right, but in a way that does not greatly influence the integral. The extent to which r influences the right-hand side of (5.1.4) determines the speed of convergence, and is measured by the absolute value of the derivative dr^*/dr, a fact demonstrated formally in books on numerical analysis, such as that of Scarborough (1958, p. 209). If $|dr^*/dr|$ is less than 1 in the neighborhood of the solution, convergence will occur; if it is much less than 1, convergence will be rapid. From (5.1.4) dr^*/dr is seen to have a factor $1-\kappa/T$, where κ is the mean age of childbearing in the stable population:

$$\kappa = \int_\alpha^\beta ae^{-ra}l(a)m(a)\,da.$$

(Since r satisfies (5.1.2), the denominator of the expression for mean age κ is unity.) The derivative dr^*/dr seems to be telling us that if we can put the arbitrary T equal to some number near κ, rapid convergence will result. In fact we do not know κ before we find r, but κ varies little among populations and T can be put at 27.5 years.

No direct use can be made of a continuous form like (5.1.4)—it must be converted to the discrete form for calculations. If T is chosen as 27.5, then with the customary approximation

$$\int_x^{x+5} e^{-ra}l(a)m(a)\,da = e^{-(x+2\frac{1}{2})r}{}_5L_xF_x,$$

where $_5L_x = \int_x^{x+5} l(a)\,da$, and F_x is the observed age-specific fertility rate for ages x to $x+4$ at last birthday, we translate (5.1.4) into calculable terms as

$$r^* = \frac{1}{27.5} \ln \left(e^{10r} {_5}L_{15}F_{15} + e^{5r} {_5}L_{20}F_{20} + {_5}L_{25}F_{25} \right.$$

$$\left. + e^{-5r} {_5}L_{30}F_{30} + e^{-10r} {_5}L_{35}F_{35} + e^{-15r} {_5}L_{40}F_{40} \right). \tag{5.1.5}$$

The expression in parenthesis contains six terms if we include births under 15 with the 15 to 19 group and those over 45 with the 40 to 44 group. Data for United States females in 1968 are shown in Table 5.1, where F_x', the birth rate of children of both sexes, is converted to F_x, the female birth rate, by multiplying by the fraction of births that were girls in 1968, that is, 0.487. The calculation of (5.1.5) starting with $r=0$ gives $r^* = \ln(2.395 \times 0.487)/27.5 = 0.00560$ and $r^{**} = 0.00587$ in two successive iterations.

Table 5.1 Second iteration of intrinsic rate of natural increase for the United States, females, 1968

x	$_5L_x$	$1000F_x'$	$_5L_x F_x'$	$e^{-\left(x+2\frac{1}{2}-27\frac{1}{2}\right)(0.0056)}$
15	4.867	67.1	0.327	1.058
20	4.851	167.4	0.812	1.028
25	4.831	140.3	0.678	1.000
30	4.807	74.9	0.360	0.972
35	4.770	35.6	0.170	0.946
40	4.714	10.2	0.048	0.919
Total			2.395	

Source: For $_5L_x$, *Vital Statistics of the United States*, 1968, Vol. 2, Section 5, pp. 5–7. : For F_x', *Statistical Abstract of the United States*, 1973, p. 52.

The method is applicable to complex as well as to real roots. With complex roots we must check to ensure that the root being approached is the one sought—the real root being unique no such precaution is needed. If all complex roots are sought, one can sweep out each as it is found, after the ith, by dividing out the polynomial in e^{-5r}; this will prevent the iteration from converging to any root more than once.

The Intrinsic Rate for Various Kinds of Data

The usual application of (5.1.2) is to the births and deaths of a particular period, 1 or 3 or 5 calendar years, as when the *Statistical Abstract of the United States*, 1973, tells us that the intrinsic rate of increase was 0.6

percent for the United States in 1968, with 0.4 percent for White and 1.6 percent for Nonwhite components (p. 56).

Male Period Intrinsic Rates. The above numbers apply to females; a corresponding calculation can be made by imputing male births to fathers, and in general it produces a different answer. Sometimes the answer is substantially different, as for the United States, 1964, data, where females show $1000r$ as 15.70, and males as 17.48. The higher male rate is largely due to fathers being older than mothers on the whole, while numbers of persons in the main childbearing ages during the 1960s reflected the rising births during the late 1930s and 1940s. If the men of an age to be fathers come from earlier smaller cohorts, their rates will be higher for the given number of births that actually took place, and it is largely this that is reported by the difference between the male and female intrinsic rates.

Table 5.2 shows some male and female rates; the differences are considerable and larger than can be explained by misstatement of age. For the United States in particular the steady increase in the gap between male and female rates seems due to the relative shortage of men of the age to be fathers in the wake of the baby boom.

Table 5.2   Male and female intrinsic rates during the 1960s

| | $1000r$ | |
Country and year	Male	Female
United States		
1966	12.82	9.70
1964	17.48	15.70
1963	18.68	17.10
1962	19.81	18.83
1959–61	20.92	20.70
Chile, 1964	23.55	21.05
Hungary, 1964	− 2.95	− 7.28
England and Wales, 1960–62	9.55	9.77

Source: Keyfitz and Flieger (1968).

Cohort Intrinsic Rate   The same equation (5.1.2) can help interpret the death and birth rates in a cohort. By following deaths and births to the individuals born in a given year or 5 years, we obtain a cohort life table and a set of age-specific birth rates that together determine r. Applied to the women who were 0 to 4 years of age in 1920 in the United States, and who therefore were 5 to 9 years of age in 1925, and so forth, they yield an intrinsic rate of 1.5 per thousand (Keyfitz and Flieger, 1968, p. 601). This means that the age-specific rates of birth and death were such that, if they persisted, the cohorts (and incidentally the period cross section) would ultimately increase at 1.5 per thousand. This value of $1000r$ is low because the group in question passed through its principal ages of childbearing in the late 1930s and early 1940s. Period and cohort influences are confounded in the concrete historical record.

Intrinsic Rate for One Family   The concept of intrinsic rate can be applied to a particular family. If a girl child is born at age a_1 of the mother and another girl at age a_2, r is found from

$$e^{-ra_1}l(a_1) + e^{-ra_2}l(a_2) = 1,\tag{5.1.6}$$

which is easily solved for r by the method of (5.1.4) or otherwise. The meaning of r is that a population in which all women married and bore girl children at ages a_1 and a_2 would increase at this rate; the r so calculated is an interpretation of the fertility behavior of the particular family. Non-marriage or sterility within marriage can be accomodated by using $l(a)$ as the probability of surviving and being married and fertile by age a.

Whatever the group to which the characteristic equation 5.1.2 applies, one of its uses is to find how the rate of increase r depends on various features of the net maternity function. We will see how this is done for an increment in the birth rate $m(a)$ at a single age x. More frequently referred to, however, are the relations between the intrinsic rate and the several moments of the net maternity function: These relations are easily found once we express the characteristic equation in terms of the moments.

5.2 A VARIANT FORM OF THE CHARACTERISTIC EQUATION

It happens that $\psi(r)$, the left-hand side of (5.1.2), when divided by R_0 is the moment-generating function of the normalized net maternity function $l(a)m(a)/R_0$:

$$\frac{\psi(r)}{R_0} = \int_\alpha^\beta e^{-ra}\frac{l(a)m(a)}{R_0}\,da.$$

The sense in which $\psi(r)/R_0$ generates the moments is that it is equivalent to the infinite series

$$\frac{\psi(r)}{R_0} = 1 - \frac{rR_1}{R_0} + \frac{r^2}{2!}\cdot\frac{R_2}{R_0} - \cdots,$$

where $R_i = \int_\alpha^\beta a^i l(a) m(a) da$, so that R_i / R_0 is the ith moment about zero of the distribution $l(a) m(a) / R_0$. But the moments about zero are large; and even though the series converges, an impractical number of terms would be required for a good approximation. A rapidly converging series is obtained by taking the logarithm of $\psi(r) / R_0$, and so generating the functions of the moments called *cumulants* (Kendall and Stuart, 1958, Vol. 1, p. 70) that we have already encountered in Section 4.3:

$$\ln \frac{\psi(r)}{R_0} = -r\mu + \frac{r^2 \sigma^2}{2!} - \frac{r^3 \kappa_3}{3!} + \frac{r^4 \kappa_4}{4!} - \dots \tag{5.2.1}$$

The cumulants expressed in terms of the R_i are as follows:

$$\mu = \frac{R_1}{R_0},$$

$$\sigma^2 = \frac{R_2}{R_0} - \left(\frac{R_1}{R_0} \right)^2,$$

$$\kappa_3 = \frac{R_3}{R_0} - 3 \frac{R_2 R_1}{R_0^2} + 2 \left(\frac{R_1}{R_0} \right)^3,$$

$$\dots \quad \dots \quad \dots \quad \dots,$$

and in terms of the moments about the mean,

$$\mu_i = \frac{\int_\alpha^\beta (a - \mu)^i l(a) m(a) da}{R_0},$$

they are

$$\kappa_1 = \mu = \mu_1,$$
$$\kappa_2 = \sigma^2 = \mu_2,$$
$$\kappa_3 = \mu_3,$$
$$\kappa_4 = \mu_4 - 3\mu_2^2,$$
$$\kappa_5 = \mu_5 - 10\mu_3 \mu_2,$$

$$\dots\dots\dots \quad .$$

Now the characteristic equation is $\psi(r) = 1$, that is, $\ln[\psi(r) / R_0] = -\ln R_0$; or, written out in terms of the cumulants, from (5.2.1) the equivalent to (5.1.2) is

$$\ln R_0 = r\mu - \frac{r^2 \sigma^2}{2!} + \frac{r^3 \kappa_3}{3!} - \frac{r^4 \kappa_4}{4!} + \dots \tag{5.2.2}$$

The successive terms diminish rapidly in value, even where the cumulants increase. For the United States, 1967 ($1000r = 7.13$), we have the following:

	Cumulant	Term of (5.2.2)
R_0	1.205	0.186
μ	26.28	0.187
σ^2	34.98	-0.000889
κ_3	127.5	0.0000077
κ_4	-120.7	0.000000013

The rate of convergence is slower for populations of higher r, and much slower for complex roots of (5.2.2).

5.3   PERTURBATION ANALYSIS OF THE INTRINSIC RATE

A main use of the foregoing theory is to compare populations that differ in some birth or death parameter, and note by how much they differ in intrinsic rate.

How the Intrinsic Rate Varies with the Moments

We are now in a position to find how the intrinsic rate varies with the several moments. To find, for example, how r in (5.2.2) varies with σ^2 we might first think of solving explicitily for r and noting how σ^2 appears in the solution. Since an explicit solution is impossible, we are fortunate that it is not necessary: the theory of implicit functions will again provide the derivative of r with respect to σ^2. If σ^2 is subject to a small increment, say $\Delta\sigma^2$, and the corresponding change in r is Δr, then, writing $\phi(r, \sigma^2)$ for the right-hand side of (5.2.2), we have in terms of partial derivatives

$$\Delta\phi(r, \sigma^2) = \frac{\partial\phi}{\partial r}\Delta r + \frac{\partial\phi}{\partial \sigma^2}\Delta\sigma^2.$$

Insofar as $\phi(r, \sigma^2)$ is a constant (namely, $\ln R_0$) for values of r satisfying the characteristic equation, its change $\Delta\phi(r, \sigma^2)$ must be zero; therefore

$$\frac{\partial\phi}{\partial r}\Delta r + \frac{\partial\phi}{\partial \sigma^2}\Delta\sigma^2 = 0,$$

and solving for $\Delta r / \Delta\sigma^2$ results in

$$\frac{\Delta r}{\Delta\sigma^2} = -\frac{(\partial\phi/\partial\sigma^2)}{\partial\phi/\partial r}. \tag{5.3.1}$$

In the limit as the increment tends to zero this gives the derivative of r with respect to σ^2 in terms of the two partials, with all other moments constant. The partials are readily calculated from (5.2.2) as

$$\frac{\partial \phi}{\partial r} = \mu - r\sigma^2 + \frac{r^2 \kappa_3}{2} - \dots, \qquad \frac{\partial \phi}{\partial \sigma^2} = -\frac{r^2}{2},$$

$$\therefore \frac{dr}{d\sigma^2} \doteq \frac{r^2}{2(\mu - r\sigma^2)}, \qquad\qquad (5.3.2)$$

if we truncate after the variance, equivalent to fitting a normal curve to the net maternity function $l(a)m(a)/R_0$.

This tells us that if two increasing populations are identical in all moments, except that one has a larger variance in age of childbearing than the other, the one with the larger variance will have the higher rate of increase. If the ages of childbearing are more spread out, apparently the gain through some children being born earlier more than offsets the loss through those born later. [What if R_0 is allowed to vary?]

Easier to understand is the relation between r and μ, the mean age of childbearing. The same technique as before gives for the required derivative

$$\frac{dr}{d\mu} = \frac{-r}{\mu - r\sigma^2}.$$

The term $r\sigma^2$ in the denominator is relatively small; therefore it seems that for an increasing population $dr/d\mu$ is negative, and the larger μ is the smaller r is, again with everything else the same. Larger μ implies slower turnover.

At one time comparison of the United States and Canada showed a contrast between larger families in Canada, and thus a higher R_0, and younger marriage and childbearing in the United States, and thus a smaller μ. The smaller μ reversed the effect of the higher R_0, and the net outcome was a higher r for the United States.

Finally, and most obviously, the intrinsic rate is positively related to R_0. Neglecting all but the first two terms on the right-hand side of (5.2.2), we have

$$\frac{dr}{dR_0} = -\frac{(\partial \psi / \partial R_0)}{\partial \psi / \partial r}$$

$$= \frac{1}{R_0(\mu - r\sigma^2)}.$$

If r is small, the intrinsic rate rises with R_0 as long as $\mu - r\sigma^2$ is positive, that is to say, always.

One kind of change can be compared with another and a set of equivalencies found. What increase in R_0 exactly offsets an increase of $\Delta\mu$ in μ and leaves the rate of increase unchanged? Should effort, say in India, go into raising the age of marriage or into disseminating birth control within marriage. India should of course do both, but the question still remains of where the marginal effort should go. With $R_0 = 1.77$, and $\mu = 25$, if raising the average age of childbearing by 3 years is easier than lowering age-specific birth rates by 5.9 percent, the effort should concentrate on age at marriage. In general if a change from R_0 to R_0^* is to be equivalent to one from μ to μ^* then if σ^2 does not change much, the equation

$$\frac{\ln R_0^*}{\mu} \doteq \frac{\ln R_0}{\mu^*}$$

holds to a close approximation. But this is true only if we can be sure that a higher rate of childbearing will not take place within the delayed marriages, and that illegitimacy will not be substantially increased.

Such statements can be made for any of the cumulants. The first three derivatives from (5.2.2), along with their values for the case of $R_0 = 2$, $\mu = 27$, and $\sigma^2 = 40$, so that $r = 0.02618$, disregarding terms beyond $r^2\sigma^2/2$, are as follows:

$$\frac{dr}{dR_0} = \frac{1}{R_0(\mu - r\sigma^2)} = 0.01927,$$

$$\frac{dr}{d\mu} = \frac{-r}{\mu - r\sigma^2} = -0.001009,$$

$$\frac{dr}{d\sigma^2} = \frac{r^2}{2(\mu - r\sigma^2)} = 0.0000132. \tag{5.3.3}$$

Thus a small increase ΔR_0 increases r by $0.01927\Delta R_0$ and so forth. In proportions the derivatives are

$$\frac{dr}{dR_0} : \frac{dr}{d\mu} : \frac{dr}{d\sigma^2} = \frac{1}{R_0} : -r : \frac{r^2}{2}.$$

The influence of successive cumulants of the net maternity function alternates in sign and decreases with the powers of r. As a matter of curiosity we can extend the series, and find the ratios

$$\frac{dr}{d\kappa_3} : \frac{dr}{d\kappa_4} : \frac{dr}{d\kappa_5} : \ldots = -\frac{r^3}{3!} : \frac{r^4}{4!} : -\frac{r^5}{5!} : \ldots.$$

Change in Births at One Age

Other calculations of the relation of rate of increase to aspects of the net maternity function depend on the form (5.1.2) of the characteristic equation. For example, we would like to know whether the use of contraception by young women will have more effect on the rate of increase than its use by older women. Suppose that for the 1-year interval around x the value of $m(x)$ is changed to $m(x) + \Delta m(x)$; our problem is to find the value Δr by which this modifies r.

The new value $r + \Delta r$ is obtained from the characteristic equation 5.1.2 in the form

$$\int_\alpha^\beta e^{-(r+\Delta r)a} l(a) \left[m(a) + \Delta m(x) \right] da = 1, \qquad (5.3.4)$$

where we have modified $m(a)$ by adding to it the quantity $\Delta m(x)$ for the 1 year x. [This unorthodox notation will not cause any trouble if we think of $\Delta m(x)$ as a function of a, defined to be zero everywhere except in the interval $x - \frac{1}{2}$ to $x + \frac{1}{2}$, where it is $\Delta m(x)$.] The left-hand side of (5.3.4) consists of two additive parts, one an integral, and the other approximately $e^{-(r+\Delta r)x} l(x) \Delta m(x)$. If for $e^{-(r+\Delta r)a}$ we write $e^{-ra}(1 - a\Delta r)$ within the integral, two integrals emerge, of which $\int_\alpha^\beta e^{-ra} l(a) m(a) da$ equals unity by our original equation (5.1.2), and $\int_\alpha^\beta a e^{-ra} l(a) m(a) da$ (without denominator) equals κ, the mean age of childbearing in the stable population. If $\Delta m(x)$ is small enough that the term involving $\Delta r \Delta m(x)$ may be ignored, we obtain

$$\Delta r \doteq \frac{e^{-rx} l(x)}{\kappa} \Delta m(x). \qquad (5.3.5)$$

Thus the intrinsic rate r is changed by $e^{-rx} l(x) / \kappa$ times the change in the age-specific birth rate $m(x)$. Note that the coefficient of $\Delta m(x)$ is proportional to the number of women in the stable age distribution. Thus the relative effect of changes in rates at the several ages is proportional to the number of women at these ages. Such sensitivity analysis is a way of exploiting models to obtain conditional statements of cause and effect in other instances where the result is less obvious.

An equivalent method of working out the effect of change in a birth or death rate involves the use of implicit functions. The interested reader can work out other examples. Here we proceed to a more general case in which not single ages but groups of ages are considered.

5.4 ARBITRARY PATTERN OF BIRTH RATE DECLINE

As the birth rate declines in the United States or any other country, it falls more rapidly at some ages than at others. For modernizing populations the initial fall has been greatest at the oldest ages of childbearing, as has been noted alike for the United States and for Taiwan. The ages that drop are partially related to the means of population control used: sterilization

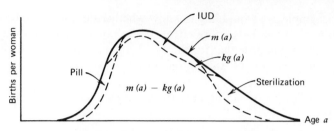

Fig. 5.2   Area $kg(a)$ removed from net maternity function by the several methods of birth control.

applies mostly to the older ages of childbearing; the pill, to younger ages (at least while it is a novelty); abortion, to all ages. The intrauterine device (IUD) is not much used by women until they have had a child, suggesting an aggregate impact on ages intermediate between the pill and sterilization. Possible cuts $g(a)$ that might be taken out of the birth function $m(a)$ by these three methods of birth control are suggested in Fig. 5.2. The fertility function that remains is $m(a) - kg(a)$, where k is a constant.

We will first consider an arbitrary function $g(a)$ and see the effect of removing it times some constant k from the birth function $m(a)$. Our analysis will concentrate on two special cases:

1. The effect on r of deducting $kg(a)$ from $m(a)$, where k is small, as though one were trying to examine the direction and pace of the first move toward fertility reduction.

2. The final condition of stationarity that will result from subtraction of $kg(a)$ from $m(a)$, where now k is large enough to produce stationarity.

The first case is simple because k is small, and the second is simple because the final condition is stationary; intermediate values of k are more difficult to handle and will not be discussed here. From the first case we will know in what direction the system starts to move, and from the second where it ends; by comparing these two we obtain at least a suggestion of how the movement is modified as k goes through intermediate finite values.

Effect of Small Arbitrary Change in Birth Function

Suppose an arbitrary function $g(a)$, positive or negative, such as unity for 1 year of age and zero elsewhere, or equal to $m(a)$, the birth function, or some other variant. We consider deductions from $m(a)$ equal to $kg(a)$, that is to say, $kg(a)$ is a bite of arbitrary shape taken out of $m(a)$. For purposes of this part of the argument k is small enough that we can neglect second-order terms like $(\Delta r)^2$ and $k \Delta r$, where Δr is the difference that the deduction of $kg(a)$ from $m(a)$ makes to r.

To find the value of Δr that corresponds to $kg(a)$ we have to solve the equation

$$\int_{\alpha}^{\beta} e^{-(r+\Delta r)a} l(a) \big[m(a) - kg(a) \big] da = 1, \qquad (5.4.1)$$

where r is defined by (5.1.2). Expanding the exponential $e^{-\Delta ra} \doteq 1 - \Delta ra$ in (5.4.1), ignoring the term involving $k \Delta r$, and solving for Δr gives

$$\Delta r \doteq - \frac{\int_{\alpha}^{\beta} e^{-ra} l(a) g(a) da}{\kappa} k, \qquad (5.4.2)$$

where κ is the mean age of childbearing in the stable population.

If $g(a) = m(a)$ for all a, (5.4.2) becomes

$$\Delta r = - \frac{k}{\kappa} \quad \text{or} \quad k = -\kappa \Delta r.$$

The question might be what fractional change in age-specific rates will bring the rate of increase down by Δr; the answer here given is that a subtraction of $100\kappa \Delta r$ percent at each age does it. A variety of results, including (5.3.5), can be obtained as special cases of (5.4.2). The method is still that of comparative statics: birth rates are taken as $m(a)$ for one population and as $m(a) - kg(a)$ for another, and the two stable conditions compared.

Amount of Change Needed for Drop to Bare Replacement

For bare replacement the net reproduction rate, the expected number of girl children by which a girl child born now will be replaced,

$$R_0 = \int_{\alpha}^{\beta} l(a) m(a) da,$$

must equal unity. If R_0 is to equal unity on the age-specific birth rates $m(a) - kg(a)$, we must have

$$\int_{\alpha}^{\beta} l(a) \big[m(a) - kg(a) \big] da = 1,$$

where the solution for k will tell just how much of the change shaped like $g(a)$ in the age pattern is required for the reduction to replacement. The answer is evidently

$$k = \frac{R_0 - 1}{\int_{\alpha}^{\beta} l(a) g(a) da}.$$

For $g(a) = m(a)$ this is $k = (R_0 - 1)/R_0$, as accords with intuition.

Effect of Uniformly Lower Death Rates

Suppose two populations of which one has the force of mortality $\mu(a)$ and the other $\mu^*(a) = \mu(a) + \delta$, where δ is the same for all ages. Then the population with $\mu(a) + \delta$ will have survivorship

$$l^*(x) = \exp\left\{ -\int_0^x \left[\mu(a) + \delta \right] da \right\} = e^{-\delta x} l(x).$$

Its characteristic equation will be

$$\int_\alpha^\beta e^{-r^* a} l^*(a) m(a) \, da = 1$$

or

$$\int_\alpha^\beta e^{-(r^* + \delta)a} l(a) m(a) \, da = 1.$$

But this is identical with the characteristic equation for $l(a)m(a)$, as given in (5.1.2), except that it has $r^* + \delta$ rather than r. And, since the characteristic equation has a unique real root, it follows that $r^* + \delta = r$, or $r^* = r - \delta$. In words, the solution with the incremented mortality is the original solution less the increment of mortality.

From this it follows that age distribution is unaffected by a constant increment of mortality. This is so because the age distribution is proportional to $e^{-rx} l(x) dx$; and if we change $l(x)$ to $l^*(x) = e^{-\delta x} l(x)$, so that r goes to $r^* = r - \delta$, then $e^{-rx} l(x) dx$ goes to $e^{-(r-\delta)x} e^{-\delta x} l(x)$, that is, it is unchanged on cancellation of $e^{-\delta x}$.

That a change in death rates that is the same at all ages has no effect on age distribution is true more generally. Suppose an age distribution, however irregular, and a decline of 0.001 in mortality rates at all ages. Then exactly one person in a thousand who would have died on the former regime now survives, age by age. This increases the number at every age by exactly 0.001, that is, multiplies it by 1.001, and multiplying every age by 1.001 can have no effect on the age distribution (Coale, 1956).

5.5 DROP IN BIRTHS REQUIRED TO OFFSET A DROP IN DEATHS

Let us find the fraction by which existing fertility must decline so as to offset an absolute decrease in mortality equal to k at every separate age. In symbols, suppose that for women who have reached age a the chance of dying between ages a and $a + da$ drops from $\mu(a)da$ to $[\mu(a) - k]da$, and this applies with the same k at all ages; by what uniform fraction f at all ages would women have to lower their birth rates in order for the intrinsic rate r to remain the same? If the drop in births takes place uniformly at all ages, the old probability of having a child between ages a and $a + da$ being $m(a)da$, and the new probability being $(1 - f)m(a)da$, we can determine the unknown f.

The effect of lowering the death rate by the amount k at each age is equivalent to increasing the survivorship $l(a)$ by the factor e^{ka}, for by definition the new $l^*(a)$ must be, as before,

$$l^*(a) = \exp\left\{ - \int_0^a [\, \mu(t) - k\,] \, dt \right\}, \tag{5.5.1}$$

and carrying out the integration gives $l^*(a) = e^{ka}l(a)$. Alongside the old characteristic equation 5.1.2 we have a new one:

$$\int_\alpha^\beta e^{-ra} e^{ka} l(a)(1 - f)m(a) \, da = 1. \tag{5.5.2}$$

We will replace e^{ka} by $1 + ka$, permissible if k is small, take advantage of (5.1.2) to cancel $\int_\alpha^\beta e^{-ra} l(a)m(a) \, da$ on the left of (5.5.2) against the 1 on the right, and solve for f as

$$f = \frac{k\kappa}{1 + k\kappa}, \tag{5.5.3}$$

where κ is again the mean age of childbearing in the stable population. Approximately, the fraction that the births would have to be reduced to offset a fall of k in the mortality of every age is $k\kappa$. For a population whose κ is 27 years, an absolute fall of 0.001 in the death rate at each separate age would require a fall of the fraction $(0.001)(27)/[1 + (0.001)(27)] = 0.0263$ in the birth rates at each age to offset it.

A variant of the same question, left to the reader, asks how much must be cut off the $m(a)$ curve at its upper end to offset a drop k in the age-specific death rates. We go on to find the drop in fertility that would offset the largest possible decrease in mortality—its complete elimination.

The Drop in Fertility That Would Offset a Drop in Mortality to Zero

The question has been raised how a drop in mortality to zero could be offset by a change in fertility at all ages of women. In the simplest form, what value of f, the fractional fall in fertility at all ages, is associated with an intrinsic rate r that would remain unchanged if mortality to the end of reproduction were to drop to zero? Putting $l(a) = 1$ and changing $m(a)$ to $m(a)(1 - f)$ in (5.1.2) provides the equation that f must satisfy:

$$\int_\alpha^\beta e^{-ra} m(a)(1 - f) \, da = 1, \tag{5.5.4}$$

while r is still subject to (5.1.2). The value of f from (5.5.4) is

$$f = 1 - \frac{1}{\int_{\alpha}^{\beta} e^{-ra} m(a)\, da}. \tag{5.5.5}$$

A fertility drop by the fraction f at all ages would preserve r, the ultimate rate of increase, against the hypothetical drop to zero of mortality up to age β. A very slightly different problem is to find the fraction f that would preserve the generation ratio of increase R_0, the net reproduction rate, defined as

$$R_0 = \int_{\alpha}^{\beta} l(a) m(a)\, da.$$

The required fraction is the solution in f of the equation

$$\int_{\alpha}^{\beta} m(a)(1 - f)\, da = R_0, \tag{5.5.6}$$

or

$$f = 1 - \frac{R_0}{\int_{\alpha}^{\beta} m(a)\, da} = 1 - \frac{R_0}{G_0}, \tag{5.5.7}$$

the integral in the denominator being the gross reproduction rate G_0 (Coale, 1973b).

Applying this to developed countries shows that a 3 or 4 percent decline in births would offset the drop to zero mortality. In 1967 the United States G_0 was 1.26 and the R_0 was 1.21 (Keyfitz and Flieger, 1971, p. 361). For less developed countries where mortality is somewhat higher, a 5 to 15 percent drop in births would suffice. No one need be concerned that a further fall in the Mexican death rate, for example, will add seriously to the demographic problem of that country. Mexico's G_0 in 1966 was 3.17, its R_0 2.71, and its birth rate $1000b = 43.96$ (Keyfitz and Flieger, 1971, p. 345). A drop to $1000b = 37.58$ would offset a transition to zero mortality.

The conclusion that further decline in mortality need not provoke any substantial rise in the rate of population growth probably applies to the world as a whole. Insofar as mortality up to the end of childbearing is already very low, further diminution in it can have only a small effect on the rate of increase, and this small effect is likely to be offset for most countries by the decline in fertility during the 1970s. The parts of the world where this conclusion does not yet apply are mostly in tropical Africa.

Diseases of Infancy versus Heart Disease: Their Effects on Population Increase

The death rate from cardiovascular renal diseases for females in the United States in 1964 was 448 per 100,000 population, and that from certain diseases of infancy (as defined) was 26 (Preston, Keyfitz, and Schoen, 1972, p. 770). Standardized, the numbers were 383 and 26, still a ratio of nearly 15 to 1. Eliminating certain diseases of infancy adds only 0.930 year to $\overset{o}{e}_0$, whereas eliminating CVR adds 17.068 years, or 18 times as much. All indications are that CVR has at least 15 times the effect on mortality of certain diseases of infancy.

But no such proportion appears in the effects on overall population increase of eliminating these diseases. Consider first the effect on the net reproduction rate. Using the life table calculated as though CVR were eliminated raises the net reproduction rate by 0.002. Eliminating certain diseases of infancy without altering the other causes raises the net reproduction rate by 0.018. Heart disease may be 15 times as prevalent as diseases of infancy, but its long-term effect on increase is only about one-ninth as great.

5.6   MOMENTS OF THE DYING POPULATION IN TERMS OF THOSE OF THE LIVING, AND CONVERSELY

If we know the age distribution of the living population of the life table, we ought to be able to find the age distribution of the dying. Stated in life table symbols, the problem is simply that of finding the distribution d_x in terms of l_x, and the answer is $d_x = l_x - l_{x+1}$.

Translating moments of the living into those of the dying is straightforward; given the moments of $l(x)$, we proceed to find the moments of $l(x)\mu(x)$, where $\mu(x) = -\dfrac{1}{l(x)}\dfrac{dl(x)}{dx}$. The result will enable us to find the mean age, variance, and other parameters of the living from those of the dying, and vice versa.

One device is to relate the cumulant-generating function of the ages of the dying to that of the ages of the living. For a general distribution function $f(x)$, define $\psi(r)$ as the transform

$$\psi(r) = \ln\left[\int_0^\omega e^{-rx} f(x)\,dx \right],$$

and define the cumulants of $f(x)$ as the coefficients of the powers of r in the expansion

$$\psi(r) = -r\kappa_1 + \frac{r^2}{2!}\kappa_2 - \frac{r^3}{3!}\kappa_3 + \ldots. \tag{5.6.1}$$

For the special case where $f(x)$ is proportional to $l(x)$, the transform is

$$\ln\left[\frac{\int_0^\omega e^{-rx}l(x)\,dx}{\int_0^\omega l(x)\,dx}\right],$$

which will be called $\psi_L(r)$; the κ_L are the cumulants of the distribution $l(x)/\int_0^\omega l(x)\,dx$. In reference to our distribution of population the mean age is μ_L, the variance σ_L^2, the skewness κ_{3L}, and the kurtosis κ_{4L}. For deaths the mean is $\kappa_1 = \overset{o}{e}_0$, the variance $\kappa_2 = \sigma^2$, the skewness κ_3, and the kurtosis κ_4.

The exponential of the cumulant-generating function of the ages of the dying is

$$\exp[\psi(r)] = \int_0^\omega e^{-rx}l(x)\,\mu(x)\,dx = -\int_0^\omega e^{-rx}\,dl(x),$$

and on integration by parts we have

$$-\int_0^\omega e^{-rx}\,dl(x) = -e^{-rx}l(x)\Big|_0^\omega - r\int_0^\omega e^{-rx}l(x)\,dx$$

$$= 1 - r\int_0^\omega e^{-rx}l(x)\,dx.$$

But the integral here is $\int_0^\omega l(x)\,dx$ times the exponential of the cumulant-generating function of the living. Hence there follows the identity

$$\exp[\psi(r)] = 1 - r\overset{o}{e}_0\exp[\psi_L(r)], \tag{5.6.2}$$

where $\psi_L(r) = \ln\left[\int_0^\omega e^{-rx}l(x)\,dx / \int_0^\omega l(x)\,dx\right]$, referring to the living, is distinguished from $\psi(r) = \ln\left[\int_0^\omega e^{-rx}l(x)\,\mu(x)\,dx\right]$, referring to the dying. Note that $\int_0^\omega l(x)\,\mu(x)\,dx = 1$; therefore we do not need a denominator for $\psi(r)$, generating the cumulants of the dying, but do require the denominator $\int_0^\omega l(x)\,dx = \overset{o}{e}_0$ for $\psi_L(r)$.

The basic result is (5.6.2); and, subject to conditions of convergence that do not seem to give trouble in practice, expanding $\psi(r)$ and $\psi_L(r)$ within it enables us to find one set of cumulants in terms of the other:

$$\exp\left(-\overset{o}{e}_0 r + \frac{\sigma^2 r^2}{2} - \frac{\kappa_3 r^3}{6} + \cdots\right)$$

$$= 1 - r\overset{o}{e}_0 \exp\left(-\mu_L r + \frac{\sigma_L^2 r^2}{2} - \frac{\kappa_{3L} r^3}{6} + \cdots\right),$$

or on expanding the exponentials

$$1 - \overset{o}{e}_0 r + \left(\sigma^2 + \overset{o}{e}_0^2\right)\frac{r^2}{2} - \cdots$$

$$= 1 - r\overset{o}{e}_0\left[1 - \mu_L r + \left(\sigma_L^2 + \mu_L^2\right)\frac{r^2}{2} - \cdots\right].$$

Equating powers of r, we get

$$\overset{o}{e}_0 = \overset{o}{e}_0,$$

$$\frac{\sigma^2 + \overset{o}{e}_0^2}{2} = \overset{o}{e}_0 \mu_L,$$

$$\frac{\kappa_3 + 3\sigma^2\overset{o}{e}_0 + \overset{o}{e}_0^3}{6} = \frac{\overset{o}{e}_0\left(\sigma_L^2 + \mu_L^2\right)}{2},$$

$$\cdots \quad \cdots \quad \cdots \quad \cdots \quad \cdots \quad .$$

Thus $\sigma^2 = 2\overset{o}{e}_0 \mu_L - \overset{o}{e}_0^2$, identically, and we have without approximation the variance in the age of dying in terms of the mean age of the living and $\overset{o}{e}_0$, all for the life table population. For example, in the case of Colombian females, 1964, where $\overset{o}{e}_0 = 61.563$ and $\mu_L = 37.360$, the variance in age at death is

$$\sigma^2 = 2(61.563)(37.360) - (61.563)^2 = 810.0.$$

Thus the four cumulants of ages in a stationary population given for some 200 populations in Keyfitz and Flieger (1968) provide five cumulants of ages of the dying for those same populations.

Expectation of Life as a Function of Crude Birth and Death Rates

If we know only the crude death rate of a population we can say little about its expectation of life; a crude death rate of 10 can apply to a country with a life expectation as high as 75 years or as low as 60 years, in the former case with a rate of increase of 0.005 and in the latter of 0.030. If we are also told the crude birth rate or the rate of natural increase, we can narrow this range considerably, as McCann (1973) has shown.

We know that d, the crude death rate in the stable population, is

$$d = \int_0^\omega b e^{-ra} l(a) \mu(a) da,$$

so that, dividing by b and noting that the right-hand side is the exponential of the cumulant-generating function of the distribution of deaths by age expressed in terms of $-r$, we have

$$\frac{d}{b} = \int_0^\omega e^{-ra} l(a) \mu(a) da,$$

or $\ln d - \ln b = \psi(r)$, and this is the same as

$$\ln b - \ln d = r \overset{o}{e}_0 - \frac{r^2 \sigma^2}{2} + \frac{r^3 \kappa_3}{6} - \cdots,$$

since in the stationary population the mean age of dying is the expectation of life $\overset{o}{e}_0$. Solving for $\overset{o}{e}_0$ gives

$$\overset{o}{e}_0 = \frac{\ln b - \ln d}{b - d} + r \left(\frac{\sigma^2}{2} - \frac{r \kappa_3}{6} + \frac{r^2 \kappa_4}{24} - \cdots \right), \tag{5.6.3}$$

where $r = b - d$. Now the expression in parentheses on the right depends on the life table in a fairly systematic way. With a set of model life tables we can iterate to the value of $\overset{o}{e}_0$, given b and d.

A different approach to the same problem is to start with the identity

$$\frac{1}{b} = \int_0^\omega e^{-rx} l(x) dx,$$

divide by $\overset{o}{e}_0 = \int_0^\omega l(x) dx$, take logarithms, and then use the fact that the right-hand side is the cumulant-generating function of the living:

$$\ln \left(b \overset{o}{e}_0 \right) = \mu_L r - \frac{\sigma_L^2 r^2}{2} + \frac{\kappa 3_L r^3}{6} - \cdots,$$

where now the cumulants are of the distribution of the living in the stationary population rather than of the dying. Hence we have

$$\overset{o}{e}_0 = \frac{1}{b} \exp \left(\mu_L r - \frac{\sigma_L^2 r^2}{2} + \cdots \right). \tag{5.6.4}$$

Applying (5.6.3) to Colombian females, 1964, and dropping terms involving third and higher cumulants, we obtain

$$\overset{o}{e}_0 = \frac{\ln 0.03840 - \ln 0.01006}{0.02835} + \frac{(0.02835)(810.0)}{2}$$
$$= 47.25 + 11.48 = 58.73$$

against the life table value of 61.56. From (5.6.4), dropping terms, we have

$$\overset{o}{e}_0 = \frac{e^{\mu_L r}}{b} = \frac{e^{(37.36)(0.02835)}}{0.03840}$$
$$= 75.10,$$

which is a much poorer approximation. But if we take one more term in the exponential of (5.6.4) with $\sigma_L^2 = 539.34$, this becomes

$$\overset{o}{e}_0 = 60.47,$$

which is the best of the three.

These results use the mean and variance of the life table, for which we are looking. In practice one would not be able to attain them in a single calculation, but would find them from the $\overset{o}{e}_0$ of the previous iteration. The method can choose an $\overset{o}{e}_0$ from a one-parameter set of life tables.

Which of (5.6.3) and (5.6.4) is preferable? The decision depends on which set of cumulants (that for the living or that for the dying) is more nearly invariant with respect to $\overset{o}{e}_0$, since that determines the number of iterations required in a given series of model life tables. The answer also depends on which is more robust with respect to the choice of the series of model tables, a line of investigation that must be left for another time. (James McCann and Samuel Preston contributed much of the foregoing argument.)

5.7   FOUR MATHEMATICAL FORMULATIONS OF THE BASIC EQUATION OF POPULATION

So far, this book has dealt with what in retrospect can be seen as special cases of a general analysis. Chapter 2 treated the pure death process of the life table, in which births, if considered at all, were just equal to deaths. Chapter 4 used the life table along with an arbitrary rate of increase r to constitute a stable age distribution. The present chapter ascertained the same r from an equation incorporating age-specific birth rates as well as the life table.

The general analysis of which all these are parts relates the entire population of each generation or period to the preceding. This can be done in the form of an integral equation, a matrix multiplication, a difference equation, and a partial differential equation.

These mathematical forms look very different from one another, though they are ultimately equivalent. The purpose of presenting them is not to exhibit the mathematical virtuosity of their several authors, but to take advantage of the fact that some applications are easier with one approach, others with another. This book is not the place to treat the mathematics in detail; that has been done elsewhere (Coale, 1972; Pollard, 1973; Keyfitz, 1968; Rhodes, 1940). Here the several approaches will be presented, and some observations made on their relation to one another and to the applications that are the subject of this book.

The Lotka Integral Equation

Historically the earliest formulation was in terms of an integral equation solved by Sharpe and Lotka (1911), whose unknown is the trajectory of births and which, under the name of the renewal equation, has become famous in many other contexts. Births $B(t)$ at time t are the outcome of the births a years earlier, where a ranges from about 15 to about 50, say from α to β in general. Newborns of a years earlier, numbering $B(t-a)$, have a probability $l(a)$ of surviving to time t: those that do survive have a probability $m(a)da$ of themselves giving birth in the time interval a to $a+da$; the total of these over ages α to β is $\int_\alpha^\beta B(t-a)l(a)m(a)da$, which ultimately must equal current births $B(t)$. But any such system has to have an initial condition to start it off; in the Lotka equation the initial condition is $G(t)$, the number of births due to the women already born at the start of the process. The function $G(t)$ is zero for $t \geqslant \beta$, when all the females alive at $t=0$ have passed beyond childbearing. Entering the known $G(t)$ and $l(a)m(a)$ in the Lotka integral equation,

$$B(t) = \int_\alpha^\beta B(t-a)l(a)m(a)da + G(t), \qquad (5.7.1)$$

determines the trajectory $B(t)$.

The method used by Lotka to solve (5.7.1) for $B(t)$ was first to deal with the homogeneous form, in which $G(t)$ is disregarded, and to try $B(t) = e^{rt}$. Entering this value for $B(t)$ and corresponding $B(t-a) = e^{r(t-a)}$ in (5.7.1) without $G(t)$ gives the characteristic equation 5.1.2, which has for the general net maternity function $l(a)m(a)$ an infinite number of roots. This is a more satisfactory way of deriving (5.1.2) than was used above. The left-hand side of (5.1.2), say $\psi(r)$, is large for negative r and diminishes toward zero as r becomes large and positive; we saw that only one of the roots can be real. Suppose that the roots in order of magnitude of their real parts are $r_1, r_2, r_3, \ldots$. The complex roots, such as the pair r_2, r_3, must be pairs of complex conjugates, say $x + iy, x - iy$, where x and y are real; if they are not conjugates, they could not be assembled into the real equation 5.1.2.

The homogeneous form [i.e., omitting $G(t)$ from (5.7.1)] is linear, and hence if $e^{r_1 t}$ is a solution so is $Q_1 e^{r_1 t}$, where Q_1 is an arbitrary constant. If a number of such terms are solutions, so is their sum. These considerations provide the general solution to the homogeneous form

$$B(t) = Q_1 e^{r_1 t} + Q_2 e^{r_2 t} + \cdots, \tag{5.7.2}$$

where the r's are the roots of (5.1.2) and the Q's are arbitrary constants. The solution to the nonhomogeneous form (5.7.1) containing $G(t)$ is obtained by selecting values of Q that accord with the births $G(t)$ to the initial population. Lotka showed that these are

$$Q_s = \frac{\displaystyle\int_0^\beta e^{-r_s t} G(t)\, dt}{\displaystyle\int_0^\beta a e^{-r_s a} l(a) m(a)\, da}, \qquad s = 1, 2, \ldots. \tag{5.7.3}$$

The constant Q_1 attached to the real term will be important in Chapter 6, where we seek the effect on the trajectory of adding one person aged x.

A less awkward way to solve (5.7.1) (Feller, 1941; Keyfitz, 1968, p. 128) is by taking the Laplace transform of the members. That of $B(t)$, for example, is

$$B^*(r) = \int_0^\infty e^{-rt} B(t)\, dt$$

and similarly for $G(t)$ and $l(a)m(a) = \phi(a)$, say. The integral on the right of (5.7.1) is a convolution, that is to say, the sum of the arguments of the two functions $B(t-a)$ and $l(a)m(a) = \phi(a)$ in the integrand does not involve a; the transform of a convolution is the product of the transforms of the two functions. The equation in the transforms (distinguished by asterisks) is thus

$$B^*(r) = G^*(r) + B^*(r)\phi^*(r),$$

and is readily solved for the transform $B^*(r)$ of the unknown function $B(t)$:

$$B^*(r) = \frac{G^*(r)}{1 - \phi^*(r)}.$$

To invert the right-hand side, expand in partial fractions, using the factors of $1 - \phi^*(r)$, obtained from the roots $r_1, r_2, \ldots$, of $\phi^*(r) = 1$, which is the same as (5.1.2). Call the expansion of $B^*(r)$

$$B^*(r) = \frac{Q_1}{r - r_1} + \frac{Q_2}{r - r_2} + \cdots .$$

The Laplace transform of $e^{r_1 t}$ is

$$\int_0^\infty e^{-rt} e^{r_1 t} \, dt = \frac{1}{r - r_1} ,$$

as appears from integration, so the inverse transform of $1/(r - r_1)$ is $e^{r_1 t}$. Using this fact permits writing the solution in the form of (5.7.2), and the coefficients Q_s are the same as before, that is, (5.7.3). Specializing (5.7.3) to $s = 1$ gives the constant Q_1 for the first term of the solution as

$$Q_1 = \frac{\int_0^\beta e^{-rt} G(t) \, dt}{\kappa} , \qquad (5.7.4)$$

where again κ is the mean age of childbearing in the stable population. The roots $r_2, r_3, \ldots$, all have real parts less than r_1, so the terms involving them become less important with time, and the birth curve $B(t)$ asymptotically approaches $Q_1 e^{r_1 t}$. This statement holds under general conditions on $\phi(a)$ analogous to those of Section 1.9.

What solution 5.7.2 amounts to is a real term that is an exponential, plus waves around this exponential, of which the demographically interesting one corresponds to the pair of complex roots of largest absolute value, has the wavelength of the generation, and accounts for the echo effect: other things being constant, a baby boom in one generation is followed by a secondary baby boom in the next generation.

The Leslie Matrix

Whelpton (1936) presented what he called the components method of population projection, in which an age distribution in 5-year age groups is "survived" along cohort lines, and births less early childhood deaths are added in each cycle of projection. The method was also used by Cannan (1895) and Bowley (1924). Later the same projection was formalized by Bernardelli (1941), Lewis (1942), and Leslie (1945, 1948), the latter in such detail that the process has come to be called after him.

Leslie noted that, if the initial population is represented by a vertical vector **P**, say in 5-year age groups,

$$P = \left\{ \begin{array}{c} {}_5P_0 \\ {}_5P_5 \\ \cdot \\ \cdot \\ \cdot \\ {}_5P_{\omega-5} \end{array} \right\},$$

then survivorships ${}_5L_5/{}_5L_0$, ${}_5L_{10}/{}_5L_5$, and so on, placed in the subdiagonal of a matrix **S** will carry the population down cohort lines when the vector is premultiplied by the matrix. Survivors after 5 years will be given by **SP**, after 10 years by $S(SP) = S^2P$, and so on. The contribution of births after the process gets under way is provided by the first row of a matrix, say **B**, with nonzero elements in the third to eleventh positions if fertility is positive from ages 15–19 to 45–49. (Note that the third element of the vector corresponds to ages 10 to 14, in which fertility may well be assumed to be zero, but the third element of the matrix takes account of the fact that individuals 10 to 14 years old at the start of each 5-year projection cycle grow into ages 15 to 19 during that cycle.) If the sum of the survivorship and birth matrices is $M = S + B$, the complete projection to time t measured in units of half-decades is

$$P^t = M^t P^{(0)}.$$

(See upper left part of Table 8.2.)

The characteristic equation is obtained by considering the stability condition, in which projection of the age distribution through one cycle does not alter relative proportions, but increases all ages in the same ratio, say λ:

$$MK = \lambda K,$$

where **K** is the vertical stable vector. This amounts to

$$[M - \lambda I]\{K\} = \{0\}, \tag{5.7.5}$$

I being the identity matrix of suitable order, 18×18 if 5-year age groups up to 90 are recognized, and $\{0\}$ is a vector of zeros. if the elements of **K** are not to be all zero, the matrix $[M - \lambda I]$ must be singular, which is to say, its determinant must be zero.

The determinantal equation $|M - \lambda I| = 0$ provides roots in λ called eigenvalues. The zero roots are not of any interest; a population with positive fertility up to age 50 has 10 nonzero roots in λ.

The eigenvalue of greatest interest is that of largest absolute value, say λ_1, corresponding to e^{5r_1} of the Lotka formulation. With finite age groups in the usual finite approximation the population grows somewhat faster on the Leslie than on the Lotka projection; for instance, over a 5-year period, using Mexican data for 1966, λ_1 was 1.1899 whereas e^{5r_1} was 1.1891. For a low-increase country like the United States the difference does not show by the fourth decimal place, and it vanishes altogether when the interval of projection is made small. In fact, as the interval becomes small, the two models become identical (Keyfitz, 1968, Chapter 8).

The real eigenvector K_1 is the stable population (4.1.1). Although there is only one set of eigenvalues, there are two sets of eigenvectors, the other being horizontal so as to multiply M on the left and satisfy the equation $HM = \lambda H$. The real H_1 contains the reproductive value at the several ages, considered from a continuous viewpoint in Chapter 6.

The Difference Equation

A third way of looking at the population trajectory, developed like the matrix during the 1930s and 1940s, by Thompson (1931), Dobbernack and Tietz (1940, p. 239), Lotka (1948, p. 192), and Cole (1954, p. 112), is in terms of a difference equation. A secondary treatment is found in Keyfitz (1968, p. 130).

Consider one girl baby together with the series expected to be generated by her at 5-year intervals, say $u_0, u_1, u_2, \ldots$, where $u_0 = 1$. The simplest way to describe the model is to bunch the person-years lived into points at 5-year intervals. The u_i will at first decrease, corresponding to the probability that the girl will die during the time before she begins to bear children; then they will start to increase, and they will increase further with the approach to u_8 just 40 years later, when her children start to bear. The series generated by the girl now alive includes the probability that she will live for 15 years and then have a child, say a probability of f_3, that she will live 20 years and then have a child, f_4, and so on. After n periods of 5 years the girl's descendants (including herself if still alive) are u_n. The u_n must be equal to the chance of her living that long and having a child then, $f_n u_0$, plus the chance of her having lived $n-1$ periods and having a child that would now have given rise to u_1, and so on. In sum,

$$u_n = f_n u_0 + f_{n-1} u_1 + f_{n-2} u_2 + \cdots \tag{5.7.6}$$

for all n. In this series the f are known quantities corresponding to the $l(a)m(a)$ of the Lotka form, or to the $_5L_x F_x$ of the matrix; the u series is the unknown function corresponding to $B(t-a)$.

Just as the integral equation was solved by the Laplace transform, so set 5.7.6 is solved by generating functions. Multiply (5.7.6) for u_n by s^n, add all such equations from $n=0$ to $n=\infty$, and then express the result in terms of

$$U(s) = u_0 + u_1 s + u_2 s^2 + \cdots,$$

$$F(s) = f_0 + f_1 s + f_2 s^2 + \cdots,$$

so that the set of equations 5.7.6 amounts to

$$U(s) = 1 + U(s)F(s),$$

which is readily solved to give

$$U(s) = \frac{1}{1 - F(s)}. \tag{5.7.7}$$

Dividing out the right-hand side would only generate again the series with which we started. But first finding the roots of $1 - F(s) = 0$, a further form of the characteristic equation, using the roots to break down the right-hand side of (5.7.7) into partial fractions of the type $d_i/(s - s_i)$, and then expanding each of the partial fractions, we get a series in powers of s that corresponds to (5.7.2) in the Lotka solution.

The descriptions read as though the Lotka model is backward looking, since it finds the relation between the present generation and the preceding one, whereas the Leslie model and the set of difference equations are forward looking, portraying the continuance of present rates into the future. These differences of direction are superficial, however, and the mathematical outcomes are essentially identical.

The von Foerster Partial Differential Equations

A fourth approach, due to von Foerster (1959), has been given less attention in demography. It is most easily visualized in terms of the Lexis diagram (Fig. 2.1), redrawn in the present context as Fig. 5.3. If $P(a,t)$ is the population (say of females) at age a and time t, the female population of age $a + \Delta a$ at time $t + \Delta t$ is $P(a + \Delta a, t + \Delta t)$. If $\Delta a = \Delta t$ the latter includes the same individuals as were counted in $P(a,t)$, only subject to deductions for mortality (as well as for emigration if one wishes, but the present section excludes migration). The equation of change involving mortality $\mu(a)$, a function of age but not of time, is

$$P(a + \Delta a, t + \Delta t) = P(a,t) - \mu(a)P(a,t)\Delta t. \tag{5.7.8}$$

Expanding $P(a + \Delta a, t + \Delta t)$ by Taylor's theorem for two independent variables and canceling $P(a,t)$ from both sides leaves

$$\frac{\partial P(a,t)}{\partial t}\Delta t + \frac{\partial P(a,t)}{\partial a}\Delta a = -\mu(a)P(a,t)\Delta t.$$

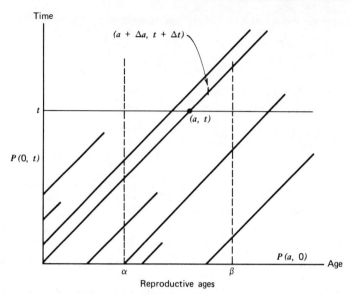

Fig. 5.3 Lexis diagram showing boundary distributions $P(a,0)$ along age axis given at the outset, and $P(0,t)$ along time axis generated by (5.7.9) and (5.7.10); (5.7.9) fills out the interior of the quadrant.

Dividing by Δa, which is equal to Δt, we have

$$\frac{\partial P(a,t)}{\partial t} + \frac{\partial P(a,t)}{\partial a} = -\mu(a)P(a,t). \qquad (5.7.9)$$

This is von Foerster's partial differential equation for one sex, for all values of $0 < a < \omega$, where ω is the oldest age to which anyone lives.

Births enter as a boundary condition at age zero:

$$P(0,t) = \int_{\alpha}^{\beta} P(a,t)m(a)\,da, \qquad (5.7.10)$$

where α is the youngest age of childbearing and β the oldest, and $m(a)$ is the age-specific birth rate, supposed to be invariant with respect to time.

The Four Presentations

The common structure of the four presentations may not stand out conspicuously, but each has the following:

1. An initial age distribution.

2. Provision for mortality; in the first three methods this is the survival probability $l(x)$ or L_x of the life table, while in the von Foerster method it

is the age-specific death rate $\mu(a)$; if age and time move forward together we have a cohort, and the partial differential equation whose solution is

$$l(x) = \exp\left[-\int_0^x \mu(a)\,da \right].$$

3. Provision for reproduction, presented as the first row of the matrix **M**, and as the boundary condition 5.7.10 in the partial differential equation.

4. A characteristic equation, whose real or positive root is the intrinsic rate or its exponential, obtained from the birth boundary condition in the partial differential equation.

5. Right eigenvectors, of which the positive one is the stable age distribution.

6. Left eigenvectors, of which the positive one is the reproductive values of the several ages taken up in Chapter 6.

[The reader may wish to identify each of these features in the four forms.]

Although in principle any property of the deterministic population process under a fixed regime is obtainable from any of the four forms, and numerical differences disappear if the interval of time and age is small enough, the projection of a population into the future, in disregard of the several roots, is simplest with the matrix (Chapter 8); the integral equation seems to give a superior finite approximation for the intrinsic rate and provides a simple perturbation analysis, as in Section 5.3. The partial differential equation has been applied to two-sex models, including marriage (Fredrickson, 1971), and the difference equation has seemed more natural than the other forms in some biological applications (Cole, 1954).

Chapter Six

REPRODUCTIVE VALUE, WITH APPLICATIONS TO MIGRATION, CONTRACEPTION, AND ZERO POPULATION GROWTH

When a woman of reproductive age is sterilized and so has no further children, the community's subsequent births are reduced. When a woman dies or otherwise leaves the community, all subsequent times are again affected. Our formal argument need make no distinction between emigration and death, between leaving the country under study for life and leaving this world altogether. A single theory answers questions about the numerical effect of sterilization, of mortality, and of emigration, all supposed to be taking place at a particular age x. By means of the theory we will be able to compare the demographic results of eradicating a disease that affects the death rate at young ages, say malaria, as against another that affects the death rate at older ages, say heart disease.

A seemingly different question is what would happen to a rapidly increasing population if its couples reduced their childbearing to bare replacement immediately. The period net reproduction rate R_0, the number of girl children expected to be born to a girl child just born, would equal 1 from then on, and ultimately the population would be stationary. But the history of high fertility has built up an age distribution favorable to childbearing, and the ultimate stationary total will be much higher than the total at the time when the birth rate dropped to bare replacement. The amount by which it will be higher is calculable, and by the same function —reproductive value—that is used for problems of migration and changed mortality.

6.1 CONCEPT OF REPRODUCTIVE VALUE

Without having these particular problems in mind, Fisher (1930, p. 27) developed a fanciful image of population dynamics that turns out to provide solutions to them. He regarded the birth of a child as the lending to him of a life, and the birth of that child's offspring as the subsequent repayment of the debt. Apply this to the female part of the population, in which the chance of a girl living to age a is $l(a)$, and the chance of her having a girl between ages a and $a + da$ is $m(a) da$, so that the expected number of children in the small interval of age specified is $l(a) m(a) da$. This quantity added through the whole of life is what was defined as the net reproduction rate R_0 in Section 5.1:

$$R_0 = \int_\alpha^\beta l(a) m(a) da,$$

where α is the youngest age of childbearing and β the oldest. The quantity R_0 is the expected number of girl children by which a girl child will be replaced; for the population it is the ratio of the number in one generation to the number in the preceding generation, according to the given $l(a)$ and $m(a)$.

Fisher's image discounts the future, at a rate of interest equal to the intrinsic rate r of Section 5.1. The value of 1 dollar, or one child, discounted back through a years at annual rate r compounded momently is e^{-ra}; therefore the value of $l(a) m(a) da$ children is $e^{-ra} l(a) m(a) da$, as in the financial calculations of Section 2.5. The present value of the repayment of the debt is the integral of this last quantity through the ages to the end of reproduction. Thus the debt that the girl incurs at birth is 1, and the discounted repayment is the integral $\int_\alpha^\beta e^{-ra} l(a) m(a) da$. If loan and discounted repayment are to be equal, we must have

$$1 = \int_\alpha^\beta e^{-ra} l(a) m(a) da,$$

and this is the same as the characteristic equation (Lotka, 1939, p. 65, and (5.1.2)), from which the r implied by a net maternity function $l(a) m(a)$ is calculated. The equation can now be seen in a new light: the equating of loan and discounted repayment is what determines r, r being interpretable either as the rate of interest on a loan or as Lotka's intrinsic rate of natural increase.

The loan-and-repayment interpretation of the characteristic equation suggests calculating how much of the debt is outstanding by the time the girl has reached age $x < \beta$. This is the same as the expected number of subsequent children discounted back to age x. Her expected births in the interval a to $a + da$, $a > x$, are $[l(a)/l(x)] m(a)$; and if these births are discounted back $a - x$ years, her debt outstanding at age x is

$$v(x) = \int_x^\beta e^{-r(a-x)} \frac{l(a)}{l(x)} m(a) \, da$$

or, as Fisher (1930) wrote,

$$v(x) = \frac{1}{e^{-rx}l(x)} \int_x^\beta e^{-ra} l(a) m(a) \, da, \qquad (6.1.1)$$

where $v(x)$ will be called reproductive value at age x. Evidently $v(0) = 1$, and, for $x > \beta$, $v(x) = 0$.

For his studies in genetics Fisher needed to know the extent to which persons of given age (say x), on the average contribute to the births of future generations. This seemingly different question is answered by a function proportional to $v(x)$; its value can be established at $v(x)/\kappa$, where, as in Section 5.1,

$$\kappa = \int_\alpha^\beta a e^{-ra} l(a) m(a) \, da, \qquad (6.1.2)$$

that is, κ is the mean age of childbearing in the stable population. The basic proposition is that the addition of a girl or woman aged x to the population at time zero adds an expected $v(x)e^{rt}/\kappa$ baby girls at time t, always supposing the continuance of the same regime of fertility and mortality. The simplest derivation of this takes off from the real term of solution 5.7.2 to the Lotka renewal equation. (A self-contained version is provided in the appendix to this chapter.)

Reproductive Value from the Lotka Integral Equation

One Woman Aged x. The continuous model of Section 5.7 provides the curve of descendants of an arbitrary initial age distribution, and its asymptotic trajectory is the real term $Q_1 e^{r_1 t}$ of (5.7.2), the value of Q_1 being given by (5.7.4). For a distribution consisting of one woman aged x, disregarding questions of continuity and of random variation, we find that the children expected at time t to $t + dt$ are $[l(x+t)/l(x)]m(x+t)\,dt$, which is therefore the function $G(t)$. Entering it in (5.7.4), that is in $Q_1 = \int_0^\beta e^{-rt} G(t) \, dt / \kappa$, we have

$$Q_1 = \frac{\int_0^{\beta-x} e^{-rt} [l(x+t)/l(x)] m(x+t) \, dt}{\kappa}, \qquad (6.1.3)$$

which except for the divisor κ is identical with $v(x)$ of (6.1.1), giving the discounted value of the expected future births to a woman aged x. In the special case of a baby just born, $x = 0$; and, by virtue of (6.1.3) and the characteristic equation (5.1.2), $Q_1 = 1/\kappa$.

Stable Age Distribution.   The same constant Q_1 can be readily evaluated for a population of unity having the stable age distribution $be^{-ra}l(a)$. We can guess in advance from the nature of stability that the asymptotic population will be e^{rt} and the births be^{rt}, so Q_1 must equal b for this case.

The proof seems simplest if we start by calculating the total expected reproductive value of a stable population:

$$\int_0^\beta be^{-rx}l(x)v(x)\,dx,$$

then cancel the $e^{-rx}l(x)$ with the denominator of $v(x)$ of (6.1.1) to find

$$b\int_0^\beta \int_x^\beta e^{-ra}l(a)m(a)\,da\,dx,$$

and finally integrate by parts to obtain

$$b\int_0^\beta ae^{-ra}l(a)m(a)\,da = b\kappa$$

as the reproductive value of a population of unity having a stable age distribution. The constant Q_1 is this total reproductive value divided by κ, that is, $b\kappa/\kappa = b$, as suggested by intuition.

Arbitrary Age Distribution.   A more general statement can be made: whatever the initial age distribution $P(x)$ of a closed population acted on by fixed rates of birth and death, its births have an asymptotic trajectory Q_1e^{rt} where Q_1, defined by (5.7.4), is equal to $\int_0^\beta P(x)v(x)\,dx/\kappa$, that is, the sum of reproductive value in the population divided by the mean age of childbearing.

To see this, note that the total reproductive value of $P(x)$ is

$$V = \int_0^\beta P(x)v(x)\,dx = \int_0^\beta P(x)\int_0^{\beta-x}e^{-rt}\frac{l(x+t)}{l(x)}m(x+t)\,dt\,dx. \quad (6.1.4)$$

But this is the same as the numerator of Q_1 in (5.7.4), where $G(t)$ is the number of children expected to be generated by the initial population $P(x)$. For the number of those children born at time t will be

$$G(t) = \int_0^\beta P(x)\frac{l(x+t)}{l(x)}m(x+t)\,dx, \quad (6.1.5)$$

and multiplying by e^{-rt} and then integrating over t gives the double integral in (6.1.4). This demonstrates that $Q_1 = V/\kappa$, where V is the number of women, each weighted by the $v(x)$ for her age x. Once again, $1/\kappa$ of the present value of the balance outstanding by age x in the hypothetical loan is equal to the contribution of a woman aged x to the ultimate trajectory, and both the loan and the trajectory are additive for a group of women of arbitrary ages.

The foregoing proof depends on the solution of the integral equation. The appendix proof, on the other hand, stands on its own feet.

Once we know the effect on the birth trajectory of adding one girl and assume a fixed birth rate b, we can obtain the effect on the population trajectory by dividing by b. This *is* obvious, for since the birth rate b is B/P, births divided by population, the population must be $P = B/b$, births divided by the birth rate. Hence the effect of adding a girl or woman aged x is to add $v(x)e^{rt}/\kappa$ to ultimate births and $v(x)e^{rt}/\kappa b$ to ultimate population.

To obtain some intuitive feeling for the reason why the effect of one child just born on the ultimate birth trajectory is to raise it by $v_0 e^{rt}/\kappa = e^{rt}/\kappa$, rather than just e^{rt} or some other value, suppose that all children are born at the same maternal age and that this age is κ. Then the birth of an additional girl child now will result in R_0 girl children in κ years, R_0^2 children in 2κ years, and R_0^n in the nth generation, where R_0 is, as before, the net reproduction rate; that is to say, a child born now outlines a birth curve (Fig. 6.1) rising in the ratio of R_0 every κ years, but with births

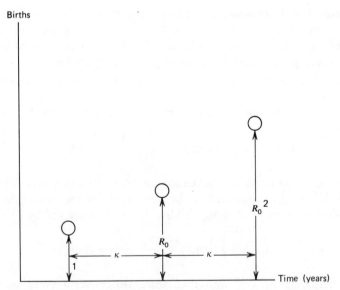

Fig. 6.1 Effect of one birth if all children are born at age κ of mother.

occurring only at κ-year intervals. In other words, the curve outlined gives the number of births per κ years resulting from one birth at the outset; it is reduced to births per year by dividing by κ: e^{r}/κ. This argument is at best heuristic; the result applies much more generally than to the primitive model in which all births occur at the same maternal age.

Numerical Calculation

The expression for $v(x)$ in (6.1.1) applies to exact age x, and an approximation analogous to that customarily made for the stable age distribution is

$$v_x \doteq \frac{e^{-2\frac{1}{2}r}{}_5L_xF_x + e^{-7\frac{1}{2}r}{}_5L_{x+5}F_{x+5} + \cdots}{l_x}. \tag{6.1.6}$$

This, with numerator and denominator multiplied by e^{-rx}, is shown in Table 6.1 for Mauritius females, 1966. Figure 6.2 shows the curves of $v(x)$ for Mauritius, the United States, and Hungary, taken from Keyfitz and Flieger (1971, pp. 315, 361, and 443).

For the average reproductive value for the age interval x to $x+4$ at last birthday the recurrence formula

$$_5V_x = \tfrac{5}{2}F_x + \frac{e^{-5r}{}_5L_{x+5}}{_5L_x}\left(\tfrac{5}{2}F_{x+5} + {}_5V_{x+5}\right) \tag{6.1.7}$$

Table 6.1   Calculation of reproductive values for females of exact ages 0, 5, 10,...,50, Mauritius, 1966; $r = 0.0305371$

Age	$_5L_xF_x$	$e^{-\left(x+2\frac{1}{2}\right)r}$	$\sum_{y=x}^{\beta-5} e^{-\left(y+2\frac{1}{2}\right)r}{}_5L_yF_y$	$e^{-rx}l_x$	v_x
x	(1)	(2)	(3)	(4)	(5)=(3)/(4)
0		0.92650	1	1	1
5		0.79531	1	0.78463	1.2745
10	0.0014	0.68269	1	0.66822	1.4965
15	0.1858	0.58602	0.99907	0.57152	1.7481
20	0.6236	0.50304	0.89019	0.48700	1.8279
25	0.6061	0.43181	0.57649	0.41212	1.3988
30	0.4730	0.37067	0.31477	0.34841	0.9034
35	0.3239	0.31818	0.13944	0.29392	0.4744
40	0.1201	0.27312	0.03639	0.24719	0.1472
45	0.0146	0.23445	0.00358	0.20816	0.0172
50	0.0008	0.20125	0.00016	0.17341	0.0009

Source: Net maternity function from Keyfitz and Flieger (1971, p. 315).

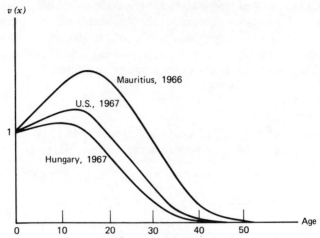

Fig. 6.2   Curves of reproductive value for females of three countries.

Table 6.2   Values of $_5V_x$, the Fisher reproductive value of females aged x to $x+4$ at last birthday, and $_5V_x/(b\kappa)$, the coefficient of the amount by which population at time t is raised by one added person aged x to $x+4$ at time zero, Mauritius, 1966

Age	$_5V_x$	$_5V_x/(b\kappa)$
0–4	1.159	1.092
5–9	1.381	1.301
10–14	1.618	1.524
15–19	1.783	1.679
20–24	1.611	1.517
25–29	1.151	1.084
30–34	0.690	0.650
35–39	0.312	0.294
40–44	0.083	0.078
45–49	0.009	0.008
$v_0 = 1$		
$v_0/(b\kappa) = \dfrac{1}{(0.03889)(27.30)} = 0.942$		

Source: Keyfitz and Flieger (1971), p. 315.

provides a reasonable approximation. However, the $_5V_x$ of Table 6.2 was calculated, not in this way, but by the method (easier if a computer is available) of finding the left eigenvalue of the projection matrix referred to in Section 5.7.

Evidently total reproductive value of a population of arbitrary age distribution acted on by a fixed regime increases at rate r in the short as well as the long run. Such a statement is conspicuously not true for the size of the total population, whose increase in the short run depends on its age distribution. Both births and population acted on by a fixed regime *ultimately* go into an exponential trajectory with parameter r; the total of reproductive values *immediately* follows an exponential trajectory (Fisher, 1930, p. 30).

The above like other pieces of theory in this book can be justified only by its ability to answer demographic questions. The following section deals with the first of a series of such questions.

6.2 ULTIMATE EFFECT OF SMALL OUT-MIGRATION OCCURRING IN A GIVEN YEAR

When people leave a crowded island like Barbados or Java, they make life somewhat easier for those who remain behind, assuming that the rates of mortality and fertility do not change as a result of their departure.

The age at which they leave determines the effect. Departures of persons who are already past the ages of reproduction cannot influence the ultimate population trajectory; the effect of their leaving is only the subtraction of the person-years they themselves will live from the time of departure to death.

A one-time departure of a person of reproductive age or below will lower the expected population trajectory, but cannot change its rate of climb as long as the age-specific rates of birth and death remain unchanged. In symbols, if the ultimate trajectory is Qe^{rt}, a one-time departure of an individual or a group under age β can lower Q but will not alter r. It follows from the theory of Section 6.1 that a female of age x leaving reduces the female births at time t by $v(x)e^{rt}/\kappa$ and the female population at time t by $v(x)e^{rt}/(b\kappa)$, where we take t to be large. Thus the change in Q for population due to the departure of one female aged x is $\Delta Q = - v(x)/(b\kappa)$.

We are still on the one-sex model and suppose female dominance, that is, that births are determined by the number of females at the several ages and not by the number of males. This would be true if males were in the majority or polygyny prevailed or artificial insemination were applied. The extension of the ideas of the present chapter to a genuine two-sex model depends on behavioral variables not readily incorporable in demographic theory.

The effect of a one-time bulge in births follows readily. With ΔB extra births in a given year the birth trajectory would be raised $e^{rt}\Delta B/\kappa$, and the population trajectory would be raised this amount divided by the birth rate b.

Does a female of random age affect the ultimate population more or less than a girl baby? The former, entering at time zero, raises the population at time t an expected e^{rt}, while the latter raises it by $e^{rt}/(b\kappa)$. The mean age of childbearing κ is never very far from 27, and the reciprocal of 27 is 0.037. For low-fertility populations b is considerably less than $1/\kappa \doteq 0.037$; hence a baby has more effect than a female between zero and ω randomly chosen from the stable age distribution. For high-fertility populations, on the other hand, b is greater than $1/\kappa$ and a baby has less expected effect than a randomly selected female. Thus for Mexico the departure of a woman of random age has more effect than averting one birth; for the United States averting a birth has more effect.

The same technique can be used to find a variety of equivalents. By what amount, for example, would births have to drop in a particular year to offset an immigration of 1000 women aged 15 to 19 in the same year? The population at distant time t resulting from 1000 women aged 15 to 19 is $1000_5V_{15}e^{rt}/(b\kappa)$. The population from B births at time t is $Bv_0e^{rt}/(b\kappa)$. Equating these two expressions, we obtain

$$B = \frac{1000_5V_{15}}{v_0}$$

as the required equivalent number of births. From the Mauritius information in Table 6.2 we have, since $_5V_x$ is normed to $v_0 = 1$,

$$B = 1000_5V_{15} = 1783.$$

In any one year (or other period) a drop of 1783 female births would be required to offset the immigration of 1000 women aged 15 to 19 at last birthday.

6.3 EFFECT OF CONTINUING BIRTH CONTROL AND STERILIZATION

Suppose that a few women each year resort to birth control when they are of age a, and this occurs year after year, so that the birth rate $m(a)$ is permanently lowered for age a, but all other age-specific birth rates remain unaltered. If the change in the age-specific birth rate in the single year of age a is $\Delta m(a)$, a quantity that will carry a minus sign for decrease in $m(a)$, the change in the intrinsic rate of the population is determined by finding the derivative $dr/dm(a)$ in the characteristic equation $\int_\alpha^\beta e^{-rx}l(x)m(x)dx = 1$ as in Section 5.3, and for finite increments Δr and $\Delta m(a)$ is approximately

$$\Delta r \doteq -\frac{e^{-ra}l(a)\Delta m(a)}{\kappa}, \tag{6.3.1}$$

the same as (5.3.5). The result depends on $\Delta m(a)$ being small enough so that e^{-ra}, as well as κ, is substantially unaffected. Subject to this same condition, we can find the combined effect of small increments at two different ages, say a and $a+1$. The effect on r will be approximately the sum of the Δr for $\Delta m(a)$ and that for $\Delta m(a+1)$, and similarly for any other groups of ages.

Now suppose a permanent change in $m(a)$ for all a from age x onward, so that the new birth function is $m(a)$, $a < x$, and $(1-f)m(a)$, $a \geq x$, f being a small positive or negative fraction. This could be the result of sterilization becoming the custom at age x, or of the fraction f of women at age x turning to conventional birth control in order to avoid all further children. If f is small we can enter $-fm(a)$ for $\Delta m(a)$ in the preceding display, and find the total effect Δr by adding the Δr's for the several ages:

$$\Delta r = -\frac{f\int_x^\beta e^{-ra}l(a)m(a)\,da}{\kappa}. \tag{6.3.2}$$

The integral here will be recognized as the same one that turned up in $v(x)$ of (6.1.1). Entering $v(x)$ makes this

$$\Delta r = -\frac{fe^{-rx}l(x)v(x)}{\kappa}.$$

In words, the decrease by the fraction f of fertility rates for all ages above x lowers the intrinsic rate by $v(x)$ multiplied by $fe^{-rx}l(x)/\kappa$. Remembering that $be^{-rx}l(x)$ is the fraction of the population at age x, where at this point it is convenient to make x integral and have it represent exact ages $x-\frac{1}{2}$ to $x+\frac{1}{2}$, we can say that the decrease in r is $f/(b\kappa)$ times the fraction of the population aged x, times the reproductive value at age x. More simply, the integral in (6.3.2) is the fraction of current mothers aged x and over, so (6.3.2) tells us that the effect on r is equal to the fraction f dropping out of childbearing, times the fraction of babies born to women aged x and over, divided by the mean age of childbearing. Designating by b_x the fraction of births occurring to mothers aged x and over, (6.3.2) can be written

$$\Delta r = -\frac{fb_x}{\kappa}.$$

Conventional birth control, sterilization, or mortality, if they take place year after year can lower births to women over age x by a small fraction f, and if they do the rate of increase r is reduced by f times the fraction b_x of children born to women aged x and older, divided by the mean age of childbearing.

The preceding discussion covers also the consequences of a fall in the death rate. Suppose that the rate at ages $x - \frac{1}{2}$ to $x + \frac{1}{2}$ goes from $\mu(x)$ to $\mu(x) + \Delta\mu(x)$ and remains at that level, or (what is practically the same) that $\Delta\mu(x)/\delta$ is permanently added to the density $\mu(x)$ over a narrow age interval δ. Then all the results of this section apply. The derivation first finds the effect of $\Delta\mu(x)/\delta$ on $l(x)$, using the approximate formula $e^{-\Delta\mu(x)/\delta} \doteq 1 - \Delta\mu(x)/\delta$. Thereafter the derivation is the same as for (6.3.1), since $l(a)$ and $m(a)$ enter symmetrically into the characteristic equation.

6.4   LARGE CHANGE IN REGIME

So far only small changes have been discussed. We now ask the same question in reference to an arbitrary, possibly large, change: if birth control is applied by women aged x and above, what fraction of births must they avoid in order to change the rate of increase from r to $r + \Delta r$?

Suppose that in every cohort women aged x and higher apply birth control to the point where they reduce their age-specific rates by the fraction f of what they were before; sterilization of f of the women reaching age x would have this effect. The original intrinsic rate of increase was found by solving for r in the characteristic equation. The equation for the new rate of increase $r + \Delta r$ breaks down into two parts:

$$\int_\alpha^\beta \exp\left[-(r+\Delta r)a\right]l(a)m(a)\,da - f\int_x^\beta \exp\left[-(r+\Delta r)a\right]l(a)m(a)\,da = 1,$$

$$(6.4.1)$$

where we suppose $\alpha \leqslant x \leqslant \beta$. Equation 6.4.1 could be solved for x if f and $r + \Delta r$ were given, or for $r + \Delta r$ if x and f were given. A simple explicit solution is available for f, the fraction of decrease above the given age x that will suffice to change the intrinsic rate from r to $r + \Delta r$:

$$f = \frac{\displaystyle\int_\alpha^\beta \exp\left[-(r+\Delta r)a\right]l(a)m(a)\,da - 1}{\displaystyle\int_x^\beta \exp\left[-(r+\Delta r)a\right]l(a)m(a)\,da}.$$

$$(6.4.2)$$

Result 6.4.2 depends in no way on Δr being small. [Find its limiting value when Δr is small.]

The numerator of (6.4.2) is bound to be positive for $\Delta r < 0$, corresponding to the birth control formulation in which f is defined as positive and birth rates go from $m(a)$ to $(1-f)m(a)$. In the special case where the desired $r + \Delta r = 0$ we would have the simpler form

$$f = \frac{\int_{\alpha}^{\beta} l(a)m(a)\,da - 1}{\int_{x}^{\beta} l(a)m(a)\,da} = \frac{R_0 - 1}{\int_{x}^{\beta} l(a)m(a)\,da}. \tag{6.4.3}$$

The f of (6.4.3) is the fraction by which women aged x and over must reduce fertility to bring the rate of population increase r down to zero. The age x is arbitrary but is required to stay within certain limits if $0 < f < 1$. For data for Colombia, 1965, one observes that no reduction of fertility in women 30 and over could bring stationarity if ages under 30 retained existing rates, for we have $R_0 = 2.267$ and $\int_{30}^{50} l(a)m(a)\,da = 1.001$, and hence a drop to $R_0 = 1$ would not occur even if all fertility above age 30 disappeared.

One would have thought that a girl child would contribute the same amount to the ultimate trajectory irrespective of the age of her mother; all babies start at age zero, after all. The expression $\Delta r = e^{-ra}l(a)\Delta m(a)/\kappa$ in (6.3.1) is consistent with this view, for it says that the effect of a small change $\Delta m(a)$ in the age-specific birth rate is proportional to $e^{-ra}l(a)$, that is, proportional to the number of women of that age in the stable population; this has to be right, in that a given change in the birth rate will alter the number of babies in proportion to the number of women to whom the change is applied. The expression for Δr in (6.3.1) supposes that $\Delta m(a)$ is small enough not to affect κ, the mean age of childbearing.

But for the ultimate effect of a large change that takes place generation after generation, it does make a difference whether women are young or old when they have their children. Avoiding births at age 40 is not as effective as avoiding them at age 20, because of the more rapid turnover of a population in which births occur to younger mothers. This is taken into account in (6.4.2) and (6.4.3).

6.5 EMIGRATION AS A POLICY APPLIED YEAR AFTER YEAR

Each year some inhabitants of Java go to Sumatra under an official transmigration program that has been government policy for two-thirds of a century. The authorities have always recognized that the amount of relief provided to Java depends on the age of the migrants at the time of their out-migration, and that young couples are the ideal ones to go, but they have tended to exaggerate the effect. Widjojo (1970) shows realistic population projections under alternative assumptions about the rate of movement, from which the consequences of different policies can be seen. In this section we will examine one aspect of policy only: the effect of the age of the migrants on the ultimate rate of increase of the population.

We can express (6.4.2) in terms of a generalization of reproductive value. In this general reproductive value, say $v_{x,\bar{r}}$, future children are discounted, not at the intrinsic rate r of the observed population, but at the rate $\bar{r}$ at which the emigration policy is to aim:

$$v_{x,\bar{r}} = \int_0^{\beta-x} e^{-\bar{r}t} \frac{l(x+t)}{l(x)} m(x+t)\,dt.$$

Then the alternative form of (6.4.2) is

$$f_x = \frac{v_{0,\bar{r}} - 1}{e^{-\bar{r}x} l_x v_{x,\bar{r}}}.$$ (6.5.4)

The argument of this section pivots on the simple result 6.5.4. If $\bar{r} = 0$, we obtain the fraction f_x emigrating out of each cohort for stationarity. In general, (6.5.4) serves to show how much emigration is required to attain the demographic objective represented by a rate of increase $\bar{r}$, given the continuance of the life table $l(a)$ and the birth rates $m(a)$.

To apply (6.5.4) we need only the net maternity function $l(a)m(a)$. For Mauritius, 1966, this is given in Table 6.1 in 5-year age intervals. The intrinsic rate of Mauritius is estimated at 30.54 per thousand. How much emigration will be required for the modest goal of bringing it down to 20 per thousand? If the emigrants are $x = 25$ years of age, (6.5.4) tells us that with $\bar{r} = 0.020$ a fraction $f_{25} = 0.417$ of each cohort must leave on reaching this age. If the emigrants are $x = 20$ years of age, the proportion that will have to leave is smaller, 0.279.

Thus, to bring about a drop from the actual increase of 30.54 per thousand to one of 20.00 per thousand, the departure of 41.7 percent of each cohort will be required if the emigrants leave at age 25, and of 27.9 percent if they leave at age 20. Emigration is not the easiest means of population control.

To find the amount of emigration that will hold the ultimate rate of increase down to zero we need the value of f_x when $\bar{r}$ is replaced by zero in (6.5.4). The integral in the numerator is then R_0, the net reproduction rate, and the integral in the denominator is the part of R_0 beyond age x. Hence we have again (6.4.3),

$$f_x = \frac{R_0 - 1}{\int_x^\beta l(a)m(a)\,da} \tag{6.5.5}$$

as the fraction of the age x that must emigrate per year to hold the ultimate population stationary, x again being low enough for f_x not to exceed unity. To see (6.5.5) independently of its derivation as a special case of (6.5.4) we note that to bring the net reproduction rate down to 1 we need to lose $R_0 - 1$ births per woman from each birth cohort. The number of births per woman lost by removing a proportion f of women at age x is

$$f_x \int_x^\beta l(a)m(a)\,da.$$

Equating this to $R_0 - 1$ yields (6.5.5).

6.6 THE MOMENTUM OF POPULATION GROWTH

The authorities of some underdeveloped countries fear that once birth control is introduced their populations will immediately stop increasing. Such fears are misplaced, partly because diffusion takes time, and even when birth control is available it is not immediately used. But let us leave aside this behavioral aspect, and consider only the momentum of population growth that arises because the age distribution of a rapidly increasing population is favorable to increase. Suppose that all couples adopt birth control immediately and drop their births to a level that permits bare replacement. With U. S. mortality rates fertile couples need on the average (Section 11.3) 2.36 children to give a net reproduction rate R_0 of unity. An average of 2.36 children covers the loss of those dying before maturity, the fact that not everyone finds a mate, and some sterility among couples.

We saw that without any change in birth rates the ultimate birth trajectory due to $P(x)\,dx$ persons at age x to $x + dx$ would be $e^{rt}P(x)v(x)\,dx/\kappa$, and for the whole population distributed as $P(x)$ would be $e^{rt}\int_0^\beta P(x)v(x)\,dx/\kappa$. For calculating the effect of the fall to bare replacement we want the trajectory based on the existing age distribution $P(x)$, but with a function $v^*(x)$, corresponding to an intrinsic rate $r = 0$. We can arrange this, without changing any other feature of the age incidence of childbearing, by replacing $m(x)$ by $m^*(x) = m(a)/R_0$, which will ensure that $R_0^* = 1$ and $r^* = 0$. Then the ultimate stationary number of births must be

$$\int_0^\beta P(x)v^*(x)\,dx/\kappa, \tag{6.6.1}$$

where κ becomes μ, the mean age of childbearing in the stationary population because $v^* = 0$:

$$\frac{v^*(x)}{\kappa} = \frac{1}{\mu l(x)} \int_x^\beta \frac{l(a)m(a)\,da}{R_0}.$$

Ascertaining the ultimate stationary total population requires dividing by b, the stationary birth rate, which is the same as multiplying by $\overset{o}{e}_0$, the expectation of life at age zero.

Expression 6.6.1 is readily usable. If we have a table of the net maternity function in 5-year age intervals up to age 49 and the initial age distribution, then, by cumulating the net maternity function to obtain $_5V_x^*$ and multiplying 10 pairs of $_5P_x$ and $_5V_x^*$, we have the ultimate stationary population

$$\overset{o}{e}_0 \Sigma_0^{\beta-5} \, _5P_x \, _5V_x^* / \mu, \tag{6.6.2}$$

where

$$_5V_x^* = \frac{(5/_5L_x)\left(\frac{1}{2}\, _5L_x F_x + _5L_{x+5}F_{x+5} + \cdots\right)}{R_0}.$$

This calculation will give the same result as a full population projection with the new $m^*(x)$.

If the initial age distribution $P(x)$ can be taken as stable, the result is even simpler. Entering $P(x) = P_0\, be^{-rx}l(x)$ in (6.6.1), where r is the intrinsic rate before the drop to zero increase, canceling out $l(x)$ in numerator and denominator, and multiplying by $\overset{o}{e}_0$ to produce the stationary population rather than stationary births, we obtain

$$(1/P_0)\overset{o}{e}_0 \int_0^\beta P(x)v^*(x)\,dx = \frac{b\overset{o}{e}_0}{\mu} \int_0^\beta \int_x^\beta e^{-rx} l(a)\frac{m(a)}{R_0}\,da\,dx \tag{6.6.3}$$

as the ratio of the ultimate stationary population to the population at the time when the fall occurs.

The double integral is evaluated by writing b_x for $\int_x^\beta l(a)m(a)\,da/R_0$; and, integrating by parts in (6.6.3) to obtain

$$\frac{b\overset{o}{e}_0}{\mu} \int_0^\beta e^{-rx}b_x\,dx = \frac{b\overset{o}{e}_0}{\mu}\left[\frac{e^{-rx}}{-r}b_x\Big|_0^\beta - \frac{1}{r}\int_0^\beta e^{-rx}\frac{l(x)m(x)}{R_0}\,dx\right],$$

we find that the right-hand side reduces to

$$\frac{b\overset{o}{e}_0}{r\mu}\left(\frac{R_0-1}{R_0}\right), \tag{6.6.4}$$

on applying the fact that $b_0 = 1$ and $\int_0^\beta e^{-rx} l(x) m(x) dx = 1$. Expression 6.6.4 gives the ratio of the ultimate population to population just before the fall to zero increase and is the main result of this section.

For Ecuador, 1965, the data are $1000b = 44.82$, $\overset{o}{e}_0 = 60.16$, $1000r = 33.31$, $\mu = 29.41$, and $R_0 = 2.59$. These make expression 6.6.4 equal to 1.69. By simple projection or by (6.6.2), which does not depend on the stable assumption, we would have a ratio of the ultimate stationary to the present population of 1.67. This experiment and others show that the degree of stability in many underdeveloped countries makes (6.6.4) realistic.

James Frauenthal has pointed out to me that $(b\overset{o}{e}_0 / r\mu)[(R_0 - 1)/R_0]$ of (6.6.4) is very nearly $b\overset{o}{e}_0 / \sqrt{R_0}$. For R_0 is approximately $e^{r\mu}$, and hence

$$\frac{b\overset{o}{e}_0}{r\mu} \left(\frac{R_0 - 1}{R_0} \right) = \frac{b\overset{o}{e}_0}{\sqrt{R_0}} \left[\frac{e^{r\mu/2} - e^{-r\mu/2}}{r\mu} \right]$$

$$= \frac{b\overset{o}{e}_0}{\sqrt{R_0}} \left(1 + \frac{r^2\mu^2}{24} + \frac{r^4\mu^4}{960} + \cdots \right)$$

on expanding both the exponentials in powers of $r\mu$. The product $r\mu$ is of the order of unity, so that $r^2\mu^2/24$ must be close to 0.05. The example of Ecuador, 1965, gives $b\overset{o}{e}_0 / \sqrt{R_0} = 1.68$ as compared with 1.69 for (6.6.4).

To obtain an intuitive meaning of this, note that the absolute number of births just after the fall must be $1/R_0$ times the births just before the fall. Births will subsequently rise and then drop in waves of diminishing amplitude, and it seems likely that the curve will oscillate about the mean of the absolute numbers before and after the fall. If the geometric mean of 1 and $1/R_0$ applies, the ultimate number of births will be $1/\sqrt{R_0}$ times the births before the fall. In that case the ultimate population will be $\overset{o}{e}_0 / \sqrt{R_0}$ times the births before the fall, or $b\overset{o}{e}_0 / \sqrt{R_0}$ times the population before the fall.

In words, the approximation $b\overset{o}{e}_0 / \sqrt{R_0}$ says that the momentum factor is proportional to the birth rate and the expectation of life, and inversely proportional to the square root of the net reproduction rate. Table 6.3 suggests to what degree the factor depends on $\overset{o}{e}_0$ and to what degree on R_0 for an initial birth rate of $1000b = 45$. The conclusion is that with an immediate fall in fertility to bare replacement Ecuador and demographically similar countries would increase by about 50 percent or more before attaining stationarity. Note that (6.6.4) or $b\overset{o}{e}_0 / \sqrt{R_0}$ is a good approximation to the degree in which the age distribution before the fall is stable.

Table 6.3   Values of $b\overset{o}{e}_0/\sqrt{R_0}$, the approximate ratio of the ultimate
to the present population if the birth rate falls immediately from
$b = 0.045$ to that needed for bare replacement, $1/\overset{o}{e}_0$

Initial	$\overset{o}{e}_0$		
R_0	40	50	60
1.5	1.47	1.84	2.20
2.0	1.27	1.59	1.91
2.5	1.14	1.42	1.71

[Using model tables or otherwise, comment on the consistency of the
pattern $b = 0.045$, $\overset{o}{e}_0 = 60$, $R_0 = 1.5$ that gives rise to the ratio 2.20 in Table
6.3.]

6.7   ELIMINATING HEART DISEASE WOULD MAKE VERY LITTLE DIF-FERENCE TO POPULATION INCREASE, WHEREAS ERADICATION OF MALARIA MAKES A GREAT DEAL OF DIFFERENCE

Age distributions of deaths from malaria and heart disease are shown in
Table 6.4 for the Philippines, 1959. Evidently malaria affects the young
ages, whereas heart disease is negligible before middle life. Though the two
causes are responsible for about equal numbers of deaths, malaria has a
much greater effect on the chance that a child will survive to reproductive
age and on the number of women living through reproduction.

Finding the effect on the population trajectory of eliminating deaths in
any one year requires that each death at age x be evaluated as $v(x)$, that is
to say, we need the sum $\int_0^\beta P(x)v(x)dx$, where now $P(x)dx$ is the population removed by death at ages x to $x + dx$. (The constants b and κ will not
affect the relative positions of the two causes.) The broad age groups and
lumping of the two sexes in Table 6.4 prevent us from attaining high
accuracy. Table 6.4 shows unweighted arithmetic averages of $v(x)$ for the
age groups required. The value of the malaria deaths, if they were female,
would be $(251)(1.21) + (156)(1.64) + (133)(2.00) + (186)(0.76) = 967$; that of
the heart disease deaths similarly calculated would be 250. In practice men
and women influence mortality in different degrees, and no easy way to
allow for this suggests itself.

But the complexities that a two-sex model would introduce would not
greatly affect the present conclusion: although absolute numbers of deaths
from heart disease are about equal to those from malaria, malaria has
nearly 4 times the effect on subsequent population.

Table 6.4   Deaths from malaria and heart disease, Philippines, 1959 and 1960

Age x to x+n	Malaria, Cause B–16, 1959	Degenerative heart disease, Cause B–26, 1959	$_nV_x$ Reproductive value for females, Philippines, 1960
All ages	913	918	
–5	251	12	1.21
5–14	156	7	1.64
15–24	133	37	2.00
25–44	186	198	0.76
45–64	138	322	0
65+	45	333	0
Unknown	4	9	
Total reproductive value for deaths of stated age	967	250	

Source: *United Nations Demographic Yearbook*, 1961, p. 498; Keyfitz and Flieger (1971), p. 411.

APPENDIX   REPRODUCTIVE VALUE AS A CONTRIBUTION TO FUTURE BIRTHS

Section 6.1 appeals to intuition to make it appear likely that the effect of adding one girl or woman aged x to the population is to raise the number of births t years hence, where t is large, in proportion to $v(x)e^{rt}$, $v(x)$ being defined as

$$v(x) = \frac{\int_x^\beta e^{-ra}l(a)m(a)\,da}{e^{-rx}l(x)}.$$

This result can be derived from the Lotka equation of Section 5.7, but here we examine a demonstration that is self contained, using the familiar device of calculating the situation at time t from two successive moments near the present. For purposes of this appendix $v(x)$ will be defined afresh, in terms of the ultimate birth trajectory.

Suppose that a woman aged x at time zero contributes $v(x)e^{rt}$ to the births at subsequent time t, where $v(x)$ is to be determined and t is large.

This means that her disappearance would lower the ultimate birth trajectory by $v(x)e^{rt}$. We assume that age-specific birth and death rates are fixed, so that her descendants will ultimately increase in geometric proportion and be unaffected by other members of the population.

The woman aged x can, in the next short period of time and age, say Δ, have a child, and whether or not she has a child can survive to the next age, $x+\Delta$. The chance of her having a child is $m(x)\Delta$, and the chance of her surviving is $l(x+\Delta)/l(x)$. By having a child she would contribute $v(0)e^{r(t-\Delta)}$ to the births at time t, and by surviving she would convert herself into a woman of reproductive value $v(x+\Delta)$ and so contribute $v(x+\Delta)e^{r(t-\Delta)}$. If the progression of childbearing and aging at the given rates over the time Δ is not to affect the ultimate birth trajectory, we can equate the two expressions for later births:

$$v(x)e^{rt} = \left[m(x)v(0)\Delta + \frac{l(x+\Delta)}{l(x)}v(x+\Delta) \right] e^{r(t-\Delta)}. \qquad (A.1)$$

If we multiply both sides of (A.1) by

$$\frac{1}{\Delta}\frac{l(x)}{v(0)}e^{-rx}e^{-rt},$$

we obtain

$$\frac{1}{\Delta}l(x)\frac{v(x)}{v(0)}e^{-rx} = m(x)l(x)e^{-rx}e^{-r\Delta}$$
$$+ \frac{1}{\Delta}l(x+\Delta)\frac{v(x+\Delta)}{v(0)}e^{-r(x+\Delta)}. \qquad (A.2)$$

Subtracting the rightmost term from both sides and letting $\Delta \to 0$, we have directly

$$-\frac{d}{dx}l(x)\frac{v(x)}{v(0)}e^{-rx} = m(x)l(x)e^{-rx},$$

and integrating gives

$$e^{-rx}l(x)\frac{v(x)}{v(0)} = \int_x^\beta e^{-ra}l(a)m(a)\,da, \qquad (A.3)$$

so that, if $v(0)$ is set equal to unity, $v(x)$ again comes out as shown in (6.1.1). No constant of integration is needed, since both sides are unity for $x=0$. Equation (A.3) establishes $v(x)$ to within a multiplicative constant.

Let us find the constant $v(0)$ that corresponds to the ultimate effect of adding one female to the population.

If the initial age distribution is stable, we know that the population at time t must be e^{rt} for each person initially present, and hence the births at time t are be^{rt}. Equating the two values for time t, we have

$$be^{rt} = \int_0^\beta be^{-rx}l(x)v(x)\,dx\,e^{rt};$$

(A.4)

since from (A.3) $v(x)$ may be written as

$$\frac{v(0)}{e^{-rx}l(x)} \int_x^\beta e^{-ra}l(a)m(a)\,da,$$

the $be^{-rx}l(x)$ within the integral of (A.4), as well as e^{rt} outside the integral, cancels, and we obtain the following equation for $v(0)$:

$$\frac{1}{v(0)} = \int_0^\beta \int_x^\beta e^{-ra}l(a)m(a)\,da\,dx.$$

(A.5)

The integral on the right-hand side is evaluated by integration by parts and turns out to be κ, the mean age of childbearing in the stable population. This proves that for the $v(x)$ function of this appendix, $v(0) = \frac{1}{\kappa}$, and that the $v(x)$ function of the main body of the chapter, defined in (6.1.1), gives the ultimate birth trajectory due to a woman aged x as $e^{rt}v(x)/\kappa$.

Chapter Seven

UNDERSTANDING POPULATION CHARACTERISTICS

To understand a phenomenon we must break it down into simple elements and then put these elements together again in such a way as to reconstruct the phenomenon. This was the method Descartes proposed for study of the physical world, and it can be used to make intelligible the population characteristics presented as census and other data. Such characteristics as age, sex, marital status, birthplace, occupation, and industry can be treated by the Cartesian method, though not all with equal effectiveness.

The transition from one year of age to the next against the hazard of death, and the population rate of increase, are elements that help to explain age distribution. The transition from one school grade to the next in the face of the hazard of dropping out has a bearing both on the grade distribution of pupils presently in the schools and on the distribution by years of schooling completed in the population at large. The transition into the labor force and that into retirement go some distance toward accounting for the distribution of the population by labor force status. These transitions can be incorporated into models capable of approximating the present distribution of ages, schooling, and labor force participation.

Explanation involves many levels arranged in an infinite regression. Why the age distribution or the sex ratio is as it is is traceable through deeper and deeper stages, involving fetal mortality and its causes and the causes of death in young and older people. The present argument can go only one short step in this regression.

7.1 ACCOUNTING FOR AGE DISTRIBUTION

Young and Old Populations

The United States is celebrating its 200th birthday; France is older, having gained its independence from Roman colonialism about the fifth century and become a unified nation in the seventeenth century; Taiwan is much younger than either, having been established in its present form after World War II. In the United States the percentage of children under 15 years of age is 30.9, while in France it is 24.6; Taiwan has a larger proportion of children, 45.2 percent (all 1965 figures). For these three countries and for many others, the older the country as a political entity the smaller is the fraction of its population under 15 years of age. Yet no one could take seriously an assertion relating political to demographic age. The correlation can only be called spurious since we have no reason in logic to think that the fraction of children is related to political youth or age. Chapter 12 shows other weaknesses of a purely empirical approach to demography.

Let us here drop political age and call a country (demographically) young if it has a large fraction of children and a small fraction of old people. "Young" and "old" in terms of this definition will be explainable by the life table and rate of increase. Of 800 age distributions for various countries and times that are available for examination, that of Honduras in 1965 is the youngest, with 50.8 percent of its population reported as under 15 years of age. The average age of Honduran males was 19.8 years; of United States males, 30.8 years; of Swedish males, 36.1 years (again all for 1965). Demographic youth or age can have direct and traceable consequences. Other things being equal, if a country has many children to support, it will be occupied in building houses and schools for them and will have fewer resources for building factories to increase its future income. This issue will reappear in Section 12.6.

Our first attempt at explanation will again be Euler's stable age distribution (4.1.1), by which, under a fixed regime of mortality and fertility including the probability $l(a)$ of surviving from birth to age a and a rate of increase r, the population between ages a and $a + da$ is $e^{-ra}l(a)da$ per current birth, and as a proportion this is divided by its integral over the range zero to ω.

A comparison of (4.1.1) with observed proportions for two age groups and three countries appears in Table 7.1, all for females. Of the difference in the under 15 group between France and Taiwan ($45.2 - 23.6 = 21.6$

Table 7.1 Percentage of females under 15 and over 65 for three countries in 1965

	Percentage under 15		Percentage over 65	
Country	Observed	Stable	Observed	Stable
Taiwan	45.2	40.2	3.1	4.5
United States	29.8	28.4	10.4	10.6
France	23.6	26.5	15.3	12.2

percent) about two-thirds ($40.2 - 26.5 = 13.7$ percent) is accounted for on the stable model. The stable model accounts for a similar fraction of the differences in the numbers over 65.

The stable model we have constructed involves nothing but the $l(a)$, which depend on the present life table, and r, the rate of increase. Since it is based only on current information on birth and death, and does not take account of migration or of past wars and epidemics, we should be impressed by its capacity to explain so large a part of the differences among real age distributions.

Age Distribution as a Function of Rate of Increase

We saw earlier how the fraction of any age in a stable population is expressible in terms of the rate of increase of the population and the mean ages of the relevant subgroup. A special case, the fraction of population 65 years of age and over was treated in Section 4.7. In general terms the fraction between any pair of ages α and β is equal to

$$_{\beta-\alpha}C_\alpha = \frac{\int_\alpha^\beta e^{-ra}l(a)\,da}{\int_0^\omega e^{-ra}l(a)\,da}. \tag{7.1.1}$$

By a proposition cited in Section 5.2, $\ln[\int_0^\omega e^{-ra}f(a)\,da]$ generates the cumulants of the density distribution $f(a)$, the first cumulant being the mean, and the second and third cumulants being moments about the mean. We may define $f(a)$ as $l(a)/\int_0^\infty l(x)\,dx$ for the denominator, and the same for the numerator between α and β, outside of which $f(a)=0$. Normalizing (7.1.1) by dividing by $\int_\alpha^\beta l(a)\,da/\int_0^\omega l(a)\,da$, taking logarithms of both sides, and expanding the two cumulant-generating functions of $-r$ gives

$$\ln {}_{\beta-\alpha}C_\alpha = \ln\left(\frac{{}_{\beta-\alpha}L_\alpha}{\overset{o}{e}_0}\right) - \left[k_1 r - \frac{k_2 r^2}{2!} + \frac{k_3 r^3}{3!} - \cdots\right.$$

$$\left. - \left(\kappa_1 r - \frac{\kappa_2 r^2}{2!} + \frac{\kappa_3 r^3}{3!} - \cdots\right)\right], \qquad (7.1.2)$$

where the k's are the cumulants of the life table distribution between α and β, and the κ's are the cumulants over the whole range of the age distribution.

Hence to a first approximation, and on taking derivatives and then entering finite increments,

$$\Delta_{\beta-\alpha}C_\alpha \doteq (\kappa_1 - k_1)\,{}_{\beta-\alpha}C_\alpha\,\Delta r, \qquad (7.1.3)$$

as was established for special cases in Sections 4.3 and 4.7.

Putting $\alpha = 0$ and $\beta = 15$ shows that the proportion under age 15 goes up as r goes up, since k_1, the mean age of those under 15, is bound to be less than κ_1, the mean age of the whole population. Similar considerations apply to other age intervals. The relation can be studied as the exponential of a quadratic or cubic wherever r is large enough to make further terms important.

The stable model does not always fit. Among 800 populations tested, that of England and Wales, 1881, comes closest; the Netherlands, 1901, is second. But even there agreement is not perfect. Females aged 0 to 14 in the actual population of England and Wales, 1881, comprised 35.5 percent; in the fitted stable model, 35.0 percent. Discrepancies between the model and the observed populations invariably demand our attention.

Since in Table 7.1 the 1965 rates of death were the source of the life table $l(a)$, and the 1965 intrinsic rate of increase was the source of r, one reason why the model can be at variance with reality is that different rates of death and increase applied in earlier years. This indeed appears to be the main source of discrepancy. In Taiwan birth rates have been falling; the 1965 birth rates are too low to represent the preceding 15 years. A calculation based on the stable model with 1959–61 birth and death rates shows 43.6 percent under 15, a value closer to the observed one.

For intervals α to β straddling the mean age, k and κ will not be very different; (7.1.3) shows that differences in r do not greatly affect the middle ages. By a similar argument drastic declines in the later ages are associated with increases in r.

Neutral and Nonneutral Change in Mortality

How do populations that have been subject to different death rates differ in age? If the difference is the same amount at all ages, it has no effect on the age distribution. If birth rates are the same and mortality at all ages has been higher by exactly 0.01 in one population than in the other, the age distributions will be identical (Coale, 1958).

This seems to be a paradox. A rise in mortality that prevents people from living to as old an age as they once did ought to make the population consist to a greater degree of young people, one would think. It certainly makes the prospect of attaining old age less than it was before for an individual; why does it not do the same for the community? Here, as in many other situations, the same rule does not apply to populations as to individuals.

When mortality is higher with fertility unchanged, the rate of increase is just enough lower to compensate as far as age distribution is concerned for the change in the life table. The canceling out is a property of exponential growth dovetailing with the exponential effect on $l(x)$ of an addition to $\mu(x)$.

If k (e.g., 0.01) is added to the mortality rate $\mu(x)$ at each age, so that it becomes $\mu^*(x) = \mu(x) + k$, the probability of surviving to age x is $l^*(x) = e^{-kx}l(x)$ instead of $l(x)$.

But if the age-specific birth rates are unchanged, the rate of increase of the population diminishes, and by exactly the same amount, k. The proof of this statement is that the new rate of increase r^* must satisfy the characteristic equation

$$\int_\alpha^\beta e^{-r^*x}l^*(x)m(x)\,dx = 1$$

or

$$\int_\alpha^\beta e^{-r^*x}e^{-kx}l(x)m(x)\,dx = 1$$

or

$$\int_\alpha^\beta e^{-(r^*+k)x}l(x)m(x)\,dx = 1.$$

Since the original r satisfied the same equation that $r^* + k$ now satisfies, by virtue of the uniqueness of the real root we have $r = r^* + k$, so that $r^* = r - k$; the new rate is exactly k less than the old rate.

Combining the preceding two paragraphs gives, for the new stable population on a radix of one current birth per year,

$$e^{-r^*x}l^*(x) = e^{-(r-k)x}e^{-kx}l(x) = e^{-rx}l(x);$$

hence the number of persons at age x per current birth is the same under the new regime as under the old.

Changes in mortality that have occurred historically can be distinguished according to whether they tended to be at younger or older ages, that is, whether or not they tended to lower the mean age of the stable population if the birth rate remained the same. We find that the improvements in England and Wales from 1861 to 1891 were on balance at younger ages, those between 1891 and 1911 were at older ages; and those from 1911 to 1931 again affected younger ages to a greater degree (Keyfitz, 1968, p. 191).

Accounting for Observed Ages

The first part of the analysis of age distributions here outlined is concerned with the regime of mortality and natural increase actually existing; the second, with trends in the regime during the lifetimes of the current population; the third, with extraordinary historical events, especially those that cause short-term fluctuations in birth and death. These events include wars, which reduce the numbers of males in their twenties; immigration, which usually consists of young adults; and famines, which especially affect young children. In this third part of the analysis theory does not help much; we must look at the record to see what happened.

Are Birth or Death Rates the Major Influence on Age Distribution?

The stable model, which can reconstruct an age distribution from a life table and rate of increase, enables us to compare two populations, say those of the United States and Madagascar, of which one is old and the other young, and to explain the difference between them. We know that the United States has lower birth rates as well as lower death rates; the question is, how much of the difference in ages is due to the difference in births, and how much to the difference in deaths?

Without the Cartesian decomposition, through the stable or some other model, no answer can be given to such a question. The rates of birth and death of both countries are what they are; their age distributions are what they are. We cannot even think of an experimental treatment of real populations that would answer the question, let alone perform one. But in a model we can vary one factor and see how the age distribution changes, and then vary the other and again see how the distribution changes. If the two kinds of change add up to the total change, we have decomposed the total; our model has paid off in providing without cost an experiment that tells the relative effects of birth and death on age when everything else remains unchanged.

Table 7.2 provides examples of the experimental treatment. For the stable model, with the female age-specific rates of birth and death observed in the United States in 1967, it shows 24.5 percent under 15 years of age (second item in second row). If we now alter the death rates to those of Madagascar, 1966, leaving the birth rates as they were, we find 22.0

Table 7.2 Features of age distribution and rate of increase obtained by combinations of female birth and death rates from five countries, stable model

Age-specific death rates of:	Age-specific birth rates of:				
	Venezuela, 1965	United States, 1967	Madagascar, 1966	England and Wales, 1968	Sweden, 1803–07
Percent under 15: $100_{15}C_0$					
Venezuela	47.7	23.9	47.8	23.6	34.2
United States	48.5	24.5	48.6	24.2	34.8
Madagascar	45.0	22.0	45.2	21.8	32.1
England and Wales	48.5	24.5	48.6	24.2	34.8
Sweden	43.6	21.0	43.8	20.8	31.3
Dependency ratio percent: $100(_{15}C_0 + {}_\infty C_{65})/{}_{50}C_{15}$					
Venezuela	102.1	58.8	102.4	58.7	70.3
United States	105.4	61.1	105.6	60.9	72.5
Madagascar	91.3	51.5	91.8	51.3	62.8
England and Wales	105.2	60.3	105.5	60.1	72.1
Sweden	85.6	46.7	86.2	46.6	58.9
Percent 65 and over: $100_\infty C_{65}$					
Venezuela	2.8	13.1	2.8	13.3	7.1
United States	2.8	13.5	2.8	13.7	7.3
Madagascar	2.7	12.0	2.7	12.2	6.5
England and Wales	2.8	13.1	2.7	13.3	7.1
Sweden	2.5	10.9	2.5	11.0	5.8
Intrinsic rate of natural increase per 1000: $1000r$					
Venezuela	38.5	4.9	38.6	4.5	19.5
United States	40.7	7.6	40.8	6.7	21.5
Madagascar	22.3	-11.3	22.5	-11.6	3.8
England and Wales	41.0	7.4	41.1	7.0	21.8
Sweden	24.3	-9.4	24.6	-9.6	6.4

percent under age 15. The higher death rates of Madagascar lower the proportion under 15 by 2.5 percentage points.

Now, retaining the death rates of the United States but entering in the stable model the birth rates of Madagascar, we find the proportion under age 15 rising from the original 24.5 percent to 48.6 percent. The higher birth rates of Madagascar raise the proportion under 15 by $48.6 - 24.5 = 24.1$ percentage points.

The two preceding paragraphs show that birth rates have about 10 times as much effect as do death rates on the proportion of a population under 15 years of age. As a check we take the differences in the other direction, starting with the same 45.2 percent for Madagascar births and deaths, subtracting 48.6 to find the effect of death rates at -3.4, and subtracting 22.0 to find the effect of birth rates at 23.2, so now births are 7 times as influential as deaths. The discrepancy is $(45.2 - 22.0) - (48.6 - 24.5) = -0.9$. This quantity is the interaction between birth and death: it is the difference between the effect of births in the presence of Madagascar deaths and the effect of births in the presence of United States deaths. It measures the uncertainty in the decomposition, and is small enough in this case not to affect our assertion that the age difference is due chiefly to the birth difference.

This may seem obvious for the proportion under age 15, which represents the births of the last 15 years and therefore ought to be closely related to the birth rate. More surprising is the outcome of the same analysis for the fraction of the population 65 years of age and older. Now we have for United States births and deaths 13.5 percent; a drop of only 1.5 to 12.0 for Madagascar with the change in deaths alone, and a drop of 10.7 to 2.8 with the change in births alone. Again births are the main factor, accounting for 8 times as much of the change as do deaths.

Similar calculations may be performed on Table 7.2 for the dependency ratio $(_{15}C_0 + _\infty C_{65})/_{50}C_{15}$, where $_nC_x$ is the population between exact ages x and $x + n$, as well as for the intrinsic rate r. Variation along rows (due to births with deaths held constant) is everywhere greater than variation down columns.

One cannot but be puzzled on noting that historically the birth rate has changed little in the countries of Asia and Africa since the time when they had a much lower proportion of young people than they now have. With little change over time in births, and much change in deaths, rates of increase and age distribution have changed drastically; how is it that Table 7.2 shows births as the cause? The answer is that cross-sectional analysis need have no relation to longitudinal (see Section 8.4). It is the fact that people are always born at age zero, whereas they die at all ages, that gives the birth rate more leverage on age distribution in a cross-sectional analysis such as that of Table 7.2; the historical trend is mostly determined by the acceleration of population increase due to falling mortality at young ages.

7.2 WHY THERE ARE MORE WOMEN THAN MEN AT OLDER AGES IN MODERN POPULATIONS

On the whole the population of the United States contains more females than males, but the difference is by no means uniform through the several ages. Males are in excess to age 20, but from then on there are more females, with large proportional differences after age 65 (Fig. 7.1). Can theory, combined with known facts of mortality, account for this difference between male and female age distributions? Specifically, can theory tell why in 1967 there are 2,236,000 men aged 70 to 74 against 2,941,000 women, a sex ratio of 76 males per 100 females? Why has the ratio of males to females in the United States declined steadily during the course of the present century? Essentially the same method of study that worked for age distribution will help to account for the varieties of sex ratios in observed populations.

Our search, as before, will start with the current age-specific rates of birth and death, now pertaining to the two sexes separately, from which a stable model may be constructed. What is left unexplained by the stable

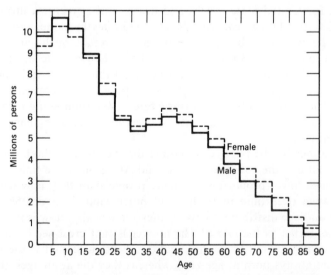

Fig. 7.1 Male and female populations by age, United States, 1967.

model based on current rates may be referred to trends in the rates in recent years; what is then still unexplained can be pursued by the study of migration and sudden changes in death rates due to wars, epidemics, and other historical events.

To convert the one-sex model used earlier for the analysis of ages into the (very primitive) two-sex model needed now, one item of data is required: the sex ratio at birth, say s. If s boys are born for each girl, and B girls are born in the current year, then the number of boys born is sB. By the same argument as was used for (4.1.1) we can write down the sex–age distribution if the regime of mortality and fertility is fixed and population is increasing in a geometrical sequence with a ratio e^{5r} of increase over any 5-year period. Births, as well as each age–sex group, are all supposed to be increasing in this ratio; hence, if currently there are B female births per year, on an approximation to the stable population argument of Section 4.1 there will be $B_5 L_0 e^{-2\frac{1}{2}r}$ females aged 0 to 4, $B_5 L_5 e^{-7\frac{1}{2}r}$ aged 5 to 9, and similarly for later ages. We are here satisfied with the common approximation

$$\int_x^{x+5} e^{-ra} l(a)\, da \doteq e^{-r\left(x+2\frac{1}{2}\right)} \int_x^{x+5} l(a)\, da = {}_5 L_x e^{-r\left(x+2\frac{1}{2}\right)}.$$

The corresponding male births are sB, and male survivors at the end of the first 5-year period are $B s_5 L_0^* e^{-2\frac{1}{2}r}$, the same as for females but using s and the male life table function ${}_5 L_0^*$. Thus the number of females is

$$B_5 L_x e^{-\left(2\frac{1}{2}+x\right)r},$$

and of males is

$$B s_5 L_x^* e^{-\left(2\frac{1}{2}+x\right)r},$$

both in the age group x to $x+4$ at last birthday, where we suppose the two sexes to be increasing at the same rate r.

Then the sex ratio in the age group is

$$\frac{B s_5 L_x^* e^{-\left(2\frac{1}{2}+x\right)r}}{B_5 L_x e^{-\left(2\frac{1}{2}+x\right)r}} = \frac{s_5 L_x^*}{{}_5 L_x},$$

in which everything has canceled but s and the life table survivors.

In application to the United States in 1967, we have $s = 1.050$, ${}_5 L_{70} = 329{,}111$, and ${}_5 L_{70}^* = 225{,}346$, so the stable model gives the sex ratio at age 70 as

$$\frac{(1.050)(225{,}346)}{329{,}111} = 0.72,$$

compared with 0.76 observed. The difference arises because the current life tables have a higher ratio of male to female mortality than the cohort in question experienced; immigration and other factors also operate.

7.3   THE STABLE EQUIVALENT

The stable equivalent Q, associated with long-run projections, helps to interpret an observed past age distribution from the viewpoint of reproductive potential, and so bridges the present chapter and the preceding one dealing with reproductive value. It is the natural companion of the intrinsic rate of natural increase r. The rate r tells us *how fast* the population would ultimately increase at present age-specific rates; Q tells us *at what level* the ultimate population curve would stand.

Population Projection and the Stable Approximation Thereto

We are given an observed (from a mathematical viewpoint an arbitrary) age distribution for one sex, which is arranged as a vertical vector $\{\mathbf{P}^{(0)}\}$, together with a set of age-specific birth and death rates arranged in the form of a matrix $\mathbf{M}$. If 5-year age groups to age 85 to 89 at last birthday are recognized, $\mathbf{M}$ has 18×18 elements and $\{\mathbf{P}^{(0)}\}$ has 18×1. The first row of $\mathbf{M}$ provides for fertility, and the subdiagonal for survivorship; this is, in fact, the Leslie matrix of Section 5.7. The age distribution projected through $5t$ years is

$$\{\mathbf{P}^{(t)}\} = \mathbf{M}^t \{\mathbf{P}^{(0)}\}. \tag{7.3.1}$$

An approximation to this projection, called asymptotic because it is approached as closely as one wishes with sufficiently large t, is

$$\{\mathbf{P}^{(t)}\} \doteq \mathbf{Q} e^{5rt}, \tag{7.3.2}$$

where $\mathbf{Q}$ is the stable equivalent of the age distribution.

To calculate $\mathbf{Q}$ choose a large t and equate the right-hand sides of (7.3.1) and (7.3.2). If the population were of stable age distribution from the start, and contained $\mathbf{Q}$ individuals at the several ages, by time $5t$ it would grow to $\mathbf{Q} e^{5rt}$. In fact, we know that it is of age distribution $\{\mathbf{P}^{(0)}\}$, and when projected it grows to $\mathbf{M}^t \{\mathbf{P}^{(0)}\}$ by time $5t$. The matrix equation for the calculation of $\mathbf{Q}$ is thus

$$\mathbf{Q} e^{5rt} = \mathbf{M}^t \{\mathbf{P}^{(0)}\}$$

or

$$\mathbf{Q} = \frac{\mathbf{M}^t \{\mathbf{P}^{(0)}\}}{e^{5rt}}. \tag{7.3.3}$$

Table 7.3 Female population total by conventional projection and by contribution of dominant root, starting from United States, 1960* (000s)

Year	t	Leslie projection with fixed 1960 rates	Contribution of positive term Qe^{rt}
1960	0	91,348	76,840
1970	10	106,220	94,986
1980	20	125,669	117,416
1990	30	150,129	145,144
2000	40	181,464	179,419
2010	50	222,196	221,789
2020	60	273,949	274,164
2030	70	338,990	338,907
2040	80	418,996	418,939

*Right-hand column is $Qe^{rt} = 76,840e^{0.0212t}$.

Table 7.4 Female population P_0 and stable equivalent number Q, United States, 1919–21 to 1965, adjusted births

Year	Observed female population (000s) P_0	Stable equivalent (000s) Q
1919–21	52,283	55,519
1924–26	57,016	61,442
1929–31	60,757	72,304
1934–36	63,141	78,879
1939–41	65,811	77,279
1944–46	69,875	72,016
1949–51	76,216	68,376
1954–56	83,248	69,535
1960	91,348	76,840
1965	98,703	98,645

Source: Keyfitz and Flieger (1968).

One way of describing (7.3.3) is to say that $\{\mathbf{P}_0\}$, the initial population, is projected *forward* t periods by the matrix $\mathbf{M}$ and *backward* an equal length of time by the real root r, that is, by dividing by e^{5rt}. The quantity $\mathbf{Q}e^{rt}$ is the real term in the solution of the Lotka equation (5.7.2), but is more complete in providing the several ages of the population rather than births alone. The total of all ages, written as italic Q, not boldface, is shown in Table 7.3 for United States females, starting with the 1960 age distribution and projected by 1960 births and life table.

The intrinsic rate of natural increase for the regime of 1959–61 being $r = 0.0212$, and the stable equivalent of the initial population being $Q = 76,840,000$, the future female population t years after 1960, if age-specific rates remained fixed and the stable model applied, would be $76,840,000e^{0.0212t}$. Table 7.3 compares this at 10-year intervals with the full projection, which implicitly uses all terms in the right-hand side of (5.7.2). By the year 2000 the discrepancy is down to 1.1 percent.

However, between 1960 and 1965 some of the postwar cohorts moved into childbearing ages, and the age distribution became more favorable, to the point where the stable equivalent and the observed total practically coincided, both being just under 99 million (Table 7.4). At the same time a drastic decline in the birth rates occurred, so that the intrinsic rate fell to $r = 0.01267$. Hence the future from the 1965 vantage point was

$$98,645,000e^{0.01267(t-5)}, \tag{7.3.4}$$

if t is still measured from 1960.

Application of the Stable Equivalent Q

Table 7.4 shows Q to be considerably above the observed female population P_0 for the United States during the 1930s, and below it in the 1950s. This reflects the tendency for there to be proportionately more women of the age of motherhood in the population for some years after a fall in the birth rate. The crude birth rate usually lags behind the intrinsic birth rate after an upturn or downturn in fertility. The stable equivalent Q measures the favorabililty of the age distribution to reproduction, given the current regime of mortality and fertility.

In Table 7.5 historical data on Q are presented for four other countries. Again a high Q relative to population after a fall in birth rates appears for England and Wales between 1901 and 1941, and for Australia and Canada before 1941. The Netherlands also shows this feature, but to a more moderate degree.

Table 7.5 Observed female population and stable equivalent, historical data for four countries

Country and year	Female population (000s) P_0	Stable equivalent (000s) Q	Ratio Q/P_0
Australia			
1911	2,152	2,395	1.11
1921	2,683	3,013	1.12
1933	3,263	4,267	1.31
1947	3,782	3,501	0.93
1957	4,758	4,215	0.89
1960	5,083	4,494	0.88
1965	5,632	5,659	1.00
Canada			
1931	5,001	5,706	1.14
1941	5,608	6,356	1.13
1951	6,751	6,431	0.95
1961	8,794	8,120	0.92
1965	9,479	9,839	1.04
England and Wales			
1861	10,324	10,802	1.05
1871	11,695	11,966	1.02
1881	13,373	13,608	1.02
1891	14,989	15,805	1.05
1901	16,845	19,047	1.13
1911	18,655	22,014	1.18
1921	19,816	22,229	1.12
1931	20,839	27,321	1.31
1941	21,515	27,522	1.28
1946	21,979	20,511	0.93
1951	22,751	22,741	1.00
1956	23,150	21,577	0.93
1961	23,820	19,764	0.83
Netherlands			
1901	2,615	2,647	1.01
1910	2,960	3,064	1.03
1920	3,419	3,615	1.06
1930	3,954	4,386	1.11
1940	4,437	4,983	1.12
1945	4,619	4,551	0.99
1950	5,074	5,077	1.00
1955	5,395	5,405	1.00
1960	5,766	5,615	0.97
1965	6,081	5,942	0.98

Source: Keyfitz and Flieger (1968).

Relation Between Q and Reproductive Value V

Reproductive value, the discounted future girl children that will be born to a woman, has a close relation to Q. [Prove that Q, like V but unlike P_t, has the property of increasing at a constant rate under a fixed regime of mortality and fertility. The proof involves the fact that $(\mathbf{M}^t/e^{5rt})\{\mathbf{P}^{(0)}\}$ is invariant with respect to t as long as t is large; in particular, $\mathbf{M}^t/e^{5rt}$ is the same when $t+1$ is written for t (Section 6.1).]

In fact, V is a simple multiple of Q. In the continuous representation, V is exactly equal to Q multiplied by the intrinsic birth rate b and by the mean age of childbearing in the stable population κ, two constants obtainable from the age-specific rates and having nothing to do with the observed age distribution. [The reader may prove this statement by rearranging the double integral contained in $\int_0^\beta P(x)v(x)\,dx$, where $v(x)$ is defined as in (6.1.1), and showing it to be the same as the numerator of the first coefficient Q in the solution (5.7.4) to the Lotka equation. In the present notation he will prove $Q = V(b\kappa)$.] Goodman (1968) shows this result to apply in the discrete case. Values of P_0, Q, and V are given in Table 7.6 for a number of countries.

A question arises of the degree to which Q, the stable equivalent, is sensitive to the particular set of age-specific birth and death rates used in its calculation. The first row of Table 7.7 shows Q for the age distribution of 1960, worked out according to the 1960 and 1965 patterns of mortality

Table 7.6 Observed female population, stable equivalent, and reproductive value (000s)

Country and year	Observed female population P_0	Stable equivalent Q	Ratio of stable to observed Q/P_0	Reproductive value in units of girl babies V
Austria, 1964	3,845	3,187	0.83	1,665
Czechoslovakia, 1964	7,198	7,312	1.02	3,253
Denmark, 1964	2,380	2,326	0.98	1,091
Fiji Islands, 1964	219	229	1.04	229
Finland, 1964	2,370	2,540	1.07	1,227
Germany (East), 1964	9,257	7,871	0.85	3,499
Germany (West), 1964	30,980	27,755	0.90	13,124
Netherlands, 1964	6,081	5,942	0.98	3,665
Norway, 1964	1,854	1,649	0.89	914
Puerto Rico, 1964	1,309	1,375	1.05	1,050
Roumania, 1964	9,665	13,250	1.37	4,088
Switzerland, 1964	2,940	2,861	0.97	1,431

Source: Keyfitz and Flieger (1968).

Table 7.7 Stable equivalents Q for United States females in 1960 and 1965, each calculated with two different matrices M (thousands)

| | Calculated with matrix M of | |
	1960	1965
Age distribution:		
1960	76,912	89,001
1965	85,478	98,645
Percent increase	11.14	10.84

and fertility as embodied in the two M's; the second row shows the corresponding Q's for the 1965 age distribution. The values obtained for Q depend greatly on the set of age-specific rates applied as M. But if we study only the *change* in Q in the United States between 1960 and 1965, it turns out that the increase is 11.14 percent on the 1960 M and 10.84 percent on the 1965 M. This way of making a comparison (applied between France and Italy) is due to Vincent (1945), who noted the virtual invariance with respect to the mortality and fertility patterns used. We are entitled to say that the age distribution of women in the United States became about 11 percent more favorable to reproduction during the 5 years in question, and the statement is true almost without regard to the fertility and mortality patterns used in making this assessment.

As an example of a place comparison, Table 7.8 shows Q values for Mexico and the United States, both for 1962. The Q for Mexico is 0.282 of that for the United States when the M of the latter is used; it is 0.272 when the M of the former is used. Jeffrey Evans has programmed place comparisons among five countries which demonstrate the same invariance.

Table 7.8 Stable equivalents Q for the United States and Mexico (thousands)

| | Calculated with matrix M of | |
	United States, 1962	Mexico, 1962
Age distribution		
United States	82,933	69,395
Mexico	23,388	18,863
Ratio, Mexico to United States	0.282	0.272

Section 8.3 below uses the stable equivalent to compare the effect on age distribution of eliminating cancer with that of eliminating heart disease.

A More General Stable Equivalent

Age is merely a special case of the stable equivalent. Any model that possesses the ergodic property, that is, that tends asymptotically to a distribution unaffected by the initial distribution, is equally capable of analysis by the methods given above. In fact (7.3.3) remains unchanged; only now the matrix $\mathbf{M}$ and the vector $\mathbf{P}^{(0)}$ provide for the two sexes, regions, married and single populations, and any other groups recognized in the model. Applications are worked out in Keyfitz (1969).

7.4 AGE AT MARRIAGE

A curve to describe proportion married with age, backed by a convincing rationale, is provided by Hernes (1972). In such an age-graded population it hardly occurs to individuals to marry when most of their contemporaries are unmarried; but as marriage gets under way after about age 18, each sees the number of his or her unmarried friends diminishing and begins to feel left out—experiences, indeed, an increasing pressure to marry. Hence, argues Hernes, we can take the rate of transfer into the married state as proportional to the fraction married. But it must also be proportional to the fraction not yet married; the marrying can come only from the stock of the unmarried. The result is a logistic curve of which Savage (1973) provides a generalization.

A Sum of Random Intervals Model

Coale (1971) found by experimenting with a number of observed distributions of age at marriage that all fitted a standard curve, provided only that the curve was adjusted for (a) the age at which girls become marriageable, (b) the proportion ever marrying by the end of life, and (c) horizontal scale. If the distributions are presented as risk functions, that is, age-specific marriage rates for the still-single population but excluding those who never marry, they take the form for first marriages

$$r(x) = 0.174 e^{-4.411 e^{-0.309 x}}, \qquad (7.4.1)$$

where x is the age of the person, measured from the origin for the particular population. Calculation yields the following values:

x	$r(x)$
0	0.0021
1	0.0068
2	0.0161
3	0.0304
4	0.0483
5	0.0679
10	0.1424
20	0.1724

This zero-parameter or three-parameter curve, depending on how one looks at it, gives close fit to data but, as Coale points out, lacks an obvious behavioral rationale.

Feeney (personal communication) suggested that the marriage curve may be composed of a random age of entry followed by a random delay. Coale and McNeil (1972) carried this thought further and developed a distribution involving three delays.

If the probability that X falls between x and $x + dx$ is $f_X(x)dx$, and the probability that Y falls between y and $y + dy$ is $f_Y(y)dy$; the joint probability is $f_X(x)f_Y(y)dx\,dy$. To find the distribution $f(z)$ of $Z = X + Y$ we need to integrate this over all x and y such that $x + y = z$, that is,

$$f_Z(z) = \int_{-\infty}^{\infty} f_X(x)f_Y(z-x)\,dx. \qquad (7.4.2)$$

This expression for $f_Z(z)$ is called a convolution, like (5.7.1), because the sum of the arguments of the functions in its integrand does not involve x, the variable of integration. It is readily applied to the sum of two negative exponential distributions, $f_X(x) = r_1 e^{-r_1 x}$ and $f_Y(y) = r_2 e^{-r_2 y}$, to obtain the distribution of $Z = X + Y$ as

$$f_Z(z) = \frac{r_1 r_2}{r_1 - r_2}(e^{-r_2 z} - e^{-r_1 z}). \qquad (7.4.3)$$

It may also be applied to more than two exponentials and to a normal curve followed by three exponentials, as long as independence holds.

This is how Coale and McNeil (1972) proceed to account for the distribution of marriage ages. They suppose a normal distribution of ages at which girls become marriageable, followed by three delays, each exponentially distributed. Fitting to data for French couples, they find the mean age of entry into a state of marriageability as 16.6 years, the mean interval between then and meeting the future husband as 4.02 years, the mean interval from acquaintance to engagement as 1.53 years, and the mean interval from engagement to marriage as 0.93 year. The closeness of fit of the convolution to the observed data for this and other populations confirms their behavioral model.

Small Marriage Circles

So much for marriage partners in a large population, where random variation in the time of individual marriage is recognized, but random variation in the number of men and women of marrying age can have only a minor effect. If in fact each individual, as he or she comes of age, seeks a marriage partner from a relatively small circle, some part of nonmarriage can be due to random differences in the numbers of men and women in these circles. Henry (1969) has addressed himself to this aspect of the problem.

He asks us to think of a circle containing candidates for marriage, whether or not they see themselves in that light. A circle may be an office or other workplace, a social club, or a neighborhood. Suppose that it contains $2n$ members, all of such age and disposition as to be candidates for marriage to one another. Let them be randomly distributed by sex; that is, the probability of a member being male is $1/2$, and of being female $1/2$. The expected number of male candidates would be n, and of females likewise n, so that in any realization of our hypothetical circle in which these expected values held all $2n$ candidates would marry. The task is to find the expected number of candidates that fail to find mates over all realizations of the circle. The following solution of Henry's problem is due to McFarland (1970).

If the chance of each individual being male is $1/2$, the chance that of the $2n$ members the numbers of males is $n+k$ and of females $n-k$ is

$$\binom{2n}{n+k}\left(\frac{1}{2}\right)^{2n}. \tag{7.4.4}$$

In this situation the nonmarrying males will number $2k = n+k-(n-k)$, $k>0$. Hence the expected number of males not marrying must be $n+k-(n-k)$ times probability 7.4.4, added through all possible constitutions of the circle that have males in excess of females:

$$\sum_1^n \left[(n+k)-(n-k)\right]\frac{(2n)!}{(n+k)!(n-k)!}\left(\frac{1}{2}\right)^{2n}$$

$$=\left(\frac{1}{2}\right)^{2n}(2n)!\left[\sum_1^n \frac{1}{(n+k-1)!(n-k)!} - \sum_1^{n-1}\frac{1}{(n+k)!(n-k-1)!}\right].$$

$$\tag{7.4.5}$$

We have made the upper limit in the right-hand summation $k = n - 1$, because $k = n$ gives a zero term owing to the factor $n - k$. Now note that the term for $k = 2$ in the left summation cancels with that for $k = 1$ on the right, both being equal to $1/(n+1)!(n-2)!$. All other terms similarly cancel, except that for $k = 1$ on the left, which is equal to $1/n!(n-1)!$. Hence the required expected number of males left over is

$$\left(\frac{1}{2}\right)^{2n} (2n)! \frac{1}{(n)!(n-1)!} = n\left(\frac{1}{2}\right)^{2n} \frac{(2n)!}{n!n!}. \qquad (7.4.6)$$

The expected number of females left over must be the same by symmetry, and hence for both sexes we have an expected

$$2n\left(\frac{1}{2}\right)^{2n} \frac{(2n)!}{n!n!}$$

persons unmarried or, as a fraction of the $2n$ individuals in the circle,

$$\left(\frac{1}{2}\right)^{2n} \frac{(2n)!}{n!n!}. \qquad (7.4.7)$$

McDonald (1965) finds the same result (7.4.7) for the matching of male and female worms in the spread of certain infestations. For no readily understandable reason, the expected fraction of marriage candidates (or worms) unmatched is the same as the probability that the group is equally divided between males and females.

Stirling's approximation to the factorial is $n! = n^n e^{-n}\sqrt{2\pi n}\,[1 + (1/12n)]$, omitting terms from $1/n^2$ onward. Entering this in (7.4.7) gives

$$\left(\frac{1}{2}\right)^{2n} \frac{(2n)^{2n} e^{-2n}\sqrt{4\pi n}\,\left[1 + (1/24n)\right]}{\left\{n^n e^{-n}\sqrt{2\pi n}\,\left[1 + (1/12n)\right]\right\}^2},$$

which after cancellation becomes

$$\frac{1}{\sqrt{\pi n}} \cdot \frac{1 + 1/(24n)}{\left(1 + 1/(12n)\right)^2} \doteq \frac{1 - 1/(8n)}{\sqrt{\pi n}}. \qquad (7.4.8)$$

Thus, if a marriage circle containing $2n$ individuals is considered, the expected fraction of excess of one sex or the other, that is to say, the average fraction who cannot marry within the circle, is slightly under $1/\sqrt{\pi n}$. For a group of 20 individuals this is $1/\sqrt{\pi n} = 0.178$, reduced to 0.176 by the factor $1 - 1/(8n)$ (Table 7.9 and Fig. 7.2).

This solution may be extended to a circle having a disequilibrium of the sexes, in the sense that the probability of a random individual being male is not $1/2$ but some other number; in this case, another device is required to sum the series.

Table 7.9   Values of $(2n)!/(2^{2n}n!n!)$ and Stirling approximations

Size of group $2n$	$(2n)!/(2^{2n}n!n!)$	$1/\sqrt{\pi n}$	$(1-\dfrac{1}{8n})/\sqrt{\pi n}$
2	0.5	0.5642	0.4937
4	0.375	0.3989	0.3740
6	0.3125	0.3257	0.3122
8	0.2734	0.2821	0.2733
10	0.2461	0.2523	0.2460
12	0.2256	0.2303	0.2255
14	0.2095	0.2132	0.2094
16	0.1964	0.1995	0.1964
18	0.1855	0.1881	0.1855
20	0.1762	0.1784	0.1762
40	0.1254	0.1262	0.1254
80	0.08893	0.08921	0.08893
120	0.07268	0.07284	0.07268
160	0.06298	0.06308	0.06298
200	0.05635	0.05642	0.05635

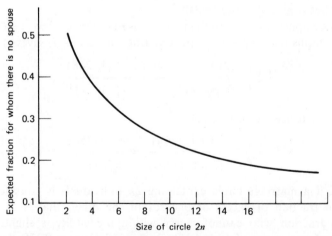

Fig. 7.2 Diminishing fraction of expected number without spouse as marriage circle increases.

How Many Households Are Implied by Birth, Death, and Marriage Rates?

Age-specific rates of birth and death, along with the fraction of women married at each age, imply an average size of nuclear family (Goodman, Keyfitz, and Pullum, 1974).

For the general case, call the age distribution of women $p(a)$, not necessarily stable, so that $\int_0^\omega p(a)\,da = P^f$, and the fraction married at age a is $q(a)$; here the total number of married women is $\int_0^\omega p(a)q(a)\,da$. It is reasonable to attach a separate family to each married woman, where for this purpose only those currently living with spouse will be defined as married. Then the total number of families is also $\int_0^\omega p(a)q(a)\,da$, and the mean number of persons per family is

$$\frac{2P^f}{\displaystyle\int_0^\omega p(a)q(a)\,da} \tag{7.4.9}$$

if the numbers of males and females in the population are equal.

To go from this to the mean size of family implied by age-specific rates in a stable population, we replace $p(a)/P^f$ by $be^{-ra}l(a)$, as in Section 4.1. Then we have for the mean number of persons per family

$$\frac{2}{\displaystyle\int_0^\omega be^{-ra}l(a)q(a)\,da.} \tag{7.4.10}$$

This is different in concept from the average we would derive from the census itself by counting persons in families and dividing by the number of families. Our (7.4.10) neglects persons living not in families but in prisons and other institutions, and implicitly somehow allocates illegitimate children to married women, but this is a minor divergence from the census. The main difference is that (7.4.10) gives what is implied by the current rates rather than by rates that have existed over the lifetimes of the people counted in a census. To reconcile these two kinds of average would be a difficult but worthwhile piece of research.

What about the size of the extended family, supposing that a separate extended family is formed by a married woman if her mother is dead? We need merely enter in (7.4.10) the probability that a woman aged a does not have a living mother, a subject to be developed in Chapter 10. If the probability that a woman aged a has a living mother is $M_1(a)$ [an expression for this is given later as (10.1.4)], the chance that she has not is

$1 - M_1(a)$, and from (7.4.9) extended families will average

$$\frac{2P^f}{\int_0^\omega [1 - M_1(a)] p(a)q(a)\,da} \text{persons,} \qquad (7.4.11)$$

or in the stable case

$$\frac{2}{\int_0^\omega [1 - M_1(a)] be^{-ra} l(a)q(a)\,da} \text{persons.} \qquad (7.4.12)$$

Intrinsic Rates of Natural Increase: Age, Parity, and Nuptiality

The intrinsic rate of growth, as defined by Lotka and discussed in Section 5.1, is that which ultimately results from the continuance of observed age-specific rates of birth and death. The intrinsic rate depends in no way on the observed age distribution, but is a means of interpreting the age-specific rates. And yet the choice of age-specific rates was in a sense arbitrary; we could have used other classifications—say rural–urban-specific rates, classified by age or not. Any characteristic that shows differentials of birth and death rates is a candidate for providing an intrinsic rate, though not all characteristics are equally logical candidates.

Oechsli (1971) has calculated rates intrinsic for age, parity, and nuptiality, and for certain combinations of these. The age–parity rate, for instance, tells what the increase of the population would be once its age-parity distribution came to be that resulting without disturbance from the observed set of rates in the several age-parity groups.

To see the meaning of various directions of adjustment consider the following five rates (per 1000 population) for United States females in 1960:

Crude	Crude rate of natural increase	14.7
A	Age intrinsic rate	20.8
$A-P$	Age–parity intrinsic rate	23.0
$A-N$	Age–nuptiality intrinsic rate	18.4
$A-N-P$	Age–nuptiality-parity intrinsic rate	19.6

The rise when we go from the crude rate in the first line to the age intrinsic rate in the second means that the observed age distribution was unfavorable to increase—that there was a smaller proportion of women of childbearing age than are present in the stable condition at 1960 age-specific rates of birth and death. This is a well-known result of the small cohorts born in the 1930s.

When we go from the age intrinsic to the age–parity intrinsic rate, we find a further increase, which can mean only that within age groups the distribution of observed parities was unfavorable to reproduction. The highest-bearing parities are the low ones; apparently the stable condition on 1960 age-parity specific rates would have relatively more individuals of low parity than the actual situation of 1960.

On the other hand, when we go from the age intrinsic rate to the age–nuptiality intrinsic rate (from 20.8 to 18.4), we find a decline; this means that the proportion of married women in the population of 1960 was greater (in the main ages of childbearing) than the proportion of married women in the stable condition. If the marriage rates, the age-specific nuptial fertility rates, and the age-specific mortality rates of 1960 were allowed to work themselves out, they would result in a lower overall birth rate than would the age-specific fertility and mortality rates of 1960, disregarding marriage.

The fall from the age–parity to the age–nuptiality–parity says that separation of the married women in the age–parity analysis brings the rate down, and the effect is so drastic that we find $A - N - P$ below the simple age intrinsic rate A. In short, the effect of nuptiality more than offsets the effect of simple parity. Karmel (1950) suggested in his comment on Whelpton (1946) that the parity correction by itself could be deceptive. Suppose from one year to the next a rise in marriages, while age–parity rates at each marriage duration remained the same. The age-nuptiality-parity intrinsic rate would be unchanged, whereas both the age intrinsic and the age–parity intrinsic rates would rise. But the latter would rise more, for the higher first births would be divided by zero-parity women rather than, as in the age-specific rate, being diluted by division by all women.

The rise from the 18.4 in $A - N$ to the 19.6 in $A - N - P$ means that within the married group, age by age, the parity distribution of the observed population was less favorable to fertility than the parity distribution of the stable condition.

All of this can be shown on a diagram. The lozenge form brings out the contrast between the effects of parity and of nuptiality (A = age; P = parity; N = nuptiality):

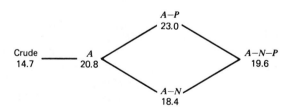

The Life Cycle

According to Glick's calculation (1955), the following changes in median ages of various events in American families took place between 1890 and 1950:

Event	Median age of husband		Median age of wife	
	1950	1890	1950	1890
First marriage	22.8	26.1	20.1	22.0
Birth of last child	28.8	36.0	26.1	31.9
Marriage of last child	50.3	59.4	47.6	55.3
Death of one spouse	64.1	57.4	61.4	53.3
Death of other spouse	71.6	66.4	77.2	67.7

Whereas in 1890 a minority of couples survived until the last child was married, by 1950 most survived, on the average by about 14 years. A new demographic element came into existence: husband and wife living together after their last child had left home—the empty nest. This corresponds to a new pattern of spatial movement as well; a couple may start out in an apartment in the city, move to a suburb when their first child is born, and remain there until their last child has left home. If the husband is middle class, his income has usually continued to climb, and his earnings are higher than when the children were at home; moreover, his wife may well take up some new kind of paid work or resume an earlier career. The couple no longer need their suburban home and schools and are in a position to move into town and pay a substantial rent. Collectively such couples have affected the skylines of many American cities as new high-rise, high-rent apartments spring up to accommodate the new demographic element.

The change in life cycle is due to improved mortality, especially for women, along with earlier marriage in both the older and the younger generation—a 1-year fall in the age of marriage subtracts 2 years from the age at which the last child is married, everything else remaining the same. Moreover the birth rate has fallen so that children are fewer; and, especially if the wife is eager to resume her career, the children that couples do have are more closely spaced. To all this is added an increased tendency for children to leave home before marriage.

We thus know to what factors the changes are due, but we do not know how much of a particular change is due to each factor. Yet it need not be difficult to break down any part of the difference. In 1890, for husbands, the first death of spouse occurred 2 years before the last child was married;

in 1950 it was 14 years after. One would like to know how much of the change was due to improved mortality, how much to earlier marriage, and so on. These effects would be ascertained by the technique exhibited in Table 7.2. The first step would be to set up a model, including death rates, marriage rates, home-leaving rates, birth rates, all by age. Then the model with the rates for 1890 would be used to generate the 1890 column of Glick's table, or an approximation to it. The same would be done for the 1950 column. Then the various elements of the models would be interchanged; for example, the marriage rates for 1950 would be combined with the other elements for 1890 to obtain an estimate of the effect of changed marriage ages. The result would be somewhat more elaborate to interpret than Table 7.2, since it would have several orders of interaction, but no new principle would be required.

This demographic theory of the life cycle needs to be further developed, and then integrated with the theory of savings and consumption over the life cycle that has become a standard part of macroeconomics. The matrix treatment developed by Rogers (1975) for migration would seem to be applicable to it; Krishnamoorthy is working on the adaptation.

Married and Divorced

The numbers of married and divorced persons counted in a census, like those of the several ages and sexes, are related to the country's previous history of marriage and divorce. It is necessary to consider the time series of marriages of preceding years, along with other series on the dissolution of marriages by death of one spouse or divorce. The present is in principle explainable by and reconcilable with the past. If the reconciliation and explanation are in a small local area, one would have to take account of immigration and emigration as well as marriages, deaths, and divorces, but this complication will be disregarded here. The discussion that follows is due to Preston (1975).

Still for simplicity, disregard the age of the individuals concerned, and take account only of duration of marriage. (First marriages fall in a relatively narrow band of ages, and the theory will apply to them more strictly than to all marriages.) Call $\mu^m(x)dx$ the chance that a marriage that has been in existence x years will break up during the time x to $x + dx$ through the death of the husband, $\mu^f(x)$ that it will break up through the death of the wife, and $\mu^d(x)$ that it will break up through the divorce of the couple. Then the argument that started in Section 1.5, of which a special case was the survivorship of an individual in the face of death (Section 2.1), is here applicable to the survivorship of a couple in the face of the death of either member or of divorce. It is as though a group of marriages, initially P_0 in number, had to run the gauntlets of death and divorce, and only a certain fraction survived in each time period. The surviving couples at the end of t years would be

$$P(t) = P_0 \exp\left\{ -\int_0^t \left[\mu^m(x) + \mu^f(x) + \mu^d(x) \right] dx \right\}. \quad (7.4.13)$$

The expected number of divorces between time t and $t + dt$ would be $P(t)\mu^d(t)dt$, assuming independence, and disregarding remarriage.

These causes of dissolution compete with one another. Higher mortality lowers the divorce rate, everything else remaining the same. The reason for this is to be seen in the expression for the number of marriages that will eventually end in divorce:

$$D = \int_0^\infty P(t) \mu^d(t) dt.$$

This, divided by the number P_0 of marriages that started the cohort off, gives the fraction expected to end in divorce. If, as between two populations otherwise similar, mortality is higher at any age in one, $P(t)$ will be lower in that one for all subsequent ages, so D will also be lower. This is analogous to the way that deaths from cancer in the multiple-decrement table of Section 2.6 depend on deaths from other causes.

The Current Divorce–Marriage Ratio.   The ratio of current divorces to current marriages, say for the year 1973, is a convenient measure of the extent of divorce. This measure is often used, and almost as often criticized on the ground that current divorces come from the marriages of a period going back a number of years, and hence the denominator of the ratio ought to be these marriages. The ideal is a schedule of divorce rates according to duration of marriage, so that duration-specific divorce rates can be calculated. But when these are not available and we resort to the current divorce–marriage ratio, we can apply an interpretation of this ratio that has been provided by Samuel Preston.

Let $D(t)$ be the curve of divorces with time, and $M(t)$ the curve of marriages. Again let the (unknown) continuous duration-specific force of divorce be $\mu^d(x)$ for marriages that have lasted x years, and call the probability of survival of the marriage for x years against the contingencies of both death and divorce $p(x)$. Then the current number of divorces $D(t)$ must be

$$D(t) = \int_0^\infty M(t - x) p(x) \mu^d(x) dx, \quad (7.4.14)$$

and under a fixed rate of increase r the current number of marriages is

$$M(t) = M_0 e^{rt}. \qquad (7.4.15)$$

Therefore, on entering $M(t-x) = M_0 e^{r(t-x)}$ in the expression (7.4.14) for $D(t)$, we have

$$D(t) = \int_0^\infty M_0 e^{rt} e^{-rx} p(x) \mu^d(x) \, dx. \qquad (7.4.16)$$

From (7.4.15) and (7.4.16)

$$\frac{D(t)}{M(t)} = \int_0^\infty e^{-rx} p(x) \mu^d(x) \, dx. \qquad (7.4.17)$$

How much does this ratio depend on the rate of increase of marriages r? Taking the logarithm and then differentiating both sides of (7.4.17) gives the simple result

$$\frac{d}{dr} \left\{ \ln \left[\frac{D(t)}{M(t)} \right] \right\} = -A_D, \qquad (7.4.18)$$

where A_D is the mean number of years of marriage at the time of divorce, calculated for the part of the population that ultimately does divorce. One could confine the argument to first marriage and first divorce, or else to first marriage and any divorce, but to take all marriages and all divorces accords with the data most commonly available.

Integrating (7.4.18) gives

$$\ln \left[\frac{D(t)}{M(t)} \right] = \ln \left[\frac{D_0(t)}{M_0(t)} \right] - rA_D,$$

where $D_0(t)/M_0(t)$ is the ratio in the stationary population. Taking exponentials provides

$$\frac{D(t)}{M(t)} = \frac{D_0(t)}{M_0(t)} e^{-rA_D}, \qquad (7.4.19)$$

which would have been obtained more directly as an approximation to (7.4.17).

For populations that have not experienced sudden changes in the marriage rate (7.4.19) enables us to infer the ratio in the stationary population, $D_0(t)/M_0(t)$, which is the same as the probability that a marriage will end in divorce. The mean number of years married for those who divorce was constant through the 1960s at about 7 (*Statistical Abstract for the United States*, 1972, p. 3). Suppose a rate of increase of about 1 percent per year. Then Preston's result (7.4.19) can be used to calculate the probability that a random marriage will end in divorce, assuming values for r and A_D and applying them to the observed $D(t)/M(t)$:

$$\frac{D_0(t)}{M_0(t)} = \frac{D(t)}{M(t)} e^{rA_D} = \frac{D(t)}{M(t)} e^{(0.01)(7)} = 1.073 \frac{D(t)}{M(t)}. \qquad (7.4.20)$$

This result is directly applicable only if birth, marriage, divorce, and death rates have all been fixed in the past. But even under instability in these rates (7.4.20) is useful, for the birth rates really do not matter; what is necessary is that marriages have been increasing in the past at a reasonably steady and known rate.

7.5 THE FOREIGN-BORN AND INTERNAL MIGRANTS

The 1970 census gives 9,619,000 foreign-born in the United States, a decline from previous censuses and considerably less than the 11,595,000 reported in 1940. If the flow of immigrants (net of those leaving) had been constant and at constant ages, improvements in mortality would have led to a steady increase in the number alive to be counted in the census; the reason for the decline must be a greater decline in entrants than the increase in fraction surviving. But the preceding decade's immigration records showed 3,322,000 entrants, the peak to date in a steady rise from the low of 528,000 immigrants in 1931–40. The number of immigrants entering the United States has been rising sharply in the postwar period; why, then, are fewer and fewer foreign-born counted in successive censuses?

The answer is that we need a longer view backward than the postwar period. The 40 years from 1931 to 1970 showed entrants numbering 7,400,000 against 22,326,000 for the preceding 40 years. This contrast is what is reflected in the declining immigrant population; the years since the 1930s have witnessed the dying off of the immigrants from a time earlier in the century. Immigrants are typically young adults who have on the average 40 or more years to live after their arrival.

Any statistical reconciliation is rendered more difficult yet by the considerable volume of illegal immigrants, who are certainly not included in the annual official numbers of entrants; some unknown fraction are picked up by the census.

A Matrix Analysis

The next stage in analysis, beyond the accounting for present numbers of foreign-born in terms of the preceding stream of immigration, is to project the consequences for future population of the present rates of immigration or of some hypothetical change in them. This takes us beyond description and reconciliation of reports into at least a primitive kind of mechanism. The mechanism is the effect of fixed (or changing) rates on the pattern of residents from abroad, where "abroad" may mean another country, state, or county.

A Markov chain comes first to mind as the language for expressing such mechanisms. If the chance that an individual residing in state j moves to state i, say Maryland to California, is m_{ij}, irrespective of the previous history of the person, and the number of individuals in the ith state is p_{it} at time t, then the distribution of individuals among states at time $t+1$ is

$$P_{t+1} = MP_t,$$

where **M** is the matrix having m_{ij} in the jth position in the ith row, and P_t is the vertical vector with p_{it} in its ith position. The argument is similar to that summarized in Section 7.3 for the Leslie matrix.

Rogers (1968) provides an exposition of the theory and examples of the migration process for the United States. In particular he considers 1955–60 migration and natural increase between California and the rest of the United States with the matrix

$$M = \begin{bmatrix} 1.0215 & 0.0127 \\ 0.0627 & 1.0667 \end{bmatrix}.$$

He starts the process with the initial 1955 vector in thousands:

$$P_{1955} = \begin{bmatrix} 12{,}988 \\ 152{,}082 \end{bmatrix}$$

and finds a 1960 distribution between California and the rest of the United States equal to

$$P_{1960} = \begin{bmatrix} 1.0215 & 0.0127 \\ 0.0627 & 1.0667 \end{bmatrix} \begin{bmatrix} 12{,}988 \\ 152{,}082 \end{bmatrix} = \begin{bmatrix} 15{,}199 \\ 163{,}040 \end{bmatrix}.$$

Continuation of the process, or use of eigenvalues, gives the ultimate ratio of California to United States population if these rates continue.

Migration and Age

Among other simplifications the models of the preceding paragraphs suffer from the omission of age. Rogers goes on to show (1968, p. 10) that one can make each of the m_{ij} itself a matrix, with nonzero elements in the first row and subdiagonal, and so he combines the migration and age effects in a single large matrix. With 50 states and 18 ages for females the matrix would be 900×900.

Arrangement of the elements within **M** and P_t is arbitrary, as long as the, same order is used in both. One could put the states in alphabetical order or in order of their 1970 populations, and even the ages could be rearranged with no loss other than inconvenience in remembering the sequence. Moreover the ages need not be a subdivision of the states; the states could just as well be a subdivision of the ages. In fact Feeney (1970) shows the advantage of considering the ages separately, making a block of the interstate migration for ages 0 to 4, then another block for ages 5 to 9, and so on. The block matrix for ages is then largely empty, and its properties are readily worked out.

The literature on migration and settlement is too extensive to refer to here in any complete way, let alone to summarize. Classic papers on the mathematics are due to Blumen, Kogan and McCarthy (1955), Goodman (1961b), and McGinnis (1968). Alonso (1972), Lowry (1964), and Stone (1971) provide theory on rural-urban movements, and an annotated bibliography is due to Price and Sikes (1975). The economics of migration is treated by David (1974) and Todaro (1969), and geographical aspects by Berry (1973) and Zelinsky (1971). Goldstein (1976) suggests some lines of future research.

Of interest as potentially unifying migration theory and integrating it with multiple decrement life tables, tables of the work force, tables of marital status, is the work of Rogers (1975) and Rogers and Willekens (1976). Their matrix formulation simplifies and generalizes the work of Schoen (1975). Alonso (1975) is developing a general framework that holds promise of being able to handle non-linearities that are important in the real world.

7.6 HUMAN STOCKS AND FLOWS

The study of population involves relating stocks to flows, as Richard Stone (1972) reminds us. Censuses report the stocks, according to the categories of age, marital status, education, occupation, and other characteristics, while vital statistics, numbers of graduates provided by schools, and similar current data report the flow. In contrast to economic data, which are more plentiful with respect to flows, social statistics are richer and higher in quality with respect to stocks. Relating the two is important in all fields.

Underlying all social statistics are individuals passing through the several states of their life cycles. They begin by being born, as reported in a flow series, spend some years at home, go into the educational system at the elementary level, sooner or later move to the intermediate and higher levels, eventually enter the labor force, where they may stay briefly or long, perhaps go back to school, and ultimately retire, possibly after several entries into and withdrawals from the labor force. At the same time they pass from a household of orientation, are married and form a household of procreation, have children, divorce, remarry, become widowed, and go through other domestic transitions. If it were useful, we could consider each economic activity state classified by the several domestic states, but it is less demanding of data to avoid this and to use two models in which the two collections of states are separately treated.

The two sequences outlined above through which individuals go are referred to by Stone as the *active* sequence, relating the individual to production and the market, including schooling and retirement, and the *passive* sequence, including the successive types of household of which he is part, the housing conditions, and his neighborhood and location. A further sequence is that of *health and medical care*, as the individual passes through the stages of being well and sick, encounters successive medical practitioners, is hospitalized and released. Some individuals go also through a sequence of *delinquency* states, starting with aberrant behavior and its consequences as they pass through the hands of police, courts, and prisons.

For each of the states in each of the four sequences mentioned above, a precise definitional boundary is required for purposes of measurement. For education it happens to be relatively easy to draw a sharp boundary around formal full-time schooling, and this is where the boundary is usually placed for statistical purposes; the important component of home and part-time learning is neglected. A conflict between precision of measurement and relevance of concept exists in any empirical science. As another example, it is sharper to restrict statistically economic production to that which goes through the market, locating self-transport to place of work and other do-it-yourself contributions outside the boundary of production.

To introduce the notation and ideas with an uncomplicated example, consider just two states, alive and dead, and the corresponding flows of birth and death. The statement is an adaptation of the Leslie (1945) model to a stationary population. Suppose a matrix S in which the subdiagonal elements are the probabilities of surviving from one year of age to the next, so that the first is, in the notation of Chapter 2, L_1/L_0, the second L_2/L_1, and so on; all elements but the subdiagonal are zero. The new population that enters each year through birth or migration is a vertical vector b. Suppose also that b consists of the number L_0 in its first position and zeros elsewhere. Then, if the population at time t is $\mathbf{P}_t$, also a vertical vector, we have

$$\mathbf{P}_1 = \mathbf{SP}_0 + \mathbf{b},$$
$$\mathbf{P}_2 = \mathbf{SP}_1 + \mathbf{b} = \mathbf{S}^2\mathbf{P}_0 + \mathbf{Sb} + \mathbf{b},$$
$$\cdot \quad \cdot \quad \cdot \quad \cdot \quad \cdot \quad \cdot \quad \cdot \quad \cdot$$

After the process has been going on for a long time, the term in $\mathbf{S}^t\mathbf{P}_0$ will have vanished; in fact all powers of $\mathbf{S}$ beyond the $(m-1)$th, if it is an $m \times m$ matrix, will consist entirely of zeros. Similarly, if t is m or greater, such terms as $\mathbf{S}^t\mathbf{b}$ will be zero, so we can add them in with impunity. This gives us the series

$$\mathbf{P}_t = \mathbf{b} + \mathbf{Sb} + \mathbf{S}^2\mathbf{b} + \cdots, \qquad t > m$$
$$= [\mathbf{I} + \mathbf{S} + \mathbf{S}^2 + \cdots]\mathbf{b}, \qquad (7.6.1)$$

which can be thought of as infinite. The sum of a geometric series of matrices is obtained in the same way as the sum of a series of scalars of which the common ratio is less than unity. Let the sum be $\mathbf{T}$:

$$\mathbf{T} = \mathbf{I} + \mathbf{S} + \mathbf{S}^2 + \cdots.$$

Multiplying $\mathbf{T}$ by $\mathbf{S}$ gives the same series, except that the $\mathbf{I}$ is missing; hence we have

$$\mathbf{T} = \mathbf{TS} + \mathbf{I},$$

or, on subtracting $\mathbf{TS}$ from both sides and factoring out $\mathbf{T}$,

$$\mathbf{T}[\mathbf{I} - \mathbf{S}] = \mathbf{I},$$

and, on multiplying on the right by the inverse $[\mathbf{I} - \mathbf{S}]^{-1}$,

$$\mathbf{T} = [\mathbf{I} - \mathbf{S}]^{-1}.$$

Entering this result in (7.6.1) gives for the population distribution by age at time t

$$\mathbf{P}_t = [\mathbf{I} - \mathbf{S}]^{-1}\mathbf{b}. \qquad (7.6.2)$$

The factor multiplying $\mathbf{b}$ is called the fundamental matrix of the original matrix $\mathbf{S}$, and it has many uses.

For our particular matrix $\mathbf{S}$ giving survivorships as the transitions between successive ages, the determinant of $[\mathbf{I} - \mathbf{S}]$ is readily seen to be unity, and the inverse is the transpose of the cofactors of the elements of $\mathbf{I} - \mathbf{S}$; that is to say, for the jth element of the ith row of the inverse we enter the determinant obtained by deleting the ith column and jth row of $\mathbf{I} - \mathbf{S}$. This procedure provides the fundamental matrix of the survivorship matrix:

$$
[\mathbf{I}-\mathbf{S}]^{-1}=
\begin{bmatrix}
1 & 0 & 0 & 0 & \cdots \\
\dfrac{L_1}{L_0} & 1 & 0 & 0 & \cdots \\
\dfrac{L_2}{L_0} & \dfrac{L_2}{L_1} & 1 & 0 & \cdots \\
\dfrac{L_3}{L_0} & \dfrac{L_3}{L_1} & \dfrac{L_3}{L_2} & 1 & \cdots \\
\vdots & & & &
\end{bmatrix}.
\qquad (7.6.3)
$$

The elements of the first column provide the probability of attaining the successive ages, starting at age zero; the elements of the second column give the same probabilities, starting at age one, and so on for the several columns. The totals of the columns are the expectations of further life, starting in the first age, the second age, and so on; expressed formally, if $\mathbf{R}$ is the vector consisting of ones

$$
\mathbf{R}=\begin{bmatrix} 1 & 1 & 1 & 1 & \cdots \end{bmatrix},
$$

then the ith element of $\mathbf{R}[\mathbf{I}-\mathbf{S}]^{-1}$, like $\mathbf{R}$ a horizontal vector, is equal to the expectation of further life for a person who has attained the ith age. (In contrast to most demographic and actuarial work, this way of developing the subject takes individuals in midstate rather than completed ages. Unless the states were age intervals much shorter than 1 year, calling the midstates $\frac{1}{2}, 1\frac{1}{2}, \cdots$ intervals would not make the expectations quite equal numerically to those calculated in the usual life table. The difference is of no consequence for the present purpose.)

Merely to arrive at a somewhat inaccurate version of the life table, the matrix analysis above is cumbersome as well as superfluous. Its advantage is that it gives stocks (of people) in terms of flows, not only for death but also for many other conditions.

We were able conveniently to sum the powers of $\mathbf{S}$ because $\mathbf{S}$ vanishes beyond a certain power. That does not happen in general, but in many situations the elements of the powers become smaller and smaller in something like a diminishing geometric progression. They do this when the matrix $\mathbf{S}$ is part of an absorbing chain; our matrix $\mathbf{S}$ above is part of an absorbing chain in the sense that everyone is absorbed by death sooner or later in the course of his progress through the several ages.

Some of the considerations just mentioned can be illustrated by a model of the school population and its emergence into the labor force. Consider only the flows portrayed in the graph of Fig. 7.3 and the corresponding matrix **S**, made by the method of Section 1.9. We embed **S** in a larger matrix **A** that includes absorption by completion of the several kinds of schooling:

$$\mathbf{A} = \begin{bmatrix} \mathbf{S} & \mathbf{O} \\ \mathbf{T} & \mathbf{I} \end{bmatrix},$$

or, writing 1 where positive transitions would be,

$$
\begin{array}{c}
 & & \text{From } j \\
 & & 1 \quad 2 \quad 3 \quad 4 \quad 5 \quad 6 \quad 7 \\
\text{To } i \;
\begin{array}{c} 1 \\ 2 \\ 3 \\ 4 \\ 5 \\ 6 \\ 7 \end{array}
& \mathbf{A} =
& \begin{bmatrix}
0 & 0 & 0 & 0 & 0 & 0 & 0 \\
1 & 0 & 0 & 0 & 0 & 0 & 0 \\
0 & 1 & 0 & 0 & 0 & 0 & 0 \\
0 & 0 & 1 & 0 & 0 & 0 & 0 \\
0 & 0 & 0 & 1 & 0 & 0 & 0 \\
0 & 0 & 0 & 1 & 0 & 0 & 0 \\
0 & 0 & 1 & 1 & 1 & 1 & 1
\end{bmatrix}
\end{array}
$$

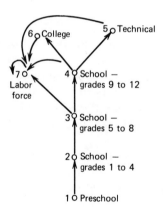

Fig. 7.3 Graph of progress through school system and points of emergence into the labor force, along with corresponding matrix **A**, disregarding mortality and repeating; time period = 4 years.

Each time period through which the process passes is represented by a multiplication by **A**; and as **A** moves on to higher powers, so does **S**:

$$\mathbf{A}^n = \begin{bmatrix} \mathbf{S}^n & \mathbf{O} \\ \mathbf{T}_n & \mathbf{I} \end{bmatrix},$$

where $\mathbf{T}_n$ represents the output of the system.

Various kinds of facts emerge from the scheme, including

1. The probability of being in the ith state after n time periods for an element that started in the jth state is $s_{ij}^{(n)}$ of $\mathbf{S}^n, i, j$ nonabsorbing.

2. The expected number of times the chain is in the ith nonabsorbing state if it starts in the jth state is n_{ij}, the jth element of the ith row of $\mathbf{N} = (\mathbf{I} - \mathbf{S})^{-1}$.

3. The expected number of steps before being absorbed for an element that starts in the jth nonabsorbing state is the jth element of $\mathbf{RN}$, where $\mathbf{R}$ is a horizontal vector consisting of ones.

4. The chance of being absorbed into state i of the large matrix $\mathbf{A}$, for an element that started in state j, is b_{ij} of the matrix $\mathbf{B}$, where $\mathbf{B} = \mathbf{TN} = \mathbf{T}(\mathbf{I} - \mathbf{S})^{-1}$. (Kemeny et al., 1974, p. 214).

7.7 THE DEMOGRAPHY OF ORGANIZATIONS

This book deals for the most part with large populations. It presents theory suited to the understanding of national populations, like those of the United States or Mexico. But this is an inappropriate restriction; every city ward, corporation, school, hospital, or seaside resort has its demography. The operations of communities and institutions depend on a flow of people, whose entries are analogous to births and their departures to deaths. For institutions that have relatively well-determined posts, differentiated by age and sex like a national population and in addition by skills and other role requirements, a thoroughgoing demography would be an extensive subject, and the pages that follow are barely an introduction to it. They draw from contributions due to Bartholomew (1967), Coleman (1973), March (1975), and Waugh (1971). Their claim to a place in this chapter is the help they offer in understanding distributions of income and similar variables.

We tackle the sheer size aspect first in political, then in economic, organizations.

Loss of Power

One aspect of the number of persons in an organization has been called by Coleman "loss of power," the diminishing influence of the individual as the organization grows in size. This appears clearly in voting, where the individual has a deciding voice only when his associates are evenly divided. The probability of such even division can be shown to be inversely proportional to the square root of the size of the voting group. If there are 100,000 individuals aside from Ego, the chance that they will split evenly is approximately one-tenth as great as if there are 1000 individuals. This inverse square root law is easily derived.

With $2n + 1$ members voting, the chance that Ego's vote will be decisive is the same as the chance that the other $2n$ individuals will split n for and n against whatever motion is under debate. The number of ways in which this can happen is the number of ways of putting $2n$ objects equally into two boxes, that is, $(2n)!/n!n!$. The total number of combinations of the $2n$ votes is 2^{2n}, since each could vote "yes" or "no." With equal chances on each vote the probability that the $2n$ votes will be evenly split is

$$p = \left(\frac{1}{2}\right)^{2n} \frac{(2n)!}{n!n!} .$$

The solution happens to be formally identical with that for the fraction unmarried in (7.4.7).

Entering as before the Stirling first approximation to the factorial, $n! = n^n e^{-n}\sqrt{2\pi n}$, we find that everything cancels except $1/\sqrt{\pi n}$. With $n = 3$, $1/\sqrt{\pi n}$ is 0.3257 against the exact 0.3125; with $n = 5$, $1/\sqrt{\pi n}$ is 0.2523 against the exact 0.2461. For higher values of n the error of the approximation is negligible, as Table 7.9 shows. This establishes the proposition that a person's power goes down as the square root of the size of the group within which he is operating provided he is the last one to vote; in the symmetrical condition before the voting starts each member can have no more and no less than $1/n$ of the power.

Organizing Political Success

As Coleman points out, one means by which an individual can apply social skill to attain power is by restructuring the electorate. In real life an electorate, whether it be a local boys' club, a town, a nation, or the Congress of the United States, is made up of cliques, factions, committees, parties, and other subgroups. In the smallest cell the probability $1/\sqrt{\pi n}$ provides an appreciable chance to the individual. Ego may well gain a sense of power through having the decisive vote in the clique with relative frequency, even though the decisions concern small matters such as how the clique as a whole will vote in a larger contest. If the voting is to be by groups, like an electoral college, Ego's chance of being the deciding voter is little different from that in individual voting. But evidently a person gains power nearly in the ratio of $\sqrt{2} = 1.41$ by being a member of a coalition containing half the members plus one. He gains if he becomes a member of a coalition of any size that votes together while others vote individually. Coleman proves that the size of coalition that maximizes the person's power is considerably less than the 51 percent that gives absolute control.

Economic Hierarchies

Economic organizations often fall naturally into hierarchies by virtue of the technical requirements of production and decision making. To simplify a typical organization, assume that there is one head of it, he has s persons reporting directly to him, and each of these has s persons reporting to him in turn, where s can be a number like 5 and is called the span of control (Cramer, 1972). If there are n levels then counted from the top downward the personnel of the organization will be distributed as follows:

Level	1	2	3	$\cdots$	n
Number of employees	1	s	s^2	$\cdots$	s^{n-1}

and the total personnel, say at time t, will be $P(t)=(s^n-1)/(s-1)$. Then, if a retirement takes place at the ith level, the chance of promotion for each individual at the $(i+1)$th level is $1/s^i$, which is a very small number for the lower echelons of the hierarchy. The theory here does not have any simple relation to that relating promotion and age of Sections 4.8 and 9.10.

Note that, as long as s is greater than 1, there are more persons in the lowest level than in all higher levels together. If seniority in promotion is maintained, the halfway point between bottom and top will always be within the lowest level. A person in an organization with $s=5$ will be 80 percent of the way to the top by the time he is promoted out of the lowest level, when the scale is in terms of individuals. But when the scale is in terms of levels, he will be only $1/n$ of the way to the top.

Suppose that the organization starts with P_0 employees, in k layers; then

$$P_0 = 1 + s + s^2 + \cdots + s^{k-1} = \frac{s^k-1}{s-1};$$

and if it is growing at rate r, its size at time t can be expressed as $P(t)=P_0e^{rt}$. Equating this to the above expression $P(t)=(s^n-1)/(s-1)$ gives

$$\frac{s^n-1}{s-1} = \left(\frac{s^k-1}{s-1}\right)e^{rt}. \tag{7.7.1}$$

Even for a small population the error in substituting s^n for s^n-1 and s^k for s^k-1 is negligible. The substitution permits solving (7.7.1) for n:

$$s^n = s^k e^{rt},$$

so that

$$n = k + \frac{rt}{\ln s}, \tag{7.7.2}$$

where k, the initial number of levels, depends only on the initial population and the span of control. The conclusion is that the creation of new levels goes on at the steady rate of $r/(\ln s)$ per unit of time or, equivalently, that each $(\ln s)/r$ units of time a new level is created.

A typical entrant who makes a career in a large organizaition virtually ensures that he will not rise far above the bottom. With a span s of 5, even spectacular success, rising above 0.999 of fellow employees, will put him only at 4.4 levels from the bottom, or in the fifth layer. This is of course modified for a two-class organization, like the traditional British army, in which one entered either as an enlisted man, with zero chance of rising above sergeant, or as an officer, with appreciable chance of rising to the highest ranks.

The boundaries of an organization are not always well defined; in fact, they may be determined by the viewpoint of the individual. An orderly in a hospital is near the bottom of the paid hierarchy; but if he thinks of patients as part of the hospital, he adds a substantial layer below him. A teaching assistant in a college is at the bottom or not, depending on whether students are included in the hierarchy. A faculty member may be high in his department, but low in the collection of departments in the country that make up his professional peer group.

Suppose that the rules of an organization call for absolute seniority, so that everyone has a turn at the top, if only for a short period. In a stationary condition the fraction of his service that he could have at the top is

$$\frac{1}{P} = \frac{s-1}{s^n - 1}.$$

If $s = 5$, $n = 9$, he could be boss for $4/(5^9 - 1) = 1/488{,}000$ of his career, which works out to 11 office minutes in the 45 years from age 20 to age 65.

But if the situation is hopeless for the mass of people in an organization, by the same logic the person who has an exceptional endowment of luck, brains, or influence can very quickly rise to the top. If the organization has 488,000 employees, and everyone in it above the bottom level has 5 people reporting to him, there are only 9 layers. A person starting at the bottom need be promoted only once every 3 years to become head of General Motors before he is 50.

Chapter Eight

PROJECTION AND FORECASTING

All statistical facts refer to the past. The United States Census of April 1970 counted 203 million of us, but no one knew this until the following November, and the details of the count were published over the course of years. The census differs only in degree from stock market prices, which are hours old before they appear in the daily press. There are no exceptions—not even statistics of intentions—to the rule that all data are to some degree obsolete by the time they reach us.

On the other hand, all use of data refers to the future; the business concern proposing to set up a branch in a certain part of the country consults the census but is interested in what it tells only as an indication of what will come in the future. The branch plant, or a school or hospital, may take 3 years to build and will be in existence over the following 30 years; whether or not the decision to build was wise depends on circumstances between 3 and 33 years hence, including the number and distribution of people over that period.

8.1 FORECASTING: BOTH UNAVOIDABLE AND IMPOSSIBLE. PAST DATA, PRESENT ACTION, AND FUTURE CONDITIONS OF PAYOFF

That all data refer to the past and all use of data to the future implies a line between past and future drawn at "now." Without continuities that make possible extrapolation across that line statistical data would be useless, indeed the very possibility of purposeful behavior would be in doubt.

The separation between a past census and the future in which action will be implemented is not only the instant of *now*, but also a finite period of time that includes the interval from enumeration of the census to publication of its results, the interval between their publication and the use of them in making a decision, and the interval between the decision and its implementation. The slab of time separating past data on population and the start of operation of a factory or school or telephone exchange decided upon by projecting these data can easily be a decade or more. Prediction often consists in examining data extending several decades back into the past and inferring from them what will happen several decades in the future, with one decade of blind spot separating past and future.

Since our knowledge of population mechanisms is weak, moreover, predictions or forecasts, more appropriately and modestly called projections, must involve some element of sheer extrapolation, and this extrapolation is from a narrow data base. Below the observations is an historical drift in underlying conditions that makes the distant past irrelevant to the future. If in the nineteenth century fluctuations in population were caused largely by epidemics, food scarcities, and other factors, and if now these factors are under better control but even larger changes in population are caused by parental decisions to defer or anticipate births, then carrying the series back through the nineteenth century will not be of much help in present extrapolations to the future. Thus, even supposing the continuity that makes forecasting possible in principle, the volume of past data enabling us to make a particular forecast is limited. Moreover, this intrinsic scarcity of relevant data is in addition to the shortcomings of past statistical collections. For such reasons some of those who are most knowledgeable refuse to take any part in forecasting. Yet ultimately the refusal to forecast is absurd, for the future is implicitly contained in all decisions. The very act of setting up a school on one side of town rather than the other, of widening a road between two towns, or of extending a telephone exchange is in itself a bet that population will increase in a certain way; not doing these things is a bet that population will not increase. In the aggregate implicit bets, known as investments, amount to billions of dollars each year. The question is only who will make the forecast and how he will do it—in particular, whether he will proceed intuitively or use publicly described methods. As Cannan (1895) said in the very first paper using the components method of forecasting, "The real question is not whether we shall abstain altogether from estimating the growth of population, but whether we shall be content with estimates which have been formed without adequate consideration of all the data available, and can be shown to be founded on a wrong principle."

In any concrete investment decision, the bet on population is combined with a bet on purchasing power, on preferences for one kind of goods rather than another, on technology as it affects alternative methods of production. The component of the bet that is our interest in this book, population, is somehow incorporated into a package of bets.

Heavy Stakes on Simultaneous Lotteries

A school construction program, for example, cannot be based on population forecasts alone; it requires participation rates as well—what fraction of the school-age population will want to attend school. These two elements have changed during the postwar period. During the 1960s United States population and participation rates both rose among youths of college age. Those 20 to 24 years of age numbered 10,330,000 in 1960 and 15,594,000 in 1970, a rise of 51 percent; the fraction enrolled at school went from 13.1 to 21.5 percent, a rise of 64 percent over the same decade. The ratio for the population being 1.51, and the ratio for participation 1.64, the combined effect of these two factors was the product of 1.51 and 1.64 or 2.48, equal to the ratio of 1970 to 1960 enrollment. Planning a school for any future period is in effect taking out a package of at least two lottery tickets.

Sometimes a movement of one of the factors counteracts a movement of the other, and in that case one turns out to be better off with the package bet than one would have been with either component alone. New college enrollments have started to decline in some parts of the country, while entrants are still the cohorts of the 1950s when births were constant or rising. Thus so far the two offset one another. But if decline in the participation rate continues through the 1980s, when the college-age cohorts will decline, the drop in attendance will be rapid.

It is often said that population forecasts should be made in conjunction with forecasts of all the other variables with which population interacts. The state of the economy is certainly related to population: marriages, and hence first births, will be numerous in good times, and will be few when incomes are low and unemployment high. This is the case in advanced countries; in poor countries births will fall with the process of economic development, and the sooner the rise in income the sooner will be the fall in births, at least on the theory that has been dominant. In both rich and poor countries shortages of land, energy, minerals, food, and other resources will, through different mechanisms, restrict population growth.

Our present capacity to discern such mechanisms is embarrassingly limited, for reasons briefly explored in Section 12.5. At best we can suggest which factors may be related to which other ones, but even the direction of effect, let alone quantitative knowledge of the relations, is still largely beyond us. That is why most of the work reported in this chapter, like most population projection as practiced, concentrates on demographic variables alone.

Projection as Distinct from Prediction

The preceding chapters, mostly based on stable theory, have also been concerned with projection in a population closed to migration, but always with *long-term* projection. They answered a variety of forms of such questions as: what will be the *ultimate* age distribution if present birth and death rates continue, or what difference will it make to the ultimate rate of increase if the birth rate to women over 35 drops permanently to half its present value, everything else remaining unchanged? The long-run answers are usually simpler than the *medium-term* ones of population projection.

The questions asked in the preceding chapters were so clearly of the form, "What will happen if ... ?" that there was no need to stress the conditional character of the statements referring to the future. Medium-term population projection offers the appearance of prediction, but the detailed reference to the future need not alter the conditional character of the numbers produced. Section 8.2 begins the treatment of projection, while Section 8.5 concerns prediction or forecasting, that is, statements intended to apply to a real rather than to a hypothetical future, but in fact the two topics are inseparable.

A projection is bound to be correct, except when arithmetic errors make the numbers constituting its output inconsistent with the assumptions stated to be its input. On the other hand, a forecast is nearly certain to be wrong if it consists of a single number; if it consists of a range with a probability attached, it can be correct in the sense that the range straddles the subsequent outcome the stated fraction of times in repeated forecasting. A probability can—indeed, should—be attached to a forecast, whereas a probability is meaningless for a (hypothetical) projection.

Despite the apparently sharp distinction, projections put forward under explicit assumptions are commonly interpreted as forecasts applying to the real future. Does the intention of the authors or the practice of the users determine whether projection or forecasting has occurred in a particular instance? Insofar as the assumptions of a projection are realistic, it is indeed a forecast. Those making projections do not regard all assumptions as equally worth developing in numerical terms and presenting to the public, but at any given moment they select a set regarded as realistic enough to be of interest to their readers. When they change to a different set, users suppose that the old assumptions have become unrealistic in view of current demographic events. More will be said later about the dangers and excitements of forecasting; the section immediately following deals with projection.

8.2 THE TECHNIQUE OF PROJECTION

Projection in demography is calculating survivors down cohort lines of those living at a given point of time, calculating births in each successive period, and adding a suitable allowance for migration. Of the four ways of looking at population dynamics described in Section 5.7, the one most convenient for the present purpose is that due to Leslie, and before him used by Cannan (1895), Bowley (1924), and especially Whelpton (1936).

Survivorship. Within the supposedly homogeneous subpopulation the first step is to convert the death rates that are assumed to apply at each period in the future into a life table, or else directly assume a life table for each future period. The column used for the purpose is the integral

$$_5L_x = \int_0^5 l(x+t)\,dt,$$

which in general varies over time as well as over age.

If the population at the jumping-off point of the projection is $_5P_x^{(0)}$ for ages $x = 0, 5, 10, \ldots$, the population 5 years older and 5 years later may be approximated as

$$_5P_{x+5}^{(5)} = {_5P_x^{(0)}} \left(\frac{_5L_{x+5}}{_5L_x} \right). \tag{8.2.1}$$

For changing rates a new life table would be assumed operative at each future 5-year interval and applied as in (8.2.1). By this means the population would be "survived" forward until the cohorts of the initial period were all extinguished.

Expression 8.2.1 is not exact even if the life table is appropriate, unless the distribution within the age group $(x, x+5)$ happens to be exactly proportional to the stationary population $l(x+t)$, $0 \leqslant t \leqslant 5$. If the population is increasing steadily at rate r, the distribution within the age interval will be proportional to $e^{-rt}l(x+t)$; and the greater r is, the more the population will be concentrated at the left end of the age interval. Being on the average younger within each age interval, it will average somewhat higher survivorship from one age interval to the next in the part of the span of life where mortality is rising with age. [Using the Taylor expansion

Table 8.1 Population and life table data for estimating survivorship of females 70–74 years of age, England and Wales, 1968

Age	$_5P_x$	$_5L_x$	l_x
65	1,280,500	391,456	82,172
70	1,033,400	339,660	73,827
75	753,600	265,710	61,324

Source: Keyfitz and Flieger (1971), pp. 152, 154.

method of Section 2.2, find a formula for the small addition to (8.2.1) to allow for this, and calculate its amount from the data of Table 8.1. A different form of correction is given as (11.1.16) in Keyfitz (1968, p. 249).]

Reproduction. To estimate the births of girl children to women in each 5-year age interval we need a set of age-specific birth rates, say F_x, for ages x to $x+4$ at last birthday (for brevity omitting the prescript). The F_x might be obtained from past experience, over 1 calendar year, say, of observed live female births $_5B_x$ to women of exact age $(x, x+5)$. If midperiod population corresponding to these births numbered $_5P_x$, then $F_x = {_5B_x}/{_5P_x}$.

In the first time period we begin with $_5P_x^{(0)}$ women aged x to $x+4$ at last birthday and applying (8.2.1) end with $_5P_{x-5}^{(0)}({_5L_x}/{_5L_{x-5}})$ women in this age class. Within the age class an estimate of the mean surviving women or the average exposure per year during the 5 years is the average of these two numbers; 5 times this average yields the total female exposure to conception during the 5 years. Multiplication of the total exposure by F_x yields the expected births to women aged x to $x+4$ ($l_0 = 1$):

$$\frac{5}{2}\left[{_5P_x^{(0)}} + {_5P_{x-5}^{(0)}}\left(\frac{_5L_x}{_5L_{x-5}}\right)\right]F_x, \qquad x = \alpha, \alpha+5, \ldots, \beta-5. \qquad (8.2.2)$$

However, since we are interested in the population aged 0 to 5 rather than the number of births, we must multiply (8.2.2) by $_5L_0/5$ and sum over all fertile ages between α and β:

$$_5P_0^{(5)} = \frac{1}{2}\sum_\alpha^{\beta-5}\left[{_5P_x^{(0)}} + {_5P_{x-5}^{(0)}}\left(\frac{_5L_x}{_5L_{x-5}}\right)\right]{_5L_0}F_x. \qquad (8.2.3)$$

To calculate the number of women exposed to the risk of childbearing as the average of the numbers at the beginning and at the end of the period is a slight overstatement of exposure if the increase is at a steady rate, that is, rising geometrically and so concave upward. The correction for this has been presented elsewhere (Keyfitz, 1968, p. 252) and will here be disregarded.

Extension to All Ages and Both Sexes. If convenience in arranging the worksheets were thereby served, we could first confine the calculation to ages under β, the end of reproduction. The survivorship and birth operations described above can be repeated for an indefinite sequence of 5-year cycles in disregard of the population beyond reproduction. Older ages can be filled in by repeated application of (8.2.1).

Males, like females beyond age β, can be dealt with after the projections for the female ages under age β are completed. Pending parental control of the sex of offspring, we can suppose a fixed ratio of males to females among births. If this ratio is taken as s, ordinarily a number close to 1.05, then multiplying the girl births by s, or the number of girls under 5 years of age by $s_5 L_0^* / {}_5 L_0$ (where ${}_5 L_0^*$ refers to the male life table, ${}_5 L_0$ to the female), will give the corresponding number of boys. The male part of the projection can then be filled out by repeated application of (8.2.1), using a life table for males.

The procedure described to this point can alternatively be arranged as matrix multiplication to secure a numerically identical result. The number of females in successive age groups is recorded in the top half of a vertical vector $\mathbf{P}$ and the number of males in the bottom half. The vector, containing 36 elements if 5-year age intervals to 85–89 are recognized for each sex, is premultiplied by a matrix $\mathbf{M}$ whose nonzero elements are in its subdiagonal and its first and nineteenth rows. Population after t cycles of projection at constant rates will be $\mathbf{P}_t = \mathbf{M}^t \mathbf{P}_0$. If fertility ends at age $\beta = 50$, the upper left-hand corner of the matrix will be a 10×10 submatrix containing birth elements in its first row, and constituting the self-acting portion of the larger matrix (Table 8.2). Every part of the preceding description can be readily altered to provide for different rates from one period to another, and in practical work rates are assumed to change.

The numerical implementation of the projection is more easily programmed but is less economical with the matrix (since it involves many multiplications by zero) than with (8.2.1) and (8.2.2), to which the matrix is equivalent. On the other hand, the theoretical properties of the projection process are more easily studied in the matrix formulation, especially the approach to stability (Lopez, 1961; McFarland, 1969; Parlett, 1970).

The upper left-hand 10×10 submatrix of $\mathbf{M}$ shown in Table 8.2 can be called $\mathbf{A}$ and analyzed with the concepts of Section 1.9. By drawing a graph, we can show $\mathbf{A}$ to be irreducible in that its positive elements are so arranged as to permit passage from any position to any other. Its primitivity—that there is at least one power N such that all elements of $\mathbf{A}^N$ are

Table 8.2 Female-dominant projection matrix M with 36 rows and 36 columns, and vector $P^{(0)}$ in 5-year age intervals, $l_0 = l^*_0 = 1$; male life table and population distinguished by asterisk

$$
M=\begin{bmatrix}
0 & 0 & \dfrac{_5L_0}{2}\left(\dfrac{_5L_{15}}{_5L_{10}}F_{15}\right) & \dfrac{_5L_0}{2}\left(F_{15}+\dfrac{_5L_{20}}{_5L_{15}}F_{20}\right) & \cdots & 0 & 0 & 0 & 0 & \cdots \\[2ex]
\dfrac{_5L_5}{_5L_0} & 0 & 0 & 0 & \cdots & 0 & 0 & 0 & 0 & \cdots \\[2ex]
0 & \dfrac{_5L_{10}}{_5L_5} & 0 & 0 & \cdots & 0 & 0 & 0 & 0 & \cdots \\[2ex]
0 & 0 & \dfrac{_5L_{15}}{_5L_{10}} & 0 & \cdots & 0 & 0 & 0 & 0 & \cdots \\[1ex]
\vdots & \cdot & \cdot & \cdot & & \vdots & \vdots & \vdots & \vdots & \vdots \\[1ex]
0 & 0 & s\dfrac{_5L^*_0}{2}\left(\dfrac{_5L_{15}}{_5L_{10}}F_{15}\right) & s\dfrac{_5L^*_0}{2}\left(F_{15}+\dfrac{_5L_{20}}{_5L_{15}}F_{20}\right) & \cdots & 0 & 0 & 0 & 0 & \cdots \\[2ex]
0 & 0 & 0 & 0 & \cdots & \dfrac{_5L^*_5}{_5L^*_0} & 0 & 0 & 0 & \cdots \\[2ex]
0 & 0 & 0 & 0 & \cdots & 0 & \dfrac{_5L^*_{10}}{_5L^*_5} & 0 & 0 & \cdots \\[2ex]
0 & 0 & 0 & 0 & \cdots & 0 & 0 & \dfrac{_5L^*_{15}}{_5L^*_{10}} & 0 & \cdots \\[1ex]
\cdot & \cdot & \cdot & \cdot & & \cdot & \cdot & \cdot & \cdot & \\
\cdot & \cdot & \cdot & \cdot & & \cdot & \cdot & \cdot & \cdot &
\end{bmatrix}
\qquad
P^{(0)}=\begin{bmatrix}
_5P_0 \\[1ex]
_5P_5 \\[1ex]
_5P_{10} \\[1ex]
_5P_{15} \\[1ex]
\cdot \\ \cdot \\ \cdot \\[1ex]
_5P^*_0 \\[1ex]
_5P^*_5 \\[1ex]
_5P^*_{10} \\[1ex]
_5P^*_{15} \\[1ex]
\cdot \\ \cdot
\end{bmatrix}
$$

208

positive for that N—follows as long as any two relatively prime ages have nonzero fertility.

This description corresponds to the usual execution of the projection in being female dominant: all births are imputed to females. The same theory is applicable to a process in which births are imputed to males. With the prevailing method of reproduction a male and a female are required for each birth, and with either male or female dominance the other sex is implicitly taken to be present in whatever numbers are required.

Age versus Other Variables

The concentration on age in the projection described above, though it follows a long and honorable tradition, may be considered arbitrary from a wider viewpoint. We know that mortality and fertility rates depend on age, but they also depend (though less decisively) on rural and urban residence, education, social class, and many other variables.

A transition matrix that recognizes rural and urban residence and disregards age can easily be devised. Such a matrix and vector are

$$\mathbf{MP}^{(0)} = \begin{bmatrix} m_{rr} & m_{ur} \\ m_{ru} & m_{uu} \end{bmatrix} \begin{bmatrix} P_r \\ P_u \end{bmatrix}, \tag{8.2.4}$$

where m_{ru} is the fraction moving from rural to urban, and m_{ur} that from urban to rural. If m_{ur} and m_{ru} were zero, m_{rr} and m_{uu} would be the change ratios of rural and urban parts. By repeated application of (8.2.4), the population at the end of t periods of 5 years is $\mathbf{M}^t\mathbf{P}^{(0)}$. The procedure would be preferred if a move to an urban area caused a change in natural increase greater than the change in going from one age group to another.

Recognition of rural and urban residence does not preclude recognition of age. We can make area the primary classification and show the breakdown by age within each area, as does Rogers (1968, p. 13), or else we can take age first and show within each age the rural and urban areas, as does Feeney (1970).

The usual model of projection recognizes age and sex, sometimes region, less often rural and urban parts, and in a few countries race. But age and sex have been the universal dimensions of population projection since the 1940s; no other is accepted as indispensable.

Yet the concentration on age and sex could represent a cultural lag. It might be that at certain times this breakdown is important, at other times less so.

To see just how much improvement results from recognizing age and sex, as against not recognizing them, the experiment of Table 8.3 was

Table 8.3 Projections for 20 populations over a 15-year time period, (*a*) neglectin age and sex, and (*b*) taking account of age and sex, in both cases neglectin migration, compared with observed populations 15 years later; closer of (*a*) and (*b* is starred

t	Population (000s) $P_t/1000$	Rate of natural increase per 1000 population $1000r$	Projected 15 Years Without age and sex $P_t e^{15r}/1000$ (*a*)	By age and sex Total of $M^3 P_t/1000$ (*b*)	Observed at time $t+15$ $P_{t+15}/1000$
United States					
1920	106,630	10.93	125,627*	123,665	127,25
1945	131,976	11.64	157,153*	150,910	179,99(
Japan, 1951	84,260	15.71	106,651	106,607*	98,85
Belgium, 1935	8,279	3.01	8,661*	8,346	8,64(
France, 1876	36,824	3.54	38,832	38,447*	38,13
Hungary, 1951	9,423	8.76	10,746	10,427*	10,17
Netherlands, 1935	8,387	11.70	9,996*	9,889	10,11
Norway, 1951	3,296	10.08	3,834	3,674*	3,75
Sweden					
1780	2,104	8.59	2,393	2,381*	2,27
1805	2,418	6.39	2,661*	2,666	2,57
1830	2,876	6.70	3,180	3,216*	3,29
1855	3,625	9.23	4,163*	4,144	4,16
1880	4,572	11.96	5,470*	5,485	4,89
1905	5,278	10.68	6,195*	6,265	5,87
1930	6,131	3.18	6,431*	6,409	6,6
1945	6,636	9.12	7,609*	7,287	7,4
Switzerland, 1951	4,749	7.39	5,306*	5,118	5,91
England and Wales					
1941	38,743	1.41	39,571*	38,259	44,66
1946	40,595	7.36	45,333*	43,273	46,16(
Australia, 1951	8,422	13.61	10,329*	9,887	11,55(

carried out. For each of 20 populations a 15-year projection was made by age and sex, using the age-sex-specific rates of birth and death for the initial moment—1 year, 3 years, or 5 years, but always symmetrically arranged around the midpoint of the stated jumping-off year. Except for the constancy of the rates assumed and the omission of migration, this is the usual projection by periods and is designated as (*b*) in the table.

Contrasted with this is the simpler projection in which no account is taken of age and sex, but the crude or observed rates of birth and death are made to provide a rate of increase, and that rate is applied to the population of the jumping-off moment. This method, which has not been used by demographers in good standing for the last 40 years or more, is shown as (a) in the table.

The observed population 15 years later is the last column of the table, and projections (a) and (b) may be compared with it. I had the intention, before I saw the outcome, of estimating quantitatively how much improvement is due to the incorporation of age and sex, by seeing how much closer column (b) was to the subsequent performance. That column (a) would turn out equally well was never anticipated. In fact, in the slight majority of the instances (marked with an asterisk) the simple projection (a) comes closer to the performance than (b), which recognizes age and sex.

There are obvious qualifications in regard to the result. An experiment involving 20 cases is too small, especially since they are not entirely independent of one another; when the European birth rate was falling, somewhat the same influences acted on age distribution in all countries. (However, a similar experiment on an additional 20 cases, using a 10-year prediction span, gave a similar result.) The use of fixed rather than changing rates of birth and death is a handicap equally to methods (a) and (b). The same is true for the absence of migration, omitted because data are more difficult to come by, and also because it presents special problems: should one use the absolute numbers of the jumping-off year or the rates, and how would they be applied by age and sex?

The conclusion from the experiment is that in some circumstances the effect of age is important, and in others it is not. The experimenting summarized in Table 8.3 hardly constitutes justification for abandoning age, especially since we usually need the forecast by age, but we should not be under the illusion that projection by age and sex is a powerful technique for discerning the future.

To find which of the other dimensions can provide real gains in accuracy of forecast will require additional experimenting similar to that of Table 8.3. We ought to be trying to project marriages, and then applying rates of nuptial fertility; perhaps not age within marriage but duration of marriage is the superior variable; perhaps first births, second births, and so on are more easily extrapolated separately than are births of all orders together, and so the model ought to be order-specific.

Whatever the variables recognized, their change from period to period is easily provided for. Each 5-year period would have its own projection matrix, so that after t periods we would have not $\mathbf{M}^t \mathbf{P}^{(0)}$ but instead, if

M_{i-1} is the matrix for the ith period,

$$P^{(t)} = M_{t-1} \ldots M_2 M_1 M_0 P^{(0)}. \qquad (8.2.5)$$

Whereas the changing matrix can be symbolically incorporated into a formula without difficulty, the attempt to determine the elements of the matrix, that is, to say what future mortality and fertility will be, is the most difficult problem of demography, and will be the subject of Section 8.4.

Projection in a Heterogeneous Population

When a heterogeneous population is projected without recognition of its subpopulations, the result is always lower than what would have been found by applying the same projection process to the subpopulations and adding. This was shown to be true in Section 1.4, without recognizing age. It is true also for projections by age, but to prove it in general for an arbitrary initial age vector is difficult.

As an example that will suggest the quantitative effect, the United States population in 1966 without breakdown by color, as projected with a life table made from the deaths in that year and the fertility rates implied by the 1966 births, results in a total population for 1981 of 230,477,000. Recognizing the two separate groups of Whites and Nonwhites, whose 1966 populations, births, and deaths add exactly to the totals for the United States, constructing life tables and age-specific birth rates for the two groups separately, and then projecting each by means of its own life table and birth rates, gives 1981 Whites as 199,287,000 and Nonwhites as 31,441,000, which add to 230,728,000. The deficiency of the projection not recognizing color is 251,000, or about 1 part in 1000, after 15 years. After 100 years the two separate projections add to 8 percent more than the projection without breakdown by color.

8.3   APPLICATIONS OF PROJECTION

Projection lends itself to making "if ... then ..." statements; indeed it consists of such statements. If England and Wales have the same age-specific birth and death rates as in 1968 for the following 25 years, the total population will grow from the 48,593,000 estimated for 1968 to 54,869,000 in 1993. The increase will average 0.0049 or 4.9 per 1000 per year, less than the intrinsic rate r of 1968, which was 6.9 per 1000. The slower rate of the projection is due to an unfavorable 1968 age distribution.

The United States 1967 population, projected at 1967 rates, amounts to 230,109,000 by 1982, an average rate of increase of slightly over 1 percent per year. In this case the rate of increase is raised by an exceptionally large proportion of women in childbearing ages; the intrinsic rate r of 1967 was only 0.74 percent.

Population Dynamics with One Cause of Death Eliminated

A transparently simple application of projection involves the effect on population growth of eliminating a particular cause of death, say cancer. We want the effect of this change separate from the effects of all other changes that may take place. Excluding the effect of the birth rate or of income incurs no difficulties, but excluding changes in other causes of death raises a problem if these causes would become more (or less) serious as a direct result of eliminating cancer. Since we know little about the interrelations of the several causes, we assume that age by age the others remain unchanged when cancer is eliminated. (Section 2.6)

A life table was calculated omitting all mortality from cancer, and another omitting all mortality from heart disease, using the technique of Section 2.6 and data for the United States, 1964. The unaltered table and each of these two modifications were applied to the 1964 female population of the United States to separate out the effects of the two causes on the rate of increase and on the age distribution of the ultimate stable population. The resulting rates and age distributions are shown in Table 8.4, always supposing that the birth rates of 1964 continue to prevail.

The intrinsic rate of natural increase is affected by less than 1 part in 200 by omission of heart disease: it rises from 0.01573 to 0.01579. Not many women are struck down by heart disease at ages before the end of childbearing. Cancer deaths are fewer in total, but they affect younger ages in somewhat more cases and so their omission produces a slightly greater rise in the rate of increase.

To represent the effect on age distribution we have used the stable equivalent $\mathbf{Q}$, corresponding to an age distribution, or an age–sex distribution $\mathbf{P}_0$, obtained in (7.3.3) as

$$\mathbf{Q} = \frac{\mathbf{M}^t \mathbf{P}_0}{e^{5rt}}, \tag{8.3.1}$$

where t is large, say 100 cycles of 5 years, and e^{5r} is the ratio of increase per cycle as t becomes large. The stable equivalent is the number of persons in each category of age and sex that could be projected to (distant) time t by multiplication by e^{rt} at all ages, with assurance that the same numbers at time t would result as from projection of the observed population by the usual components method described in Section 8.2.

Table 8.4   Ultimate age distribution and intrinsic rates corresponding to United States 1964 population, with (a) all causes of death, (b) all causes except heart disease, and (c) all causes except cancer (thousands of persons)

Age	(a) All causes of death		(b) Death from heart disease removed		(c) Death from cancer removed	
	Stable equivalent		Stable equivalent		Stable equivalent	
	Males	Females	Males	Females	Males	Females
0–4	10,535	10,125	10,537	10,127	10,537	10,126
5–9	9,698	9,329	9,699	9,330	9,700	9,330
10–14	8,943	8,609	8,942	8,608	8,944	8,609
15–19	8,229	7,941	8,227	7,939	8,230	7,940
20–24	7,545	7,317	7,543	7,315	7,546	7,315
25–29	6,910	6,737	6,911	6,737	6,914	6,736
30–34	6,326	6,195	6,332	6,198	6,332	6,197
35–39	5,774	5,682	5,795	5,693	5,786	5,693
40–44	5,238	5,193	5,290	5,216	5,260	5,219
45–49	4,700	4,719	4,808	4,762	4,740	4,768
50–54	4,141	4,249	4,335	4,326	4,212	4,332
55–59	3,547	3,780	3,864	3,906	3,662	3,902
60–64	2,921	3,299	3,390	3,503	3,088	3,463
65–69	2,268	2,788	2,907	3,109	2,485	2,992
70–74	1,629	2,242	2,429	2,721	1,872	2,474
75+	2,003	3,491	7,833	11,856	2,596	4,168
Total	90,407	91,696	98,842	101,346	91,904	93,264
Total both sexes	182,103		200,188		185,168	
Females $\frac{15-44}{\text{Total}} \times 100$	42.60		38.57		41.92	
Female mean age	31.32		36.79		32.03	
Intrinsic rates						
Birth	0.02348		0.02124		0.02308	
Death	0.00774		0.00546		0.00726	
Natural increase	0.01573		0.01579		0.01582	
Sex ratio						
All ages	0.986		0.975		0.985	
Ages 75+	0.574		0.661		0.623	

The stable equivalent shown in Table 8.4 is little affected at younger ages by the omission of heart disease or cancer, and even by age 50 the increase is less than 5 percent for males and 2 percent for females. At the very oldest ages of 75 and over, however, the effect of eliminating heart disease is dramatic: a nearly fourfold rise for men and well over a threefold increase for women.

The net result is a rise in the average age of females from 31.32 to 36.79 years with the elimination of heart disease, and to 32.03 with the elimination of cancer. The percentage of females in the childbearing ages 15 to 44 falls from 43.21 to 39.56 with the elimination of heart disease, and to 42.54 with the elimination of cancer.

The main limitation of the result given in Table 8.4 is the certainty that if heart disease were eliminated other causes would also be affected. They would be increased insofar as heart disease selects weaker individuals, more subject to other ailments than randomly selected members of the population, an issue raised in Section 3.4.

Effect of Immediate Drop to Replacement Fertility

Continuing with the effort to make population projection perform experiments, we ask another question: "What would be the ultimate stationary population if birth rates were to drop immediately and permanently to bare replacement level?" Though a drop to bare replacement would sooner or later terminate growth, a large concentration of women at childbearing ages exists as a result of growth in the past, and the ultimate level would be considerably higher than the present population.

The question may be answered by a population projection, applying the observed life table and observed age-specific birth rates divided by R_0, the net reproduction rate. We refrain from trying to guess what mortality is going to do, nor do we suppose changes in the age distribution of childbearing. The object is to see the outcome of a drop to replacement fertility if everything else remains unchanged.

Taking the birth and death rates for the year listed, making a life table from the death rates, dividing the birth rates by R_0, and projecting some 500 years into the future gives the results shown in Table 8.5 for six countries. Thus Colombia showed 17.993 million people in 1965; the projection climbed to 29.786 million, a rise of 65.5 percent. Such a projection takes full account of the initial age distribution.

The results can be compared with the corresponding calculation on the stable age distribution. We saw in Section 6.6 that the ratio of the ultimate stationary to the present population, on the assumption of an immediate

Table 8.5 Current and ultimate stationary populations, on assumption that birth rates drop immediately to stationary level, for six countries

| | Number (000s) | | Percent increase |
Population	Current	Ultimate	to ultimate
Chile, 1965	8,584	12,916	50.5
Colombia, 1965	17,993	29,786	65.5
Ecuador, 1965	5,109	8,518	66.7
Italy, 1966	53,128	62,189	17.1
Peru, 1963	14,713	23,080	56.9
United States			
1966	195,857	259,490	32.5
1967	197,863	267,096	35.0

drop to bare replacement fertility, is

$$\frac{b \overset{o}{e}_0}{r\mu}\left(\frac{R_0-1}{R_0}\right),$$

(8.3.2)

where the birth rate b, the rate of natural increase r, the net reproduction rate R_0, and the mean age μ of childbearing in the stationary population are all calculated before the fall. Applying (8.3.2) to Colombian females of 1965 gives 1.59, that is, an ultimate rise of 59 percent over the 1965 population. This is somewhat less than the 66 percent rise on the projection, so presumably the observed 1965 Colombian sex–age distribution departed from the stable one in a direction favorable to reproduction. However, the departure could be an artifact due to defects in the statistics. In the face of inaccurate primary data it is an advantage to have available both the projection and the stable formula (8.3.2).

A number of such experiments are described by Frejka (1973). He sees what the ultimate stationary population will be with an immediate drop and with a drop spread over 25 years. He does not keep other factors constant at their base values, but supposes that mortality will fall according to a certain curve. This has the advantage of greater realism if indeed the projected fall of mortality occurs. On the other hand, it has the drawback of requiring us to keep in mind a particular fall in mortality rather than just constancy. Such a conflict between realism and simplicity is typical of demographic projection.

We have all thought how convenient it would be if we knew the condition at some distant future and could interpolate between the jumping-off point and then. Sooner or later the population must cease to grow; and if we could only guess the date at which it would become stationary, most of the problem of forecasting would be solved, for the interpolation could not involve the gross errors to which extrapolation is subject. Frejka's treatment is an attempt along this line.

8.4 THE SEARCH FOR CONSTANCIES

Any forecasting method, whether naive or sophisticated, depends on some function being approximately constant. For the short term it may be sufficient to suppose that the absolute number of births of the current year will be repeated over the next few years, and the same for deaths and migration. More convincing is to suppose that the crude rates will be constant for the next few years. Insofar as age distribution is changing, the rates that are supposed fixed had better be age specific. Insofar as a visible trend appears in the age-specific rates, one may wish to take year-to-year differences of the age-specific rates as fixed; if $_5M_x^t$ is the death rate at time t for the age interval x to $x+4$, then $_5M_x^t - {_5M_x^{t-1}}$ being constant will give $_5M_x^{t+1} = 2{_5M_x^t} - {_5M_x^{t-1}}$. If the past trend looks to be exponential, the logarithm of the numbers in previous years can be supposed to have fixed first differences.

If the trend in total population can be assumed to be logistic, what is fixed is the ratio of the difference of reciprocals in successive years; with p_t standing for the population in year t,

$$\frac{1/p_t - 1/p_{t-1}}{1/p_{t-1} - 1/p_{t-2}}$$

is constant.

Better adapted ways of choosing the entities that are to be held constant are provided by relational methods, which deserve a more detailed treatment.

Relational Methods

To project mortality or fertility or nuptiality—indeed, any component that varies with age—we need to determine not only overall trends but also what is going to happen to the several ages. We could suppose that all ages are affected in the same way, either adding to all age-specific rates some constant for each year that goes by, or multiplying them by some constant. But actual changes are far from being either constant increments or constant multiples applicable to all ages. We could meet this objection by extrapolating each age separately, but that would produce gratuitous errors, as well as inconvenient discontinuities; with most data age distributions would become less and less smooth as we went forward in time on separate projections for the several ages.

We could observe how past changes have occurred, for instance, how successive mortality tables for Sweden differ, and use the Swedish trend as showing the future for countries that are not yet down to the Swedish level of mortality. Similar possibilities exist for fertility and nuptiality. This method has been used, but it presents difficulties. The problem is to find some way of relating the future to the past that involves a small number of parameters, say two, and that is a sufficiently good fit to all times for the two parameters extrapolated to produce acceptable curves for future dates.

Mathematical curves would serve this purpose if any could be found that fitted closely enough. If the age distribution of childbearing could be satisfactorily fitted by a normal curve, for example, we could extrapolate the total, mean age, and variance of ages to find the age distribution of childbearing at future times. But Lotka's (1939, p. 70) normal curve does not fit past data well enough to justify its use for prediction, nor does the incomplete gamma function applied by Wicksell (1931) or Hadwiger's (1940) more elaborate exponential. (Keyfitz, 1968, Chapter 6, is a secondary source on these.) Murphy and Nagnur (1972) tried a Gompertz curve, long used for mortality, with some success.

Success in specifying algebraic or transcendental curves has been incomplete enough that most workers resort to sets of model tables, for fertility as well as for mortality. A set of useful model fertility tables has been published by Coale and Trussell (1974), which do for this component what the Coale and Demeny (1966) tables did for mortality.

An alternative is the relational method evolved by Brass (1974) over the course of some years of experimenting. Instead of aiming at the desirable but unavailable mathematical curve, or attempting to sum up the entire range of empirical materials in a set of model tables, the relational method embraces changes through time in a flexible description involving two (or at most three) parameters. Let us see how the Brass method fits mortality; fertility and nuptiality may be treated in a similar way.

Mortality. In the first application, to mortality, Brass found that to go from one life table to another was easy if both were translated into logits, that is, their $l(x)$ columns were transformed by

$$Y(x) = \tfrac{1}{2} \ln \left[\frac{1 - l(x)}{l(x)} \right].$$

If the early table is distinguished by a subscript s, the relation is the linear

$$Y(x) = \alpha + \beta Y_s(x),$$

or, written out in full,

$$\tfrac{1}{2}\ln\left[\frac{1 - l(x)}{l(x)}\right] = \alpha + \frac{\beta}{2}\ln\left[\frac{1 - l_s(x)}{l_s(x)}\right].$$

In forecasting one would take a life table for time t_s as $l_s(x)$ and fit to it the table for later time t_1, finding the constants α_1 and β_1, say. A new α_2 and β_2 would be found on fitting the table for t_2 to t_1, and α_3 and β_3 on fitting the table for t_3 to t_2. The several fittings would indicate a trend in α and in β that could then be extrapolated into the future. The extrapolated α and β for future dates, along with the base life table $l_s(x)$, would carry the life table to the dates in question. Studying mortality trends of the past half-century in England and Wales, Brass considers it possible that in the future β may well come close to unity, and α decrease by 0.5 every 40 years. The trend in α and in β must be worked out for each population on which the method is tried. The method imports nothing—neither a mathematical curve nor model tables—from the experience of other populations than the one under consideration: for England and Wales β and the first difference of α are constant, but other functions of α and β would be used in other populations.

Are Longitudinal Relations Demonstrated by Cross-Sectional Data?

In seeking a constancy of some function of the population variables through time one is tempted to transfer a relation found in cross-sectional data. Constancy from place to place at a given time ought to be evidence of constancy through time. The provinces of India whose mortality is low seem also to be the ones whose fertility is low; does it not follow that, as mortality falls in the years ahead for the whole of India, so also will fertility? And—only a short step further—the low mortality may be argued to *cause* the low fertility, among other reasons because parents aim to have a certain number of children who survive to maturity. These statements may be true, and if they are they would be very helpful in forecasting. But other evidence than the cross-sectional relation is required to prove them, as can be seen from the very simple cases of Figs. 8.1 to 8.3.

Figure 8.1 is a stylized illustration of the problem for three provinces or other population groups, A, B, and C, with deaths in Fig. 8.1a and births in Fig. 8.1b. From the birth and death rates of the provinces at t_0, i.e., taking vertical cross sections of the two families of curves at t_0, we can

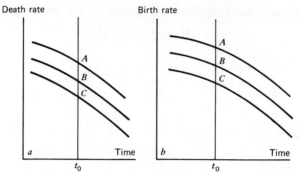

Fig. 8.1 Demographic transition for three provinces or other groups designated as *A*, *B*, and *C*.

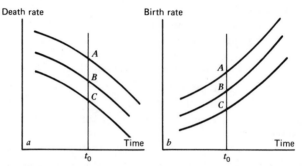

Fig. 8.2 Opposite to demographic transition for three provinces *A*, *B*, and *C*.

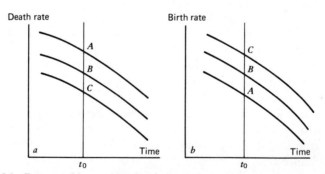

Fig. 8.3 Demographic transition for three provinces with sequence reversed.

obtain a cross-sectional correlation of birth rates and death rates, and it would be positive; the provinces are in the same sequence A, B, and C. On the other hand, we obtain a longitudinal correlation by comparing birth and death rates through time for any particular province. In Fig. 8.1 the longitudinal, like the cross-sectional, correlations of birth and death rates are positive.

But we could draw the curves differently and obtain the opposite result, as has been done in Fig. 8.2, where deaths are declining and births are rising. The correlation of birth and death rates through time for any of the provinces *A*, *B*, or *C* would be negative, though that for the cross section at any given time would again be positive.

Is the cross-sectional correlation even *necessary* to the correlation in time? Examine Fig. 8.3, drawn in the same way as Fig. 8.1, except that in Fig. 8.3*b* the births have been labeled differently. In this diagram the cross-sectional correlation is negative, while the correlation through time is positive. There is nothing impossible a priori about this arrangement. The cross-sectional correlation is neither necessary nor sufficient for the longitudinal one (Janowitz, 1971). This is part of the elusiveness of the inference of future trends from past conditions.

8.5 FEATURES OF FORECASTING AND FORECASTING ERROR

No one expects botanists, geographers, or anthropologists to make declarations regarding the future. Physicists do make predictions, but within an experimental situation closely protected against interference from outside events in the real world. Demographers, on the other hand, are expected to predict future population as it will actually occur. And they respond as best they can; much of the published literature in demography, and even more of the unpublished, whether written by amateurs or by professionals, consist in statements about the future.

We saw that a projection over t units of time can be written as $\mathbf{M}^t\mathbf{P}$, where $\mathbf{M}$ is a projection matrix and $\mathbf{P}$ the initial population vector. If we know the elements of $\mathbf{M}$ and of $\mathbf{P}$, the estimate of the future consists in the multiplication. We may incorporate in $\mathbf{M}$ and $\mathbf{P}$ several regions, rural and urban populations, ethnic and racial groups, or other divisions. We may admit that the transition probabilities are a function of time and say (equation 8.2.5) that at time t the population is

$$\mathbf{P}^{(t)} = \mathbf{M}_{t-1}\mathbf{M}_{t-2}\cdots\mathbf{M}_0\mathbf{P}^{(0)}.$$

The preceding paragraph, like Section 8.2, is complicated enough to have the effect of concealing the logical status of what we are doing. Age and other distinctions do matter, but their numerical effects are often small in comparison with the prediction error within any category. Let us drop the categories and think only of total population projected over one period, say of 30 years; thus we are back to $P_1 = MP_0$, but now the symbols are scalars. For example, the population of the United States was counted in 1970 at 203 million; what will be its number in the year 2000? The ultimate in simplicity is to say that, *if* the population increases by 33 percent, it will number 270 million. Most projections snow us with breakdowns by age, sex, race, and region, and take a number of time intervals, all of them valuable, but in their combination causing us to lose perspective on the problem. By peeling off the breakdown, we arrive at the essence of calculation of future population in its two aspects of projection and prediction.

Projection is where the 33 percent is hypothetical. All projection consists of such statements as the following: "*If* (which we do not assert) the population grows at 33 percent in 30 years, then by the year 2000 it will have increased to $203 \times 1.33 = 270$ million." The projection consists in performing the multiplication, is conditional on the 33 percent, and is as unassailable as the laws of arithmetic. No projection risks being in error; it cannot be proved or disproved by what the population actually turns out to be in the year 2000.

Stated in this stripped-down form, the result is wholly uninteresting. At most it does the reader the service of performing the multiplication, and in an age of computers no one would pay much to be told the bare arithmetical fact that $203 \times 1.33 = 270$. The demographer's service surely starts with his comment on the realism of the 1.33, and with that he enters the field of forecasting.

Forecasting is where the 33 percent is taken as the real prospective increase: "The population *will* grow 33 percent in 30 years." Unless this is to be soothsaying, we now need evidence for the 33 percent. Such evidence may be one or another kind of extrapolation; in the simplest case the argument would be that the next 30 years will show an increase of 33 percent because the last 30 years showed such an increase. A more sophisticated version would assert, not that the ratio will be constant, but that the rate of change in the ratio will be constant. In the most general statement the forecast asserts that some more complex function, possibly involving economic, ecological, psychological, or other variables sufficient to determine the future population numbers, will remain constant into the future, and the task of forecasting consists in the search for such a functional invariance.

One circumstance that can make prediction interesting is what makes a poker game interesting: the fact that the cards, first hidden as the future is hidden, are later turned face upward on the table, and so test the accuracy of the forecast. In economic forecasting a frequent span is 6 months or 1 year; such a period is not too long for the predictor to see whether he guessed right, or at least more accurately than someone else, and to learn from the experience. But 30 years, which is a typical span for demographic forecasting, is too long a wait for learning to occur. To wait 30 years to see the cards removes the interest inherent in the rapid alternation of fore-cast–verification–forecast–verification that holds us at the poker table.

Extrapolation Versus Mechanism

Any forecasting that takes itself seriously tries to base itself on the underlying mechanisms operating, rather than merely extrapolating trends. Yet the distinction is not always sharp. The components projection on which much stress is laid is indeed a mechanism, but it still depends on extrapolation of birth, death, and migration rates.

A mechanism that lends itself to prediction is Easterlin's model described in Section 9.11, in which age-specific birth rates depend negatively on the size of the cohort of an age to marry and bear children at the given time. In effect it predicts waves of twice the length of generation, so that in the United States birth rates would be low for the next decade or more, and only in the 1990s would they pick up again. (Of course, even if the mechanism is operative exactly as described, the intensity of its operation, measured by the constant γ of (9.11.1), would still have to be ascertained by extrapolation.)

Other mechanisms are less useful for forecasting. That working women have fewer children than nonworking women is true without telling us whether seeking work is primary and lack of children the result, or whether selection is involved–women who do not have children take jobs. But suppose the first case: that the fall in births during the 1960s was due to more and more women preferring work outside the home to child raising. Perhaps they needed the income; perhaps outside work came to carry greater prestige. Certainly women's liberation will reduce childbearing, at least until the day when men take over the unpaid work of child raising. To use this in prediction we would need some way of knowing in advance about the shifting preferences for work and income versus the satisfactions of motherhood. Will the uptrend in the former continue over the next decade and so maintain the downtrend in births?

The difficulty of answering this question suggests that the mechanism in question is an ad hoc explanation of the past, to be retained as long as women increasingly enter the labor force and the birth rate falls, but to be quickly dropped and replaced by some other mechanism as soon as births turn upward. One can imagine, after births do start to rise, articles showing how inevitable is the reassertion of the durable values of motherhood as opposed to ephemeral economic interest. Whether such explanations are true or false, if they come after the fact they are too late to forecast turning points.

In this difficult situation it is natural to resort to asking women what their childbearing intentions are—just as people are queried about their house-buying intentions, and firms their investment plans. Such data help but only in short-term forecasting. Most of the children born more than 5 years from now will be to mothers who are presently still in their teens, unmarried, in no position to provide a realistic statement of their futures as mothers (Ryder and Westoff, 1967; Siegel and Akers, 1969). For the shorter term, intentions may predict well; Westoff, Potter, and Sagi (1963) found that about the best predictor of whether or not a couple with two children will have a third is their own statement.

Even for estimating turning points in the birth curve less than 5 years ahead, however, the statements of wives have not always been borne out. Women may declare an intention that accords with present rates of childbearing, but once the future becomes the present they are influenced by whatever the fashion is at the time. It is too much to say that current childbearing influences stated intentions more than intentions anticipate future childbearing, but some hint of this does appear in the time series of intentions, on the one hand, and performance, on the other.

We have some evidence (Masnick and McFalls, 1976) that women's attitudes toward childbearing are formed (or manifest themselves) early in their married careers. If they start married life in a time of low fertility when contraception is practiced rigorously, they tend to continue to practice it. Such a fact, if the manner and degree of its operation could be established, would facilitate forecasting.

Shape of the Projection Fan

If we know the past, and must make estimates of the future, the population trajectory starts out as a single, somewhat jagged line, and at the moment where past and future meet fans out into a set of relatively smooth lines representing the several possibilities. Disregarding for the moment the errors, incompleteness, and delays in statistics on the past, the question is how the single line or curve, representing more or less certain past knowledge, fans out into the future to make the horn shape familiar in graphical representations of projection.

If the lines of the fan were straight, each would require only one parameter—say, the angle made with the time axis—for its full description.

Such straight lines imply that uncertainty increases in equal increments with time from the present—that if we know in 1970 that the population for 1980 will be in a certain range with a certain probability, the population for 1990 will be in twice that range, both expressed in numbers of persons (Fig. 8.4a).

If, on the other hand, one could say that for all future time the (fixed) rate of increase r would be within the range r_1 to r_2, the horn would take the shape of exponentials as in Fig. 8.4b. Drawn on semilog paper, this would be back to the form of Fig. 8.4a.

Only slightly more difficult is thinking that the future rate of increase would be $r(t)$ at time t, drawn from a specified probability distribution. Since, as in (1.5.1), population at time t is $P_t = P_0 \exp[\int_0^t r(\tau)\,d\tau]$, what is operative is the sum of $r(t)$. If the increases at the several times in the future are drawn independently at random, the variance of $\int_0^t r(\tau)\,d\tau$ is

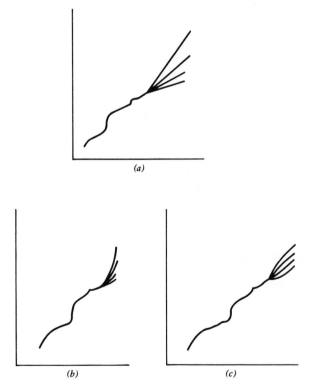

(a)

(b)   (c)

Fig. 8.4 Shape of the fan under various conditions. (a) Ignorance of population increasing with time in equal increments. (b) Ignorance of (fixed) rate of increase. (c) Future subject to diminishing variation.

proportional to the time t, the standard deviation to $\sqrt{t}$. The range in this case would be a curve like $e^{\sqrt{t}}$, in suitable units. Or under other circumstances the curve might be of the form $\exp(\sqrt{\sqrt{t}}\,)$ (Fig. 8.4c). A priori the possibilities are unlimited.

But now recall that we can predict survivorship better than births. As time moves on, more and more of the population will have been born since the jumping-off point, and a smaller and smaller fraction will consist of survivors from that point. As a larger fraction passes into the group known less well, the fan widens more rapidly than is shown in any of the three diagrams of Fig. 8.4.

In symbols, suppose that at a given future time f of the population will have been born since the jumping-off point and will be known with uncertainty represented by the standard deviation σ, and $1-f$ of the population with uncertainty $k\sigma$, where $k<1$. Then the accuracy with which the whole population is known has the standard deviation

$$\sigma^* = \sigma\sqrt{f^2 + (1-f)^2 k^2}\ .$$

The spread can be expressed directly in terms of survivors and births. For *ex ante* evaluation the population t years hence may be written as

$$P_t = \int_0^t B(\tau) l(t-\tau)\, d\tau + \int_0^\omega p(a)\frac{l(a+t)}{l(a)}\, da + I_t - E_t,$$

where

$B(\tau) =$ the births at time τ,

$l(t-\tau) =$ the probability of survival of a birth to
  age $t-\tau$, that is, to time t,

$p(a)\, da =$ the number of persons age a to $a + da$
  at the jumping-off point where $t=0$,

$I_t =$ the cumulative number of immigrants by time t, as
  projected from immigration statistics by a
  survivorship function,

$E_t =$ the cumulative number of emigrants, also as projected
  to time t.

The quantities in the equation are subject to different amounts of error—current population $p(a)$ is best known, prospective survivorship $l(a+t)/l(a)$ next best, future births $B(\tau)$ only poorly. Emigrants present more difficulties than immigrants in current statistics as well as in the future. Separate estimates need to be made of the precision of each of these components. As time goes on from the jumping-off point, the dependence of the forecast on future births increases, and hence the precision decreases. The fan of projections will correspondingly open out more widely than in straight lines or exponentials.

8.6   THE COMPONENTS OF FORECASTING ERROR EX ANTE

The errors that arise in estimates of the future are classifiable under five headings. This analysis is my interpretation of that due to Paul Meier, Lincoln Moses, Richard Savage, and others at the Hawaii Conference on Statistical Problems in Population Research, August 1971. Arrangement is in ascending order of difficulty of estimation, and probably also of magnitude.

1. There is random variation from the deterministic model on which the estimate was made. Corresponding to the deterministic model used for forecasting, one can construct many stochastic models, all with expected values equal to the forecast. The most obvious of these stochastic models allows the same probability to act on the several individuals independently.

In application to a single item, say births numbering B, the coefficient of variation (standard deviation divided by expectation) can be calculated as a function of the numbers involved, for example the number of births B. For large, closed populations, assuming statistical independence between individuals gives a coefficient of variation equal to $1/\sqrt{B}$. When births are in millions, the error is trifling; with even as few as 10,000 births the coefficient of variation is only 1 percent. This component of forecasting error is important only for populations as small as a neighborhood or a village.

2. The constants in the models are not known exactly. The projection may suppose the age-specific rates of birth and death, first differences of these rates over time, ultimate family size, or something else to be fixed into the future. If whatever is taken as constant really is constant but is improperly measured or assessed, the future will to that extent be incorrectly estimated. These errors of the past may be amplified in a forecast, but they still add little to the other, deeper errors inherent in forecasting and considered below.

3. The quantities supposed constant, which constitute the parameters of the model, really vary in time. Only a finite past record, a short sample of time periods, is available for estimating their paths. Often the sample of time periods is a single past year or decade. It is hardly a properly drawn sample, yet the forecaster has no other way of estimating the future values of the needed parameters.

4. Probably more important than any of the foregoing, the model itself is incorrectly specified. The main fault is not the bad estimates of parameters, but an altogether inappropriate function supposed to hold for all time. For example, the period age-specific rates of birth are held constant, when what is really constant is their first differences, or else not period rates at all but the average number of children born to a cohort. The finite past experience that can be brought to bear has little power to discriminate among models, as can be seen by experimenting with the logistic and explosion models of Section 1.6. It is not easy to compel the past to inform us which of several models that fit indifferently well will give the best forecast, yet the futures given by these models can be very different. Insofar as the underlying process has been really homogeneous over time, one can seek data extending further into the past, and so widen the base of experience on which the model is selected, but both the availability of the historical record and the homogeneity of the process set limits on this capability.

5. Finally, even perfect use of exact facts regarding a homogeneous past may be frustrated by the future being genuinely different. The uncertainty about the future is superimposed on projections of past data at the disposal of the demographer, and such uncertainty does not lend itself to estimation in advance. In some countries and epochs this fifth component of error will be small, but the twentieth century is not such an epoch. This component is wholly distinct from sampling error and is the characteristic special difficulty of prediction.

Of the five components of error the first three are, at least in principle, accessible to statistical analysis, and the fifth is not accessible by any means. A rough technique may be devised for handling the fourth component or, more strictly, the first four combined. This provides a lower bound for the overall error *ex ante*, that is to say, made at the same time as the estimate itself. This is contrasted below with the error *ex post*, calculable after the event predicted, the predictand is known, and which does include all five sources of error.

In the course of estimating the future many separate decisions have to be made, and none of these follows uniquely from any accepted principles. Extrapolation of death rates can proceed from a shorter or longer experience; it can be done separately for the several age–sex groups or for all groups together, supposing that mortality will improve according to the pattern of a series of model tables. If each time such a decision is made one or more other reasonable possibilities are also followed through, a large number of combinations of these alternatives will be available. Extrapolation from short versus long experience of deaths, and from separate ages versus all ages together following a series of model tables, and similarly for births, alone gives 16 combinations and therefore 16 forecasts. The variation among these provides an *ex ante* estimate of error.

Alternatively, if the calculation is more intuitive than these mechanical extrapolations, and a 2 percent per year decline in fertility is proposed, the estimator can ask himself whether 1 percent and 3 percent are also reasonable, or whether he would bet 19 to 1 odds that the range is limited to $1\frac{1}{2}$ to $2\frac{1}{2}$ percent. Similarly in regard to mortality and migration. The aggregation of these sources of error provides upper and lower bounds for the future population. The aggregation may be based on the assumption that the several errors act independently, that is to say, their squares are added, and at the end the square root taken, or more conservatively the errors may themselves be added.

The Length of the Experience Base

Every forecast works from some period in the past. As a minimum it takes the population of an initial year as its jumping-off point and assumes that the age-specific rates of birth, death, and migration of the initial year remain constant into the future. To derive a trend in such age-specific rates requires at least 2 past years; better estimates of trend can be obtained from 5, 10, or more years, using least squares or other fitting. The longer base will be of value also in providing an estimate of error of the fit. If the past were homogeneous, we could never have too much of it, and would incorporate the whole available statistical record in the forecast.

Since we always suspect heterogeneity in the past, under what circumstances is it desirable to use a long experience base and when is a short base to be preferred (Anderson, 1971)? If sudden or sharp changes occur from time to time, or a gradual drift in relationships is taking place, the experience base should be confined to the most recent time and be relatively short, in the hope that the part of the past used is homogeneous with the future. A prediction for the United States today would not be greatly aided by what happened before World War I, even if we had good data for that long past time.

The forecaster who would provide a distribution needs data even more badly than the one content to produce a single figure. He is even more tempted to go back in time to increase his stock, and also more concerned about the danger that his results will be distorted by changes in the system the further back he goes.

To ascertain what part of the past record is relevant to the future being predicted is a subsidiary but not unimportant subject of investigation.

8.7   EX POST EVALUATION OF POINT ESTIMATES

To check on the *ex ante* estimate of error of a particular forecasting approach, one can apply the approach to the past, noting, say, the differences between the population in 1970 as predicted in 1935 and the observed 1970 population now available. Experiments on the experience base should lead to improved estimates of future population and their variance.

After all justifiable use of the past has been made, concentrated on a point estimate for a future moment, and after the moment arrives and a census is taken, one would think that then, at least, we would be in a position to judge the estimate unambiguously. But further problems arise; surprisingly, even the possession of the actual population count, with which the forecast made earlier can be compared to provide an *ex post* assessment of its accuracy, leaves some residual difficulties. Statement of the accuracy of prediction attained is not unambiguous even after the event, at least if we want to compare two predictions made at different times for the same future date, and more generally to compare estimates over different time intervals and in different countries.

For all such purposes a benchmark of some kind is needed, an extension of the "persistence" (forecasting that tomorrow's weather will be the same as today's) that meteorologists use to see how well their elaborate methods have served, and that Mosteller et al. (1949, p. 297) have applied to election polls. The benchmark may be a naive estimate of the kind discussed above, a standard form of projection by age and sex with fixed rates, or some other, as will be suggested below.

The Scripps medium projection made in 1935 for the 1970 population of the conterminous United States was 155 million. The actuality as counted in the 1970 census was 203 million for the same area. Was 48 million a large error? The estimate was 76 percent of the true figure, or 24 percent short, but was this good or bad? If one could predict the national income of the year 2012, 35 years from now, within 24 percent, he would be doing well; on the other hand, 24 percent error in predicting next year's federal tax collections would be decidedly poor. The only way to assess the quality of a point forecast is to compare it with some standard way of forecasting.

If the quality of a prediction has plainly to be assessed in relation to some other prediction produced by a standard method that can be taken as a base or benchmark, it is much less obvious how this base should be selected. One benchmark corresponds to persistence in weather forecasting: assume that the population will not change from the 1935 level. The 1935 level was 127 million, so the true increase over the whole period from

1935 to 1970 was the difference between this and the realization: $203 - 127$ $= 76$ million. This was the error to which the use of the 1935 figure for 1970 would have been subject.

Somewhat more formally, the general expression for the quality of a forecast as measured *ex post* is

$$\text{Quality of forecast} = \frac{\text{Forecast} - \text{Benchmark}}{\text{Realization} - \text{Benchmark}}. \qquad (8.7.1)$$

In effect, our first effort was to use a benchmark of zero, giving for 1970

$$\text{Quality} = \frac{155 - 0}{203 - 0} = 0.76, \qquad (8.7.2)$$

the complement of which, 24 percent, is one way of describing the error.

The second effort described above, is to use the 1935 observed population of 127 million as a benchmark, and we find, again for 1970,

$$\text{Quality} = \frac{155 - 127}{203 - 127} = \frac{28}{76} = 0.37. \qquad (8.7.3)$$

The more precise benchmark provides a more rigorous evaluation, as though we estimate not the 1970 population but the increase from 1935.

We now proceed to a yet tighter measure of quality. The forecast will not be credited with the fraction of the increase from the jumping-off point that it includes, but only the part of it not covered by a projection at 1935 rates of birth and death. Such a projection from 1935 gives 148 million for 1970, so we have

$$\text{Quality} = \frac{\text{Forecast} - \text{Projection at rates of 1935}}{\text{Realization} - \text{Projection at rates of 1935}}$$

$$= \frac{155 - 148}{203 - 148} = \frac{7}{55} = 0.13. \qquad (8.7.4)$$

This last measure of quality in effect recognizes that whoever made the forecasts in 1935 knew the 1935 population, birth rates, and death rates. He could have projected with these rates, but used his knowledge and intuition to improve on them. We will credit him with good judgment only to the degree that he bettered that fixed-rate forecast.

The same expression (8.7.1) can be applied to assess 1950 and 1960 as well as 1970, and Table 8.6 shows the results. Note that (8.7.2) seems to give worse results as one proceeds in time, and so does (8.7.3). Only (8.7.4) constitutes a measure of quality that is virtually the same for 1950, 1960, and 1970.

Population 10 to 30 years ahead is better predicted than income, demand for housing, interest rates, unemployment, prices, technology, weather, earthquakes, or any other common subject of forecasting. But we

Table 8.6   Three retrospective or *ex post* evaluations of the 1935 Scripps Medium Projection to 1950, 1960, and 1970

Year	Forecast as percent of census count (8.7.2)	Estimated increase from 1935 as percent of census increase (8.7.3)	Departure from fixed-rate benchmark as percent of census departure (8.7.4)
1950	94	61	12
1960	84	43	12
1970	76	37	13

cannot take much satisfaction in this superiority. Our sophisticated techniques are effective only in the degree to which they produce better results than naive methods. Thus one direction of evaluation of population projections is how they compare with simple straight-line extrapolation and other naive methods (Agnew, 1972).

The benchmark is a simple-minded, conventional, stylized standard. It is intended to judge how good refined methods are, and to compare one refined method with another. The refined methods can use intuitive elements that do not have to be justified; the benchmark to judge them must be entirely objective, so that it can be constructed after the event, the predictand, is known. If the benchmark is made too good, the forecasts being judged by it look too bad. Some of my correspondents have argued that the benchmark ought to be nothing but the actual population at the jumping-off point, but this seems to let the forecaster off too lightly, since anyone can improve on such a benchmark. In principle the benchmark should incorporate the minimum knowledge that the forecaster should have taken into account, and so it records how much more than the minimum skill he possessed.

Future Percentage Increase

To regard projections in terms of the percentage increase they imply accords with the wider range of uncertainty in prospective population as we go forward in time. Table 8.7 shows the angle of climb of the curve, expressed in terms of the average percentage increase from 1972, implied by the four official projections, C, D, E, and F, for the United States.

The differences between 1972–80, 1972–90, and 1972–2000 are small compared with the differences between projections C, D, E, and F, and one can summarize the whole table by its bottom line, which says that the projected rate of increase is between 0.65 and 1.30 percent. For the

Table 8.7 Annual rate of future increase implied
by official United States projections (percents)

Period	C	D	E	F
1972–1980	1.26	1.13	0.88	0.76
1972–1990	1.35	1.19	0.92	0.75
1972–2000	1.30	1.12	0.84	0.65

Source: Statistical Abstract of the United States (1973), p.
6.

increase of the whole period the C estimate comes out just double the F
estimate.

8.8 A DIVISION OF LABOR

Who ought to estimate future population? Is it true that in a free-enterprise
society the risks of decision are taken by the entrepreneur, that these risks
include the danger of being wrong regarding the future population, and
that if we leave things alone there will be a natural selection of en-
trepreneurs favoring those who have, among other talents, a superior
ability to forecast population (or who can hire better demographers)? In
this scheme there is no room for official forecasting of population.

Yet such an austere view has never been held in regard to knowledge in
general, whose officially sponsored diffusion is, rather, part of the in-
frastructure on which a free-enterprise system functions. If there is some
information regarding the future that can serve everyone and improve
many decisions, then let it be assembled, published, and paid for by the
public authorities. This is so notwithstanding the fact that mistakes are
made in forecasting the future; the test is whether forecasts add more to
the quality of decisions than is spent in making them.

Among other difficulties, all users do not want the same forecast. One
user needs a conservative estimate of the future—a figure that he is
reasonably sure will be exceeded. Another needs a high figure; he wants to
guard especially against any possibility that the estimate he uses will be
exceeded by the realization. How can we separate the task of forecasting
from the adaptation of the forecast to a particular use? The loss function
does this in a precise way.

The Loss Function Permits a Three-Way Division of Labor

Only the user can know how much he stands to lose through a projection
being wrong in one direction or the other, or by a certain amount. His loss

function may be strongly asymmetric. Suppose that the future population of a town is wanted for deciding the capacity of a new water reservoir. If the reservoir turns out to be too small, another will soon have to be built, and this will be expensive. If it turns out to be too large, it will be underutilized, and the loss is only the marginal cost of the excess capacity, which may be small.

The logic for arriving at exactly the right prediction $\hat{x}$ for a particular use is based on developments in statistics going back to the 1930s, and in its application to demography is set forth by Muhsam (1956). Suppose that the user has studied his own application enough to be able to judge how much loss he would suffer with a particular departure of the estimate $\hat{x}$ from the true population x (not knowable until the future date has arrived), and suppose that he can express this in the form of a loss function $L(\hat{x}, x)$ or, less generally but more simply, $L(\hat{x} - x)$.

He is given the population forecast in the form of a probability distribution $P(x)$ by the official agency mentioned above. Not being able to control x, the user integrates it out to provide his total expected loss:

$$R(\hat{x}) = \int_{-\infty}^{+\infty} L(\hat{x} - x) P(x) dx. \tag{8.8.1}$$

It remains only to choose $\hat{x}$ so as to minimize the total expected loss $R(\hat{x})$; the value of $\hat{x}$ required is the solution of the equation $dR(\hat{x})/d\hat{x} = 0$, provided that the functions $P(x)$ and $L(\hat{x} - x)$ are well behaved.

For a highly simplified numerical example, suppose the official estimate to be discrete and to have the following form:

Forecast x Persons	Probability $P(x)$
50,000	0.25
60,000	0.50
70,000	0.25

Now suppose that the user's loss function is as follows:

Forecast error $\hat{x} - x$	Loss $L(\hat{x} - x)$
−20,000	$2,000,000
−10,000	500,000
0	0
10,000	100,000
20,000	200,000

Thus, if he uses $\hat{x} = 50,000$ and the performance turns out to be $x = 70,000$, he loses $2,000,000, and so on.

We can make a two-way table of loss, $L(x - \hat{x})$:

$\hat{x}$	x		
	50,000	60,000	70,000
50,000	0	500,000	2,000,000
60,000	100,000	0	500,000
70,000	200,000	100,000	0

The table can be summarized by the sum $\Sigma P(x)L(x - \hat{x})$ for each possible forecast $\hat{x}$:

Forecast $\hat{x}$	Expected Loss $\Sigma P(x)L(x - \hat{x})$
50,000	$750,000
60,000	150,000
70,000	100,000

The right forecast for the particular purpose is 70,000.

8.9 INTERVAL ESTIMATES AS CURRENTLY PROVIDED

Ex post we know in what fraction of cases the upper and lower projections straddle the subsequent performance. If a collection of projections is in any sense homogeneous, and the method currently in use is similar to the techniques employed in the collection, the fraction of instances in which the subsequent census was straddled constitutes a level of confidence for the present method. A large collection of early projections is available to be compared with subsequent actuality.

Such material may be used to test various hypotheses about the process of projection as it has been practiced in the past. One of these is that, after a steady movement of births and population in a consistent direction (such as occurred from the 1870s to the 1930s), confidence increases, and the range of admitted future possibilities narrows—the projection fan is made smaller. When a sudden change (especially in the birth series) creates uncertainty the fan is made very large. A second hypothesis is that series that are abandoned may ultimately turn out unexpectedly well, perhaps better than those that are continued. Third, the level of births anticipated may be too sensitive to current birth rates; one could test the hypothesis that waves in future population estimates correspond to waves in current births. I am grateful to George C. Myers for these suggestions.

Official Agencies Have Backed into Confidence Intervals

What has happened as a result of the insistence on neutral projections rather than forecasts, and on making several so that the user can choose among them, is that the agencies involved have backed into confidence intervals. I know of no user who does what the theory of projections says he should do—examine the assumptions of the several sets, given more or less completely in fine print in the introduction, use personal judgment as to which is right, and only then look at the corresponding projection and adopt it for use. A user frequently picks the series that seems to him to give the right answer, and pays only secondary attention to the fine print describing the assumptions. Insofar as he does this, the whole theory of projections is subverted, for he could just as well choose among a set of random numbers.

But users do want the government estimates; they may pick a middle figure from the assortment presented, or a high or low figure according to their need, and suppose that the assumptions made by the official demographers represent the range of reasonable possibilities. This is to say that they are using the published high and low series as defining a confidence interval. Like the producer of the series, they do not formally attach a probability to the range, but even brief experience shows them that there is a finite chance that the performance can fall outside the range given.

My own informal estimate, based on 30 cases, is that the confidence attachable to responsible official estimates is about two-thirds. My hypothesis is that some such number has implicitly been playing the role in projection that 0.95 plays in tests of statistical significance. Because the instruments are much cruder, no one is interested in 95 percent limits for forecasts; they are apparently too wide for planning purposes. But much more research is needed, especially *ex post* studies that look back on earlier projections and note what fraction turns out to straddle the population performance.

The need for projections steadily increases, and the demand bears no relation to accuracy or inaccuracy as demonstrated *ex post*. The Bureau of the Census will always be required to make projections, independently of how good these projections are in an absolute sense: the least bad forecasts available are what people seek. It can be criticized, not for failing to predict what subsequently occurs, but only for failure to use sound methods and to take account of all relevant data.

Chapter Nine

SOME TYPES OF INSTABILITY

A population can be stable in only one way: by the constancy of its birth and death rates over time, and hence the constancy of its rate of increase. It can be unstable in infinitely many ways: by falling or rising birth rates, by falling or rising death rates, by either birth or death rates rising at some ages and falling at others, by the rise or fall being moderate or rapid, by its being linear, quadratic, or of higher degree. Any and all of these and their combinations could be given the same detailed attention as stability. Needless to say that will not be done here, nor is it likely to be done anywhere else.

The stable model has been studied in detail because it is more informative than any single case of instability. The diversity of kinds of instability distracts attention from the interest in any one kind. To keep down the complexity in the treatment here, either fertility or mortality will be allowed to vary, but not both, and populations will be assumed to be closed to migration as before.

Falling death rates are conspicuous in most of the world today; our first task is to see how their recognition alters the stable model of Chapter 4.

9.1 ABSOLUTE CHANGE IN MORTALITY THE SAME AT ALL AGES

Coale (1963) opened up this subject by analyzing the effects of a steady fall in death rates; he called *quasi-stable* a population in which birth rates remain constant while death rates decline uniformly. The quantitative effect of this on rates of increase from the stable model was calculated by

Coale and Demeny (1967). The following is an attempt to see the effect in general terms. In the first example death rates rise or fall by the same absolute amount at all ages. This is hardly realistic, but it will show the approach.

Suppose a rise each year at all ages equal to the constant k (which would be negative to provide for a fall, say of magnitude 0.0001, in which case $k = -0.0001$; the constant k is restricted to values that leave probability positive and less than 1 at all ages). After n years the mortality at age a will not be $\mu(a)$, as it was at the beginning, but $\mu^*(a) = \mu(a) + nk$. If the initial probability of survivorship was $l(x) = \exp[-\int_0^x \mu(a)\,da]$, the survivorship n years later, subject to $\mu^*(a) = \mu(a) + nk$, will be $l^*(x) = \exp\{-\int_0^x [\mu(a) + nk]\,da\} = l(x)e^{-nkx}$. This is true whether both the initial $\mu(a)$ and the subsequent $\mu(a) + nk$ apply to periods or to cohorts.

Inferring the Increase in Births

Apply the cohort case to an observed age distribution to ascertain the rate of increase in births. If $k = 0$, the stable assumption for ascertaining the rate of increase in the population from a census, derived as (4.2.4), gives

$$r_0 = \frac{1}{y - x} \ln\left[\frac{B(t - x)}{B(t - y)}\right] = \frac{1}{y - x} \ln\left[\frac{c_x/l_x}{c_y/l_y}\right], \qquad (9.1.1)$$

where the c_x and c_y are the fractions in finite intervals around ages x and y (Fig. 9.1) and are to be identified with observed populations. This is modified to estimate the increase in births between y and x years ago, $y > x$, (once we abandon stability, we have to specify the time to which the rate of increase refers). If death rates increase at k per year between cohorts, and the life table for the cohort born y years ago is given by $\mu(a)$ and that for the cohort born x years ago by $\mu^*(a) = \mu(a) + k(y - x)$, then $l_x^* = l_x e^{-k(y-x)x}$, and the estimate becomes

$$r_1 = \frac{1}{y - x} \ln\left(\frac{c_x/l_x^*}{c_y/l_y}\right)$$

$$= \frac{1}{y - x} \ln\left(\frac{c_x/(l_x e^{-k(y-x)x})}{c_y/l_y}\right)$$

$$= r_0 + kx, \qquad (9.1.2)$$

on simplifying and expressing the result in terms of (9.1.1).

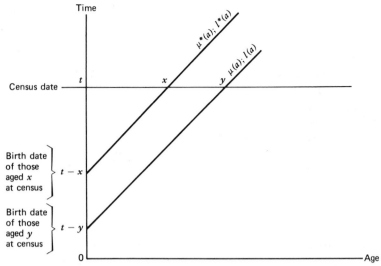

Fig. 9.1 Lexis diagram showing census date and comparison of those enumerated at age x and y to ascertain increase between x and y years ago.

For $y > x$ and falling mortality (i.e., $k < 0$), we have $r_1 \leqslant r_0$. In words, under a regime of falling mortality use of the customary formula (9.1.1), which assumes a fixed life table, gives a rate of increase in the earlier births that is too high by $-kx$, the fall in mortality since the younger age group was born. The usual formula (9.1.1) gives too high an r because it disregards the fact that the younger age with the life table l_x^* originates in fewer births than the life table l_x implies.

Let us generalize this to find the average rate of increase in persons aged z between the y cohort and the x cohort, where $x < z < y$. The c_y projected back to age z number $c_y(l_z/l_y)$, and the c_x projected forward to age z number $c_x e^{-k(y-x)(z-x)}(l_z/l_x)$. The average rate of increase r_z is found from

$$\exp[r_z(y-x)] = \frac{c_x e^{-k(y-x)(z-x)}(l_z/l_x)}{c_y(l_z/l_y)}$$

$$= \frac{c_x/l_x}{c_y/l_y} e^{-k(y-x)(z-x)},$$

or, on solving for r_z,

$$r_z = r_0 - k(z-x), \tag{9.1.3}$$

which reduces to (9.1.2) for $z = 0$. For k negative, the increase in any age z greater than x will be more rapid than r_0, the rate inferred on the stable model. [Show that the result applies to any z, whether or not it is between x and y.]

Increase in person-years in cohort. To proceed from how persons aged z were changing over some particular interval to rate of increase in population, a first approach is to compare person-years in the two cohorts that are x and y years of age, respectively, at time t. Person-years in a cohort are births times expectation of life, that is to say, births times the integral of the survivorship function. This is not the usual way to estimate population increase, but is worth starting with because of its mathematical convenience. [Prove that the estimate of change is approximately

$$r_2 \doteq r_0 - k(\bar{a} - x), \tag{9.1.4}$$

where $\bar{a}$ is the mean age.]

9.2 PROPORTIONAL CHANGE IN MORTALITY

Now instead of a fixed change k at all ages suppose a fractional change—that mortality for a given cohort (or period) is $\mu(a)$, while n years later it is $\mu^*(a) = \mu(a)(1 + nk)$. Then that later cohort (or period) will have survivorship $l_x^* = l_x^{1+nk}$. If $k < 0$, then $l_x^* > l_x$.

Rate of Increase of Births. From the numbers c_y enumerated at time t and age y the births $B(t-y)$ must be $B(t-y) = c_y/l_y$, again taking as the standard life table the cohort passing through age y at census time t. The table for the younger cohort aged x at the census must have $\mu^*(a) = \mu(a)(1 + nk)$, so its survivorship to age x will be $l_x^* = l_x^{1+nk} = l_x^{1+(y-x)k}$. Then the number of births $B(t-x)$ from which the c_x are the survivors is

$$B(t-x) = \frac{c_x}{l_x^*} = \frac{c_x}{l_x^{1+(y-x)k}}. \tag{9.2.1}$$

The rate of increase in births between y and x years ago is estimated as

$$r_3 = \frac{1}{y-x} \ln \left[\frac{B(t-x)}{B(t-y)} \right]$$

$$= \frac{1}{y-x} \ln \left[\frac{c_x/l_x^*}{c_y/l_y} \right]$$

$$= r_0 + \frac{1}{y-x} \ln l_x^{-(y-x)k}$$

$$= r_0 - k \ln l_x. \tag{9.2.2}$$

We could have taken our standard $\mu(a)$ to apply to the cohort midway between that aged x and that aged y at the time of the census and obtained approximately the symmetrical expression

$$r_4 \doteq r_0 - k \ln \sqrt{l_x l_y} \ . \tag{9.2.3}$$

[Prove this.] Both (9.2.2) and (9.2.3) show that a negative k for declining mortality, along with $\ln l_x$ or $\ln \sqrt{l_x l_y}$, which are always negative, gives a subtraction from the r calculated from (9.1.1); under the conditions of declining mortality (9.1.1) suffers from an upward bias in estimating the rate of increase of births.

But once again the historic rate of increase of births is not what we need most. We want change in population, and the survivorship will more than offset the correction in (9.2.3). First we review what we know from Section 3.3 of the effect on $\overset{o}{e}_0$ of a proportional change in mortality.

Change of $\overset{o}{e}_0$. The ratio of expectations of life for populations of different periods or cohorts with $l(a)$ changing by fixed fractions will depart substantially from unity, but never by as much as the ratio of age-specific mortality (Section 3.3). If one of two populations has mortality $\mu(a)$ and the other $\mu^*(a) = \mu(a)(1+k)$, the ratio of the expectation of life of the second to the first is

$$\frac{\overset{o}{e}_0^*}{\overset{o}{e}_0} = \frac{\int_0^\omega l(a)^{1+k} \, da}{\int_0^\omega l(a) \, da} ,$$

and, on expanding around $k=0$ to the first term of a Taylor series, this becomes

$$\frac{\overset{o}{e}_0^*}{\overset{o}{e}_0} \doteq \frac{\int_0^\omega [l(a) + k l'(a)] \, da}{\int_0^\omega l(a) \, da} , \tag{9.2.4}$$

where $l'(a)$ is the derivative of $l(a)^{1+k}$ with respect to k evaluated at $k=0$. Now $dl(a)^{1+k}/dk = \ln l(a) l(a)^{1+k} = l(a)\ln l(a)$ at $k=0$. Then we have to the linear approximation

$$\frac{\overset{o}{e}_0^*}{\overset{o}{e}_0} = 1 + k \frac{\int_0^\omega l(a)\ln[l(a)] \, da}{\int_0^\omega l(a) \, da}$$

$$= 1 - kH, \tag{9.2.5}$$

where the quantity H, defined in Section 3.3, is minus the average $\ln l(a)$ weighted by $l(a)$. The parameter H of the life table is shown in Table 3.3 as about 0.20 for contemporary male populations and about 0.16 for females, these values being substantially lower than those for a generation earlier. We will apply (9.2.5) with $(y-x)k$ in place of k, since our assumption is that mortality increases by k per year.

Increase in Total Cohort Population. To approach the rate of increase in population rather than in births, we again calculate two cohorts, and compare the number of person-years lived in the cohort born at time $t-y$ with the number for that born at time $t-x$.

For the number of person-years in the cohort we multiply the births by the expectation of life, as was done for r_2 to obtain (9.1.4), and the outcome reduces to

$$r_5 = r_0 - k \ln l_x + \frac{1}{y-x} \ln \left[\frac{\overset{o}{e}{}_0^*}{\overset{o}{e}{}_0} \right], \tag{9.2.6}$$

on entering the values of (9.2.2). [Prove this.] On applying (9.2.5) with $(y-x)k$ in place of k, we obtain

$$r_5 = r_0 - k \ln l_x + \frac{1}{y-x} \ln \left[1 - (y-x)kH \right]. \tag{9.2.7}$$

Approximating with $\ln(1-\alpha) \doteq -\alpha$, this becomes finally

$$r_5 = r_0 - k (\ln l_x + H). \tag{9.2.8}$$

Similarly to the case in which we assumed a constant absolute change in mortality rates, this will apply a positive correction to r_0 when the death rate is falling ($k < 0$), whenever x is a young age.

Increase of Persons of Arbitrary Age. For arbitrary z, whether or not $x < z < y$, we can find the overall rate of increase by comparing the number of individuals in the cohort aged y at time t with those in the cohort aged x at time t. The ratio of the latter to the former is equated to $e^{r_z(y-x)}$, where r_z is the rate of increase sought. Thus we have the equation in r_z, the rate of increase of persons aged z,

$$e^{r_z(y-x)} = \frac{c_x(l_z/l_x)^{1+k(y-x)}}{c_y(l_z/l_y)},$$

and the solution in r_z is

$$r_z = r_0 + k \ln \left(\frac{l_z}{l_x} \right), \tag{9.2.9}$$

for the average increase during time $t-y+z$ to $t-x+z$. [Use (9.2.9) to provide an alternative derivation of (9.2.8).]

The correction to r_0 is negative for $z < x$ and positive for $z > x$. The general form (9.2.9) would be a good starting point for deriving the previous expressions of this section as well as others that will occur to the reader. For $x = 0$, $k = -0.01$ and $r_0 = 0.03$ this gives the rate of increase at four ages, with Mexican male mortality of 1966 as the base:

$$
\begin{array}{rl}
z = \ 0 & r_z = 0.0300 \\
20 & 0.0314 \\
40 & 0.0323 \\
60 & 0.0347
\end{array}
$$

The steady rise in the inferred rate of increase with age is clearly exhibited.

Demeny (1965) comes a step closer to realism by showing the effect of a decline of mortality (a one-year gain in $\overset{o}{e}_0$ per calendar year) that continues over a limited time (5 years, 10 years, ..., 40 years). Unfortunately this effect cannot be expressed analytically.

9.3 CHANGING BIRTH RATES

The effect of changing birth rates on the population rate of increase and on its age distribution is easily determined to a good approximation if the changes are the same for all maternal ages. The following is a generalization of stable theory that permits drawing conclusions as to rates of increase in a population, given its age distribution. In symbols, suppose that the birth rate for women aged a at time t is $m(a,t) = m(a)f(t)$ (Coale, 1963, p. 8; Coale and Zelnik, 1963, p. 83). The argument that follows shows how to infer the rates of birth and natural increase with some relaxation of the restriction on (4.2.4), though not without specializing $f(t)$.

The homogeneous form of the renewal equation (5.7.1) becomes

$$
B(t) = \int_\alpha^\beta B(t-a) l(a) m(a) f(t)\, da.
$$

In the birth function $B(t-a)$ under the integral sign, express both time t and age a as departures from A, the mean age of childbearing, so that $B(t-a)$ becomes $B[(t-A)-(a-A)]$, and then expand the birth function as a Taylor series around $t - A$:

$$
B(t) = \int_\alpha^\beta B\big[(t-A)-(a-A)\big] l(a) m(a) f(t)\, da
$$

$$
= \int_\alpha^\beta \bigg[B(t-A)-(a-A)B'(t-A)
$$

$$
+ \frac{(a-A)^2}{2!} B''(t-A) - \cdots \bigg] l(a) m(a) f(t)\, da.
$$

Dividing by $R_0 = \int_\alpha^\beta l(a)m(a)\,da$ and carrying through the integration expresses the right-hand side in terms of moments about A, the mean age of childbearing. The first moment is zero, and the second σ^2, the variance of ages of childbearing. Dividing by $B(t-A)$, taking logarithms, and then expanding the logarithm of the series of moments, gives, up to second derivatives,

$$\ln B(t) - \ln B(t-A) = \ln R_0 + \ln f(t) + \frac{B''(t-A)\sigma^2}{2B(t-A)}. \qquad (9.3.1)$$

Since the term involving the second derivative is only about 2 or 3 percent of the value of the main term, it may be neglected in what follows. This amounts to the outrageous assumption that all children are born at the same age of mother. No argument could show that this assumption is reasonable, but numerical tests demonstrate that it makes little numerical difference in this particular application. If the assumption seems objectionable, however, the solution below could be regarded as a first approximation, $B''(t-A)$ calculated and entered in (9.3.1), and a more exact result obtained. (Alternatively, the second derivative could be replaced by a second difference.) Adding both sides over every A^{th} value and canceling leaves a summation of $\ln f(t)$ at intervals of A, the mean age of childbearing:

$$\ln B(t) = \ln B_0 + \frac{t}{A}\ln R_0 + \Sigma \ln f(t),$$

and taking exponentials and writing e^{rt} for $R_0^{t/A}$, approximately true when the unit of time is very nearly a generation, gives

$$B(t) = B_0 e^{rt}\exp\{\ln f(0) + \ln f(A) + \cdots$$
$$+ \ln f[(n-1)A]\}. \qquad (9.3.2)$$

After the particular function $f(t) = \exp[k_1 t + k_2 t(t - A)]$ is entered, the summation is evaluated to $t = nA$ as

$$B(t) = B_0 \exp\left[rt + k_1\frac{t(t+A)}{2A} + k_2\frac{t(t^2 - A^2)}{3A}\right]. \qquad (9.3.3)$$

The intended application being to an age distribution with typical age a, we are interested in births at time $-a$, and these are obtained by putting $t = -a$ in (9.3.3) and then dividing by the current population P:

$$\frac{B(-a)}{P} = b\exp\left[-ra + \frac{k_1 a(a - A)}{2A} - \frac{k_2 a(a^2 - A^2)}{3A}\right], \qquad (9.3.4)$$

where b is the current birth rate. Once an age distribution $c(a)$ is given for a population that can be assumed to be closed and whose life table is $l(a)$,

$B(-a)/P$ can be estimated by $c(a)/l(a)$. Taking logarithms and fitting to at least four ages produces the four constants b, r, k_1, and k_2. A more detailed derivation of (9.3.4) and the fitting to data are given in Keyfitz et al. (1967).

If $k_1 = k_2 = 0$, (9.3.4) reduces to an equation of Bourgeois-Pichat (1958), shown in Section 4.5. In the more general case where only $k_2 = 0$, we have the result due to Coale and Zelnik (1963, p. 83).

Fitting (9.3.4) to an age distribution, when we are given or may assume a life table, estimates not only the rate of increase and the birth rate but also the change in the latter as indicated by k_1 and k_2. Based on four or more ages, the four constants b, r, k_1, and k_2 are obtained, and these permit a reconstruction of the age distribution by multiplying the right-hand side of (9.3.4) by $l(a)$. The age distribution so obtained can be compared with the observed age distribution. The fit may be compared with that resulting when k_2 is put equal to zero, and when $k_1 = k_2 = 0$. Unless it is substantially better, one would avoid the complication of the additional constants; but if the reconstruction of ages is markedly improved with the nonstable method here described, so presumably also are the estimates of b and r.

Table 9.1   Estimates of birth rates and other parameters from (9.3.4) for five populations, fitted to ages 5 to 74

Country and year	$1000b$	$1000r$	$1000k_1$	$1000k_2$
Fiji Islands, 1964	38.7	31.9	-6.0	0
France, 1899–1903	19.2	-4.6	-23.5	-0.3
Honduras, 1965	42.9	34.4	-5.6	0
Japan, 1962	16.8	-3.5	-51.6	-0.5
Netherlands, 1901	31.8	14.7	-12.1	-0.2

Table 9.1 gives estimates for certain countries of the four constants contained in (9.3.4). The usefulness of these is suggested by the fact that in all five cases the model reproduces their age distribution at ages 5 to 74 appreciably better than does the stable model with $k_1 = k_2 = 0$. In two instances the k_2 did not appreciably improve the fit; in the other three it did, but the calculated k_2 was small. Note that k_1 always turned out negative, reflecting falling birth rates.

9.4   ANNOUNCED PERIOD BIRTH RATE TOO HIGH

When successive cohorts bear children at younger and younger ages, each period cross section will tend to catch more births than any cohort. The period births are "too many" in the sense that no one cohort of women has so high an average; the childbearing of successive cohorts overlaps in each period. In the early 1940s there were many marriages and hence first births, and Whelpton (1946) showed from the 1942 registrations that if the pace continued women would average 1.084 first births each. Conversely, when couples are having their children later and later, a given period will catch less than its share of births, that is to say, fewer than pertain to any cohort.

To prove this and similar propositions requires a formal means of translating cohort moments into period moments and vice versa. The problem in its general form has been solved by Ryder (1964). What follows is a self-contained adaptation of his solution.

If the same life table applies at all times, and the probability at time t of a woman of age x to $x + dx$ having a child is $m(x,t)dx$, the net reproduction rate R_0 is

$$R_0 = \int_\alpha^\beta l(x)m(x,t)dx,$$

where α and β are the youngest and oldest ages, respectively, of childbearing, and $l(x)$ is the chance that a child just born will live at least to age x. The R_0 is a function of time; the fact that fertility varies with time as well as with age is what gives rise to our problem.

The nth period moment at time zero about age A chosen arbitrarily is defined as

$$\frac{R_n(A)}{R_0} = \frac{\int_\alpha^\beta (x-A)^n l(x)m(x,0)dx}{\int_\alpha^\beta l(x)m(x,0)dx},$$

where the R_0 does not depend on A. The nth cohort moment is similarly

$$\frac{R_n^*(A)}{R_0^*(A)} = \frac{\int_\alpha^\beta (x-A)^n l(x)m(x,x-A)dx}{\int_\alpha^\beta l(x)m(x,x-A)dx},$$

in which $R_0^*(A)$ does depend on A. The cohort moment contains a time argument $x - A$, contrived so that $m(x, x-A)$ follows the group of women born A years before time t down their life lines. It selects out of the period births as officially published for successive years those appropriate to the particular cohort (Fig. 9.2).

The cohort $R_n^*(A)$ is expressible in terms of $R_n(A)$, $R_{n+1}(A),\ldots$, by means of a Taylor expansion of $m(x, x-A)$ about time $t = 0$. For this expansion $m(x, x-A)$ is treated for any fixed age x as a simple function of

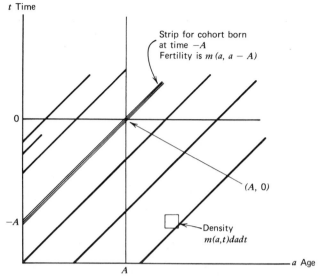

Fig. 9.2 Cohort and period fertility.

time, so that for each x

$$m(x, x-A) = m(x,0) + (x-A)\dot{m}(x,0) + \frac{(x-A)^2}{2!}\ddot{m}(x,0) + \cdots, \quad (9.4.1)$$

the dots representing differentiation with respect to time. The accuracy of approximation by a given number of terms will depend on the smoothness of whatever changes are taking place in the birth function.

Entering the Taylor expansion (9.4.1) in the expression for $R_n^*(A)$ gives

$$R_n^*(A) = \int_\alpha^\beta (x-A)^n l(x)\left[m(x,0) + (x-A)\dot{m}(x,0) + \cdots \right] dx. \quad (9.4.2)$$

To put this into convenient form we have to convince ourselves that the integral $\int_\alpha^\beta (x-A)^{n+1} l(x)\dot{m}(x,0)\,dx$ is the derivative with respect to time of the period moment, that is, equals $\dot{R}_{n+1}(A)$, and similarly for later terms. The proof consists in representing $\dot{m}(x,0)$ as a difference between two values, $m(x,\Delta)$ and $m(x,0)$, divided by Δ. Before letting Δ tend to zero, note that the integral $\int_\alpha^\beta (x-A)^{n+1} l(x) m(x,\Delta)\,dx$ is $R_{n+1}(A)$ at time Δ, say $R_{n+1}(A,\Delta)$, and similarly when Δ is replaced by zero. The difference of the two integrals divided by Δ is

$$\frac{R_{n+1}(A,\Delta) - R_{n+1}(A,0)}{\Delta},$$

and this becomes $\dot{R}_{n+1}(A,0) = \dot{R}_{n+1}(A)$ as Δ tends to zero. A similar proof would show that later terms of (9.4.2) become $\ddot{R}_{n+2}(A)/2$, and so on. Expressed more briefly, the fact we are using is that the integral of a derivative equals the derivative of an integral under conditions far more general than are required for the demographic application.

On incorporating this fact, expansion 9.4.2 leads to the fundamental result

$$R_n^*(A) = R_n(A) + \dot{R}_{n+1}(A) + \frac{\ddot{R}_{n+2}(A)}{2!} + \cdots, \qquad (9.4.3)$$

which estimates the nth cohort moment in terms of the nth and higher period moments (Ryder, 1964). The most interesting application of (9.4.3) will be for $n = 0$, and, truncating the series at the second term on the right, we obtain

$$R_0^*(A) \doteq R_0 + \dot{R}_1(A)$$

$$\doteq R_0 \left[1 + \frac{\dot{R}_1(A)}{R_0} \right], \qquad (9.4.4)$$

the zeroth period moment not depending on the arbitrary A. In words, we can say that the cohort net reproduction rate is equal to the period net reproduction rate plus the change over unit time in $R_1(A)$.

The theoretical result 9.4.4 can be illustrated arithmetically. To do so, the net maternity function for United States females in 1967 was graduated by a Hadwiger function (Keyfitz, 1968, p. 149); then, leaving R_0 and the variance σ^2 the same in all periods as in 1967, the mean μ was shifted upward by 0.1 year per 5-year period. This produces the results shown in Table 9.2 for 1972 to 2012. It is seen that the period net reproduction rate remains always at 1.205. A change in the mean of 0.1 year per 5 years is a change at the rate of 0.02 per year. The right-hand side of (9.4.4) is therefore $1.205(1 + 0.02) = 1.229$.

If we add the diagonals for the three completed cohorts in Table 9.2, we find $R_0^* = 1.230$, different from the 1.229 of (9.4.4) by rounding error only.

A virtually identical argument expresses the period $R_n(A)$ in terms of the series of cohort moments $R_n^*(A)$, $R_{n+1}^*(A)$, ... :

$$R_n(A) = R_n^*(A) - \dot{R}_{n+1}^*(A) + \frac{\ddot{R}_{n+2}^*(A)}{2!} - \cdots, \qquad (9.4.5)$$

the difference from (9.4.3) being that the signs on the right-hand side here come out alternately positive and negative.

Table 9.2 Net maternity function for United States females, 1967, as graduated by Hadwiger function; later periods supposing increase of 0.1 in mean age μ of each successive period, with total R_0 and variance σ^2 fixed at those of 1967

Year	10–14	15–19	20–24	25–29	30–34	35–39	40–44	45–49	Total
1967	0.0095	0.1512	0.3876	0.3656	0.1926	0.0710	0.0208	0.0066	1.205
1972	0.0088	0.1462	0.3846	0.3685	0.1960	0.0727	0.0213	0.0068	1.205
1977	0.0082	0.1413	0.3814	0.3714	0.1995	0.0744	0.0219	0.0071	1.205
1982	0.0076	0.1365	0.3781	0.3742	0.2030	0.0761	0.0224	0.0073	1.205
1987	0.0070	0.1318	0.3746	0.3769	0.2065	0.0778	0.0230	0.0074	1.205
1992	0.0065	0.1271	0.3711	0.3795	0.2100	0.0796	0.0236	0.0076	1.205
1997	0.0060	0.1226	0.3674	0.3821	0.2136	0.0814	0.0242	0.0079	1.205
2002	0.0055	0.1182	0.3636	0.3845	0.2171	0.0833	0.0248	0.0080	1.205
2007	0.0051	0.1138	0.3597	0.3869	0.2207	0.0851	0.0255	0.0082	1.205
2012	0.0047	0.1095	0.3557	0.3891	0.2244	0.0871	0.0261	0.0085	1.205

Note that all totals on rows are 1.205, the period R_0; totals on the three complete cohorts shown are $R_0^* = 1.230$. The purpose of this hypothetical table is to show that the cohort NRR can be constant and different from the period NRR if the timing of fertility undergoes a steady change.

Note that (9.4.3) and (9.4.5) serve quite different purposes. The first is useful because it can incorporate the latest period information to suggest how current cohorts are likely to be completed, on which definitive statistics await their members reaching age 50 or so if they are women, older if they are men. Equation (9.4.5), on the other hand, shows how the cohorts, considered as the basic units underlying the process, are translated or distorted in the course of expressing themselves in successive periods.

Among other uses such results provide information on the relative variation through time of cohort and period fertility. If it were true historically that when R_0 rises $R_1(A)$ tends to fall, that is, $\dot{R}_1(A)$ is negative, and when R_0 falls $R_1(A)$ tends to rise, then the variation of $R_0^*(A) = R_0 +$

$\dot{R}_1(A)$ would be smaller than the variation of R_0 by itself. Changes in the period net reproduction rate being in these circumstances offset by contrary changes in the mean age of childbearing, and the cohort R_0^* being subject to less variation than the period R_0, R_0^* is useful in predicting future population, since all prediction depends on finding functions that are relatively constant. (Section 8.4)

If we knew that every cohort was aiming at exactly three children, (9.4.3) and (9.4.5) would not be needed; we would simply deduct the average number of children already recorded from three, and suppose the remainder to be distributed over time and age in the future in some suitable way. If, on the other hand, cohorts had nothing to do with the matter, we would treat the births to women of given age in successive periods as an ordinary series and extrapolate. The theory of this section is especially useful for the intermediate case in which the R_0^* for cohorts are shifting, but less rapidly than the R_0 for periods.

We could have gone through the argument with gross reproduction rates and obtained the same results, simply by omitting the $l(x)$ throughout. Even more generally, the $m(a, t)$ function and the R's representing the moments of $m(a, t)$ could be interpreted, not as childbearing, but as mortality, marriage, school attendance, income, or some other attribute of individuals. The foregoing relation of periods and cohorts applies to any such characteristic.

9.5 BACKWARD POPULATION PROJECTION

One may need to project a population backward, for instance to estimate age distribution of a period before the first of a series of censuses. Under stability all ages increase in the same ratio; therefore one can calculate the number living at the earlier period by dividing by this ratio. With or without stability one can simply divide the total for an age group by the probability of surviving to obtain the age group one time period earlier. This gives the best possible answer in practice for all ages but the last, to which it is inapplicable. The Leslie matrix of Section 5.7 is useless for such purposes, being singular for any population that lives beyond its reproductive span; it is of rank $n-1$, where n is the number of age groups recognized.

An easy way to retrieve the last age interval is by supposing that it has been increasing at the intrinsic rate of the population. But in some circumstances one can do better than this by using the generalized inverse, which does not require the assumption of stability (Greville and Keyfitz, 1974).

First we express the projection backward along cohort lines in matrix form as

$$
\mathbf{X}_0 =
\begin{bmatrix}
0 & \dfrac{L_0}{L_5} & 0 & 0 & \ldots & 0 \\[2ex]
0 & 0 & \dfrac{L_5}{L_{10}} & 0 & \ldots & 0 \\[2ex]
0 & 0 & 0 & \dfrac{L_{10}}{L_{15}} & \ldots & 0 \\[2ex]
\vdots & & & & & \vdots \\[2ex]
0 & 0 & 0 & 0 & \ldots & \dfrac{L_{5n-10}}{L_{5n-5}} \\[2ex]
0 & 0 & 0 & 0 & \ldots & 0
\end{bmatrix},
$$

which premultiplies the vector (say of females) to provide an estimate for the preceding period in all age intervals except the last, say 85 and over. This contains the main elements of the required backward projection, and is therefore at least a commonsense inverse of the forward projection $\mathbf{M}$ defined in Section 5.7.

There are many generalized inverses of a given singular matrix, and the choice of one from among them depends on the use to be made of it. If $\mathbf{A}$ is the given matrix, it is usual to choose a generalized inverse $\mathbf{X}$ that satisfies at least one and preferably both of the two relations (Rao and Mitra, 1971)

$$\mathbf{AXA} = \mathbf{A} \tag{9.5.1}$$

and

$$\mathbf{XAX} = \mathbf{X}; \tag{9.5.2}$$

the first says that the backward form $\mathbf{X}$ must be such that projecting forward, then backward, and then forward again is equal to projecting once forward, and an equally obvious interpretation applies to the second.

In fact $\mathbf{X}_0$ is a reasonably satisfactory generalized inverse of $\mathbf{M}$. Like $\mathbf{M}$, it is of order n and rank $n-1$. One can easily verify that it satisfies both (9.5.1) and (9.5.2). A disadvantage of $\mathbf{X}_0$, however, lies in the fact that by its use the population in the oldest age interval always comes out zero.

This is easily remedied by observing that properties (9.5.1) and (9.5.2) are retained if the zeros in the bottom row of $\mathbf{X}_0$, except the first, are replaced by arbitrary elements. The last-row elements estimate the number in the final age interval at time t as some linear combination of the numbers at time $t + \Delta t$ in all age intervals except the youngest.

Of the many ways of arriving at such a linear estimate the most direct is to use the eigenvalues and eigenvectors of the two matrices. For the classical inverse of a nonsingular matrix $\mathbf{H}$, if

$$\mathbf{H}\mathbf{x} = \lambda \mathbf{x},$$

then

$$\mathbf{H}^{-1}\mathbf{x} = \lambda^{-1}\mathbf{x}.$$

In words, we can say that a nonsingular matrix and its inverse have identical eigenvectors, associated with respective eigenvalues that are reciprocals of each other. It has been shown (Greville, 1968) that something of the same kind is true of a singular matrix and its generalized inverse.

The three important eigenvalues of the matrix are the real root, say λ_1, and the conjugate pair of complex eigenvalues closest to the real root in absolute value, denoted as λ_2 and $\bar{\lambda}_2$. The real root is the ultimate ratio of increase in the population that would result if the mortality and natality conditions reflected in the Leslie matrix were perpetuated, while the pair of complex roots is related to the amplitude and period of the oscillations that would precede the attainment of a stable state.

The real cubic polynomial with leading coefficient unity whose three zeros are the reciprocals of these three eigenvalues is $(\lambda_1 > 0)$

$$q(z) = \left(z - \lambda_1^{-1}\right)\left(z - \lambda_2^{-1}\right)\left(z - \bar{\lambda}_2^{-1}\right) = z^3 + c_2 z^2 + c_1 z + c_0. \quad (9.5.3)$$

To form a polynomial whose roots are the reciprocals of those of a given polynomial all we need do is reverse the order of the coefficients. [Show that the roots of

$$c_0 z^n + c_1 z^{n-1} + \ldots + c_n = 0$$

are the reciprocals of the roots of

$$c_n z^n + c_{n-1} z^{n-1} + \ldots + c_0 = 0.]$$

Then, if λ_1 is the real root, and $\lambda_2 = a + ib$ and $\bar{\lambda}_2 = a - ib$ are the main complex roots, the characteristic equation with these roots is

$$(z - \lambda_1)(z - \lambda_2)\left(z - \bar{\lambda}_2\right) = 0,$$

or

$$z^3 - \left(\lambda_1 + \lambda_2 + \bar{\lambda}_2\right)z^2 + \left(\lambda_1\lambda_2 + \lambda_1\bar{\lambda}_2 + \lambda_2\bar{\lambda}_2\right)z$$
$$- \lambda_1\lambda_2\bar{\lambda}_2 = 0,$$

or

$$z^3 - (\lambda_1 + 2a)z^2 + (2\lambda_1 a + a^2 + b^2)z - \lambda_1(a^2 + b^2) = 0,$$

and the equation with the reciprocals of these roots is the same with coefficients reversed:

$$\lambda_1(a^2 + b^2)z^3 - (2\lambda_1 a + a^2 + b^2)z^2 + (\lambda_1 + 2a)z - 1 = 0.$$

Hence the coefficients of (9.5.3) are

$$c_2 = -\frac{2\lambda_1 a + a^2 + b^2}{\lambda_1(a^2 + b^2)}, \qquad c_1 = \frac{\lambda_1 + 2a}{\lambda_1(a^2 + b^2)}, \qquad c_0 = -\frac{1}{\lambda_1(a^2 + b^2)}.$$

Let p_i denote the survival rate from the ith age interval to the $(i+1)$th (which is the ith subdiagonal element of $\mathbf{M}$). Then, if we take $\mathbf{X}_1$ to be a matrix like $\mathbf{X}_0$ except that the last three elements of the bottom row are

$$-c_0 p_{n-1} p_{n-2}, \qquad -c_1 p_{n-1}, \qquad -c_2 \tag{9.5.4}$$

(instead of zeros), it is easily verified that the characteristic polynomial of $\mathbf{X}_1$ is $z^{n-3}q(z)$. Thus the eigenvalues of $\mathbf{X}_1$ consist of $n-3$ zeros and the reciprocals of λ_1, λ_2, and λ_3. It is possible to show that $\mathbf{M}$ and $\mathbf{X}_1$ have in common the eigenvectors associated with these three eigenvalues.

The rule seems to be that for long-term projection backward one cannot improve on the dominant root to estimate the oldest age group. For backward projection over a short interval, however, the first three roots often seem to help. In general, the shorter the interval over which one projects backward the more possible it is to preserve minor roots without finding erratically large and impossibly negative populations.

Application

Let us test these suggestions by backward projection of the older United States female population from 1967: using data from that year only, we will estimate for 1962. For all age intervals but the last this will of course be done by the reciprocal of the survival ratio, a procedure whose properties are straightforward and well known.

From the vital statistics for 1967 the real root is $\lambda_1 = 1.0376$, and the roots following are $\lambda_2, \bar{\lambda}_2 = 0.3098 \pm 0.7374i$. The polynomial $q(z)$ of (9.5.3) is

$$q(z) = z^3 - z^2(1.9323) + z(2.4966) - 1.5065.$$

The probability of survival into the last age interval is $p_{n-1} = 0.8024$, and into the second-to-last interval is $p_{n-2} = 0.7030$. Hence the bottom row of the inverse matrix ends up with the three numbers

$$\begin{bmatrix} \cdots & \cdots & \cdots & \cdots \\ \cdots & 0.8498 & -2.0032 & 1.9323 \end{bmatrix},$$

and they are to premultiply the last three intervals (75 to 79, 80 to 84, 85 +) of the 1967 age distribution:

$$\begin{bmatrix} \cdots \\ 2198 \\ 1286 \\ 727 \end{bmatrix}$$

expressed in thousands. The inner product of the two triplets of numbers above constitutes the estimate in this particular way of forming the inverse, and it turns out to be 696 thousands. The observed 1962 figure was 602 thousands. With the procedure of projecting backward by the reciprocal of the real root alone we obtain $727/1.0376 = 701$, which is a slightly larger discrepancy.

For some other populations the superiority of the three roots method shows more clearly. For example, using data for Belgium, 1960, to estimate women aged 85 and over for 1955, we find that the three roots method gives 31,323 and one root gives 33,543 against an observed 1955 figure of 27,880. Bulgaria, 1965, projects backward to 1960 on three roots at 17,550, and on one root at 23,567, against an observed 15,995. In terms of percentage error, the three cases show the following results:

Data	Three Roots	One Root
United States, 1967	15.6	16.4
Belgium, 1960	12.3	20.3
Bulgaria, 1965	9.7	47.3

The idea of using the generalized inverse occurred to Thomas Greville as a way of formalizing and extending the projection backward along cohort lines, sometimes called *reverse survival*, that is used by demographers. This method contrasts with projecting backward by truncating the projection matrix **M** of Section 5.7 at the last age of reproduction and then using its ordinary inverse. Numerical experiments show no circumstance in which such a method is comparable in accuracy with reverse survival; working back from an observed age distribution gives large negative numbers from the first or second 5 year period onward. If one starts with the artificial age vector obtained by projecting forward on the Leslie matrix, it is possible to project backward on the inverse of the truncated matrix for a few periods, but this serves no purpose, except possibly to study the accuracy attained in double precision by the particular computer in use. All these statements reflect the severely ill-conditioned nature of the truncated matrix.

9.6   THE TIME TO STABILITY

A baby boom or other irregularity in the time curve of births tends to be echoed in each later generation insofar as the subsequent age-specific rates of birth and death are constant. The mechanism, expressed in words, is that, when the girls born in a baby boom are of reproductive age, mostly about 20 to 30 years later, there will be more mothers in proportion to the population, and consequently again more children. Still in commonsense terms, the narrower and less skewed the range of ages in which women bear children, the more concentrated will be the echo, and the larger the ratio to the original disturbance. With a broad range of ages of childbearing, especially one skewed to older ages, the waves would seem likely to disappear more quickly, again supposing fixed subsequent rates.

Insofar as such fluctuations incur social cost in first overcrowded and then underutilized facilities such as schools, one is interested in the quickness of convergence to stable form of a population that has undergone a perturbation. In recent decades the variance of ages of childbearing in the United States has diminished. Does this mean a slower reversion to stability after a disturbance? Or does skewness help more than variance to speed the convergence to stability? One way of answering these questions is in terms of the main complex roots of the Lotka equation.

The literature on time to convergence was initiated by Coale (1968, 1972), and contributions have been made by Sivamurthy (1971), Stone (1973), Trussell (1975), and others.

The Criterion of Convergence

Underlying and facilitating all this work is the fact that the real part of the second largest root in absolute value, r_2 in (5.7.2) largely determines the time to convergence. The magnitude of contribution of the term $e^{r_2 t}$, which can be written as $e^{(x + iy)t}$, depends on e^{xt}. The ratio of the asymptotic effect of the second root to that of the first, as these are projected to t years, is e^{xt}/e^{rt}; suppose that we want to know when the ratio will be less than ϵ:

$$e^{(x-r)t} < \epsilon.$$

Remembering that $x - r$ is negative, we have

$$t > \frac{\ln \epsilon}{x - r}. \tag{9.6.1}$$

Note that this studies convergence in terms of the exponentials in t of (5.7.2) and takes the constants Q into ϵ.

Use of the Characteristic Equation

Start with equation 5.1.2,

$$\int_\alpha^\beta e^{-ra} l(a) m(a)\, da = 1,$$

divide both sides by R_0, the net reproduction rate, take logarithms, expand the exponential, and so obtain the series of cumulants

$$\mu r - \sigma^2 \frac{r^2}{2!} + \mu_3 \frac{r^3}{3!} - \ldots - \ln R_0 = 0 \tag{9.6.2}$$

which is Lotka's equation 161 (1939, p. 69) and is the same as (5.2.1) if $\psi(r)$ is put equal to unity. Entering $r = x + iy$ gives for the real part

$$\phi = \mu x - \frac{\sigma^2 (x^2 - y^2)}{2} + \frac{\mu_3 (x^3 - 3xy^2)}{6}$$
$$- \frac{\kappa_4 (x^4 - 6x^2 y^2 + y^4)}{24} + \frac{\kappa_5 (x^5 - 10x^3 y^2 + 5xy^4)}{120}$$
$$- \ldots - \ln R_0 = 0, \tag{9.6.3}$$

and for the imaginary part

$$\theta = \mu y - \sigma^2 xy + \frac{\mu_3 (3x^2 y - y^3)}{6} - \frac{\kappa_4 (x^3 y - xy^3)}{6}$$
$$+ \frac{\kappa_5 (5x^4 y - 10x^2 y^3 + y^5)}{120} - \ldots = 0. \tag{9.6.4}$$

The characteristic equation 5.1.2 is expressed as $\phi + i\theta = 0$. Designate derivatives of the real and complex parts with respect to the second cumulants as ϕ_2 and θ_2, respectively, with respect to the third cumulants as ϕ_3 and θ_3, with respect to x as ϕ_x and θ_x, and with respect to y as ϕ_y and θ_y, and similarly for x and y with respect to the cumulants. In this shorthand $\partial x / \partial \sigma^2$, for example, will be written as x_2, and $\partial x / \partial \mu_3$ as x_3. Completely differentiate the real part, $\phi = 0$, by σ^2 and μ_3 in turn:

$$\phi_x x_2 + \phi_y y_2 + \phi_2 = 0, \tag{9.6.5}$$

$$\phi_x x_3 + \phi_y y_3 + \phi_3 = 0, \tag{9.6.6}$$

and the same for the imaginary part, $\theta = 0$:

$$\theta_x x_2 + \theta_y y_2 + \theta_2 = 0, \tag{9.6.7}$$

$$\theta_x x_3 + \theta_y y_3 + \theta_3 = 0. \tag{9.6.8}$$

The first and third of these equations in partial derivatives can be solved for x_2, the derivative of x with respect to variance:

$$x_2 = \frac{\begin{vmatrix} -\phi_2 & \phi_y \\ -\theta_2 & \theta_y \end{vmatrix}}{\begin{vmatrix} \phi_x & \phi_y \\ \theta_x & \theta_y \end{vmatrix}},$$

and the second and fourth for x_3, the derivative with respect to the third moment:

$$x_3 = \frac{\begin{vmatrix} -\phi_3 & \phi_y \\ -\theta_3 & \theta_y \end{vmatrix}}{\begin{vmatrix} \phi_x & \phi_y \\ \theta_x & \theta_y \end{vmatrix}}.$$

The denominators are the same for x_2 and x_3, and we want the ratio

$$\frac{x_2}{x_3} = \frac{\begin{vmatrix} -\phi_2 & \phi_y \\ -\theta_2 & \theta_y \end{vmatrix}}{\begin{vmatrix} -\phi_3 & \phi_y \\ -\theta_3 & \theta_y \end{vmatrix}} = \frac{\phi_y \theta_2 - \theta_y \phi_2}{\phi_y \theta_3 - \theta_y \phi_3}.$$

This simple expression provides the ratio of the effect of σ^2 on x to the effect of μ_3 on x, since x_2 / x_3 is shorthand for $(\partial x / \partial \sigma^2)/(\partial x / \partial \mu_3)$. It assumes that the second and third moments can vary independently of one another, and that all other moments are fixed, including R_0, the net reproduction rate.

An Exact Ratio of Partial Derivatives and an Approximation Thereto

To evaluate x_2/x_3 we refer back to the expansions of ϕ and θ and calculate the partials:

$$\phi_x = \mu - \sigma^2 x + \frac{\mu_3(x^2 - y^2)}{2} + \ldots,$$

$$\phi_y = \sigma^2 y - \mu_3 xy + \ldots,$$

$$\theta_x = -\sigma^2 y + \mu_3 xy - \ldots,$$

$$\theta_y = \mu - \sigma^2 x + \frac{\mu_3(x^2 - y^2)}{2} - \ldots,$$

$$\phi_2 = \frac{y^2 - x^2}{2}, \qquad \theta_2 = -xy,$$

$$\phi_3 = \frac{x^3 - 3xy^2}{6}, \qquad \theta_3 = \frac{3x^2 y - y^3}{6}.$$

Entering these in the expression for x_2/x_3, we have

$$\frac{x_2}{x_3} = \frac{\phi_y \theta_2 - \theta_y \phi_2}{\phi_y \theta_3 - \theta_y \phi_3}$$

$$= \frac{(\sigma^2 y - \mu_3 xy + \ldots)(-xy) - (\mu - \sigma^2 x + \ldots)\left[(y^2 - x^2)/2\right]}{(\sigma^2 y - \mu_3 xy + \ldots)\left[(3x^2 y - y^3)/6\right] - (\mu - \sigma^2 x + \ldots)\left[(x^3 - 3xy^2)/6\right]},$$

$$(9.6.9)$$

which is readily evaluated to as many terms as desired.

Choosing the terms that seem most to affect the answer gives the approximation

$$\frac{x_2}{x_3} \doteq \frac{(\sigma^2/\mu)(2x) + 1}{(\sigma^2/\mu)(y^2/3) - x}. \qquad (9.6.10)$$

If σ^2/μ, the ratio of variance to mean in the net maternity function, is 1.3, and $r_2 = x + iy$ is $-0.03 + 0.22i$, then (9.6.10) works out to 18.

Allowance for Different Ranges of Variance and Skewness among Observed Populations

For a typical population with given age-specific rates of birth and death, we have found that the ratio of the effect of variance to that of skewness, x_2/x_3 above, is about 18. Except for the approximations made after in the

Table 9.3 Ratio of Effect of Second Moment to That of Third Moment, All Others Constant: $x_2/x_3 = (\partial x/\partial \sigma^2)/(\partial x/\partial \mu_3)$

Country and year	x_2/x_3 (9.6.9)	x_2/x_3 (9.6.10)	x_2^*/x_3^* (9.6.11)
Algeria, 1965	16.670	16.805	2.673
Austria, 1968	12.636	13.052	2.027
Bulgaria, 1968	15.480	16.273	2.137
Canada, 1968	14.740	15.170	2.385
Colombia, 1965	19.708	19.886	3.276
England and Wales, 1968	16.959	17.330	2.952
France, 1967	17.861	18.322	2.893
Germany, West, 1967	18.834	19.146	3.448
Greece, 1968	18.831	19.094	3.699
Honduras, 1966	16.127	16.090	2.970
Ireland, 1967	38.027	37.953	12.340
Jamaica, 1963	15.219	15.438	2.881
Madagascar, 1966	11.419	11.795	1.553
Mexico, 1966	18.777	18.722	3.906
Nicaragua, 1965	16.034	16.147	2.811
Panama, 1966	15.027	15.362	2.275
Puerto Rico, 1965	8.979	9.638	1.142
Taiwan, 1966	36.809	37.195	5.409
Togo, 1961	11.360	11.660	1.663
Trinidad and Tobago, 1967	13.774	14.057	2.237
United States, 1966	13.713	14.183	2.131
Males	16.172	17.249	1.604
Venezuela, 1965	19.292	19.445	3.316

Female populations only, except for the United States. Based on data in Keyfitz and Flieger, (1968, 1971).

interest of ease of calculation, (9.6.9) is an exact result, allowing the several moments to vary independently of one another, and taking account of as many moments as are needed for fit to the net maternity function. But among real populations skewness varies more than variance. Variances are mostly between 25 and 55, whereas skewnesses are between 50 and 200, that is, the range of skewness is 5 times that of variance.

Can we escape this difficulty by somehow finding theoretically comparable measures of dispersion and skewness? A change in the scale on which fertility is measured affects the square root of the variance to the same degree as the cube root of the skewness. Would we have been better off to start from the beginning with the standard deviation and the cube root of the third moment?

It is easy enough to convert our results to what would have been obtained with that procedure. We write $\partial x / \partial \sigma$ as x_2^* and $\partial x / \partial \sqrt[3]{\mu_3}$ as x_3^*. Then

$$x_2^* = \frac{\partial x}{\partial \sigma} = \frac{\partial x}{\partial \sigma^2} \cdot \frac{\partial \sigma^2}{\partial \sigma} = 2\sigma \frac{\partial x}{\partial \sigma^2},$$

$$x_3^* = \frac{\partial x}{\partial \sqrt[3]{\mu_3}} = \frac{\partial x}{\partial \mu_3} \cdot \frac{\partial \mu_3}{\partial \sqrt[3]{\mu_3}} = 3\mu_3^{2/3} \frac{\partial x}{\partial \mu_3},$$

so that the new ratio, x_2^* / x_3^*, is

$$\frac{x_2^*}{x_3^*} = \frac{2\sigma}{3\mu_3^{2/3}} \cdot \frac{x_2}{x_3}. \tag{9.6.11}$$

This modifies the result (9.6.9) by an amount easily evaluated and shown in table 9.3 for 23 populations, along with (9.6.9) and (9.6.10).

The preceding pages offer a way of finding the relative influence x_2 / x_3 of the second and third cumulants (or any other pair) on the real part of the first complex root. It can be used also to find the absolute effect on the root of any cumulant; this would consist of x_2 for the influence of the second moment, x_3 for that of the third, and so on. These methods and results can now be applied to finding the time to convergence.

Time to Convergence

What determines the time to convergence is not x alone but $\ln\epsilon / (x - r)$, as in (9.6.1). We need to know, for comparing the second and third moments,

$$\frac{\dfrac{\partial \left[\ln\epsilon / (x - r) \right]}{\partial \sigma^2}}{\dfrac{\partial \left[\ln\epsilon / (x - r) \right]}{\partial \mu_3}} = \frac{-\dfrac{\ln\epsilon}{(x - r)^2} \cdot \dfrac{\partial (x - r)}{\partial \sigma^2}}{-\dfrac{\ln\epsilon}{(x - r)^2} \cdot \dfrac{\partial (x - r)}{\partial \mu_3}}$$

$$= \frac{\partial x / \partial \sigma^2 - \partial r / \partial \sigma^2}{\partial x / \partial \mu_3 - \partial r / \partial \mu_3} = \frac{x_2 - r_2}{x_3 - r_3}, \tag{9.6.12}$$

in an obvious extension of the earlier notation.

The derivatives of r with respect to the moments are obtained from equation 9.6.2 involving r, that may be called $\psi = 0$; by differentiation we have

$$r_2 = \frac{-\psi_2}{-\psi_r} = \frac{r^2/2!}{\mu - r\sigma^2 + \mu_3(r^2/2!) - \dots}$$

and

$$r_3 = \frac{-\psi_3}{-\psi_r} = \frac{r^3/6}{\mu - r\sigma^2 + \mu_3(r^2/2!) - \dots} ;$$

and assembling these with what we found earlier for x_2 and x_3 gives

$$\frac{\dfrac{\partial\left[\ln\epsilon/(x-r)\right]}{\partial\sigma^2}}{\dfrac{\partial\left[\ln\epsilon/(x-r)\right]}{\partial\mu_3}} = \frac{x_2 - r_2}{x_3 - r_3}$$

$$= \frac{\psi_r(\phi_y\theta_2 - \phi_2\theta_y) - \psi_2(\phi_x\theta_y - \phi_y\theta_x)}{\psi_r(\phi_y\theta_3 - \phi_3\theta_y) - \psi_3(\phi_x\theta_y - \phi_y\theta_x)}, \qquad (9.6.13)$$

on substituting the previously obtained x_2, r_2, x_3, and r_3. This result is exact, but unfortunately it includes a score or more terms, even if we stop at squares in r and x and fourth powers in y. To make (9.6.13) tractable for calculation and thinking about, we need to discard smaller terms. The bare minimum appears to be

$$x_2 = \frac{\sigma^2 x/\mu + \frac{1}{2}}{\mu/y^2 + \sigma^4/\mu}, \qquad x_3 = \frac{\sigma^2 y^2/6\mu - x/2}{\mu/y^2 + \sigma^4/\mu},$$

$$r_2 = \frac{r^2}{2\mu}, \qquad r_3 = \frac{r^3}{6\mu}. \qquad (9.6.14)$$

For a population with $r = 0.03$, $x = -0.03$, $y = 0.22$, $\mu = 27$, and $\sigma^2 = 35$, the result is

$$\frac{x_2 - r_2}{x_3 - r_3} = \frac{0.000764 - 0.000017}{0.0000422 - 0.0000002} = 17.8$$

against $x_2/x_3 = 18.1$. Apparently even a high rate of increase has little effect on the time to convergence.

Theoretical versus Empirical Relations

The effect of each moment on the real part of the second root is also obtainable from empirical materials. But this, like all correlations taken from the real world, has a different meaning. It tells what the effect is *when other things vary as they vary*. The formulas of the preceding pages tell what the effect is *when other things are held constant*. Both kinds of information are useful for understanding, but they are not the same. The difference between theoretical and empirical facts in demography is a main subject of Chapter 12.

Proceeding to the implications of instability in financial, economic, and social matters, we will discuss as a first aspect old-age security.

9.7 RETIREMENT PENSIONS: PAY-AS-YOU-GO VERSUS ACTUARIAL RESERVES

The cost of pensions to the wage-earner differs according to whether actuarial funding is used. On pay-as-you-go each year's pensions come out of the same year's receipts; the receipts are a tax, whose amount is in principle adjusted to the requirements of the scheme, that is to say, by the number of pensioners and the average amount of payment to them in relation to the number of contributors. Actuarial or reserve plans, on the other hand, are based on calculation of the expected cost to each individual; his premiums are cumulated at interest, and their amount is in principle just sufficient to cover his expected withdrawals from retirement to death. In the actuarial scheme, the expected costs of each individual are covered, which is another way of saying that each cohort pays for itself; in pay-as-you-go each period pays for itself. The two approaches can be compared for cost and equity.

In the stable condition, say with the population growing at rate r, a payment of unity to pensioners will cost

$$\int_{\beta}^{\omega} e^{-ra} l(a)\, da,\tag{9.7.1}$$

per current birth, where β is the age of retirement and ω the oldest age to which anyone lives. Contributions will be equal to

$$p\int_{\alpha}^{\beta} e^{-ra} l(a)\, da,\tag{9.7.2}$$

where α is the age at which uniform contribution begins, and p is the annual uniform payment by each person of working age, again per current birth. Equating (9.7.1) and (9.7.2) and solving for p:

$$p = \frac{\int_{\beta}^{\omega} e^{-ra} l(a)\, da}{\int_{\alpha}^{\beta} e^{-ra} l(a)\, da}, \tag{9.7.3}$$

and this is the premium for a simple case of pay-as-you-go, in accord with the argument of Section 4.7.

The above statements apply whether or not money bears interest. A pay-as-you-go scheme in principle holds no reserves that can accumulate interest, but dispenses what it takes in year by year.

As we saw in Section 2.5, an actuarial scheme is built on reserves that draw interest. If the rate is i per annum, compounded momently, so that the amount of one dollar at the end of t years is e^{it} dollars, then discounting a benefit of 1 dollar per year back to the moment of birth gives $\int_{\beta}^{\omega} e^{-ia} l(a)\, da$. If this amount is to be paid for by a premium of p dollars per year from ages α to β, the present value of the premium to the moment of birth must be $p \int_{\alpha}^{\beta} e^{-ia} l(a)\, da$. Equating the two present values gives for the annual premium p

$$p = \frac{\int_{\beta}^{\omega} e^{-ia} l(a)\, da}{\int_{\alpha}^{\beta} e^{-ia} l(a)\, da}. \tag{9.7.4}$$

Note that the two expressions, 9.7.3 and 9.7.4, for the annual cost of the pension are identical, with the sole difference that one contains the rate of interest i in the place where the other contains the rate of increase in the population. If r is greater than i, the average person will do better in a pay-as-you-go scheme. To prove this we need only note that p is a decreasing function of i. In fact, by taking logarithms of both sides of (9.7.4) and differentiating, we find

$$\frac{1}{p}\frac{dp}{di} = -(m_r - m_w),$$

where m_r is the mean age of the retired persons and m_w is the (necessarily younger) mean age of the working population. In finite terms

$$\frac{\Delta p}{p} \doteq -(m_r - m_w)\Delta i; \tag{9.7.5}$$

and, if $m_r - m_w$ is about 30 years, each rise of 1 percent in the rate of interest will lower the premium by 30 percent of itself. This fact is very little affected by variations in the mortality level prevailing under modern conditions. Expression 9.7.5 is formally analogous to (4.7.4), though the two have different content.

When money carries a rate of at least 5 percent and population increases at 0 to 3 percent, why does anyone want a compulsory pay-as-you-go scheme? The answer is that the rate of interest people have in mind is in terms of goods, not money, and in times of inflation the two are not the same. What counts in the comparison of (9.7.3) and (9.7.4) is the increase in the amount of goods that one can have by temporarily foregoing the use of his money. If prospective price inflation is 6 percent per year, and money interest is 5 per cent per year, the goods rate of interest is negative. The decline of the real rate of bank and bond interest virtually to zero helps account for the popularity of pay-as-you-go schemes. A further reason is that the latter are more painless at initiation, when noncontributors can simply be blanketed in, in effect at the cost of a later generation.

Pay-as-you-go is largely proof against inflation, but has demographic troubles. These are suggested in Table 9.4, showing the ratio of working to pensionable ages over a century. In the United States the main pressure will come after the year 2000, with a rise of 50 percent over the years about 2020. The only thing that could prevent this is a large increase of births before the year 2000 that would raise the 21st century labor force, which seems unlikely.

The Social Security scheme can be seen as a way of borrowing from future generations, like the national debt. Besides lacking a contractual character, it differs from the national debt in being five times as large. Martin Feldstein (1976) shows that the scheme reduces private savings: people do not save as much because they are implictly promised support

Table 9.4 Persons of working and pensionable ages in the United States, 1950–2050

Year	Age 21–64	Age 65+	Percent 65+/21–64
1950	85,944	12,397	14.42
1960	92,181	16,675	18.09
1970	103,939	20,085	19.32
1980	122,115	24,523	20.08
1990	137,500	28,933	21.04
2000	148,589	30,600	20.59
2025	146,645	45,715	31.17
2050	147,635	45,805	31.03

Source: U. S. Statistical Abstract, 1975, p. 6.

by the next generation when they are old. But at the same time their smaller savings mean smaller investment than would otherwise occur, so the incomes of the next generation will be less than with private savings for retirement or an actuarial reserve scheme. Our children's having to pay larger benefits to us out of incomes that are smaller than they otherwise would be because of our failure to save may be offset by our having paid for their education; on present trends expenditures on old-age security could substantially exceed those on education. If, however, as many think, our children will be much richer than we are, some borrowing from them is permissible.

But the subject of intergenerational equity is much too big for treatment here. All we need notice is that fluctuations in births are what bring the problem to the fore; under stable population growth most of these issues would not arise (Clark and Spengler, 1976).

9.8   THE DEMOGRAPHY OF EDUCATIONAL ORGANIZATIONS UNDER CHANGING AGE DISTRIBUTIONS

The 1950s and 1960s, with all their difficulties, attained a happy balance between graduate teaching and research. At the pinnacle of the academic profession was the faculty member of a major university, whose teaching was largely of graduate students and included or even centered on his own research. His students were in effect apprentices who would be certified by doctorates, often at the rate of one every year or two, as qualified to take posts in other graduate schools, where they would be a prolongation of the master's research and teaching. One's weight in the university depended on his own discoveries and publications, as well as on former students who would teach his work and cite his publications; and these former students would in due course replicate the process and send forth their graduates.

We know now that this process of reproduction cannot always be as rapid as in the 1960s. Even a much slower rate is out of the question in the long run. If the master is 40 years of age, and he turns out a student aged 25, and does the same again when he is 50 and a third time when he is 60, and these immediately go into graduate teaching and follow the same pattern, the population of graduate faculty is approximately trebling each 25 years. Its annual average rate of increase is given by the difference equation

$$B(t) = B(t-15) + B(t-25) + B(t-35);$$

to solve this we try $B(t) = e^{rt}$ and obtain the equation in r:

$$1 = e^{-15r} + e^{-25r} + e^{-35r}.$$

For an iterative solution we multiply through by e^{25r} and then take logarithms:

$$r^* = \tfrac{1}{25}\ln(e^{10r}+1+e^{-10r}).$$

Starting with $r=0$ on the right, we find for the successive values of r^* 0.0439, 0.0465, 0.0468, and 0.0468. A rate of 4.68 per cent cannot be maintained over any long period of time. If the general population increases at 1 percent then the fraction who are graduate school teachers would go up over 35 times in a century.

Such pencil-and-paper calculations requiring no data could have been made when the graduate student boom was at its height and would have shown its temporary character. The basic demographic point is that, in the stationary condition that is inevitable sooner or later, a faculty member, in a graduate school or anywhere else, is on the average succeeded by one faculty member.

The system is very sensitive to the rate of increase. If it is expanding at 7 percent per year, and the difference in age between a teacher and his students is 20 years, each teacher is not restricted to one replacement, but will be succeeded by four tenured members on the average. This is so because 7 percent increase is a doubling in 10 years, or two doublings in 20 years. With the same rate of increase, if the time in nontenure is 6 years and in tenure 24 years, then the stable ratio of nontenure to tenure is

$$\int_0^6 e^{-0.07x}\,dx : \int_6^{30} e^{-0.07x}\,dx$$

or

$$1 - e^{(-0.07)(6)} : e^{(-0.07)(6)} - e^{(-0.07)(30)}$$

which is $1:1.56$, as against $1:4$ with the same age limits under stationarity, disregarding mortality while in service.

In public institutions where staffing is based on fixed student–teacher ratios, the slowing down of college entrants results in a sharp deceleration of faculty appointments. And what is true formally in public institutions is true practically in private ones—as their students stabilize or decline, so do tuition and other income, with inevitable consequences for faculty numbers. The greater difficulty of entering college teaching especially is felt by women and minorities, who are just beginning to qualify. To hire them and give them chances for promotion is far harder when the system is contracting than when it was expanding.

9.9 TWO LEVELS OF STUDENTS AND TEACHERS

Extrapolation of the trend of the 1950s and 1960s could lead only to the conclusion that the entire population would attain the Ph. D. and become college teachers.

A very simple model, recognizing only two levels of education, can avoid such a nonsensical result (Correa, 1967). Suppose that the two levels are college and graduate school, and the unit of time is 4 years. Let $S_t^{(1)}$ be the number of students at time t at the lower level, and $S_t^{(2)}$ the number of students at time t at the higher level; let $T_t^{(1)}$ and $T_t^{(2)}$ be the corresponding numbers of teachers at the two levels. If ρ_1 and ρ_2 are the ratios of teachers to students at the two levels, then two equations express the demand for teachers:

$$T_t^{(1)} = \rho_1 S_t^{(1)}, \tag{9.9.1}$$

$$T_t^{(2)} = \rho_2 S_t^{(2)}. \tag{9.9.2}$$

If σ_1 is the fraction of the students in level 2 who will become teachers in level 1, and σ_2 the fraction of the students in level 2 who will become teachers in level 2, we have for the supply of teachers in period $t+1$:

$$T_{t+1}^{(1)} = (1 - \mu_1) T_t^{(1)} + \sigma_1 S_t^{(2)}, \tag{9.9.3}$$

$$T_{t+1}^{(2)} = (1 - \mu_2) T_t^{(2)} + \sigma_2 S_t^{(2)}, \tag{9.9.4}$$

where μ_1 and μ_2 represent the loss of teachers through death, retirement, and other causes at the two levels. To complete the model, suppose that a fraction ϕ of the students at the lower level go on to the higher level:

$$S_{t+1}^{(2)} = \phi S_t^{(1)}. \tag{9.9.5}$$

If the unknowns are the students and teachers at the two levels, the system has four unknowns and five equations; it is overdetermined. The unknowns can be increased to 5 by supposing that any one of the seven Greek letter constants is unknown. Not all of the constants are equally likely candidates for this; I would say that σ_1 and σ_2, the fraction of Ph. D. students who become teachers, or else ϕ, the fractions of college students who go on to graduate school, should be the first to be examined. Alternatively, the system could be made solvable by disregarding one of the equations.

The system ought to be considered as dynamic: some of the variables drive the others. If the upper level does the driving, that is, if the number of Ph. D.s determines the number of teaching positions and the number of students at the lower level, so that the operative equations are (9.9.2) and

(9.9.4), we have a first-order system, of which the solution is

$$T_t^{(2)} = \left(1 + \frac{\sigma_2}{\rho_2} - \mu_2\right)^t T_0^{(2)}. \tag{9.9.6}$$

The system expands steadily, without oscillations. In this unlikely model the number of persons who want to attend graduate school and become teachers determines the number of undergraduates. It is worth mentioning here only because it is implicit in some of the educational perspectives of the 1960s.

Taking the more realistic condition that the students at the lower level determine the system, we find that cycles in the number of college students give rise to amplified cycles in the number of new teachers demanded. Any reasonable way of making the system determinate will show that the *absolute demand* for Ph. D.s is closely related to the *increase* in the number of college students (Correa, 1967).

The model enables us to follow what happens in the wake of a baby boom. About 17 years after the rise in births comes a rise in the number of college applicants. Every effort is made to satisfy this demand for entrance: teachers are asked to defer retirement; somewhat less qualified persons are given appointments as teachers; newly established colleges take some of the new students and hire as teachers persons who would not earlier have aspired to this occupation. In our model the increase of applicants acts initially on (9.9.1), resulting partly in an immediate expansion of $T_t^{(1)}$, and partly in allowing ρ_1, the fraction of teacher per student, to become smaller, which is the same as class sizes becoming larger. Somehow the demand constituted by the rise in applicants for college entrance is *immediately* met; applicants are not ordinarily asked to come back in 8 or 10 years, which could make the system more stable.

The college teacher shortage at this stage is intense, and graduate schools receive applications from many who in earlier times would have been satisfied to leave school with a B.A. The graduate schools, like the applicants, perceive a strong demand for Ph. D.s and accept more than they otherwise would. Even if ϕ of (9.9.5) were fixed, there would be an increase in the number of recruits to graduate school the next period; but in fact ϕ increases in such times, and the graduate schools expand in higher ratios than the increase in the number of undergraduates.

Two periods later, that is to say, 8 years after the baby boom has hit the college level, the first Ph. D.s of the new wave are available. They are seeking jobs in colleges, and particularly in graduate schools, having oriented themselves to the institutions of highest prestige. The supply of graduate school teachers is now given by (9.9.4) with a high $S_t^{(2)}$. The μ_t, coefficients of death and retirement, are small over the short period here involved. The timing in this crude representation involves the 17 years from the start of the baby boom to college entry of the larger cohorts, plus the 8 years through college and graduate school, a total of 25 years from the first rise in births to the start of an employment crisis for Ph. D.s. Twenty-five years is about the interval from the later 1940s to the early 1970s.

9.10   MOBILITY IN AN UNSTABLE POPULATION

The mobility model of Section 4.8 exhibited the demographic factor in promotion, finding it faster for members of populations in rapid growth than for members of stationary populations. A person will get to a middle-level position about 9 years earlier in the fastest growing population than in a stationary one. Mortality also helps (at least for those who survive) but much less; a very high mortality population ($\overset{o}{e}_0 = 35$ years) will advance its surviving members to middle positions only 2 to 3 years sooner than the lowest mortality population known (say $\overset{o}{e}_0 = 75$ years). High subsequent birth rates advance a person's promotion more than do high death rates.

The above results are comparative rather than dynamic—they compare the age of attaining a given level in a fast- and in a slow-growing population, but supposing for each that its rates have been fixed and continuing over a long period. A separate question concerns the slowing down of an actual population: what difference does it make to individuals now alive that the United States was growing at 1.5 percent per year in the late 1950s and is dropping from this rate toward stationarity? Stable population theory, assuming as it does fixed rates, cannot by its very nature answer a question about the effect of change in rates over time.

As an introduction to the problem consider the present United States age distribution in the stylized version of Fig. 9.3. Those approaching retirement are members of the large cohorts born in the 1920s and earlier. The working population now in its forties consists of the very small cohorts born in the 1930s, and new entrants up to now have been larger, steadily increasing toward the left in Fig. 9.3, up to those born about 1960. Following that comes a downturn, so that the new entrants of the 1980s will be fewer and decreasing.

Those now in their forties are fortunate in two distinct ways. On the one hand, they are called on to replace the large number of their elders retiring

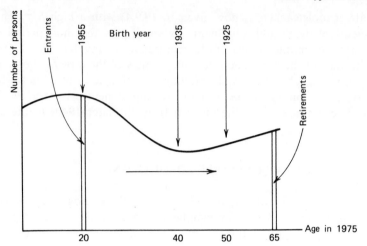

Fig. 9.3 Stylized representation of the supply of labor in the United States.

from senior posts. On the other hand, they have been drawn upward by the large number of new entrants who are younger than themselves. Supervisors and teachers are required in relation to workers and students; the tests of competence for supervisors and teachers are less stringent in times when more are required.

Thus those born in the 1930s, having been pushed upward by the young people coming in behind them, can now look forward to further promotion as their seniors retire. On the other hand, those born at the peak of the baby boom in the 1950s and early 1960s will never in their later careers be in such great demand as supervisors and teachers, for they are followed by sparse cohorts, nor will they be drawn up as strongly to fill posts vacated by retirement, because these will be less numerous.

9.11   THE EASTERLIN EFFECT

The high United States fertility of the 1950s and the subsequent decline have puzzled observers who believe that there are strong economic determinants of age-specific fertility. The phenomenon could not be due to prosperity, since income in the 1950s was not as high as in the 1960s. That children are positively related to income in time series did not seem to help here, until Easterlin (1961, 1968) noted that the prosperity of couples of childbearing age is what we should look for, not general prosperity. He pointed out that couples of childbearing age in the 1950s, born between the humps of the 1920s and the 1940s, were located in a hollow similar to that of Fig. 9.3. Not only was their promotion relatively rapid, but also in any one position, insofar as there is age complementarity in production, they frequently had the advantage of meeting situations in which they were too few to do the necessary work, with resulting appreciation of their services. This was often expressed in material terms and resulted in high wages and good prospects relative to what people of their age would have been paid in a different age configuration; hence these people have enjoyed a sense of security and well-being. Their confidence is well founded, for they will spend their whole working lives in the same advantageous position. They have translated their advantage into childbearing, perhaps projecting their security into the next generation and feeling that their children will be in demand just as they are.

So strong was this effect in the 1950s that it entirely reversed the tendency of the classical model with fixed age-specific rates of Chapter 5. Instead of a dip, echoing that of the 1930s, the 1950s showed births at the highest level in half a century. The 1930s gave a relative advantage to their children by producing few of them, and these later repaid the advantage by having many children. Such a mechanism could produce a very stable result if the rise in birth rates was of just the right amount to compensate for the few parents. In the actual case, however, the rise overcompensated.

The subsequent steady fall of the birth rate in the 1960s might well have been due to the entry into childbearing ages of the large cohorts born in the 1940s. If this was the dominant mechanism operating, we can predict continued low birth rates at least through the 1970s. Not until about 1990 will the parental generation again be small enough to be encouraged to have large families. Instead of the waves of generation length in the free response of the demographic model we find waves two generations in length.

To translate this into quantitative terms we consider females only, and simply suppose that all children are born at the same age of parent, say 25 years or the mean length of generation. If the "normal" female growth ratio is R_0 per generation, births in the tth generation are $B_t = R_0 B_{t-1}$. The conditions imply geometric increase and lead to the solution $B_t = B_0 R_0^t$.

Suppose now that superimposed on this is a component of births in the tth generation that depends on how small is the number of couples aged 25 compared with the number of couples aged 50. When the couples aged 25 are relatively few, that is to say, when B_{t-1} is less than its "normal," suppose an additional $\gamma(R_0 B_{t-2} - B_{t-1})$ births in the tth generation, γ positive. These conditions mean that the sizes of cohorts are related by

$$B_t = R_0 B_{t-1} + \gamma(R_0 B_{t-2} - B_{t-1}) \qquad (9.11.1)$$

where R_0 is no longer necessarily the net reproduction rate.

To solve (9.11.1) we try $B_t = x^t$ and find

$$x^2 - (R_0 - \gamma)x - \gamma R_0 = 0 \qquad (9.11.2)$$

of which the roots are conveniently $x = R_0$ and $-\gamma$. Thus the solution of (9.11.1) is

$$B_t = k_1 R_0^t + k_2 (-\gamma)^t, \qquad (9.11.3)$$

where k_1 and k_2 depend on the initial conditions. The term in $(-\gamma)^t$ tells us that cycles will be generated two generations in length. If the factor for normal increase R_0 is greater than γ, any waves once started will diminish as a proportion of the geometric increase. If γ is less than unity, they will diminish absolutely.

Lee (1968) applied Easterlin's theory in a much more refined model, one recognizing individual age groups. He also traced out its historical antecedents, starting with a quotation from Yule (1906): "If...the supply of labour be above the optimum, the supply of labour being in excess, the birth rate will be depressed, and will stay depressed until the reduction begins to have some effect on the labour market. But this effect will not even commence for fifteen or twenty years, and the labour supply may not be adjusted to the demand for, say, thirty years. The birth rate may now have risen again to normal, but the labour supply will continue to fall owing to the low birth rates formerly prevalent. The birth rate will therefore rise above normal and continue above normal so long as the labour supply is in defect, and so matters will go on, the population swinging about the optimum value with a long period of perhaps fifty to one hundred years, and the birth rate following suit." The germ of this idea is to be found as far back as Adam Smith, who considered that the supply of labor, like the supply of shoes, was determined by demand. Smith did not go the one further step of recognizing that the period of production of labor is longer than the period of production of shoes, with resulting longer and deeper cycles. Samuelson (1976) has further developed the subject.

Some apology is needed for the heterogeneous material contained in the present chapter, which reflects the fact that populations can be unstable in many different ways. To write about stable theory in a coherent fashion is bound to be more straightforward than to attempt to write about everything that is not stable theory. Furthermore the range of applications here attempted or recounted is especially wide, including estimating the rate of increase of a population when its death rate or its birth rate is falling, backward projection under instability, finding the time to stability after a disturbance, old-age pensions under reserve and nonreserve systems, and the consequences for the educational system, the labor market, and the birth rate of the baby boom and its aftermath.

Chapter Ten

THE DEMOGRAPHIC THEORY
OF KINSHIP

This chapter will extract information on kinship numbers from the age-specific rates of birth and death of a population. A fixed set of age-specific rates implies the probability that a girl aged a has a living mother and great-grandmother, as well as her expected number of daughters, sisters, aunts, nieces, and cousins. Certain assumptions are required to draw the implications, some stronger than others. The formulas of this chapter in effect set ,up a genealogical table, giving not the names of incumbents in the several positions but the expected number of incumbents. Those of Fig. 10.1 are based on birth and death rates of the United States in 1965, whose net reproduction rate R_0 was 1.395 and $\overset{o}{e}_0$ was 73.829, all for females. They offer a different kind of knowledge from what would be provided by a kinship census.

Like earlier chapters, this one supposes a population generated by birth and death with overlapping generations. (Generations do not overlap in annual plants, where all the parents have disappeared before the children come to life, a circumstance that requires a different kind of population analysis from that of this book.) The considerable longevity of human beings after the birth of their offspring produces simultaneously living kin of many kinds—not only parents and children, but also grandparents, nephews, and cousins. Human beings produce most of their offspring in births of discrete individuals, but this is not recognized in the present analysis, which supposes $m(x)dx$ of a daughter in each dx of maternal age. For certain kin this introduces serious qualifications, specified in Section

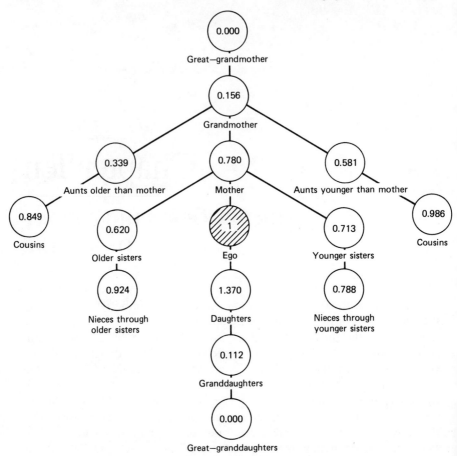

Fig. 10.1 Expected number of female kin alive when Ego (hatched circle) is aged 40, based on birth and death rates of the United States, 1965.

10.3. Development of this field is due to Lotka (1931), Burch (1970), Coale (1965), Goodman, Keyfitz, and Pullum (1974) and LeBras (1973).

Explicit recognition of the several degrees of living and dead kin varies from one culture to another, and indeed from one family to another. We disregard here cultural, social, and psychological definitions and deal with numerical relations among average numbers of biological kin as they are determined by birth and death rates. To avoid undue complication, all of the discussion following recognizes female kin only.

10.1 PROBABILITY OF LIVING ANCESTORS

Deterministic models concern both population numbers and probabilities. The two perspectives are at least on the surface distinct.

Counting Method. A large population can be seen as developing according to given rules, and in effect we can make counts of the number of individuals having the kin relations of interest. This is an extension of the notion that l_0 is the number of births occurring at one moment and $l(x)$ is the number of those surviving x years later, the cohort conception of the life table $l(x)$ referred to in Section 2.1. (But we still keep $l_0 = 1$.)

Probability Method. We can start by thinking of an individual and work out probabilities and expected values for his various kin. This is an extension of the interpretation of the life table $l(x)$ as the probability that a child just born will survive for x years.

Living Mother by the Counting Method

Our first approach to finding the probability that a girl aged a has a living mother is to see how a population would have developed starting from B girl children born at a moment $a + x$ years ago. At age x of this maternal generation cohort the survivors were $Bl(x)$, and during the interval x to $x + dx$ they could be expected to give birth to $Bl(x)m(x)l(a)dx$ daughters who would live to age a. Of the mothers who gave birth at age x a fraction $l(x + a)/l(x)$ would survive over an additional a years; hence the number of living mothers must be $Bl(x)m(x)dx[l(x + a)/l(x)]l(a)$. A woman is counted once for each birth that survives.

All this concerns one cohort of the mother generation. But we seek the probability that a girl aged a, standing before us, has a living mother, without any knowledge of which cohort her mother belonged to, or indeed any knowledge other than the regime of mortality and fertility supposed to apply to all generations and at all times. If births as a function of time are $B(t)$, and the present is time t, girls born $x + a$ years ago numbered $B(t - a - x)$, and the number of living mothers (counted once for each daughter) of all cohorts who gave birth to girls now alive and a years of age is the integral

$$\int_\alpha^\beta B(t - a - x)l(x)m(x)\frac{l(x + a)}{l(x)}l(a)dx. \qquad (10.1.1)$$

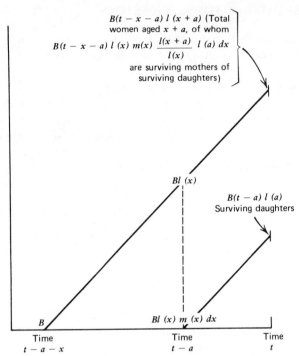

Fig. 10.2 Cohort of mothers giving birth at age x, and of daughters born at age x of mother.

For the same birth function $B(t)$ the number of daughters, that is, girls born a years ago and surviving to the present, is

$$B(t-a)l(a). \tag{10.1.2}$$

Hence the average number of mothers per daughter at time t is the ratio of (10.1.1) to (10.1.2).

Now, if the age-specific rates of birth and death have been in effect for a long period of time, the births will be growing exponentially, say according to the curve $B_0 e^{rt}$, where r is determined by (5.1.2). Entering this for the birth function in each of (10.1.1) and (10.1.2), taking the ratio of the first to the second, and canceling $l(a)B_0 e^{r(t-a)}$ from numerator and denominator gives

$$M_1(a) = \int_\alpha^\beta \frac{l(x+a)}{l(x)} e^{-rx} l(x) m(x) \, dx \tag{10.1.3}$$

for the probability that a girl aged a has a living mother under the given regime of mortality and fertility (Lotka, 1931).

All of the problems of this chapter can be solved in this way, by following cohorts through time, then in effect taking a census at a certain moment, and finding the ratio of one census aggregate to another. This does not of course constitute a census of the real population, which would show the result of changing death rates over time, but is at best a simplified abstract argument devised by analogy to counting population by means of a census and births by means of registrations. Made possible by the deterministic assumption of Section 2.1, it requires no explicit considerations of probability, yet it is both unnecessarily complicated and unnecessarily restricted.

Living Mother by Conditional Probability

Alternatively, the life table $l(x)$ column is taken, not as a cohort, but as the probability of living to age x for a child just born, on the regime of mortality assumed, with $l_0 = 1$. The corresponding approach will provide a result for $M_1(a)$ identical with (10.1.3).

In seeking the probability that a girl chosen at random out of a population with birth rates $m(x)$ and survivorship $l(x)$ has a living mother, we first note that the conditional case is easily solved. *If* the mother was a known x years old when she gave birth to the girl, *then* the chance that the mother is alive a years later must be $l(x+a)/l(x)$. This probability, conditional on the mother's age at bearing the girl having been x, is the first part of the solution.

It remains to remove the condition, which is not part of the problem; we do not care about the age x of the mother at childbearing. To eliminate the condition we average over all ages x, giving each x a weight proportional to the number of births occurring at that age of mother under the regime in question. The number of the stable population of ages x to $x + dx$ per current birth is $e^{-rx}l(x)dx$, from Euler's argument of Section 4.1, and the births to this fraction are $e^{-rx}l(x)m(x)dx$, still taken per one current birth. The last expression is the fraction of births occurring to women aged x to $x + dx$; once again, its total over all x is unity by the (5.1.2) defining r. Hence the unconditional probability that the mother of the girl in question is still alive is obtained by multiplying $e^{-rx}l(x)m(x)dx$ by the survivorship $l(x+a)/l(x)$ and totaling over all x.

This is the same expression, derived more compactly, that we obtained as (10.1.3). Because of its compactness the probability method will be preferred in what follows. Note that (10.1.3) is more general than appeared in our interpretation. The derivation did not require the fact that the girl born a years ago is still alive, but consisted in finding the probability of survival of the mother a years after a random birth. Whether the girl born survived does not affect the value of $M_1(a)$, given independent regimes.

Probability of Living Grandmother

Now think of the grandmother of the girl aged a; we once again provisionally take the latter as having been born at age x of her mother. The grandmother has to live $x + a$ years after the birth of her daughter (the mother of our girl aged a) to be alive now. The chance of a woman living $x + a$ years after the birth of her daughter as calculated above is $M_1(x + a)$. This is now to be seen as the (conditional) probability that the grandmother of the girl aged a is alive, given that the girl aged a was born when her mother was x years old. To obtain the unconditional probability we again multiply by $e^{-rx}l(x)m(x)$ and integrate out x:

$$M_2(a) = \int_\alpha^\beta M_1(x + a)e^{-rx}l(x)m(x)\,dx. \tag{10.1.4}$$

Note that (10.1.4) again does not require the survival of the mother of the girl aged a. It is merely the probability that the grandmother of a randomly selected girl birth of a years ago is now alive.

The procedure supposes not only that the regime is fixed, but also that successive generations are independently subject to the given mortality and fertility. Independence of fertility between generations means, for example, that there is no tendency for daughters born to young mothers themselves to give birth at a young age, and it also disregards social class and other differences in mortality and fertility within heterogeneous populations. This is in addition to requiring birth and death to be independent, both in the same and in different generations; it excludes the possibility that some families have both high birth rates and high death rates. Finally, the chance of a woman having a child at ages x to $x + dx$ is taken as $m(x)\,dx$, whether or not she had a child immediately before this. These several unrealistic features of the model seem to have only a small effect on the probability of living ancestors and descendants, though they are important for number of sisters, aunts, and nieces.

Once we have $M_2(a)$, the chance that a girl aged a has a living grandmother, we can similarly use it to find the chance of a living great-grandmother. Again suppose that the mother of the girl aged a was x years old at the time of childbearing; the question whether a girl aged a has a living great-grandmother is the probability that the grandmother of the mother, born $x + a$ years ago, is still alive. That the grandmother survives $x + a$ years after her granddaughter was born has probability $M_2(x + a)$, so the unconditional probability that a girl aged a has a living great-grandmother is

$$M_3(a) = \int_\alpha^\beta M_2(x+a)e^{-rx}l(x)m(x)dx. \qquad (10.1.5)$$

Once more, this does not require the mother or grandmother of the girl aged a to be alive. The argument may be readily extended to even more remote progenitors (Goodman et al. 1974).

Numerical Examples

These and the other formulas of this chapter have been programmed by Tom Pullum, and Table 10.1 shows his results for three countries—strictly speaking, for three regimes of mortality and fertility—the United States, 1967; Venezuela, 1965; and Madagascar, 1966. The first two resemble one another in mortality and the last two in fertility, as the following standardized rates per thousand population having the United States, 1960, age distribution show:

Country and year	Birth rate	Death rate
United States, 1967	16.71	9.12
Venezuela, 1965	41.82	10.97
Madagascar, 1966	44.48	29.10

Thus Venezuela and Madagascar both have about 2.5 times the fertility of the United States, and Madagascar has about 3 times the mortality of the United States and Venezuela. We will later seek a more precise way of connecting the input mortality and fertility with the output kinship probabilities, but the present comparison is suggestive.

Table 10.1 shows, for example, that the chance that a woman aged 20 has a living mother is about 0.96 for the United States, 0.93 for Venezuela, and 0.71 for Madagascar. The complements of these numbers, 0.04, 0.07, and 0.29, are the probability of orphanhood on the mother's side. It was in an effort to see how serious was the problem of orphanhood that Lotka (1931) first developed (10.1.3). The greater difference between Venezuela and Madagascar than between the United States and Venezuela is to be expected; the chance of having living ancestors depends much more on mortality than on fertility rates. Insofar as fertility affects orphanhood, it is through the age of childbearing rather than through the number of children born, as will appear in Section 10.6.

Noreen Goldman has computed kin for a number of populations and is studying the relations that emerge.

Table 10.1 Probability of living mother, grandmother, great-grandmother, and great-great-grandmother, for a female aged $a = 0, 20, 40, 60$, based on mortality and fertility regimes of the United States, Venezuela, and Madagascar

Ancestor and country	Age a			
	0	20	40	60
Living mother $M_1(a)$				
United States, 1967	1.000	0.959	0.785	0.298
Venezuela, 1965	1.000	0.932	0.707	0.223
Madagascar, 1966	1.000	0.713	0.386	0.061
Living grandmother $M_2(a)$				
United States, 1967	0.919	0.653	0.165	0.000
Venezuela, 1965	0.867	0.553	0.112	0.000
Madagascar, 1966	0.600	0.256	0.032	0.000
Living great-grandmother $M_3(a)$				
United States, 1967	0.507	0.090	0.000	0.000
Venezuela, 1965	0.397	0.058	0.000	0.000
Madagascar, 1966	0.164	0.017	0.000	0.000
Living great-great-grandmother $M_4(a)$				
United States, 1967	0.049	0.000	0.000	0.000
Venezuela, 1965	0.030	0.000	0.000	0.000
Madagascar, 1966	0.009	0.000	0.000	0.000

Stable Results versus a Kinship Census

These formulas and the numbers of Table 10.1 have been worked out for the specified regimes of mortality and fertility, taken as fixed through time and the same in all generations. They are meant to answer the question: what probability of having a living mother, grandmother, and so on does the given schedule of birth and death rates imply?

The fraction of women aged 20 in the United States having living mothers as ascertained by a survey or census would disagree with the result of calculation by (10.1.3) for several reasons: changing mortality and fertility over the preceding years, presence of immigrants from countries with different regimes, misstatement of age in the survey and in the vital statistics on which our calculations are based, failure of the various independence assumptions. Probability of living grandmother $M_2(a)$ requires independence of two generations, and $M_3(a)$ of three generations. We know that longevity runs in families, as well as being different for social classes, and experimenting would be required to find the effect of the mortality correlation between generations. All the formulas would become much more complicated if they took account of such departures from the assumptions of fixity and independence of the vital rates. One can only repeat that the kinship implication of fixed and independent rates constitutes a different kind of knowledge from a kinship census.

An Approximation

Insofar as the net maternity function is concentrated close to the mean age of childbearing κ, the quantity $l(\kappa + a)/l(\kappa)$ ought to be an approximation to our $M_1(a)$. For United States, 1967, females with $a = 20$ this would be $l(46.281)/l(26.281)$. The life table shows $l(x + 20)/l(x)$ for $x = 25$ as 0.96724, and for $x = 30$ as 0.95122; straight-line interpolation between these values gives $l(46.281)/l(26.281) = 0.963$. This compares with the more precisely calculated $M_1(20) = 0.959$ of Table 10.1; the approximation $l(\kappa + 20)/l(\kappa)$ is slightly high, because the curve of $l(x)$ is at this point concave below.

In the same way we would expect that the chance of a living grandmother would be something like $l(2\kappa + a)/l(\kappa)$. For United States women aged 20 the value is

$$\frac{l(2\kappa + 20)}{l(\kappa)} = \frac{l(72.562)}{l(26.281)} = \frac{0.65431}{0.96734} = 0.676,$$

against the $M_2(20) = 0.653$ in Table 10.1, or about 4 percent high. The greater error for grandmothers than for mothers is due to greater variation in age for the former.

Most of the difference between the crude and the correct estimate is accounted for by the concavity of the survivorship curve, along with the variance of ages of childbearing. To establish this, expand the ratio $l(x + a)/l(x)$ in $M_1(a)$ of (10.1.3) around κ by Taylor's theorem, writing the derivative of $l(x + a)/l(x)$ at $x = \kappa$ as $[l(\kappa + a)/l(\kappa)]'$, and so on:

$$\frac{l(x + a)}{l(x)} = \frac{l(\kappa + a)}{l(\kappa)} + (x - \kappa)\left[\frac{l(\kappa + a)}{l(\kappa)}\right]'$$

$$+ \frac{(x - \kappa)^2}{2!}\left[\frac{l(\kappa + a)}{l(\kappa)}\right]'' + \cdots; \qquad (10.1.6)$$

integrate over x after multiplying by $e^{-rx}l(x)m(x)$, so that the term in $x - \kappa$ vanishes; call the variance of ages of mothers σ^2; and then factor out

$l(\kappa+a)/l(\kappa)$ to obtain

$$M_1(a) \doteq \frac{l(\kappa+a)}{l(\kappa)} \left[1 + \frac{\dfrac{\sigma^2}{2} \left(\dfrac{l(\kappa+a)}{l(\kappa)} \right)''}{\dfrac{l(\kappa+a)}{l(\kappa)}} \right]. \qquad (10.1.7)$$

The correction in square brackets equals 0.9957 for United States females of 1967, and produces $(0.9631)(0.9957) = 0.9590$ for $M_1(20)$ versus 0.9594 from the printout on which Table 10.1 was based.

For grandmothers the square bracket of (10.1.7) for the correction holds approximately, but with 2κ in place of κ in each numerator. The correction then is 0.963, and multiplying by $l(2\kappa+20)/l(\kappa)$ gives 0.651, versus the true 0.653.

Presenting $M_1(a)$ in the form of (10.1.7) serves to show what feature of the net maternity function mainly determines the probability of a living grandmother: the mean age of childbearing κ acting through the factor $l(\kappa+a)/l(\kappa)$. The total of the net maternity function is absent, so to the (fairly close) approximation provided by (10.1.7) the level of fertility has little effect on probability of living ancestors. The variance of ages of childbearing has a small effect, whose amount depends mostly on the second derivative (i.e., the curvature) of $l(\kappa+a)/l(\kappa)$. The $l(x)$ curve is for the most part concave downward up to about age 65, so that its second derivative is negative. That the survival of mothers is negatively related to the variance of ages of childbearing wherever $l(\kappa+a)/l(\kappa)$ is concave downward is the conclusion from (10.1.7), but the effect is small.

Further conclusions from (10.1.7) are drawn in Section 10.6.

10.2 DESCENDANTS

To illustrate how this chapter is an extension of standard demographic techniques the familiar net reproduction rate R_0 will be put into a form suitable for the counting of descendants.

If a cohort of girl births numbers B, born at time zero, the number of survivors to age x will be $Bl(x)$ on the deterministic model, and in the interval x to $x+dx$ these will bear $Bl(x)m(x)dx$ girl babies. The total number of daughters to which the cohort will give birth during its existence will be the integral of this last expression over x, and the average number of daughters will be this integral divided by the girl births B:

$$R_0 = \frac{\int_\alpha^\beta Bl(x)m(x)\,dx}{B}$$

$$= \int_\alpha^\beta l(x)m(x)\,dx. \tag{10.2.1}$$

This, the expected number of girl children to which a girl child will give birth under the regime $l(x)m(x)$, may be regarded as the ratio of one generation to the preceding.

For the number of granddaughters we use (10.2.1) in relation to each of the daughters. Thus, if the average number of girl babies at age x to the mother cohort is expected to be $Bl(x)m(x)\,dx$, and if each of these is expected to have R_0 births, we multiply by R_0 and again integrate up to age β, now to find R_0^2 granddaughters. Similarly the average number of great-granddaughters expected by a girl child will be R_0^3.

For incomplete generations the multiple integrals are formed in the same way, but β is no longer the upper limit. If we want only girl children that will have been born to a female by the time she is age a, where $\beta \geqslant a \geqslant \alpha$, the argument gives an expected

$$\int_\alpha^a l(x)m(x)\,dx \tag{10.2.2}$$

girl children. The expected number of granddaughters by the time the original cohort is aged $a \geqslant 2\alpha$ can be obtained by noting that $l(x)m(x)\,dx$ daughters would be expected to have been born when the woman aged a was $x \geqslant \alpha$ years of age; since each of these has up to age $a - x$ in which to bear children, each would be expected to bear

$$\int_\alpha^{a-x} l(y)m(y)\,dy$$

daughters in turn. Thus the total number of granddaughters will be the product of this and (10.2.2) added through the possible x:

$$\int_\alpha^a l(x)m(x) \int_\alpha^{a-x} l(y)m(y)\,dy\,dx. \tag{10.2.3}$$

All the above concerns prospective descendants.

Now we want to find the average number of girl children that have already been born to women aged a. The same cohort of B births has been followed down from time zero, and by the time it reaches age a there are $Bl(a)$ survivors. The total number of children that have been born up to this time is the integral $\int_\alpha^a Bl(x)m(x)\,dx$, but we do not want to include all of them in our average—we are concerned only with those born to mothers that lived at least to age a. The fraction of mothers that lived from age x to age a is $l(a)/l(x)$, and this is the fraction that we will take of the daughters born at age x of the mothers. Hence we have, for the total daughters expected to be born to the mothers that survived to age a,

$$\int_{\alpha}^{a} \frac{l(a)}{l(x)} Bl(x) m(x) \, dx = \int_{\alpha}^{a} Bl(a) m(x) \, dx,$$

and on dividing this by $Bl(a)$ mothers living at age a we have the average number of such daughters:

$$B_1(a) = \int_{\alpha}^{a} m(x) \, dx. \tag{10.2.4}$$

This result is obvious when we consider that any woman alive at age $a > \alpha$ was also alive at age $x \leqslant a$, and that her probability of bearing a daughter in the interval x to $x + dx$ was $m(x) \, dx$. Her total female births to age a must therefore be given by (10.2.4), in which the $l(x)$ function does not enter. One minor difficulty is our assumption, unavoidable if existing fertility tables are to be used, that the $m(x)$ function is the same for women who survived to age a as for all women.

How many of the $\int_{\alpha}^{a} m(x) \, dx$ daughters will still be alive by the time the mother cohort is aged a? The fraction of daughters born at age x of their mothers that survive to age a of their mothers, or $a - x$ years, must be $l(a - x)$. Hence the number of daughters still alive of women aged a must on the average be

$$BL_1(a) = \int_{\alpha}^{a} m(x) l(a - x) \, dx. \tag{10.2.5}$$

We can build on these results to find expected granddaughters already born for a woman aged a. Consider a daughter born at age x of the original cohort. By the time the original cohort is aged a, the daughter herself will have averaged $\int_{\alpha}^{a-x} l(y) m(y) \, dy$ daughters as in (10.2.3). Integrating over all daughters born to the original cohort gives us the double integral

$$B_2(a) = \int_{\alpha}^{a} m(x) \int_{\alpha}^{a-x} l(y) m(y) \, dy \, dx \tag{10.2.6}$$

for the average number of granddaughters so far born to women aged a.

To find the number of such granddaughters who are still alive we must multiply within the inner integral by the chance of survival through the years to the time when the original cohort is aged a (i.e., $a - x - y$ years), that is, by the factor $l(a - x - y)$. Great-granddaughters and further direct descendants raise no new problem.

10.3 SISTERS AND AUNTS

To find the number of older sisters that a girl now aged a is expected to have, we again set the provisional condition that she was born at age x of her mother, when according to (10.2.4) her mother would be expected to have had $\int_\alpha^x m(y)dy$ children. The condition on x is removed as before by multiplying by $e^{-rx}l(x)m(x)dx$ and then integrating over x. Thus the expected number of older sisters, say S^{old}, still alive or not, is

$$S^{\text{old}} = \int_\alpha^\beta \int_\alpha^x m(y)e^{-rx}l(x)m(x)\,dy\,dx. \tag{10.3.1}$$

Because a mother aged x was necessarily alive at ages y younger than x, we need no allowance for survivorship of the mother. Note that S^{old} does not depend on the age a; a girl can hardly acquire additional older sisters as she ages, and older sisters once born cannot decrease. Some of them, however, are no longer living; to find older sisters now alive we need only include the factor $l(a+x-y)$ in the inner integral of (10.3.1), and this makes the double integral a function of a, the age of the girl with whom the calculation starts.

Younger sisters ever born require an allowance for survivorship beyond the birth of the girl aged a, and their number must depend on a. If the girl aged a was born when her mother was x years old, the chance that the mother lived on to age $x+u$ and then bore a child is $[l(x+u)/l(x)]m(x+u)du$; integrating this over the possible values of u, then multiplying by $e^{-rx}l(x)m(x)dx$, and again integrating gives

$$S_a^{\text{young}} = \int_\alpha^\beta \int_0^a \left[\frac{l(x+u)}{l(x)}\right]m(x+u)\,du\;e^{-rx}l(x)m(x)\,dx \tag{10.3.2}$$

for the number of younger sisters. Again this result may be interpreted more generally as the number of girls expected to be born to the mother of a random birth in the a years following.

A Paradox: The Average Girl Seems to Have Too Many Sisters

We find that the average number of sisters ever born according to the United States regime of mortality and fertility was 1.251 for a randomly chosen woman aged $a=60$ (Table 10.2), while the average number of girls in the completed sisterhood or sorority was 1.26, the gross reproduction rate. The two numbers are very close, yet no allowance has been made for the woman aged a herself—one would have thought that the gross reproduction rate would equal $S^{\text{old}} + S_a^{\text{young}} + 1$. Have we inadvertently included the woman as her own sister? An examination of the argument leading to (10.3.1) and (10.3.2) will satisfy the reader that we have not. Nevertheless, how can the sisters of a randomly selected girl number 1.251, so that with her the sisterhood numbers 2.251, whereas the average number of girls obtained as the gross reproduction rate is only 1.26? (Goodman, Keyfitz and Pullum, 1975).

The answer lies in the manner of selection: the number of daughters of a randomly selected mother is decidedly smaller than the number of sisters plus one of a randomly selected girl. Consider the following hypothetical distribution of total number of daughters (i.e., of completed sororities):

Number of Daughters	Proportion of Cases
0	0.79
6	0.21

This would give the same gross reproduction rate of 1.26, but now all girls have five sisters, as needs no calculation to establish. The mean size of sororities when a *girl* is chosen at random is 6, very much larger than the average of 1.26 when a *family* is chosen at random. Whenever there is variation among mothers in childbearing, the estimate of the size of sorority from a sample of daughters will be larger than the estimate from a sample of families.

The difference between these two means can be expressed in terms of the variance. Suppose that of completed sisterhoods fraction f_0 is 0, f_1 is 1, and so on in the following scheme:

Number of daughters	Relative frequency
0	f_0
1	f_1
2	f_2
$\vdots$	$\vdots$

where $f_0 + f_1 + f_2 + \cdots = 1$. Then the gross reproduction rate G is

$$G = 0f_0 + 1f_1 + 2f_2 + \cdots,$$

the mean of the distribution, and the variance of the distribution is σ^2, where

$$\sigma^2 = 1^2 f_1 + 2^2 f_2 + \cdots - G^2.$$

The probability that a randomly chosen girl is a member of a sorority with zero members is 0, that she is a member of a sorority with one member is proportional to f_1, that she is a member of a sorority with two

Table 10.2 Older and younger sisters ever born of a female aged a, birth and death rates of the United States, 1967

			a	
Sisters	0	20	40	60
Older S^{old}	0.610	0.610	0.610	0.610
Younger S_a^{young}	0.000	0.625	0.641	0.641
Total $S^{\text{old}} + S_a^{\text{young}}$	0.610	1.235	1.251	1.251

members is proportional to $2f_2$, and so on. This distribution is very different from the preceding one:

Size of sorority	Relative frequency of girls
0	0
1	$1f_1$
2	$2f_2$
3	$3f_3$
$\vdots$	$\vdots$

Now the total frequency is $0 + 1f_1 + 2f_2 + \cdots = G$, and the mean is

$$\frac{0 + (1)(1f_1) + (2)(2f_2) + (3)(3f_3) + \cdots}{0 + 1f_1 + 2f_2 + 3f_3 + \cdots} = \frac{\sigma^2 + G^2}{G} = \frac{\sigma^2}{G} + G, \quad (10.3.3)$$

without approximation. The number of sisters of a randomly selected girl equals this minus 1: $S = (\sigma^2/G) + G - 1$.

If the random selection was of families, the sorority would average G. The fact that the selection is of girls adds the term σ^2/G, the variance of the distribution of girls in families divided by the mean. Random selection of a daughter will always give a larger sorority than random selection of a family, as long as $\sigma^2 > 0$, that is, as long as there is any variation in family size. In the numerical calculation based on the formulas of this chapter the variance of the distribution is nearly equal to its mean, a relation characteristic of the Poisson distribution.

This does not arise from data but from the model. Recall that we made the probability of birth at any moment independent of births at all other moments. No heterogeneity was allowed for among women. That is why we ended with a Poisson distribution. In real populations some women are sterile and others have many children. Such heterogeneity among women negates the independence assumption and tends to make the variance greater than the mean. On the other hand, insofar as a two-child family is popular in birth-controlling populations, the variance is reduced.

Age Incidence of Childbearing Conditional on Birth of One Child

Within any homogeneous group expressions 10.3.1 and 10.3.2 are exact if $m(y)$ in the first and $m(x+u)$ in the second are conditional on the birth of a girl aged a at age x of the mother. Lacking data showing birth rates at the several ages for women who have had a birth at each age x, one is tempted to use overall values of $m(y)$ and $m(x+u)$. Insofar as the chance of another birth is zero in the months after a birth, a further impropriety is thereby added to the one discussed in detail above. The notch in the curve allowing for pregnancy and postpartum sterility would be compensated for in other parts of the range of mothers' childbearing ages by the conditional $m(y)$ being higher than the average $m(y)$ for the entire population. Moreover the selection of mothers implicit in the fact that the ones we are concerned with are of proven fertility would probably add further to the conditional $m(y)$ in those ages y where it is nonzero.

The points raised above for sisters apply also to aunts, cousins, nieces, and other kin that are related through sisters.

Aunts

Sisters are aunts when seen from the viewpoint of the daughter of one of them. For the number of aunts that are older sisters of the mother the matter is simple; since S^{old} in (10.3.1) does not depend on the age of the girl, it must be invariant when taken in relation to the daughter of the girl. Thus S^{old} of (10.3.1) is also the expected number of aunts of a girl aged a who are older sisters of the mother. Under a fixed regime of birth and death, the same in both generations, a girl has the same expected number of older sisters and of maternal aunts older than her mother. This of course is not true of surviving sisters or aunts.

Aunts who are younger sisters of the mother, say A_a^{young}, are again first obtained conditionally on the mother having been of age x at the birth of girl now aged a (Fig. 10.3). A mother who was then aged x must now be aged $x+a$, if she is alive. The number of younger sisters expected for a woman aged $x+a$ is S_{x+a}^{young}, entering the argument $x+a$ in (10.3.2). As earlier, we can use this result whether or not the mother is now alive. All that remains is to integrate out the condition that the girl aged a was born

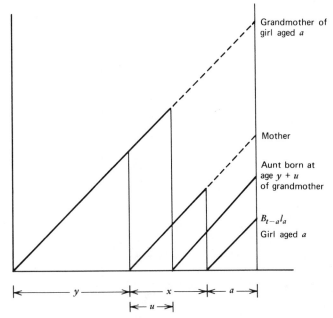

Fig. 10.3   Lexis diagram for aunt born after mother.

when her mother was aged x:

$$A_a^{\text{young}} = \int_\alpha^\beta S_{x+a}^{\text{young}} e^{-rx} l(x) m(x) \, dx,$$

or written out in full so as to accord with Figure 10.3,

$$A_a^{\text{young}} = \int_\alpha^\beta \int_\alpha^\beta \int_0^{x+a} \frac{l(y+u)}{l(y)} m(y+u) \, du \, e^{-ry} l(y) m(y) \, dy \, e^{-rx} l(x) m(x) \, dx$$

The application of the same principles to nieces and first cousins (Fig. 10.4) is found in Goodman, Keyfitz, and Pullum (1974). [The reader can show how to go on to second and higher order cousins, as well as great aunts and other distant relatives.]

10.4   MEAN AND VARIANCE OF AGES

For each kin whose expected number can be calculated, so can the mean age. Consider the descendants, for example, of daughters already born to a

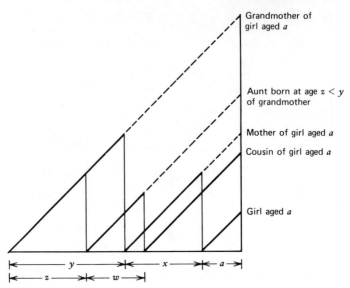

Fig. 10.4 Lexis diagram for cousin of a girl aged a through mother's elder sister.

woman aged $a > \alpha$. These number $\int_\alpha^a m(x)\,dx$, and their mean age must be

$$\frac{\int_\alpha^a (a-x)m(x)\,dx}{\int_\alpha^a m(x)\,dx} = a - \bar{x}_a, \qquad (10.4.1)$$

where $\bar{x}_a$ is the mean age of the childbearing function $m(x)$ up to age a. The mean age of children still alive to the same woman aged a is

$$\frac{\int_\alpha^a (a-x)m(x)l(a-x)\,dx}{\int_\alpha^a m(x)l(a-x)\,dx}. \qquad (10.4.2)$$

The mean age of granddaughters of women aged $a > 2\alpha$ is similarly

$$\frac{\int_\alpha^a l(x)m(x)\int_\alpha^{a-x}(a-x-y)l(y)m(y)\,dy\,dx}{\int_\alpha^a l(x)m(x)\int_\alpha^{a-x} l(y)m(y)\,dy\,dx}. \qquad (10.4.3)$$

One can go on to the variance of ages of descendants in the successive generations. Thus for the variance of ages of living daughters of a woman aged a we would have

$$\sigma_a^2 = \frac{\int_\alpha^a (x - \bar{\bar{x}})^2 m(x)l(a-x)dx}{\int_\alpha^a m(x)l(a-x)dx}, \qquad (10.4.4)$$

where $\bar{\bar{x}}$ is the mean age of women up to age a at the birth of their children, weighted by the survival function $l(a-x)$. Here, as elsewhere, no account is taken of heterogeneity in ages and rates of childbearing, or of the spacing of children imposed by the sterile period of pregnancy and afterward. The simplification has negligible consequences for the expected number of daughters, or for the probability of a living grandmother, but does matter for expected sisters, aunts, and more distant collateral relatives, as well as for variances in all kin.

Ascertainment

Such results illustrate the concept of ascertainment, the way information has been obtained, used in genetics and applied in demography by Mindel C. Sheps. Consider the expected children of a given person. When the person is a child just born, her expected future daughters are $\int_\alpha^\beta l(x)m(x)dx$ prospectively; once she has passed age β, they are $\int_\alpha^\beta m(x)$ dx retrospectively; the corresponding mean ages are $\int_\alpha^\beta xl(x)m(x)$ dx/R_0 and $\int_\alpha^\beta xm(x)dx/G_0$, the latter always being greater. The expected grandchildren calculated retrospectively for a woman of 85 differ from the prospective number of grandchildren of a child just born. In a cohort, individuals may be ascertained by the occurrence of a "signal" event at some point in their lives—the signal event may be having a second child, or being caught in a survey at time t. (Sheps and Menken, 1973, p. 341.) Expressions for extended kin provide further illustrations.

10.5 GENERALIZATION TO CHANGING RATES OF BIRTH AND DEATH

This chapter has been restricted to the stable case, in which we suppose a fixed regime of mortality and fertility to be in force over a long past period and continuing into the present. Yet the theory can be extended to cover certain kinds of change in the regime.

For an example of how changing rates would be accommodated, let us reconsider the probability that a woman aged a has a living mother, the expression $M_1(a)$ of (10.1.3). The conditional probability that the mother is alive, $l(x+a)/l(x)$, must now be determined by the chance of survival appropriate to the changing death rates actually experienced by the cohort aged $x+a$ at time t, that is, born at time $t-x-a$. The ratio $l(x+a)/l(x)$ in the formula would have to be taken from the appropriate cohort life tables, a different table for each value of x. This is certainly possible, though awkward enough that no one is likely to do it.

In addition the distribution of x, the age at childbearing, is affected by the instability; if, for instance, the actual age distribution is younger than the stable one, (10.1.3) has to be modified to allow a greater weight to $l(x+a)/l(x)$ for younger x, thereby increasing the probability that the mother is still alive. Thus the factor $e^{-rx}l(x)m(x)$ in $M_1(a)$ would have to be replaced by numbers proportional to the actual ages of mothers prevailing a years earlier, say $w(x|t-a)$. Result 10.1.3 would thus be replaced by

$$M_1'(a) = \int_\alpha^\beta \frac{l(x+a)}{l(x)} w(x|t-a)\,dx,$$

where $w(x|t-a)$ is the age distribution of women bearing children a years ago, or at time $t-a$.

Analogous considerations permit a straightforward rewriting and reinterpreting of all the formulas of this chapter in a way that dispenses with the stable assumption insofar as it affects earlier age distributions. Goodman, Keyfitz, and Pullum (1974) provide these more general formulas. Interpretation for fixed rates is simple: the given schedules $l(x)$ and $m(x)$ imply certain mean numbers of kin. The corresponding statement for changing rates is unavoidably more complicated.

10.6 SENSITIVITY ANALYSIS

A main use of the kinship formulas here developed is to ascertain the effect of changes in the demographic variables on kinship. How much does a younger age of marriage and of childbearing reduce the number of orphans? What is the effect of a fall in the birth rate on the number of grandchildren of a person of given age chosen at random? What does a uniform improvement in mortality at all ages do to the number of living aunts of a girl of given age?

Merely looking at the formulas does not tell much more than we know without them. Intuition suggests that the fraction of girls aged a who have living mothers must depend primarily on death rates (specifically those between the time of childbearing and a years afterward) and secondarily on birth rates—most of all, on whether children are born at young or older ages of mothers. In a smaller way yet it ought to depend on the overall rate of increase, because with given death rates and with birth rates in a given proportional distribution a faster growing population has somewhat younger mothers. But a quick look at (10.1.3) reveals only that $M_1(a)$ is a function of birth and death rates, without clearly suggesting the amount or even the direction of the relation.

Decomposition of $M_1(a)$, the Probability of a Living Mother

Once a computer program for an expression such as (10.1.3) for $M_1(a)$ is available, it is possible to make small variations in any part of the input—add 10 percent to the birth rates at certain ages while leaving the life table intact, for instance—and see the effect on the probability of a living mother. This has been done by Noreen Goldman and by Robert Sembiring, using the program devised by Thomas Pullum, and is useful in permitting one to see how the several factors operate numerically. Here we will try to see how they operate theoretically, by using the approximation to $M_1(a)$ developed as (10.1.7) or, written slightly differently,

$$M_1(a) \doteq \frac{l(\kappa + a)}{l(\kappa)} + \frac{\sigma^2}{2} \left[\frac{l(\kappa + a)}{l(\kappa)} \right]''. \tag{10.6.1}$$

The main effect of raising the mean age of childbearing is to replace mortality in an interval at the original κ with mortality around $a + \kappa$, as is evident from application of (1.5.5):

$$\frac{l(\kappa + a)}{l(\kappa)} = \exp\left[-\int_{\kappa}^{\kappa + a} \mu(t)\,dt \right]. \tag{10.6.2}$$

If the death rates are nearly constant with age, or if a is small, $M_1(a)$ depends little on the value of κ. The second term on the right-hand side of (10.6.1) is negative through most of the life table and is considerably smaller than the first, unless a is a very old age. The rate of increase of the population enters only through κ, which for a given life table is younger the higher the rate of increase.

If mortality $\mu(x)$ between κ and $\kappa + a$ increases by an amount k at every age, the survivorship $l(\kappa + a)/l(\kappa)$ will diminish in the ratio e^{-ka}, and this is the only effect of a constant mortality addition on $M_1(a)$. Hence the new $\overline{M}_1(a)$ is equal to $e^{-ka}M_1(a)$. The reason that the weighting factor $e^{-rx}l(x)m(x)$ in (10.1.3) remains unaffected is that a uniform change in mortality causes a change in r that offsets the change in $l(x)$ as far as age distribution is concerned, a matter discussed in Section 7.1.

Other Progenitors

If mortality at all ages is increased in the uniform amount k, the probability of a living grandmother will change to

$$\overline{M}_2(a) = \int_\alpha^\beta e^{-k(a+x)} M_1(a+x) e^{-rx} l(x) m(x) dx, \qquad (10.6.3)$$

which cannot be simplified without approximation. But let x be replaced in $e^{-k(a+x)}$ by κ', the mean age at childbearing for the mothers still alive. Then, taking the exponential outside the integral, we have approximately

$$\overline{M}_2(a) \doteq e^{-k(a+\kappa')} M_2(a).$$

For great grandmothers

$$\overline{M}_3(a) \doteq e^{-k(a+\kappa'+\kappa'')} M_3(a),$$

where κ'' is the mean age at childbearing for grandmothers still alive. In practice we do not have data on κ' or κ'' and would suppose them to be close to κ; hence the outcome in general is

$$\overline{M}_i(a) \doteq e^{-k[a+(i-1)\kappa]} M_i(a). \qquad (10.6.4)$$

If k is small, so that e^{-ka} is nearly $1-ka$, we obtain the following finite approximations for the difference in the several $M_i(a)$ on adding k to the force of mortality:

$$\Delta M_1(a) = -kaM_1(a),$$
$$\Delta M_2(a) = -k(a+\kappa)M_2(a),$$
$$\Delta M_3(a) = -k(a+2\kappa)M_3(a).$$

With these approximations, if one of two populations has mortality higher at every age by 0.003, and if κ is 27.5, for women aged $a = 20$ the chance of having a living mother is 0.94 as high as in the other population; of a living grandmother, 0.86; and of a living great-grandmother, 0.78. On the more precise (10.6.4) the last three numbers become 0.942, 0.867, and 0.799 respectively.

Venezuela has somewhat higher mortality than the United States; we note from Table 10.1 that for a Venezuelan girl aged 20 the probability of having a living mother is in the ratio $0.932/0.959 = 0.97$; of a living grandmother, in the ratio 0.85; of a living great-grandmother, in the ratio 0.64, all ratios to the United States. The gradient as one advances to more remote ancestors is steeper than that of (10.6.4) based on fixed differences of $\mu(x)$.

A more complete analysis would decompose the difference between the two countries in, say, the probability of a living grandmother into two components: (1) that due to mortality differences, and (2) that due to differences in the pattern of births. This is readily accomplished arithmetically, once an appropriate computer program is available, simply by permuting the input data, as was done in Table 7.2.

Effect of Birth Pattern on Living Progenitors

The main variation in $M_1(a)$ as far as births are concerned occurs through the mean age of childbearing κ. We found that

$$M_1(a) \doteq \frac{l(\kappa + a)}{l(\kappa)};$$

therefore taking logarithms of both sides and differentiating gives

$$\frac{1}{M_1(a)} \frac{dM_1(a)}{d\kappa} = -\left[\mu(\kappa + a) - \mu(\kappa)\right],$$

where $\mu(\kappa)$ is the force of mortality at age κ. In finite terms

$$\frac{\Delta M_1(a)}{M_1(a)} \doteq -\left[\mu(\kappa + a) - \mu(\kappa)\right]\Delta\kappa;$$

that is, the proportionate change in the chance of a living mother is minus the difference in death rates over an a-year interval times the absolute change in κ. With the death schedule of Madagascar, 1966 (Keyfitz and Flieger, 1971), and its κ of about 27.5, using for $\mu(27.5)$ the approximation $_5M_{25} = 0.01740$, and for $\mu(\kappa + a) = \mu(27.5 + 20) = \mu(47.5)$ the rate $_5M_{45} = 0.02189$, we have

$$\frac{\Delta M_1(a)}{M_1(a)} \doteq -(0.02189 - 0.01740)\Delta\kappa = -0.0045\Delta\kappa.$$

For each year later of average childbearing the chance of a woman of 20 having a living mother is lower by 0.45 percent.

The change with a is found in the same way to be

$$\frac{\Delta M_1(a)}{M_1(a)} = -\mu(\kappa + a)\Delta a,$$

and for $a = 20$, $\kappa = 27.5$, this is

$$-\mu(47.5)\Delta a = -0.02189\,\Delta a.$$

For a 5-year interval the proportionate decrease in $M_1(20)$ ought to be 5 times as great or 0.109. In fact Table IIIa of Goodman, Keyfitz, and Pullum (1974) shows

$$\frac{M_1(25) - M_1(15)}{2} = -\frac{0.7817 - 0.6421}{2} = -0.0698;$$

and as a proportion of $M_1(20) = 0.7126$, this is $-0.0698/0.7126 = -0.098$, about as close to -0.109 as we can expect with the crude approximations used.

To find the effect of a change in fertility at particular ages one can run the program twice, once with the observed regime of mortality and fertility, once with the specific birth rate for age 20-24 lowered by 0.01. Differences for progenitors are shown in Table 10.3. A drop in fertility at age 40-44 lowers the average age of childbearing and hence raises the chance of living grandmother. Other items can be similarly interpreted.

Comparison of Effect of Birth and Death Rates

Robert Sembiring has experimented to determine whether the numbers of particular kin are affected more by birth or by death rates. As an example of the procedure we consider the number of female cousins that a girl aged

Table 10.3   Effect of changed birth rate on probability of ancestor being alive, Madagascar females, 1966

Age of woman a	Difference in Probability of Having a Living:		
	Mother $\overline{M}_1(a) - M_1(a)$	Grandmother $\overline{M}_2(a) - M_2(a)$	Great-grandmother $\overline{M}_3(a) - M_3(a)$
	After Lowering the Birth Rate for Women 20–24 by 0.01		
0	0.	− 0.00268	− 0.00529
20	− 0.00025	− 0.00423	− 0.00109
40	− 0.00228	− 0.00103	− 0.00000
60	− 0.00067	− 0.00000	− 0.00000
	After Lowering the Birth Rate for Women 40–44 by 0.01		
0	0.	+ 0.00395	+ 0.00404
20	+ 0.00109	+ 0.00345	+ 0.00057
40	+ 0.00199	+ 0.00051	0.00000
60	+ 0.00036	0.00000	0.00000

a would be expected to have through her mother's sister and use the technique of permuting the input data, as in Section 7.1.

To separate the effects of mortality from those of fertility nine calculations were made of the curve of expected cousins by age. Three levels of fertility were used, those of Costa Rica for 1960, the United States for 1959–61, and Sweden for 1958–62, all pertaining to 1960 or thereabout. The gross reproduction rates of the three countries were 3.891, 1.801, and 1.080, respectively. Each of these levels of fertility was paired with each of three levels of mortality taken from the Coale and Demeny West series model tables, with $\overset{o}{e}_0$ values of 70, 55, and 40. The numbers chosen represent approximately the range of mortality and fertility among human populations. The resulting nine curves for the average number of living cousins in the female line (i.e., daughters of maternal aunts) are shown in Fig. 10.5.

The three curves for high (Costa Rican) fertility are above those for intermediate fertility, and these again are mostly above those for low fertility. Apparently fertility has more effect on the number of living cousins than does mortality. With high fertility the number of cousins reaches a sharp peak at ages 25 to 45; with lower fertility and lower mortality the curve peaks less sharply. Note that no actual population combines a gross reproduction of 3.891 with an expectation of life of 70 years; therefore the peak of 12.633 female maternal parallel cousins is purely hypothetical. The combination of United States or Swedish fertility with this high expectation of life represent possible real situations.

All of the expressions in this chapter apply to male as well as to female kin, but with one difference. This difference arises out of the fact that we know the mother was alive at the birth of her child, but we know only that the father was alive 9 months before the birth. To apply to males, the formulas would have to be adjusted for the three-quarters of a year of additional mortality, which could be appreciable for certain kin in populations subject to high death rates.

A rough approximation to the total number of first cousins (i.e., of both sexes) would be obtained by multiplying the maternal parallel female cousins here given by 8; this would be improved by making the corresponding calculation for the male line and for mixed lines. An approximation to the number of cousins implied by other schedules of mortality and fertility would be obtained by two-way quadratic interpolation, using $\overset{o}{e}_0$ and the gross reproduction rate as indices. This is especially feasible for mortality; note that the number of cousins for $\overset{o}{e}_0 = 55$ is almost exactly the mean of the numbers for $\overset{o}{e}_0 = 40$ and $\overset{o}{e}_0 = 70$ (Table 10.4). Interpolation may be useful even with an available program because of the large amount of computer time required for the exact calculation.

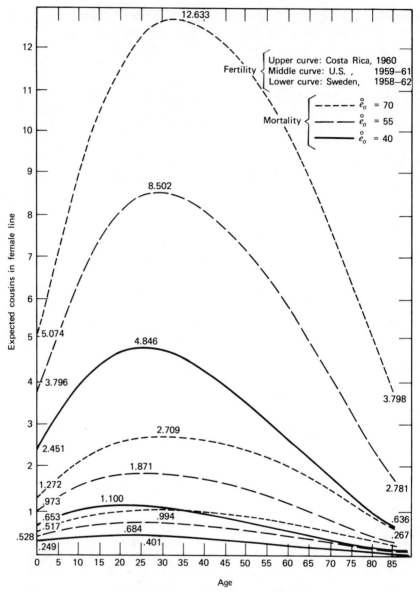

Fig. 10.5 Expected number of cousins still alive.

Table 10.4 Mean number of living first cousins in the female line of a woman aged 20, for artificial populations constructed by fertility of Costa Rica, the United States, and Sweden, about 1960, in all combinations with mortality of Coale–Demeny Model West tables having $\overset{o}{e}_0$ values of 40, 55, and 70 years

	Fertility		
Mortality	Costa Rica $G_0 = 3.891$	United States $G_0 = 1.801$	Sweden $G_0 = 1.080$
$\overset{o}{e}_0 = 40$	4.7292	1.0998	0.4009
$\overset{o}{e}_0 = 55$	7.9888	1.8502	0.6789
$\overset{o}{e}_0 = 70$	11.3518	2.6006	0.9657

10.7 THE INVERSE PROBLEM: DERIVING RATES FROM GENEALOGIES

The inverse problem is of practical interest to those who must make inferences regarding birth and death rates for areas or times for which registration systems are not in existence, or if in existence are grossly incomplete. For a given genealogy, the problem now is to find the regime of mortality and fertility.

If one-half of women aged 40 have living mothers in a certain population, what is the expectation of life? According to Table 10.1, Venezuela showed a probability of 0.707 and Madagascar of 0.386, and these had $\overset{o}{e}_0$ values of 67.7 and 38.5 years, respectively. By straight-line interpolation, supposing ages at childbearing to be sufficiently similar among all three populations to leave the answer unaffected, we find $\overset{o}{e}_0 = 48.9$ corresponding to our $M_1(40) = 0.5$.

Looked at formally, what were relatively simple integrals to evaluate when the regime of mortality and fertility was given become difficult—in most instances unsolvable—integral equations when the mean number of kin is known but the regime is unknown. If we observed mean numbers of the various living kin, we would have a set of equations, most of them containing multiple integrals, and they would have to be solved as a simultaneous set. Thus all of the expressions for different kin might be equated to observations and solved simultaneously for the unknown rates of birth and death.

Yet for many practical purposes we can avoid most of the difficulties just mentioned by supposing that all life tables can be laid out in a straight line, indexed by the expectation of life at age 0 or age 10, and correspondingly that schedules of childbearing can be arranged according to the gross reproduction rate G_0. All variations in mortality and fertility beyond these two dimensions will be neglected in this simple method.

If the number of cousins to women aged 20 is represented as a height above the $(G_0, \overset{o}{e}_0)$ plane, so that the collection of such information regarding women aged 20 is a quadric surface over the plane, an observed number of cousins can be represented by a plane parallel to the $(G_0, \overset{o}{e}_0)$ plane and cutting the quadric surface in a second-degree curve, which may now be projected down onto the $(G_0, \overset{o}{e}_0)$ plane. To make the regime entirely determinate we need some other fact about kin. Continuing to confine ourselves to age 20 for the sake of this example (though we need not stay with the same age), we note the fraction of women aged 20 having a living mother. This also can be represented as a quadric surface over the same $(G_0, \overset{o}{e}_0)$ plane, and the given observation as a plane again cutting the quadric surface in a quadratic. The intersection of the two quadratics gives the regime of mortality and fertility. The object is to choose kin that provide curves intersecting as nearly as possible at right angles to one another. Examples are probability of living mother (or grandmother) and number of daughters (or granddaughters) ever born.

In practice any one pair of observations will be unacceptable as neglecting most of the data. Indeed, errors are so pervasive that we will do none too well using all of the information available. A large number of data pairs will each provide a point of intersection, and with given accuracy of enumeration the precision of any point will be greater the closer the lines defining it come to making a right angle with each other. The several estimates obtained from pairs of kin can be weighted by the sine or other suitable function of the angle that the lines make with one another.

10.8   INCEST TABOO AND RATE OF INCREASE

An incest taboo has the advantage for the group that adheres to it of compelling biological and social mixing, and of stirring individual initiative in the search for a mate. In addition, it avoids the confusion that would result if one's father were also one's uncle, these being very different roles in most societies. It promotes political alliances among families, and it avoids intrafamilial conflict over women. Most such advantages are greater the wider the degree of incest prohibition: a taboo reaching as far as second cousins will compel more mixing than a taboo against brother–sister matings only.

But a price has to be paid for the advantages—the wider the taboo, the more individuals will fail to find mates, especially in sparsely settled populations. From the viewpoint of reproduction the incest taboo is a luxury, and the question is how much of it a group can afford. The ideal approach would be an analysis of tradeoffs: find the point at which the advantages of increased mixing are exactly offset by the lesser reproduction. Unfortunately the elements of this equation are incommensurable, and no theory seems to exist that will provide a quantitative measure of the net advantage of mixing.

However, it is possible to deal with one side of the problem: the cost in rate of increase of various degrees of incest taboo. Though determinate, this is mathematically difficult, as are all questions of population increase in which the rate of reproduction depends on the size of the group and the random number of possible mates. Having little hope of finding a closed solution, Hammel (1972, 1976) and his coworkers addressed the problem by simulation.

They used mortality rates assembled from the Maghreb and ancient Rome, and fertility rates from the Cocos-Keeling Islands, reduced by 20 percent to be slightly below stationarity without any incest taboo. A group of 65 individuals with a kinship structure of three generations of genealogical depth was derived from the previous evolution of the model. Five runs were then made with no incest prohibition, five with a prohibition of one degree (sibling and parent–child), five with a prohibition of two degrees (up to first cousin), and five with a prohibition of three degrees (effectively up to second cousin). All runs covered 100 years.

The outcome, as anticipated, was a more rapid rate of population decrease the broader the taboo. With no taboo the mean of the five runs was a rate of $r = -0.001$; with sibling and parent–child exclusion the mean was -0.006; with exclusion up to first cousin the mean rate was -0.018; with exclusion up to second cousin the rate was -0.036. The one-degree prohibition apparently costs 0.005, the two-degree an additional 0.012, and the three-degree a further 0.018 lowering of r, on this rough model.

Insofar as the rates used were realistic, a breeding group of the order of 65 individuals could not afford any exclusion, not even siblings. However, as mentioned above, the authors had reduced the Cocos-Keeling fertility by 20 percent. A group that would increase at 1 percent per year with no taboo at all could tolerate the sibling and parent-child taboo, which would reduce it to $0.01 - 0.005 = 0.005$; but it could not afford to go as far as the first cousin taboo, which would bring it down to $0.005 - 0.012 = -0.007$, or a half-life of a century. The calculation suggests that the incest tabu, aside from its other functions, is capable of holding down the rate of increase in small, dispersed populations.

10.9 THE BIAS IMPOSED BY AGE DIFFERENCE ON CROSS-COUSIN MARRIAGE

Among social groups practicing cross-cousin marriage, more instances have been observed of Ego, a male, marrying his mother's brother's daughter (MBD) than his father's sister's daughter (FSD). It is also usual for men to marry women younger than themselves. The question is whether the age bias by itself would lead to the bias toward MBDs. A realistic model would be complicated, but the effect of brides being younger than grooms can be shown with some simplified arithmetic (Hammel, 1972).

Consider a population in which men marry 5 years older than women, and children are born to the couple when the husband is age 25 and the wife age 20. Brothers and sisters are all the same age. Then, if Ego (male) is age E, his father will be age $E + 25$, and his father's sister also $E + 25$. His FSD will be $E + 25 - 20 = E + 5$. On the other hand, his mother will be $E + 20$, his mother's brother also $E + 20$, and his MBD $E + 20 - 25 = E - 5$. Thus, of the two kinds of cross-cousins, the FSD is 5 years older than Ego. If he is seeking a bride 5 years younger, he will find the MBD the right age.

A similar calculation can be made for parallel cousins. Ego's father being $E + 25$ years of age and his father's brother also $E + 25$, his FBD is $E + 25 - 25 = E$, and similarly for the other parallel cousin, designated as MSD. Parallel cousins are the same age as Ego on this simple model.

These purely demographic (some would say, merely logical) considerations mean that a tendency for men to marry kinswomen younger than themselves leads to the MBD marriage. Of the four kinds of cousins only MBDs are the right age to permit men to be older than their brides generation after generation.

Hammel was the first to point out that age preferences for *either* older or younger wives would have equivalent effects, and indeed that any heritable property would work as well as age. The contribution of Hammel and Wachter was to show by simulation that the effect remains considerable even in the face of all the obvious sources of randomness and to study the dependence of the effect on the size of the age gap. Simulation has been useful here and in other instances where analytic solutions are out of reach. Kunstadter et al (1963) used it to find the fraction of individuals who would have an MBD cousin to marry in a tribe when that was preferred.

In this book most of the theory of the 10 chapters through this one considers large populations for which deterministic models are appropriate. The study of these may be called *macrodemography*, following a usage going back through sociology, economics, and physics, ultimately to a source in Greek metaphysics. Chapter 11 introduces *microdemography*, in which properties of individuals and their random variation are recognized as the source of change in population aggregates.

Chapter Eleven

MICRODEMOGRAPHY

Physics accounts for heat by the motion of molecules, medicine accounts for disease by the action of germs, economics accounts for aggregate prices and production by the activities of individuals seeking to maximize their utility. The fact that nontrivial problems of aggregation arise, and that the microelements often turn out on closer examination to be unrealistic constructions, does not deprive them of explanatory and predictive value.

Through the work of Louis Henry, Mindel C. Sheps, Robert G. Potter, and others a microdemography has come into existence in recent years that helps us to understand such macrophenomena as birth rates of regions and nations. How much reduction of the birth rate results from couples substituting 99 percent efficient contraception for methods 95 percent efficient? If the number of abortions was equal to the number of births in a country, could we conclude that suppression of abortion would double the number of births? How can the probability of conception be measured? What difference does it make to the increase of a population if parents aim for three children rather than two? These and other questions of microdemography are the subject of the present chapter.

11.1 BIRTHS AVERTED BY CONTRACEPTION

The theory of birth as a Markov renewal process has been developed by Sheps (1964; Sheps and Perrin, 1963; Sheps and Menken, 1973), and Potter (1970) has shown how this theory can be applied to calculate births averted. Tietze (1962) was a pioneer in this field and Lee and Isbister (1966) made important early suggestions.

In conception and birth models a woman is thought of as going through pregnancy and birth, and then again pregnancy and birth, in periodic fashion, with a longer or shorter cycle. Our main effort here is devoted to finding the length of the cycle under various conditions, and to showing how that tells us the birth rate. First consider a couple who have just married, engage in intercourse without using birth control, and are fecund. Let the probability of conception for a nonpregnant woman in any month be p, and of not conceiving be $q = 1 - p$. Until further notice, all conceptions leading to miscarriage or stillbirth will be disregarded. Thus p is the probability of a conception leading to a live birth. The first question is the expected time to conception.

The probability that the time to conception will be 1 month is p, that it will be more than 1 month is q, that it will be 2 months is qp, that it will be 3 months is q^2p, and so on. Multiplying the probability of exactly 1 month by 1, of 2 months by 2, and so on, gives t, the mean number of months of waiting until conception:

$$t = p + 2qp + 3q^2p + \cdots .$$

To evaluate this we replace each p by $1 - q$ to obtain

$$t = 1 - q + 2q(1 - q) + 3q^2(1 - q) + \cdots ,$$

which permits canceling and leaves only the geometric progression

$$t = 1 + q + q^2 + \cdots ,$$

which converges for q less than 1. To find the sum we multiply by q and note that the right-hand side is the same infinite series for t, except that the 1 is missing. This provides the equation $qt = t - 1$, from which t equals $1/(1 - q)$, a result familiar in high-school algebra. Hence the mean time to conception is $t = 1/(1 - q) = 1/p$. If the chance of conception is zero, the waiting time is infinite and the argument loses its interest. Hence we consider fecund women only, defined as those for whom p is a positive number; the argument does not apply to perfect contraception.

The time to conception is the first of two intervals that make up the conception and birth cycle. The second is the nonfecund period that includes about 270 days of pregnancy plus postpartum sterility. The length of the postpartum anovulatory period depends on lactation and other factors, and we need not be detained by variation and uncertainty regarding its length, but will simply call the entire expected period of pregnancy and postpartum sterility s. This period also includes any time lost by spontaneous or voluntary abortion.

Then the average length of the cycle is

$$w = \frac{1}{p} + s \quad \text{months.} \tag{11.1.1}$$

Knowing the length of the cycle is the equivalent of knowing the birth rate for the population; if all women produce a child every w months, the average monthly birth rate is $1/w$, and the annual birth rate is $12/w$.

To illustrate (11.1.1) numerically, if $p = 0.2$ and the mean value of s is 17 months, the length of the cycle between births is 22 months, and the birth rate is $1/[(1/0.2) + 17] = 1/22$ per month, or $12/22$ per year. The problem of measuring p will be the subject of Section 11.2; in this section it is assumed to be known.

The argument resembles that underlying the stationary population in Chapter 2, except that here no variation in the probability in successive months is allowed. If the death rate is $\mu \, dx$ from age x to $x + dx$, μ being the same for all ages, then the expectation of life at any age, as we saw, is $1/\mu$ years. Month-to-month variation in the probability of conception needs to be recognized, just as variation with age was recognized for deaths, and the life table technique applied to conception is discussed in Section 11.2.

The purpose of contraception is to reduce the probability of conceiving, which has the effect of increasing the time between successive births. We call the efficiency of contraception e, defined by the reduction in the probability of conceiving: if the probability for a given month is p without protection, a contraceptive of efficiency e reduces this to $p(1-e)$, say p^*. Conversely, if we know that the probability of conception without protection is p, and with a certain contraceptive is p^*, then solving for e in the equation $p^* = p(1-e)$ gives $e = 1 - p^*/p$. If the probability is $p = 0.2$ without protection and $p^* = 0.02$ with a given contraceptive, the efficiency is $1 - 0.02/0.2 = 0.90$ or 90 percent.

To find w^*, the length of the cycle with contraception, we need not begin the argument over again, but only multiply p by $1-e$ in the expression for w to obtain the new lower probability of conception, and enter this product in (11.1.1):

$$w^* = \frac{1}{p(1-e)} + s. \tag{11.1.2}$$

Contraception is considered to have no effect on the sterile period s.

Imagine two groups of women, the first group not practicing contraception and having length of cycle $w = (1/p) + s$, and the other practicing contraception of efficiency e, with length of cycle w^* as in (11.1.2). Then w^*/w of the cycles of the first group fit into each of the cycles of the second group (Fig. 11.1), and this is the ratio of the birth rates for the two

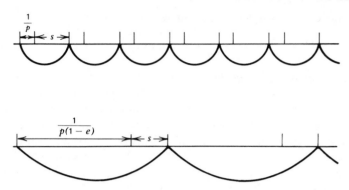

Fig. 11.1 Hypothetical average cycles of conception and birth for natural fertility and for contraception of 90 percent efficiency.

groups. In other words, if the birth rate for the unprotected group is $1/w$ and for the contracepting group is $1/w^*$, the first has a birth rate $(1/w)/(1/w^*) = w^*/w$ times that of the second.

The model is crude in omitting many factors, including end effects that could dominate if birth rates are very low. But it suffices to show that 90 percent efficient contraception does not lower the birth rate by 90 percent. For if, as before, the probability of conception with unprotected intercourse is 0.2 and the sterile period of pregnancy and afterward is 17 months, the waiting time will average $(1/0.2) + 17 = 22$ months. With 90 percent efficient contraception this increases to $1/[(0.2)(0.1)] + 17 = 67$, or just 3 times as long. Ninety percent efficient contraception reduces the birth rate by only two-thirds, rather than the nine-tenths that would apply if there were no sterile period. To put the matter intuitively, contraception can serve no purpose during a time when a woman is sterile anyway.

The technique of comparing two groups of women, one using no contraception and the other using a method of given efficiency, disregards the facts that women differ from one another in fecundity, that each woman does not continue to use a particular method indefinitely, and that the natural fecundity of each woman declines, ultimately to zero around age 50. The model hardly simulates what happens when contraception is used for a relatively short period of time like a year or two by a heterogeneous group of women; it offers a way of thinking about the matter that retains some of the essential features, and it helps to avoid some gross fallacies.

Abstention. One absolutely certain method of contraception is complete abstention from intercourse, but this is too drastic for general use, and partial abstention is the utmost that can be aspired to in practice. Suppose that a couple decide to abstain on every second occasion, without regard to the time of month. Even this represents a considerable degree of restraint; what is its effect on births? Insofar as the restraint reduces the probability of conception by one-half, it is equivalent to a contraceptive of efficiency $e = 0.5$. With parameters $p = 0.2$ and $s = 17$ months, the ratio of monthly birth rate with 50 percent abstention to that with no abstention must be

$$\frac{1/w^*}{1/w} = \frac{w}{w^*} = \frac{(1/p) + s}{\left[1/p(1 - e)\right] + s}$$

$$= \frac{(1/0.2) + 17}{\left[1/(0.2)(1 - 0.5)\right] + 17} = \frac{22}{27} = 0.81. \qquad (11.1.3)$$

The 50 percent restraint would reduce the birth rate by only about 19 percent. This would be improved if something better than random timing of intercourse could be arranged.

Births Averted—the Causal Inference

The original inspiration for such models as these was the attempt to relate activity in the dissemination of the means of contraception to decline in the birth rate. A typical question concerns the effect on births of inserting intrauterine devices (IUDs) in 1000 women. First suppose that the IUDs are of 97 percent efficiency, that they will remain in place indefinitely, and the women in question have previously been unprotected. With our same p and s again, the ratio of the new to the old birth rate would be

$$\frac{1/w^*}{1/w} = \frac{w}{w^*} = \frac{(1/0.2) + 17}{\left[1/(0.2)(1 - 0.97)\right] + 17}$$

$$= \frac{22}{184} = 0.12,$$

which tells us that 88 percent of births would be averted from then onward. In absolute numbers, without the IUDs the 1000 women would have $1000(12/22) = 545$ births per year; with the IUDs they would have $1000(12/184) = 65$ per year, so that 480 births would be averted.

This calculation may well be correct. Natural fertility is indeed to be found in some places. But far more common, even in very high fertility populations with birth rates of 40 per thousand or above, are primitive but not wholly ineffective means of contraception. Even when the population as a whole shows a very high birth rate, it can contain some couples practicing relatively efficient contraception.

The crucial assumption of the above calculation that 88 percent of births are averted is that the IUDs would take the place of unprotected intercourse. The question, "How many births would be averted by the insertion of 1000 IUDs?" implies a causal analysis and cannot be answered without first answering a subsidiary question: "What would the women be doing in the absence of the IUDs?" If there was a selection of the women who turned up for insertion of IUDs, by which most were in any case practicing relatively effective birth control, the answer in regard to births averted would be very different from the 88 percent above.

To go to an extreme, suppose that the couples were using periodic abstention in the hope of avoiding the fertile period, or condoms, or a combination, and somehow attaining 90 percent efficiency. This means that in the absence of the IUDs the probability of conception would be 0.1 of the chance with unprotected intercourse, and hence the interval between pregnancies, again supposing $p = 0.2$ and $s = 17$ months, would be $1/[(0.2)(1 - 0.90)] + 17 = 67$ months.

If the same conditions applied in the future, the birth rate would be $1/67$ per month without the IUDs, and $1/\{[1/(0.2)(1-0.97)] + 17\} = 1/184$ per month with them. Now births would be $67/184 = 0.36$ of what they would have been, so 64 percent would be averted. Births per year among the 1000 couples would be $12,000/67 = 179$ without the IUDs, and 65 with them. On these assumptions the credit to the activity of fitting 1000 IUDs would be 114 births per year. If, however, the alternative that the couples would use in the absence of IUDs was 95 percent efficient, avoidance of only $103 - 65 = 38$ births could be credited to the IUDs.

To suppose that no contraceptive would be used in the absence of the IUD gives 480 births averted per 1000 insertions; if the alternative to the IUD is 90 percent efficient contraception, 114 births are averted; if the alternative is 95 percent efficient contraception, the births averted are 38. The variation in the apparent effectiveness of the family planning effort with seemingly small variation in the assumptions is distressing, but any attempt to get around it must face the basic fact that no birth can be averted that was not going to occur.

An example of the way the arithmetic operates is given by comparing two cases: (1) a population using contraception of 50 percent efficiency, and (2) another population of which half use contraception of perfect efficiency and the other half use no contraception. The birth rate per month for the first case is $1/[(\frac{1}{2}p) + s]$; for the second, $\frac{1}{2}\{1/[(1/p) + s]\} + \frac{1}{2}(0)$. With $p = 0.2$ and $s = 17$, the first is $1/27$, the second $1/44$. Thus the birth rate in the first case would be $44/27$ times the birth rate in the second, that is, 63 percent higher.

Marginal Effect

One of the applications of this approach is to determine the result of a slight improvement in efficiency—a better IUD, a superior condom, slightly more careful use of the condom. Suppose that efficiency is raised from e to $e + \delta$. Then average births averted per year are

$$\begin{matrix} \text{Births averted} \\ \text{per year per woman} \end{matrix} = \frac{12}{[1/p(1-e)]+s} - \frac{12}{[1/p(1-e-\delta)]+s}.$$

If $f(e) = 12/\{[1/p(1-e)]+s\}$, the additional births averted are approximately equal to $f'(e)\delta$; hence we need the derivative $f'(e)$, which is

$$f'(e) = -\frac{12}{\{[1/p(1-e)]+s\}^2} \cdot \frac{1}{p(1-e)^2}.$$

Thus the additional births averted by a year of increase δ in efficiency, as a fraction of the number that would otherwise have occurred, are

$$-\frac{f'(e)\delta}{f(e)} = \frac{\delta}{(1-e)[1+sp(1-e)]}. \tag{11.1.4}$$

The values of this expression for four values of e and $p = 0.2$, $s = 17$ are as follows:

e	Further fraction averted by improvement δ in efficiency
0	0.23δ
0.9	7.46δ
0.95	17.09δ
0.97	30.25δ

Evidently to go from no protection to a contraceptive of 1 percent efficiency averts only $0.23\delta = (0.23)(0.01) = 0.23$ percent of births. On the other hand, to go from a contraceptive of 97 percent efficiency to one of 98 percent efficiency averts over 30 percent of births. The extra 1 percent of efficiency is 130 times as effective in lowering pre-existing births at the 97 percent level as at the 0 percent level. [Express the relative efficiency in terms of possible births.]

Table 11.1   Birth rates per month with various degrees of contraceptive efficiency, based on $p = 0.2$ without protection, and $s = 17$

e	$\dfrac{1}{\dfrac{1}{p(1-e)} + s}$
0.00	0.04545
0.01	0.04535
0.05	0.04492
0.50	0.03704
0.75	0.02703
0.90	0.01493
0.94	0.00997
0.95	0.00855
0.96	0.00704
0.97	0.00544
0.98	0.00375
0.99	0.00193
1.00	0.00000

Table 11.1 provides both a verification of these numbers and an illustration of their meaning. To go from 0 to 0.01 efficiency (a difference $\delta = 0.01$) decreases the monthly birth rate by $0.04545 - 0.04535 = 0.00010$ on 0.04545, or 0.0022, which is $0.0022/0.01$ or 0.22, and multiplying by δ this is the same except for rounding as the 0.23δ above. To go from 0.96 to 0.98 efficiency is to lower the birth rate from 0.00704 to 0.00375, a difference of 0.00329, or 0.00164 per 0.01 of increase in efficiency. As a fraction of births at 0.97 efficiency (Table 11.1) this is $0.00164/0.00544 = 0.301$, or 30.1δ, since $\delta = 0.01$, in agreement except for slight curvature and rounding with the 30.25δ given above.

Figure 11.2 shows monthly birth rates as a function of efficiency of contraception for the simple model here used. The numbers in the table following (11.1.4) give the relative slope at four points in the curve.

Dropping the Contraceptive

We have been considering an IUD, a supply of pills, or other "segment," as Tietze and Potter call it, of contraception, and have calculated the effect per year, as though everyone would use the supply according to instructions and without interruption. But we know that different individuals continue to be careful for different lengths of time. A rough way of taking

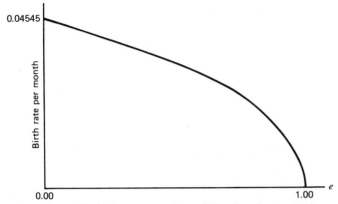

Fig. 11.2 Curve of monthly birth rates at various efficiencies of contraception, $p=0.2$ and $s=17$ months.

this into account is to suppose each woman has a probability d of dropping the contraceptive in each month. During one segment the probability of conception in a given month is p' (supposed the same for all women and for all times), and the probability in any month of dropping the contraceptive for the women who do not become pregnant while using it is d.

All of the above refers to a particular month, and we suppose that the women are followed through time until they either become pregnant or drop the contraceptive. One of these happening in the first month has probability $p'+d$; its not happening in that month but happening in the next month has probability $(1-p'-d)(p'+d)$; its happening in the third month for the first time has probability $(1-p'-d)^2(p'+d)$; and so on. If we write q for $1-p'-d$, the sequence is

$$(1-q), \qquad q(1-q), \qquad q^2(1-q), \qquad \dots .$$

The mean number of months of exposure is

$$(1-q)+2q(1-q)+3q^2(1-q)+\cdots$$

$$=1+q+q^2+\cdots = \frac{1}{1-q}$$

$$= \frac{1}{1-(1-p'-d)} = \frac{1}{p'+d},$$

before the woman passes out of the group either through becoming pregnant or dropping the contraceptive.

Among the women who leave the group of nonpregnant wearers during a particular month, the proportion $d/(p'+d)$ do so through dropping the contraceptive, and $p'/(p'+d)$ do so through becoming pregnant. If, in each case, this is the fraction in every single month, it is also the fraction in all months together. Thus $d/(p'+d)$ of the original group of women will sooner or later drop the contraceptive and we suppose that they revert to natural fertility; their chance of conceiving in any month becomes p. The model follows all women to pregnancy, either while wearing the contraceptive or subsequently. With the same argument, now applied to p rather than to $p'+d$, their mean time to pregnancy after dropping the contraceptive will be $1/p$.

Thus all women average $1/(p'+d)$ months until they drop the contraceptive or become pregnant; $d/(p'+d)$ of them drop the contraceptive, and these take another $1/p$ months, on the average, to become pregnant. Then the expected time to pregnancy for all of the women is

$$t = \frac{1}{p'+d} + \frac{d}{p'+d}\left(\frac{1}{p}\right). \tag{11.1.5}$$

The model for births averted once again consists of comparing two groups of women, one group initially wearing the contraceptive and the other never wearing it, and following through successive segments. Those initially wearing the contraceptive will take an average of t months to become pregnant; those not wearing it, an average of $1/p$ months. Suppose again that the nonfecund time of childbearing plus the postpartum anovulatory period is s months for all women, and that we count only pregnancies leading to live births (i.e., disregarding miscarriages and stillbirths). Then those practicing contraception will average a live birth every $t+s$ months, that is to say, their monthly birth rate will be $1/(t+s)$. The group not using the contraceptive will average a birth every $(1/p)+s$ months, and the corresponding rate is $1/[(1/p)+s]$. The problem is now solved: the reduction in monthly birth rates due to the contraceptive is the difference

$$\frac{1}{(1/p)+s} - \frac{1}{t+s},$$

and as a fraction of the birth rate without the contraceptive this reduces to

$$1 - \frac{(1/p)+s}{t+s}. \tag{11.1.6}$$

If an IUD is 95 percent efficient and is inserted in each of a group of women of natural fertility with $p = 0.2$ chance of a pregnancy leading to a live birth each month, so that for protected women the chance of an accidental pregnancy is 0.01 each month, and if the chance of a woman's dropping the contraceptive and reverting to natural fertility in any given month is $d = 0.03$, and if the nonfecund period of pregnancy and its aftermath is $s = 17$ months, then $t = 28.75$ months. Expression 11.1.6 says that users of the method avert 0.52 of the births that would otherwise occur.

But we should take account of the fact that women do not ordinarily go directly from natural fertility to modern contraception. The recruits to an IUD program have ordinarily been restricting their births in one way or another. Suppose that they have been practicing rhythm with care and attaining 90 percent efficiency, so that the chance of childbearing if they did not have the IUD is $p = 0.02$, and it is to this practice that they revert if they drop the IUD. Then $t = 62.5$; and, entering $p = 0.02$ in place of $p = 0.2$ in (11.1.6), we find the fraction of births averted to be 0.16 rather than 0.52 as in the preceding paragraph.

The above argument, due to Potter (1970), illustrates once more the general point of causal inference that nothing can be said about the effect of the IUD without specifying what the couples concerned would be doing without it. That such specification is important appears from our numbers: with natural fertility as the alternative to the IUD 52 percent of births are averted, whereas with 90 percent efficient contraception in the background only 16 percent are averted.

The above argument emerges in the simplest possible form when we try to see the effect of abortion on the birth rate.

Why 1000 Abortions Do Not Prevent 1000 Births in a Population

That the logic of individuals becomes grossly misleading when applied to populations is implicit in much of the work in this book. The contrast between individuals and populations is especially sharp in regard to births averted by abortion. If we think of a woman aborting a pregnancy that would have led to a live birth, then one abortion has indeed prevented one birth. But 1000 abortions in a population generally prevent far fewer than 1000 births. To find how many they do prevent we must reckon in terms of each woman's time—how long she takes to have a birth, how long she is tied up in having an abortion. Once again only conceptions potentially leading to live births will be considered, that is to say, spontaneous abortions will be disregarded (Potter, 1972).

A woman who has just conceived may decide to have an abortion in the second month and be sterile for 1 further month, a total time from conception of 3 months. Suppose that she is then fecund again, with the same probability 0.2 of conceiving in each month without contraceptive protection. To arrive at this point from the last previous fecund condition has taken her the 3 infertile months before and after the abortion, plus the preceding expected 5 months to pregnancy, 8 months in all. The 8 months represent the time out from childbearing due to one abortion. Only if this length of time were sufficient to have a child would one abortion prevent one birth in the population. If the cycle for having a child is 22 months on the average, as in this illustration, the abortion has prevented only 8/22 of a birth. On these assumptions nearly three abortions are required to avert one birth.

More generally, we can see how many births are prevented by abortions taking place at such time after the onset of pregnancy that the woman is infecund for an expected a months. The length of the cycle involving one abortion averages $(1/p) + a$, and the length of the cycle involving one birth averages $(1/p) + s$; the number of the former that will fit into the latter is

$$\frac{(1/p) + s}{(1/p) + a}. \tag{11.1.7}$$

This being the number of abortion cycles required to fill the time that will be taken by one birth cycle, it is also the number of abortions that will prevent one birth. The model is deterministic; it compares two women going through repeated cycles, one involving births and the other involving abortions, without allowing for variation in the length of cycle or in fecundity among women.

Abortion as a Backup to Contraception

Expression 11.1.7 refers to a population that does not use contraception. In populations that do practice birth control, the fractional effect of abortion is much greater, and (11.1.7) can be readily modified to show how much.

To apply the argument to our new problem we write $p(1 - e)$ in place of p as the probability of conceiving in a particular month and again go through the whole of the preceding argument. The mean length of time to pregnancy for fertile couples becomes $1/p(1 - e)$, and the number of abortions that will prevent one birth is now

$$\frac{[1/p(1 - e)] + s}{[1/p(1 - e)] + a}. \tag{11.1.8}$$

Entering $p = 0.2$, $e = 0.95$, $s = 17$ months, and $a = 3$ months gives

$$\frac{(1/0.01) + 17}{(1/0.01) + 3} = \frac{117}{103} = 1.14$$

abortions to prevent one birth.

This is a very different outcome from the no-contraception case. With unprotected intercourse nearly three abortions are required to prevent one birth. With 95 percent efficient contraception only about one and one-seventh abortions are needed to prevent one birth. If the efficiency of contraception was higher than 0.95, an abortion would have even more impact.

11.2   MEASUREMENT OF FERTILITY AND FECUNDITY

According to the usual English language definitions. fecundity is the uninhibited biological capacity of women to bear children; fertility is the number of children borne under existing social conditions. Fertility is fecundity modified by contraception and other kinds of intervention.

Fertility is directly measurable—the birth of a child is a publicly recognized event, and its recording is merely a matter of organization and attention, especially by those, parents and doctors, who are in a position to observe the event as it occurs and so have the necessary facts about it. But the underlying fecundity depends on decidedly private circumstances not generally known even to the couples concerned. These include viability of sperm and ovum as this affects the length of the fertile period, and other factors hidden from direct observation. The problem of measuring these and their influences on the birth rate will be the subject of this section.

Probability of Conception by Days of the Month

A rough way of calculating probability of conception, making use only of the frequency of intercourse and the length of the fertile period, is implied in the work of Glass and Grebenik (1954). Suppose that a couple have intercourse n times in the menstrual cycle, which includes a fertile period of f days out of a total of 25 nonmenstruating days per month. Then, if coitus is unplanned in relation to the fertile period, the probability that it will occur at least once during the f fertile days is the complement of the probability that it will not occur at all during those days: the chance that any particular coitus will take place during the nonfertile period is $1 - f/25$. If different occurrences of intercourse are independently random, with no spacing, the chance that all n will take place during the nonfertile period is this quantity to the nth power: $(1 - f/25)^n$. The chance p that at least one coitus will take place during the fertile period must be the complement of this last:

$$p = 1 - \left(1 - \frac{f}{25}\right)^n,$$

and if ovum and sperm are healthy and behave as expected, this is the chance of conception during the month in question.

For a given n the probability is increased insofar as there is a degree of regularity in intercourse, for instance if it occurs only once in each 24-hour period (Jain, 1969). Divide the nonmenstruating part of the month into 25 separate days, each a 24-hour interval, and suppose that in f of these the woman is fertile; then the chance of avoiding the first of the f days with coitus on n (separate) random days is $1 - n/25$. The chance of avoiding all f days with n acts of coitus spread over different days is $(1 - n/25)^f$, and hence the chance of conception is

$$p = 1 - \left(1 - \frac{n}{25}\right)^f.$$

We need to allow not only for frequency of intercourse but also for the moment when intercourse occurs in relation to the moment of ovulation, using the best knowledge or guesses regarding the probability of conception for intercourse on the day of ovulation, 1 day earlier, 2 days earlier, or 1 day later. Lachenbruch (1967) set up a model that incorporates these probabilities and simulated it by computer to obtain numerical results. For couples using rhythm as a means of contraception and having their intercourse in two "humps," one before and one after ovulation, he found probabilities of conception of 0.07 to 0.20, and commented that the time he allowed for intercourse would be too short for most couples. "Bracketed rhythm," in which the couple have intercourse on the last "safe" day before ovulation and the first "safe" day after, leads to a fairly high value of the probability of conception—0.20 with the assumptions made. A feature of bracketed intercourse is that the total frequency of intercourse has almost no effect on conception.

To estimate probabilities on conception on the several days of the cycle, Barrett and Marshall (1969) followed 241 fertile British couples, mostly 20 to 40 years of age and not using birth control. They obtained from each couple each month a calendar showing dates of intercourse, and a temperature chart from whose rise at midmonth the time of ovulation could be read. Then, if p_i is the probability that intercourse on the ith day will lead to conception, the chance $1 - p$ that conception did not occur during a particular month must be the product

$$1 - p = \prod_i (1 - p_i)^{x_i}$$

taken over the days of the month, where x_i is 1 if intercourse took place on the ith day and 0 if it did not.

One would like to find values of p_i such that the above product for $1 - p$ comes as close as possible to 1 for the months when conception did not occur, and to 0 for the months when it did. Barrett and Marshall took the logarithm of the likelihood and maximized for the whole sample of cycles. Their estimates for the 5 days before ovulation and the 1 day after it were as follows:

$p_{-4.5}$	0.13
$p_{-3.5}$	0.20
$p_{-2.5}$	0.17
$p_{-1.5}$	0.30
$p_{-0.5}$	0.14
$p_{0.5}$	0.07

Thus the highest probability of conception, 0.30, was for the day 24 to 48 hours before ovulation. Outside of the above 6-day range the probabilities were not significantly different from zero.

From these numbers it follows that daily intercourse gives a probability of conception

$$p = 1 - (1 - 0.13)(1 - 0.20)\ldots = 0.68.$$

The probability is 0.43 for intercourse every second day, 0.31 for every third day, and 0.24 for every fourth day (numbers rounded after calculation, and without making allowance for the effect of frequency of intercourse on the production of sperm).

Mean Fecundity from Surveys

The probability p of conceiving in a given month for a group of fertile women is typically sought in order to compare it with p', the corresponding ratio for another group of women. When p applies to women not practicing contraception, it is an estimate of fecundity or natural fertility; the amount by which p', for a group of women practicing contraception, is lower measures the efficiency of that form of contraception. The most obvious way of obtaining estimates is by observing waiting times until pregnancy, a subject to which we proceed.

Homogeneous Populations. The measurement of fertility, either natural or with contraceptive protection, depends on data for a group of women all of whom are having intercourse and are nonpregnant; suppose all to be subject to the same probability p of conceiving in each month, where p is greater than zero. Suppose that N fertile women, just married, are surveyed month by month until they become pregnant; as each becomes pregnant, she drops out of observation. Let the number who become pregnant in the first month be N_1, the number who become pregnant in the second month

N_2, and so on. Then the probability of conception in any month, p, is estimated from the first month's data as the ratio N_1/N. This leaves $N - N_1$ women starting the second month in a fecund condition, and the estimate of p from that month's data is the ratio $N_2/(N - N_1)$, and similarly for later months. A series of estimates of p is thus provided

$$\hat{p}_1 = \frac{N_1}{N},$$

$$\hat{p}_2 = \frac{N_2}{N - N_1},$$

$$\hat{p}_3 = \frac{N_3}{N - N_1 - N_2},$$

$$\vdots$$

$$\hat{p}_m = \frac{N_m}{N - N_1 - N_2 - \cdots - N_{m-1}},$$

where observation stops after the mth month.

To make use of all the information we must average the several values of $\hat{p}_1, \hat{p}_2, \ldots$. If the true probability p is the same for all women and for all months, the right average is one that weights the several months by their sample sizes: we need to weight our $\hat{p}_1, \hat{p}_2, \ldots, \hat{p}_m$ by the number of exposed women on which each is based. Since $\hat{p}_1$ is based on N women, $\hat{p}_2$ on $N - N_1$, and so on, the estimate is

$$\frac{N\hat{p}_1 + (N - N_1)\hat{p}_2 + \cdots + (N - N_1 - N_2 - \cdots - N_{m-1})\hat{p}_m}{N + (N - N_1) + \cdots + (N - N_1 - N_2 - \cdots - N_{m-1})},$$

or, entering the estimates $\hat{p}_1, \hat{p}_2, \ldots$ from above,

$$\frac{N_1 + N_2 + \cdots + N_m}{N + (N - N_1) + \cdots + (N - N_1 - N_2 - \cdots - N_{m-1})}, \quad (11.2.1)$$

supposing that all women are followed to the mth month.

This widely used index, due to Pearl (1939, p. 296), will be referred to as $\hat{p}_p$. It contains the total number of conceptions during the m months of observation in its numerator, and its denominator is the number of woman-months of exposure, if the month of conception is counted into the exposure. The index is intuitively appealing quite apart from the statistical argument above. Multiplied by 1200, it gives pregnancies per 100 woman-years of intercourse, and this rate is often calculated and published. Not only does $\hat{p}_p$ seem intuitively reasonable, but also, if all women were equally susceptible, it would be the correct measure, and we would need to go no further in the search for a measure of fecundity.

A Heterogeneous Population with Fecundity Constant for Each Woman. However, we know that some women are more fecund than others, and we seek from the survey a suitable average of their several p values. The women who are most fecund will tend to become pregnant first, so the $\hat{p}_1, \hat{p}_2, \ldots$ for the several months are estimating different quantities. The estimate for the first month $\hat{p}_1 = N_1/N$, refers to unselected women and is an unbiased estimate of the mean p. Since those who become pregnant drop out of observation, no later month refers to unselected women. The ith month, for any $i > 1$, omits some women selected for their fecundity, and so the estimate derived from it, $N_i/(N - N_1 - N_2 - \cdots - N_{i-1})$, must be an underestimate of the fecundity of the original N women.

The p values differed from month to month in the sample size on which they were estimated in the model underlying p_p, and they differed in no other way. With such homogeneous material the correct way to weight a number of estimates of the same parameter is by the quantity of information contained in each estimate, that is, by the size of sample available in each month. With heterogeneity among women the pregnancy ratios are genuinely different in the different months, and to weight by the quantity of information, that is, the sample size, would be incorrect. To avoid considering two different problems at once we will now suppose that the sample is large, so that random variation can be disregarded. What is wanted is a population average, in which each woman counts once, and hence we must weight the women of a given fecundity class according to the number of women in that class in the population.

Suppose (Sheps, in Sheps and Ridley, 1966) that the N representative women with whom we start out include $Nf(p)\,dp$ women of susceptibility or fecundity between p and $p + dp$, where dp is small. Among women of fecundity p we will expect the fraction p to become pregnant in the first month, $1 - p$ to go on to the second month and, of these, $(1 - p)p$ to become pregnant then, and so on. In other words, we will expect

$$Npf(p)\,dp$$

women to become pregnant in the first month,

$$N(1-p)pf(p)\,dp$$

in the second month,..., and

$$N(1-p)^{m-1}pf(p)\,dp$$

in the mth month—all this for a given susceptibility p.

To find the corresponding numbers for all women we add through the several susceptibility groups, which in the limit is the same as integrating with respect to p. The total expected conceptions for the ith month will be

$$N \int_0^1 (1-p)^{i-1} pf(p)\, dp. \tag{11.2.2}$$

Expression 11.2.2 shows that for $0 < p < 1$ the number of conceptions steadily decreases with time. Most of the decrease is due to women dropping out through pregnancy, and there is no provision for bringing them back in this way of measuring fertility.

The number of conceptions cannot but decline to zero in the course of time as the entire group drops out through pregnancy.

But aside from this gross fact, which applies to a homogeneous group as well, there is a selection factor that can be important if the variation in p, expressed by $f(p)$, is substantial. The pregnancy rate during the ith month is (11.2.2) divided by the number of women still under observation

$$p_i = \frac{\displaystyle\int_0^1 (1-p)^{i-1} pf(p)\, dp}{\displaystyle\int_0^1 (1-p)^{i-1} f(p)\, dp}, \tag{11.2.3}$$

which can be regarded as the mean of p weighted by $(1-p)^{i-1} f(p)$. Because $1-p$ is less than unity, the weighting function $(1-p)^{i-1} f(p)$ shifts downward (i.e., to the left on the usual form of chart) as i increases, so p_i must decline steadily with i. This is a selection arising from the removal by pregnancy of the more fertile women.

The two processes are shown in Table 11.2, with a simple example in which half the women have $p = 0.2$ and half have $p = 0.3$, and q is written for $1-p$ in (11.2.2) and (11.2.3). It shows in column 1 the chance of becoming pregnant in the ith month as forecast for a woman when she comes under observation in month 1, and also (column 3) the chance of a pregnancy in the ith month for a woman who has gone through the first $i-1$ months without becoming pregnant. The rapid decline in the first column is no surprise, while the third column exhibits the more subtle selection effect, which is appreciable even with the small variation of our example. The mean fecundability started at $p = 0.25$, the mean of 0.2 and 0.3, and by the tenth month had fallen to 0.223. The drop is more than halfway to 0.2, to which it would ultimately tend as i became large. The greater the variation, the more rapid is the decline in average fertility among the women who remain.

To express (11.2.3) in terms of variation among women, expand $(1-p)^{i-1} p$ of the numerator and $(1-p)^{i-1}$ of the denominator in a Taylor series around $\bar{p}$, the mean $\int_0^1 pf(p)\, dp$. The constant terms are $(1-\bar{p})^{i-1}\bar{p}$ in

Table 11.2 Example of removal of more fertile women in successive months, using $f(p) = 0.5$ for $p = 0.2$ and $f(p) = 0.5$ for $p = 0.3$, that is, half the women are of fecundability $p = 0.2$ and half are of fecundability $p = 0.3$

Month	Probability of conceiving in ith month for all women entering $\int_0^1 pq^{i-1}f(p)\,dp$	Fraction of women remaining at beginning of month $\int_0^1 q^{i-1}f(p)\,dp$	Probability of conceiving in ith month for women who have not conceived by $(i-1)$th month $\dfrac{\int_0^1 pq^{i-1}f(p)\,dp}{\int_0^1 q^{i-1}f(p)\,dp}$
1	0.25	1.000	0.25
2	0.185	0.750	0.247
3	0.138	0.565	0.243
4	0.103	0.428	0.240
5	0.077	0.325	0.237
6	0.058	0.248	0.234
7	0.044	0.190	0.231
8	0.033	0.146	0.228
9	0.025	0.113	0.226
10	0.019	0.087	0.223
15	0.0054	0.025	0.213
20	0.0016	0.0078	0.207
30	0.00016	0.00079	0.2020
50	0.0000018	0.0000089	0.20014

the numerator and $(1 - \bar{p})^{i-1}$ in the denominator, and the linear terms vanish, with the result

$$p_i \doteq \bar{p} - \frac{(i-1)\sigma^2}{1 - \bar{p}}, \qquad (11.2.4)$$

on using the fact that $1/(1 + \alpha) \doteq 1 - \alpha$ for α small.

In application to the distribution of Table 11.2, consisting of two spikes, $\bar{p} = 0.25$. The general rule is that the standard deviation of two numbers is half the interval between them; if the numbers are a and b, their variance is

$$\sigma^2 = \frac{a^2 + b^2}{2} - \left(\frac{a+b}{2}\right)^2 = \left(\frac{a-b}{2}\right)^2.$$

In this case $a = 0.2$ and $b = 0.3$, so $\sigma^2 = 0.0025$. Then from (11.2.4) we have for p_{10}

$$p_{10} \doteq \bar{p} - \frac{(i-1)\sigma^2}{1 - \bar{p}}$$

$$= 0.25 - \frac{(9)(0.0025)}{0.75} = 0.220,$$

as opposed to the 0.223 shown in Table 11.2. The difference is due to neglect of higher moments and other approximations, the effect of which becomes more serious as i increases.

The Pearl Index is the Harmonic Mean of the Distribution

The Pearl index $\hat{p}_p$ of (11.2.1) is shown to estimate the harmonic mean of the several p. For the expected value of N_1 is the initial number N times p, of N_2 is Nqp, of N_3 is Nq^2p, and so on. The denominator of (11.2.1) can be taken as the numbers of women nonpregnant at the beginning, after 1 month after 2 months, and so on. Entering these for any fixed p and then integrating over the range of p (overlooking that $E(X/Y) \neq EX/EY$):

$$p_p = \frac{\int_0^1 pf(p)\,dp + \int_0^1 (1-p)pf(p)\,dp + \cdots}{\int_0^1 f(p)\,dp + \int_0^1 (1-p)f(p)\,dp + \cdots},$$

where we suppose that the survey continues until the last woman becomes pregnant, or, more reasonably, that nonpregnant women left at the end of the survey are excluded from all of its records. In the numerator again we change p to $1 - q$ and assemble the integrals to obtain

$$p_p = \frac{\int_0^1 \left[(1-q) + q(1-q) + q^2(1-q) + \cdots \right] f(p)\,dp}{\int_0^1 (1 + q + q^2 + \cdots) f(p)\,dp}$$

$$= \frac{\int_0^1 f(p)\,dp}{\int_0^1 (1 + q + q^2 + \cdots) f(p)\,dp}$$

$$= \frac{1}{\int_0^1 [1/(1-q)] f(p)\,dp} = \frac{1}{\int_0^1 (1/p) f(p)\,dp}. \tag{11.2.5}$$

The quantity p_p, of which $\hat{p}_p$ given by (11.2.1) is an estimate, is thus shown to be the harmonic mean of the p's, a statement that is meaningful once all infecund women have been removed from the records.

The Gini Fertility Measure

Gini's (1924) way of providing a measure of fertility that is unbiased in the face of variation among women is effectively to confine the index to the pregnancies and exposure of the first month, bound to be unselected for susceptibility if the sample is unselected. His index is

$$\hat{p}_g = \frac{N_1 - N_{m+1}}{N_1 + N_2 + \cdots + N_m}, \tag{11.2.6}$$

where the denominator totals the women of proven fertility, and the numerator has the relatively unimportant subtraction, if m is large, of those who become pregnant in the $(m+1)$th month.

If one wants to see formally what is happening in $\hat{p}_g$ when those not pregnant by the mth month cannot be neglected, the algebra is only slightly more involved:

$$\hat{p}_g = \frac{N_1 - N_{m+1}}{N_1 + N_2 + \cdots + N_m}$$

is an estimate of

$$\frac{N \int_0^1 pf(p)\,dp - N \int_0^1 pq^m f(p)\,dp}{N \int_0^1 (p + pq + pq^2 + \cdots + pq^{m-1}) f(p)\,dp} = \frac{\int_0^1 p(1 - q^m) f(p)\,dp}{\int_0^1 (1 - q^m) f(p)\,dp}.$$

$$\tag{11.2.7}$$

This is the arithmetic mean value of p, not quite in the original distribution $f(p)$, but in the slightly different distribution proportional to $(1 - q^m) f(p)\,dp$.

Comparison of Pearl and Gini Estimates.   If p does not vary among fertile women, or does not vary greatly, we can be indifferent as to whether their arithmetic or harmonic mean is estimated. Thus in the homogeneous case $\hat{p}_p$ is the best estimate of the common p in that it has the smallest sampling error. If, however, p does vary considerably, the harmonic mean is no substitute for the arithmetic, being always below it, and to use $\hat{p}_p$ is to minimize sampling error at the cost of substantial bias. Take the arithmetic example of Table 11.2, in which a group of women is equally divided among those with probability of conceiving 0.2 and those with probability 0.3; then the arithmetic mean of their fecundity is 0.25 and the harmonic mean is 0.24, a small difference. For a group equally divided among those with probabilities of conceiving of $\frac{1}{6}$, $\frac{1}{4}$, and $\frac{1}{2}$, the arithmetic mean is

$$\frac{\frac{1}{6}+\frac{1}{4}+\frac{1}{2}}{3} = \frac{0.917}{3} = 0.306.$$

The harmonic mean is

$$\frac{3}{1/\frac{1}{6}+1/\frac{1}{4}+1/\frac{1}{2}} = \frac{3}{6+4+2} = 0.25,$$

or about 18 percent low.

Thus mean fecundity is understated by $\hat{p}_p$ whenever variation among women is considerable. The Pearl index, given as pregnancies per 100 woman-years of exposure, if unadjusted for selection will underestimate the average probability of conception per month for all women in the unselected group. In commonsense terms this is so because $\hat{p}_p$ puts weight on later months when the less fecund women are disproportionately represented. This defect of $\hat{p}_p$ is unimportant if couples are followed over a short period. It is not a defect at all if we are interested in the mean fecundity over a period of time of a group of initially fecund women, in which those who become pregnant drop out and are not replaced. Moreover, the mean waiting time to pregnancy in a heterogeneous group of women will be approximated by $1/\hat{p}_p$, so that, if waiting time is the subject of interest, the harmonic mean implicit in $\hat{p}_p$ is the one wanted.

Excursus on Averages

In the present section we have a type of selection to produce p_p that lowers the average below the unselected p_g. The opposite occurred in Section 10.3, where it appeared that choosing a woman at random gave the expected number of her daughters as the arithmetic mean $\Sum_i if_i$, where f_i is the fraction of women who have i daughters; choosing a girl at random and asking how many daughters her mother had gave a larger average. It is worth contrasting the four main kinds of average that enter demographic work.

If families are chosen with probability proportional to number of daughters, the expected value is found by weighting by i and dividing by the total number of daughters ($\Sum f_i = 1$ but $\Sum if_i \neq 1$):

$$\frac{\Sum (i)(if_i)}{\Sum if_i} = \frac{\Sum i^2 f_i}{\Sum if_i}.$$

This has the old name of contraharmonic mean (according to the *Oxford English Dictionary*). If it is designated as C and the arithmetic mean as A, the difference is (Section 10.3)

$$C - A = \frac{\Sigma i^2 f_i}{\Sigma i f_i} - \Sigma i f_i$$

$$= \frac{\Sigma i^2 f_i - (\Sigma i f_i)^2}{\Sigma i f_i} = \frac{\sigma^2}{A},$$

where σ^2 is the variance of the distribution. Thus C is always greater than A, except in the trivial case where the numbers being averaged are the same.

A similar aspect of selection, but over time, appears in Feller (1971, p. 12), who explains why we have to wait so long at a bus stop. Suppose, for example, that the buses arrive independently at random according to a Poisson process with constant α, so that the mean time between buses is $1/\alpha$. When a would-be rider shows up at the stop, he ought on the average to be midway between two buses and have to wait only $\frac{1}{2}(1/\alpha)$. That is one way of calculating. The second is to say that, since the Poisson process has no memory, and one moment of arrival has the same waiting prospect as another, the time to the next bus must on the average be $1/\alpha$. Unfortunately the second answer is the correct one. A selection occurs by which one more often arrives in a long interbus period than in a short one.

A different aspect of waiting times is evident when women are subject to different chances of having a child. What is the mean interchild period in a group of women if the probability of pregnancy is p_i for the ith woman, say in a given month? The expected period for the ith woman is $1/p_i$, and the mean time to conception $(1/n)\Sigma(1/p_i)$ months. This is the reciprocal of the harmonic mean of the probabilities of conception; it is not $n/\Sigma p_i$, the reciprocal of the arithmetic mean. The Pearl index p_p is another example of the same harmonic mean.

The geometric mean turns up in applications of the life table. The chance of a person surviving from age 30 to age 40, say, is the geometric average chance of surviving over the 10 years taken to the tenth power. It has to be a geometric average because the chance of survival is

$$\frac{l_{40}}{l_{30}} = \left[\sqrt[10]{\left(\frac{l_{40}}{l_{39}}\right)\left(\frac{l_{39}}{l_{38}}\right)\cdots\left(\frac{l_{31}}{l_{30}}\right)} \right]^{10}.$$

Alternatively, if the chance of dying in the ith of n years is μ_i, with an arithmetic average $\bar{\mu}$, the chance of surviving over the period is $(e^{-\bar{\mu}})^n$, and this is the geometric mean G of the chances of surviving the individual years.

Thus we have instances of the arithmetic (A), geometric (G), harmonic (H), and contraharmonic (C) means. For integral variables i with weights f_i such that $\Sigma f_i = 1$, these may be written, respectively, as

A	G	H	C
$\sum if_i,$	$\Pi i^{f_i},$	$\dfrac{1}{\Sigma(f_i/i)},$	$\dfrac{\Sigma i^2 f_i}{\Sigma if_i}.$

For N unweighted values X_i, integral or not, these means are

$$\frac{\Sigma X_i}{N}, \quad \sqrt[N]{\Pi X_i}, \quad \frac{N}{\Sigma(1/X_i)}, \quad \frac{\Sigma X_i^2}{\Sigma X_i}.$$

Differences are not trifling. For a population with two values, $X_1 = 1$ and $X_2 = 4$, we have for the four averages

$$2.5, \quad 2, \quad 1.6, \quad 3.4.$$

[Show that the contraharmonic mean is as much greater than the arithmetic as the arithmetic is greater than the harmonic, that is, $C - A = A - H$. Show also that $G = \sqrt{AH}$. Under what conditions do they hold?]

Graduation Uses Information Efficiently

Given that in practice samples used for fertility studies are small, one would like to avoid the sampling instability of the Gini index, as well as what is, from one point of view, the bias of the Pearl index. One would also like to know something of the variation in fecundity among women, which is not revealed by $\hat{p}_p$ or by $\hat{p}_g$. Variance could be inferred from the difference by solving (11.2.4) for σ^2, but this would have substantial error. Fortunately a graduation due to Potter and Parker (1964) provides variance, along with low sampling error and absence of bias in the mean.

Mean and Variance Simultaneously Estimated by Graduation

Potter and Parker (1964) fitted a beta distribution proportional to $p^{a-1}(1-p)^{b-1}$ whose mean fecundity $\bar{p}$ and variance σ^2 are as follows:

$$\bar{p} = \int_0^1 pf(p)\,dp = \frac{a}{a+b},$$

$$\sigma^2 = \int_0^1 (p-\bar{p})^2 f(p)\,dp = \frac{ab}{(a+b+1)(a+b)^2}. \tag{11.2.8}$$

The a and b are not directly known, but we do know the mean and variance of the waiting times of those becoming pregnant in terms of the same constants a and b:

$$\bar{w} = \frac{a+b-1}{a-1}, \quad a>1; \quad \sigma_w^2 = \frac{(ab)(a+b-1)}{(a-1)^2(a-2)}, \quad a>2.$$

All that is needed is to solve for a and b in terms of the known $\bar{w}$ and σ_w^2. After extended but straightforward algebra the estimates

$$a = \frac{2\sigma_w^2}{\sigma_w^2 - \bar{w}^2 + \bar{w}}, \quad b = (\bar{w}-1)(a-1) \tag{11.2.9}$$

are reached. Substituting for a and b in (11.2.8) would give the mean and variance of the probabilities of conceiving (not directly observable) in terms of the mean and variance of waiting times as observed. In the example used by Potter and Parker, $\bar{w} = 5.47$ months and $\sigma_w^2 = 89.98$, and from (11.2.9) these provide $a = 2.746$ and $b = 7.806$; therefore mean fecundity $\bar{p}$ is 0.260 and the standard deviation of p among women is $\sigma = 0.129$. (A more detailed secondary account is found in Keyfitz, 1968, p. 386.)

Improvements on the moments fitting sketched above have been published by Majumdar and Sheps (1970). They develop maximum likelihood estimators that make more effective use of the data, these data still consisting of waiting times for the whole group of women followed.

There is a certain arbitrariness in picking a family of probability distributions to represent fecundity on the basis of mathematical convenience rather than empirical evidence, and then drawing conclusions without at least trying alternative distributions. In spite of numerous papers on the subject, little is known about patterns of heterogeneous fecundity among women or how they vary among different populations. This has been a special handicap in studies of the effects of heterogeneous fertility on variance in completed family size, or the relative effects of male and female fecundity within marriage.

The variation among couples is especially great for a contraceptive method that is ineffective for some users. The ineffective users are selected out by pregnancy, leaving a residue of effective users whose probability of conception is very low. For this reason and others, surveys of groups of women practicing contraception are often tabulated by periods—first year, second year, and so on, so that the decline in the conception rate can be traced. Tabulating in periods has the advantage that cases subsequently lost to follow-up can be included as long as they are observed. The life table method described below rescues the incomplete records.

Life Table Methods for Fertility

The theory so far has dealt with two cases—homogeneous, where all women have the same probability of conception p, and heterogeneous, where their several p values are distributed according to an (unknown) probability distribution. In both we supposed that any given woman has an unchanging probability of conception. If the sample is to be followed for a long period, however, we need to allow also for change in individual women, either because of a decline in fecundity with age or because of increased motivation and skill in using contraception. The life table method in a fashion embraces both factors. It also allows for the selection effect of pregnancy.

To make the table we first calculate the probability of conception month by month. Like any life table, that for conception is based on two kinds of data: numbers of events, and numbers exposed to risk. In the present case the events are pregnancies, and the exposed are the women under observation, for each month. If P_i women are under observation through the ith month, and A_i (standing for "accident") conceptions occur among them, the conception rate for the group in that month is $p_i = A_i / P_i$, and the probability of not conceiving is $1 - p_i$ (Potter, 1967).

We can multiply together the $1 - p_i$ for successive months, and obtain a column analogous to the life table l_i that represents the chance of a child just born surviving to exact age i. The technique is identical with that for mortality, discussed at length in Chapter 2.

The life table model in which allowance is made for the single decrement of pregnancy can be extended to provide for other risks, including the death of the person, divorce of the couple, discontinuance of contraception, and other contingencies. Among these the possibility that the couple will drop the contraceptive is of the greatest interest for our analysis. Tietze (1962) tells us that pregnancy rates for various IUDs during the 2 years after insertion were considerably lower than discontinuance rates. This is a standard problem in competing risks, of the kind dealt with in Section 2.6, and any of the methods there used would serve in this case too. But the refinements useful for mortality are not necessary for conception, where small samples and biased data are general.

Relation of Micro to Population Replacement

We saw that the replacement of a population, the ratio of girl children in one generation to girl children in the preceding generation, is given by

$$R_0 = \int_\alpha^\beta l(a)m(a)\,da.$$

We can factor $m(a)$ into $\nu(a)f(a)$, where $\nu(a)$ is the fraction married at age a, and $f(a)$ is the marital fertility rate. We can also go one step further and say of married fertility that

$$f(a) = \frac{12}{1/\{p(a)[1-e(a)]\}+s},$$

where $p(a)$ is natural monthly probability of conceiving at age a, and $e(a)$ is the efficiency of contraception, both in a particular population. Then we have for the net reproduction rate

$$R_0 = \int_{\alpha}^{\beta} l(a)\nu(a) \frac{12}{1/\{p(a)[1-e(a)]\}+s} \, da, \qquad (11.2.10)$$

but this remains purely formal without some source of information on $p(a)$ and $e(a)$.

How Surer Contraception Reduces the Interval between Births

At one time "child-spacing" was a euphemism for contraception, and much was said about the benefits to the mother's health if she spaced out her children. This may have been good public relations at a time when authorities frowned on contraception intended simply to reduce family size. While the supposed healthful effects of spacing are still referred to in some countries, yet in fact with the spread of safe and certain contraception women often *reduce* the interval between such births as they decide to have. For the mother who must give up a job in order to look after the family, two or three children of about the same ages cost less in lost earnings than would the same number of children spread over her reproductive life.

Whatever the motivation to compress childraising into a small time interval, the couple could not afford to yield to it when contraception was uncertain. Compromise was necessary; the number of planned children would be held below what was desired in order to allow for accidents. Even if the chance of conception in any one month is as low as 0.01, and the couple have 240 fertile months ahead of them, their expected prospective children are 2.4, whether they want them or not. If they want 2 or 3 children, they cannot afford to have any deliberately. Even if they can achieve a probability of conceiving in any month as low as 0.003, the chance of an accidental pregnancy during 240 months is over one half:

$$1 - (0.997)^{240} = 0.514.$$

Thus only perfect contraception, or its equivalent in the form of easy legal abortion, permits thoroughgoing family planning, and when such planning is aimed at saving the time of the mother it will space the children as closely as possible.

11.3 WHY THREE-CHILD FAMILIES CONSTITUTE A POPULATION EX-PLOSION, WHEREAS TWO-CHILD FAMILIES WOULD LEAD TO THE EXTINCTION OF MANKIND

Let us see what three children mean for the growth of a population subject to United States mortality. There are four steps in the calculation, which we will carry out for females; the first three steps establish by how many fertile women a woman past childbearing will be replaced in the next generation.

1. If fertile women surviving through childbearing average three children in all, they will average 0.488×3 or 1.464 girls, the proportion of United States, 1967, births that were girls being 0.488.

2. Not all of the girls will live to reproduce in turn. Again according to data for the United States in 1967, the average fraction who survive to childbearing, that is, the ratio of the net to the gross reproduction rate, is 0.9665. By multiplying 0.9665 by 1.464 we go from gross to net reproduction and find $0.9665 \times 1.464 = 1.415 = R_0$.

3. An unknown fraction of girls are physiologically incapable of having children or do not wish to have them; let us allow 10 percent to cover these. This brings us to $1.415 \times 0.9 = 1.273$ as the number of fertile women by which a fertile woman is replaced on the average.

4. The period over which this replacement ratio applies is one generation, or 26.14 years for 1967 in the United States, about the same as the mean age of childbearing. We need the 26.14th root of the replacement ratio 1.274 to obtain the annual ratio of increase:

$$1.274^{1/26.14} = 1.00931,$$

or, as an annual rate compounded momently, $\ln 1.274/26.14 = 0.00926$, either way an increase of 0.0093 or 0.93 percent.

Thus, with the assumptions here made, including that the ages of childbearing are the same as those of the United States in 1967, and that 10 percent of women do not have any children, a three-child average for fertile couples implies an increase of 0.93 percent per year. This works out to a doubling in 75 years, and a multiplication by 16 in less than 300 years. With three-child families from now on the United States would have a population of about 3 billion within three centuries.

On the other hand, an average of two children per fertile married woman would not suffice to maintain the population. Calculation similar to that above shows that the population would ultimately change in the ratio of $2 \times 0.488 \times 0.9665 \times 0.9 = 0.849$ per generation, or the 26.14th root of this, 0.9938 per year, which is a decline of 0.62 percent per year. The half-life would be 111 years, and with two-child families to fertile women the United States population would fall to 30 million in a little over three centuries.

Interpolation from the above will give the average that would hold the population stationary. More directly, call the number x, and solve the equation

$$x \times 0.488 \times 0.9665 \times 0.9 = 1.$$

The result is 2.36 children per fertile married woman. In summary, with present United States death rates an average of three children leads to a population of more than 3 billion in three centuries, and an average of two children to 30 million in three centuries; what we need is an average of just 2.36 children.

An average of 2.1 children is often quoted as the bare replacement level. What is meant is 2.1 children averaged over all women, married and fertile or not. This is obtained by some such equation for the net reproduction rate as $x \times 0.488 \times 0.9665 = 1$, or $x = 2.12$, still with United States, 1967, data. Our 2.36 is the average number of children for couples who will have children. Its greatest weakness is the 10 percent allowance for celibacy and sterility.

These numbers show that the average family size over a period of time must be finely adjusted; even small departures continued for long lead to intolerable increase or decrease. Our present average for fertile married women is about two children. This number is less than we want indefinitely, but we have time to make the adjustment; intolerable changes come only over the course of generations and centuries.

Mexico, on the other hand, is not in a position to wait. Its fertile women average six children each, and this implies a growth rate of 3.5 percent per year, a doubling in 20 years, and a multiplication by 16 in 80 years. Mexico would have 800 million people within 80 years on its present course.

When both mortality and fertility are very high, as they must have been through most of unrecorded history, say at 40.00 and 40.02 per thousand, respectively (Section 1.1), an equilibrium mechanism analyzed by Frisch (1972) could have been operative. Undernourished women reach menarche later and menopause sooner than well-nourished women. They are also subject to more gaps in fecundability during the course of their reproductive lives. Hence periods of severe food scarcity result in lower births, by a purely biological causation, and when death rates are high this means population decrease. Although the mechanism does not produce stability in the face of short-period fluctuations, it can adapt population numbers to long-term declines or increases in food supplies. Evidently no such mechanism can produce an optimum population under modern conditions, where the gap between birth and death rates in many countries has become very wide.

11.4 A FAMILY-BUILDING STRATEGY TO AVOID EXTINCTION

Common sense suggests that the more children one has the less likely is the extinction of one's line of descent. This is only partly true, however, for extinction depends especially on the *variation* in the number of children in later generations, and in particular on the chance of having zero children. In avoiding the extinction of family lines a high average birth rate does not necessarily provide an advantage over a low birth rate.

Observing that many of the great men of the past had no living descendants, some writers inferred the deterioration of the race. Galton responded that before drawing such a conclusion one must know what fraction of people in general have no descendants. He initiated branching theory (Galton and Watson, 1874), which subsequently became a rich field of mathematical research with many and diverse applications. The analysis shows that in an increasing population each member either has zero descendants or has many—the chance that any of us will have exactly one descendant after 10 generations is remote. For the mathematics to explore this aspect and others see Harris (1963). Fortunately it is possible to derive the probability of extinction with virtually no theory at all. The exposition below, like Galton's statement of the problem, is given in terms of the male line.

Call the probability of having no sons p_0, of having one son p_1, of having two sons p_2, and so on, these probabilities applying independently to all males in all generations, and to be interpreted as sons living to maturity. Designate the chance of extinction of a male line starting with one person as x. Then the chance of extinction of two separately and independently developing male lines must be x^2, of three lines x^3, and so on. If a man has no sons his (conditional) chance of extinction is one, if he has one son his chance of extinction is x, if he has two sons his chance of extinction is x^2, and so on. Thus his whole (unconditional) chance of extinction through his sons is $p_0 + p_1 x + p_2 x^2 + \cdots$, and by definition this must be equal to his chance of extinction x. Hence the equation for x is

$$x = p_0 + p_1 x + p_2 x^2 + \cdots. \tag{11.4.1}$$

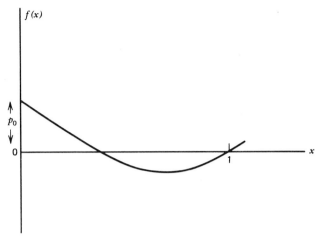

Fig. 11.3 General form of the curve $f(x) = p_0 + p_1 x + p_2 x^2 + \cdots - x$, when the derivative $f'(x) = p_1 + 2p_2 x + \cdots - 1$ is positive at $x = 1$, so that mean children are more than 1, showing $f''(x)$ always positive.

If $f(x) = p_0 + p_1 x + p_2 x^2 + \cdots - x$, we have $f(0) = p_0$, a positive quantity, and $f(1) = 0$; $f''(x)$ is always positive so $f(x)$ is concave upward. The question whether $f(x) = 0$ has a root between 0 and 1 is answered by whether it approaches 1 on the left from below, the condition for which is $f'(1)$ greater than zero or

$$p_1 + 2p_2 x + 3p_3 x^2 + \cdots - 1 > 0,$$

and $f'(x)$ is greater than zero at the point $x = 1$ if the mean number of sons is greater than one. Thus, if the mean is greater than one, the curve is sloping upward towards zero at $x = 1$, and there will be at least one root in the interior of the interval between zero and one. In this case the curve will have the general shape of Table 11.3 and Fig. 11.3 and the chance of extinction is greater than zero and less than one.

Why do irrelevant roots, such as that at $x = 1$, appear so often in applied work? The reason can be seen only if we make a distinction between the substantive problem and its mathematical formulation. In demography, as in other fields, the substantive problem facing us is identified with a mathematical formulation that is somehow broader, and after solving the mathematical formulation we have to hand-pick among its answers the one that corresponds to our narrower substantive concern. In a sense we ourselves unknowingly put extra roots into the mathematical representation, and we have no easy mathematical way of eliminating them.

Table 11.3   Values of $f(x) = \dfrac{1}{4} + \dfrac{x}{4} + \dfrac{x^2}{4} + \dfrac{x^3}{4} - x, f'(x) = \dfrac{1}{4}$

$+ \dfrac{x}{2} + \dfrac{3x^2}{4} - 1, f''(x) = \dfrac{1}{2} + \dfrac{3x}{2}$

x	$f(x)$	$f'(x)$	$f''(x)$
0	0.25	−0.750	0.50
0.1	0.178	−0.692	0.65
0.2	0.112	−0.620	0.80
0.3	0.054	−0.532	0.95
0.4	0.006	−0.430	1.10
0.5	−0.031	−0.312	1.25
0.6	−0.056	−0.180	1.40
0.7	−0.067	−0.032	1.55
0.8	−0.062	0.130	1.70
0.9	−0.040	0.308	1.85
1.0	0.000	0.500	2.00
1.1	0.060	0.708	2.15
1.2	0.142	0.930	2.30

Let us try to get some feeling for what it is in the pattern of childbearing that most affects the chance of extinction of a family line. First the case (Table 11.3) in which the chance of having no sons surviving to maturity is 0.25, of having one son is 0.25, of having two sons is 0.25, of having three sons is 0.25. (This would be an easy population to simulate with a pair of coins.) The equation for x, the probability of extinction, is

$$x = 0.25 + 0.25x + 0.25x^2 + 0.25x^3, \qquad (11.4.2)$$

which is

$$x^3 + x^2 - 3x + 1 = 0.$$

The equation is satisfied by $x = 1$, a root of no demographic interest, so we divide by $x - 1$ to obtain the quadratic

$$x^2 + 2x - 1 = 0$$

containing the other roots. This is solved by completing the square as $x = -1 + \sqrt{2} = 0.414$, the negative root being extraneous.

The above hypothetical population has a net reproduction rate of 1.5, which is somewhere between the values for presently less developed and more developed countries. Mexico in 1959–61 had much higher fertility, its net reproduction rate being over 2.5, and yet the chance of extinction (Keyfitz, 1968, p. 409) at 0.4066 was just about as high as that of our hypothetical population. (The extinction calculation was on 1960 census data following the female line for Mexico.)

A population could have even higher fertility than Mexico and yet also show a greater probability of extinction. Suppose that the chance of having no sons surviving to maturity is 0.5 and the chance of having six sons is 0.5. This would give a net reproduction rate of 3.0—higher than the values for recorded populations. But the probability of extinction of a male line would be the zero of $x = \frac{1}{2} + x^6/2$, or $x^6 - 2x + 1 = 0$. A convenient iterative form for solution is obtained by rearranging the equation as $x = (x^6 + 1)/2$. Starting with $x = 0$ on the right-hand side, the iterates are 0.5, 0.508, and 0.509, the root being 0.50866.

At the opposite extreme, a population in which everyone married and each couple had exactly one son (and one daughter) surviving to maturity would be stationary, but the probability of extinction of either line would be zero.

Couples in the United States and Europe seem (a) to devote much effort to overcoming sterility, (b) to aim at having two children with a uniformity unknown in the fertility schedules of the past, and (c) to want to have at least one boy and one girl child. Whether or not they have such an objective in mind, couples act as though each is doing its utmost to maintain both its male and female lines and wants the smallest possible number of children consistent with a high chance of infinite lines of descent.

11.5 SEX PREFERENCE AND THE BIRTH RATE

Insofar as parents wish to have at least one boy, or at least one boy and one girl, and keep having children until they attain their wish, the birth rate is higher than it would otherwise be. A considerable literature (Goodman, 1961; Repetto, 1972; Hatzold, 1974; Sheps, 1963; McDonald, 1973) analyzes the magnitude of this effect, using observed births to infer preferences, and assesses by how much the ability to control the sex of children would lower the birth rate.

If the probability of a boy on a particular birth is p, and of a girl is $q = 1 - p$, and we think of couples whose sole aim in family building is to have at least one boy, the proportion of such couples who will stop after exactly one child is p, who will stop after exactly two children is qp, who will stop after exactly three is q^2p, and so on. For them the mean number of children is

$$p + 2qp + 3q^2p + \cdots,$$

which as we saw on p. 304 is

$$1 - q + 2q(1 - q) + 3q^2(1 - q) + \cdots,$$

or, on canceling,

$$1 + q + q^2 + q^3 + \cdots = \frac{1}{1-q} = \frac{1}{p}.$$

If, for example, the chance of a boy is 0.5, couples who continue to have children until a boy arrives will average two children. (Note the formal analogy to the number of months to pregnancy in Section 11.1; births have taken the place of months and a boy takes the place of conception.)

For these couples the fraction of boys is 1 divided by the mean number of children, that is, $1/(1/p) = p$. Just as a gambler cannot influence his winnings by choosing the time of leaving a fair game, so parents cannot influence the proportion of boys by a stopping rule. This argument applies to any target number of children, so long as the couples considered are homogeneous, in that all have the same chance p of a boy on any birth.

If the couples are not homogeneous, a selective effect can occur in the population. Suppose that p is distributed according to $f(p)$, where $\int_0^1 f(p)\,dp = 1$, so there are $Nf(p)\,dp$ couples between p and $p + dp$. [We need to suppose that $f(0) = 0$, that is, no couples incapable of having boys are included.] Then for the $Nf(p)\,dp$ couples with a given p the average number of children is $1/p$, as appeared above, so the total number of children contributed by those between p and $p + dp$ is $(N/p)f(p)\,dp$; adding through the distribution of p gives the grand total of children, $N\int_0^1 (1/p)f(p)\,dp$. Since the total number of boys is N, one to each couple in this problem, the fraction of boys in the population is

$$\frac{N}{N\int_0^1 (1/p)f(p)\,dp} = H, \text{ say,}$$

which is the harmonic mean of the p's (Goodman, 1961a).

Since the harmonic mean is less than the arithmetic mean, we have proved two things about the effect of heterogeneity on the outcome of this stopping rule: the fraction of boys is H, which is smaller than the fraction of boys if no stopping rule were used, and the average number of children per couple is $\int_0^1 (1/p)f(p)\,dp = 1/H$, and hence is greater than the $1/p$ that would occur with homogeneity. Though an individual couple of fixed p cannot affect the proportion of boys among its offspring by any stopping rule, a population can: each couple continuing until it attains a boy reduces the fraction of boys in the population, as though parents were testing themselves to see whether they were boy-producers or girl-producers, and only in the latter case having further children.

As an indication of the numerical effect of this rule, suppose that one-third of parents have $p = 0.25$, one-third $p = 0.50$, and one-third $p =$

0.75. Then the harmonic mean is

$$\frac{1}{(1/0.25)\cdot \frac{1}{3} + (1/0.50)\cdot \frac{1}{3} + (1/0.75)\cdot \frac{1}{3}} = \frac{9}{22} = 0.4091,$$

as against the arithmetic mean of 0.50.

An Approximation to the Harmonic Mean. For small variations in the p values pertaining to the several couples in the population we can find a general expression for the amount by which parents following the rule of stopping with a boy will decrease the proportion of boys in the population. We first need an expansion of $1/p$ (where $0 < p \leqslant 1$) around the reciprocal of the mean value $\bar{p}$. By Taylor's theorem

$$\phi(p) = \phi(\bar{p}) + (p - \bar{p})\phi'(\bar{p}) + \frac{(p - \bar{p})^2}{2!}\phi''(\bar{p}),$$

where we suppose $p - \bar{p}$ to be small enough that $(p - \bar{p})^3$ and higher powers are negligible. Then, if the function $\phi(p)$ is $1/p$, $\phi'(\bar{p})$ is $-1/\bar{p}^2$ and $\phi''(p)$ is $2/\bar{p}^3$. Hence

$$\frac{1}{p} = \frac{1}{\bar{p}} + (p - \bar{p})\left(-\frac{1}{\bar{p}^2}\right) + \frac{(p - \bar{p})^2}{2!}\frac{2}{\bar{p}^3} + \cdots,$$

and, entering the right-hand side in place of $1/p$ in the expression for the harmonic mean, we have approximately

$$\frac{1}{\displaystyle\int_0^1 \frac{f(p)}{p}\,dp} \doteq \bar{p} - \frac{\sigma^2}{\bar{p}}. \tag{11.5.1}$$

This follows from the definition of the mean, $\bar{p} = \int_0^1 pf(p)\,dp$, and of the variance, $\sigma^2 = \int_0^1 (p - \bar{p})^2 f(p)\,dp$, the approximation in (11.5.1) requiring the variation of p to be small.

To test the approximation on the numerical example above, in which parents are equally divided among those having 0.25, 0.50, and 0.75 probability of producing a boy on each birth, we find that σ^2 is 0.04167, and hence that the estimate of the harmonic mean $\bar{p} - \sigma^2/\bar{p}$ is $\frac{1}{2} - (0.04167/\frac{1}{2}) = 0.4167$, only 2 percent higher than the 0.4091 above.

What in fact are the sex preferences of parents? We ought to be able to find out by observing, for example, in what proportion of cases parents with given constitutions of family go on to further children. The proportions of first children, of second children, and so on that are boys are out of the parents' control and so can tell us nothing about parental preferences; on the other hand, the proportions of the last child and the second-to-last child are determinable by parents, even without any ability to determine a given birth. If couples with one girl go on to a further child in a higher fraction of cases than those with one boy, this suggests a wish for boys; if those with one boy and one girl go on to a further child less often than those with two boys or two girls, this shows a wish for at least one child of each sex. How subtly do parents play the game? If they conclude, after having a girl, that they tend to be girl producers, at least some of those with boy preference will stop at that point.

Some data that classify children according to birth order and sex are available, but the complexities of their analysis will not be undertaken here. Instead we go on to anticipate the time when parents will have a measure of control over the sex of their offspring. (Some assert that techniques for this are available now, but their effectiveness is controversial.)

11.6 FAMILY-BUILDING STRATEGY WITH PARENTAL CONTROL OVER SEX OF CHILDREN

If parents want at least one son and one daughter and the chance of either is one-half on a given birth, they have no choice but to proceed at random, and they will average three children. Suppose that the chance of having a boy when they are trying for a boy is b and of having a girl when trying for a girl is g, both b and g being appreciably larger than one-half. A couple want at least B boys and at least G girls; what should they do to attain these while exceeding $B + G$ total children by as small a number as possible? A direct attack on this problem would be complicated; we will see that it can be made simple by proceeding one step at a time (McDonald, 1973).

The problem can be represented on paper as a lattice of points (Fig. 11.4), of which the one on the upper right is labeled zero. The several points represent the number of children needed to attain the target. Thus at the points on the top, reading from right to left, the couple wants zero, one, two, ... boys to complete its (self-determined) total. At the points along the right, reading from top to bottom, the couple wants zero, one, two, ... girls to complete the number sought. At the interior point A the couple want one boy and one girl, and so on. The problem is then to calculate at each such point the expected number of further children in total to reach the desired constitution of family. One visualizes families climbing toward the target, one child at a time, and we can take advantage of the additivity over the several steps of the expected number of children acquired.

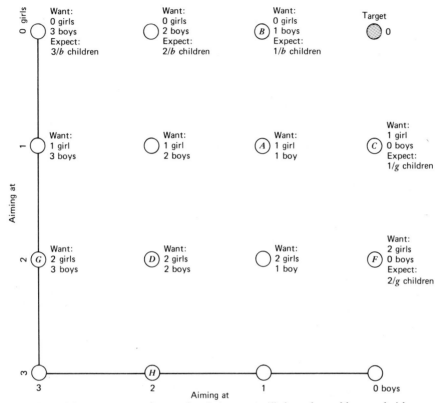

Fig. 11.4   Distance to target for couples aiming at specified numbers of boys and girls.

Consider the couple that are lacking exactly one girl (point C). Suppose that they try for a girl and stop as soon as they have one. They stand a probability g of having a girl first, in which case they add just one child, a chance $(1-g)g$ of having first a boy and then a girl (i.e., two children), a chance $(1-g)^2 g$ of having three children, and so on; hence their expected number of children is

$$g + 2(1-g)g + 3(1-g)^2 g + \cdots,$$

or, using the by now familiar device of putting $f = 1 - g$ and then consolidating terms,

$$1 - f + 2f(1-f) + 3f^2(1-f) + \cdots = 1 + f + f^2 + \cdots$$

$$= \frac{1}{1-f} = \frac{1}{1-(1-g)} = \frac{1}{g}.$$

The expected number of children is $1/g$, and we have labeled the point just below the target accordingly (Fig. 11.4). With $g = 0.7$ the expected number of children is $1/0.7 = 1.43$. With $g = 0.5$, that is, no sex control, the expected value is $1/0.5 = 2$.

Suppose that the couple wants two girls. Now they would be starting at the second point below zero. If they try for a girl, they stand a chance g of getting one, which will move them up one point and give them an expected number of children $1 + (1/g)$, so we can write $g[1 + (1/g)]$ in respect to this possibility. If they fail to have a girl, they have one more child and still need two girls, so the expectation for this is $(1 - g)(1 + e)$, where e is the expected number of children when one is trying for two girls. Then, adding both possibilities, we have

$$e = g\left(1 + \frac{1}{g}\right) + (1 - g)(1 + e),$$

or, on solving the simple equation for e,

$$e = \frac{2}{g}.$$

We could have anticipated this by noting that to move up one girl takes on the average $1/g$ children; hence to move up two girls takes $2/g$ children. To move up three girls takes an average of $3/g$ children, and similarly for higher numbers. The cells for boys only, across the top of the diagram, are the same but with b replacing g.

Hence the expectations shown on the right-hand points and across the top of the diagram; having attached probabilities to these boundary points, we now turn to the interior. Consider the interior point marked A in Fig. 11.5, standing for a couple wishing one girl and one boy, either altogether or in addition to the children they already have.

Suppose they try for a girl first. Then the chance of moving up in the diagram is g, and if they succeed they reach the point just above, from which the expectation is $1/b$. If they fail they reach the point at the right, from which the expectation is $1/g$. Hence the total expected number of children from point A is

$$A_g = g\left(1 + \frac{1}{b}\right) + (1 - g)\left(1 + \frac{1}{g}\right),$$

where 1 has been added within the parentheses to allow for the girl or boy born in the move. On cancellation this reduces to

$$\frac{g}{b} + \frac{1}{g},$$

and with $b = 0.8$ and $g = 0.7$ equals $0.7/0.8 + 1/0.7 = 2.30$.

Using the opposite strategy of trying for a boy first (Fig. 11.5) would

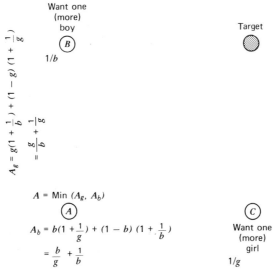

Fig. 11.5 Enlargement of part of Fig. 11.4, showing expected children for couple wanting one boy and one girl (position A). Trying for a boy first gives an expected $A_b = b(1 + 1/g) + (1 - b)(1 + 1/b) = b/g + 1/b$ children. Trying for a girl first gives $A_g(1 + 1/b) + (1 - g)(1 + 1/g) = g/b + 1/g$ children, where b is the chance of having a boy if the couple try for a boy, and g is the chance of having a girl if they try for a girl.

give

$$A_b = b\left(1 + \frac{1}{g}\right) + (1 - b)\left(1 + \frac{1}{b}\right) = \frac{b}{g} + \frac{1}{b},$$

or, with our numbers, $0.8/0.7 + 1/0.8 = 2.39$. Evidently the right strategy is to try for a girl first. This suggests a general rule: parents should leave the more controllable contingency to the last if they seek equal numbers of boys and girls.

We want always to choose the strategy that gives the minimum number of total children, for example, that corresponds to

$$\text{Min}\left(\frac{g}{b} + \frac{1}{g}, \frac{b}{g} + \frac{1}{b}\right).$$

If $b > g$, that is, if we are surer to get a boy if we aim at a boy than a girl if we aim at a girl, it is easily seen by algebra that $b/g + 1/b > g/b + 1/g$. This is so because, if $b > g > \frac{1}{2}$, then $b - \frac{1}{2} > g - \frac{1}{2}$ and $(b - \frac{1}{2})^2 > (g - \frac{1}{2})^2$, or $b^2 - b > g^2 - g$; therefore $b^2 + g > g^2 + b$, and, on dividing both sides by bg, $b/g + 1/b > g/b + 1/g$. If $b > g$ we should try for a girl first to minimize total children.

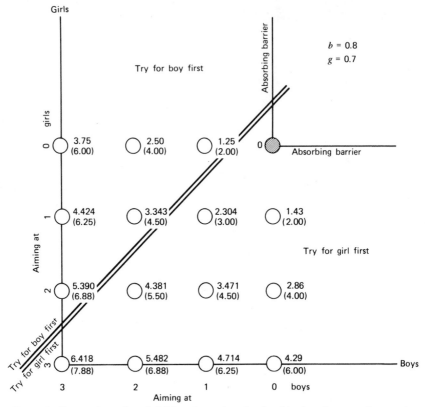

Fig. 11.6 Expected number of children for various family objectives from zero boys and zero girls up to three boys and three girls, when $b = 0.8$, $g = 0.7$, and (in parentheses) when $b = g = 0.5$.

The ability of parents to influence the sex of their children will reduce the average number of offspring for parents targetting on a minimum number of boys and of girls. Figure 11.6 shows expected numbers from various points with $b = 0.8$, $g = 0.7$, and in parentheses with $b = 0.5$, $g = 0.5$.

Let us see how sensitive the result is to the degree of reliability with which sex is determined. Table 11.4 shows the cases of parents aiming at one boy, and at one boy and one girl. Making $b = g = 0.5$, 0.6, ..., we see the average numbers of children they will have. If $b = g = 0.8$ rather than $b = g = 0.5$, the expected total drops from 2.0 to 1.25 for couples aiming at one boy, and from 3.0 to 2.25 for couples aiming at one boy and one girl. In both cases the reliability of 0.8 in sex determination eliminates three-quarters of the unwanted children.

Table 11.4   Expected number of children born to couples who stop after one boy, and who stop after one boy and one girl

	Expected total stopping after	
	One boy	One boy and one girl
$b = g$	$\dfrac{1}{b}$	$\dfrac{g}{b} + \dfrac{1}{g} = \dfrac{b}{g} + \dfrac{1}{b} = 1 + \dfrac{1}{b}$
0.5	2.0	3.0
0.6	1.67	2.67
0.7	1.43	2.43
0.8	1.25	2.25
0.9	1.11	2.11
1.0	1.00	2.00

A number of surveys have asked newly married couples how many boy and how many girl children they want. One such survey in Hull, England, showed 45.7 percent wanting one boy and one girl, 15.4 two boys and one girl, and 12.6 two boys and two girls; the average was 2.55 children. Under present circumstances, that is to say with $b = g = 0.5$ approximately, we find by applying the numbers in parentheses in Fig. 11.6 to these percentages that the average attained would be 3.74 children, or 1.19 more than wanted (Table 11.5).

With $b = 0.8$, $g = 0.7$, numbers chosen because they are about halfway to

Table 11.5   Application of average numbers of expected children to sex preferences of parents in survey in Hull, England

	Number of children			
Parents' preferences	Percent	Wanted	Average born with $b = g = \frac{1}{2}$	Average born with $b = 0.8$, $g = 0.7$
One boy, one girl	45.7	2	3.0	2.304
Two boys, one girl	15.4	3	4.5	3.343
Two boys, two girls	12.6	4	5.5	4.381
Average of survey		2.55	3.74	2.88
Excess with $b = g = \frac{1}{2}$			$3.74 - 2.55 = 1.19$	
Excess with $b = 0.8$, $g = 0.7$			$2.88 - 2.55 = 0.33$	

complete sex control represented by $b = g = 1.0$, the average would be 2.88 children, or only 0.33 more than wanted.

A technology that goes halfway to sex control would eliminate nearly three-quarters of the unwanted children born because of the sex preferences of parents. Full sex control would reduce the birth rate for these parents by 32 percent; half sex control would reduce their birth rate by 23 percent.

Five kinds of qualification are required. The least important is that children are born one at a time in the model, which has no easy way of taking account of multiple births. Moreover, not all parents have preferences regarding the sex composition of their families, and the model deals only with parents whose preferences are strong enough to be overriding. In fact, they must be willing and able to have an infinite number of children if necessary. The model also supposes that the parental decision regarding composition is made at the outset rather than in stages, or child by child. It supposes homogeneity—that all parents have the same chances b and g.

The advent of partial or complete control of the sex of children would have the effect of changing the sex of the new generation, in some cultures in favor of boys; in those cultures the advent of a high sex ratio in the new generation would reduce the number of marriages; when the children came to childbearing age marriages would be limited by the less numerous sex. Unwed males would decrease the overall birth rate. But well before that came about the culture would shift in favor of the initially less favored sex. Within a decade or so of the birth of a disproportionate number of boys couples would come to value girls more highly. Perhaps a series of waves would ensue, not unlike those familiar in a market economy arising from the interval of time between capital investments and the returns therefrom (Westoff and Rindfuss, 1974).

11.7 MEAN FAMILY SIZE FROM ORDER-OF-BIRTH DISTRIBUTION

Birth certificates almost invariably require that mothers report whether a particular birth is their first, second, third and so on. The resultant order-of-birth tabulations are available for many countries and regions, and one would like to extract their implication for the mean number of children born to mothers. The problem was considered by Burks (1933), and others.

The early writers assumed a stationary condition, in which the distribution of births by order in a calendar year or other period of observation is the same as in the cohorts of mothers that are passing through the period in question; the several cohorts are taken as of equal size. Suppose that the observed number of first births is N_1, of second births is N_2, and so on, and that these numbers apply in all periods and for all cohorts. This is to say that N_1 is the total of women who have any children at all, N_2 the number who have two or more children, N_3 the number who have three or more children, for all periods and all cohorts. If we call ϕ_1 the number who stop with one child, ϕ_2 the number who stop with two children, and so on, the N's are the cumulative sums of the ϕ's:

$$N_1 = \phi_1 + \phi_2 + \phi_3 + \cdots$$
$$N_2 = \qquad \phi_2 + \phi_3 + \cdots$$
$$N_3 = \qquad\qquad \phi_3 + \cdots$$
$$\vdots$$

and the ϕ's are the differences of the N's:

$$\phi_1 = N_1 - N_2$$
$$\phi_2 = N_2 - N_3$$
$$\phi_3 = N_3 - N_4$$
$$\vdots$$

The mean number of children in a family that has children is

$$\frac{\phi_1 + 2\phi_2 + 3\phi_3 + \cdots}{\phi_1 + \phi_2 + \phi_3 + \cdots} = \frac{N_1 + N_2 + N_3 + \cdots}{N_1}$$

$$= \frac{N}{N_1} = \frac{\text{Total births}}{\text{First births}}. \qquad (11.7.1)$$

This highly simplified formula applied to United States data for 1933 requires only the fact that births in that year were 74 per thousand native white women 15 to 44 years old, and first births were 24, making a mean family size of 3.1 children. For 1956 the corresponding figures were 115, 33, and a mean family size of 3.5 children; for 1973 the mean was 2.40.

11.8 PARITY PROGRESSION AND POPULATION INCREASE

How parents decide the size of their families has been the subject of much investigation since effective birth control has made that size subject to deliberate decision. Some may have a concept at the beginning that they retain throughout—they are fixed on three children, say. The majority, however, seem to make up their minds as they go along—they have one child and then, depending on how things look, they decide whether to have another. The following argument suggested by Norman Ryder formalizes parental decision in terms of the probabilities of successively proceeding to each further child.

Disregard time and consider the married couples that have children of successive orders. Suppose that a certain fraction of women have a first child; of these a certain fraction have a second child; of those that have two children a certain fraction go on to a third; and so on. We might take as the cohort a group of couples that married at the same time, or a group of women born at the same time. We could include a symbol for the fraction r_0 of the cohort that survives, and another for the fraction that marries, but simplicity is served by just supposing that r_1 of the girls born at a given moment will grow up and have a first child, of these the fraction r_2 will go on to a second child, and so on.

Then the probability that a girl child will have at least one child is r_1, that she will have two children is $r_1 r_2$, and so on. Suppose that the ratio of boys to girls among the births of any order is s, so the fraction $1/(1+s)$ of the births are girls. The net reproduction rate of the cohort of which the girl in question is a member is

$$R_0 = \frac{1}{1+s}(r_1 + r_1 r_2 + r_1 r_2 r_3 + \cdots). \qquad (11.8.1)$$

Due allowance is implicitly made for mortality, nonmarriage, illegitimacy, and voluntary or involuntary sterility within marriage.

We can enable the notion of parity progression to serve us better by reducing the parameters in (11.8.1) from one for each child to just two in all. Ryder found that $r_1 \doteq r_2 = h$, say, and that $r_3 \doteq r_4 \doteq r_5 \doteq \cdots = k$, say. Then (11.8.1) becomes

$$R_0 = \frac{1}{1+s}(h + h^2 + h^2 k + h^2 k^2 + h^2 k^3 + \cdots)$$

$$= \frac{1}{1+s}\left(h + \frac{h^2}{1-k} \right).$$

Table 11.6 shows values of R_0 for various combinations of h and k; the combinations on the lower right give an increasing population.

With this result we can do experiments of various kinds. We can, in particular, see how R_0 would be modified by lowering k, which is the way in which fertility change seems largely to have taken place in the United States. Now, since

$$R_0 = \frac{1}{1+s}\left(h + \frac{h^2}{1-k} \right), \qquad (11.8.2)$$

Table 11.6 Net reproduction rate corresponding to mothers'
parity progression ratio, h for first and second child, and k
for subsequent children, according to (11.8.2)

h	k						
	0.40	0.45	0.50	0.55	0.60	0.65	0.70
0.60	0.59	0.61	0.64	0.68	0.73	0.79	0.88
0.65	0.66	0.69	0.73	0.78	0.83	0.91	1.00
0.70	0.74	0.78	0.82	0.87	0.94	1.02	1.14
0.75	0.82	0.86	0.91	0.98	1.05	1.15	1.28
0.80	0.91	0.96	1.01	1.08	1.17	1.28	1.43
0.85	1.00	1.06	1.12	1.20	1.30	1.42	1.59

we have

$$\frac{dR_0}{dk} = \frac{1}{1+s}\left(\frac{h}{1-k}\right)^2.$$

Around $s = 1.05$, $h = 0.80$, $k = 0.65$, we have $dR_0/dk = 2.55$, so that each
increase of 0.01 in k produces an increase of 0.0255 in R_0, and similarly for
decreases.

To see the effects of successive childbearing decisions on population
growth we need also to take account of timing. The age at which a woman
has her first child, and the successive interbirth intervals, will evidently
make a difference in the rate at which the population grows. Timing is the
one element lacking in the present model. For the effect of its omission,
consider $h = 0.80$ and $k = 0.65$, so that $R_0 = 2.63/2.05 = 1.28$. If the mean
age of childbearing (strictly, the length of generation) is 25 years, the
intrinsic rate is 0.0099; if it is 30 years, the intrinsic rate is 0.0082.

11.9 FOR A GIVEN PROBABILITY OF SURVIVORS LOWER MORTALITY LOWERS THE RATE OF INCREASE

When mortality is high, a man who wants to have a son who will see him
through his old age requires many children. This point has often been
made before, but we still need clarification of the relation between mortality and the rate of population increase among people who want a certain
assurance of *surviving* children. With number of births given, the rate of
increase r goes up as mortality μ_x goes down; we will see that the relation
between r and μ_x is reversed if the birth rate is determined by the wish to
have surviving sons.

Call the probability of at least one surviving son p; this must equal one minus the probability that all sons will die. Consider survivorship to father's age 60; then the probability that not all sons will die is

$$1-\left(1-l_{60-a_1}\right)\left(1-l_{60-a_2}\right)\cdots\left(1-l_{60-a_n}\right)=p \qquad (11.9.1)$$

if the first son is born at age a_1 of the father, the second at age $a_2,\ldots,$ and the nth at age a_n.

Now the rate of increase of the population for this particular family, still on the one-sex model but for males, is the real root in r of the equation

$$\sum_{i=1}^{n} e^{-ra_i}l_{a_i}=1. \qquad (11.9.2)$$

This discrete form of Lotka's characteristic equation can be solved for r to tell us what r would be in a population if the mortality and childbearing patterns of a particular family were general.

Our problem is to find r as a function of the life table l_a from (11.9.2), given that the number of children n will be determined by (11.9.1). Even to define the solution of this would be awkward, so we approximate by supposing all the children to be born at the same age of the father: $a_1=a_2=\cdots=30$, say. Then the first equation, (11.9.1), is

$$1-\left(1-l_{30}\right)^n=p,$$

or

$$n=\frac{\ln(1-p)}{\ln(1-l_{30})}. \qquad (11.9.3)$$

The second equation, (11.9.2), is

$$ne^{-30r}l_{30}=1;$$

and substituting n from (11.9.3) and taking logarithms gives

$$r=\tfrac{1}{30}\ln\left[l_{30}\frac{\ln(1-p)}{\ln(1-l_{30})}\right]. \qquad (11.9.4)$$

The values of r are shown in Table 11.7, whose most important message is that each rise in l_{30} of 0.1 causes a decline in r of 0.003 to 0.008. The point seems to be that the improvement in mortality permits a decline in the number of children sufficiently great that the births drop more than enough to offset the fall in mortality. Heer (1966) has applied simulation to this problem, and his more complex model produces an inverted U-curve in r.

Note that n, being the number of children, ought to be an integer, and if p is to be assured it ought to be the next higher integer to the expression on

Table 11.7 Rate of increase r of populations with values of l_{30} from 0.5 to 0.9 and probability p of at least one living son of 0.8 and 0.9; tabulation of (11.9.4)

l_{30}	$p = 0.8$	$p = 0.9$
0.5	0.0050	0.0169
0.6	0.0017	0.0137
0.7	-0.0022	0.0097
0.8	-0.0074	0.0045
0.9	-0.0155	-0.0035

the right-hand side of (11.9.3). For some combinations of high p and low l_{30} the n implied in (11.9.3) will be an impossibly large number of children. This does not apply, however, to the range shown in Table 11.7, for which 1 to 4 male children suffice.

Note that as l_{30} moves toward unity a discontinuity exists, for r goes steadily downward with $1 - l_{30}$ for any fixed value of p; but we know that $l_{30} = 1$ and $r = 0$ will provide with certainty the one child living at age 60 of the father. Evidently (11.9.4) is not to be taken seriously as mortality falls very low, or when other than small positive values of $n \geqslant 1$ are implied.

Chapter Twelve

EPILOGUE:
HOW DO WE KNOW THE FACTS
OF DEMOGRAPHY?

Demographers know that a slowly increasing population has a higher proportion of old people than one that is increasing rapidly, and that differences in birth rates have a larger influence on the age distribution than do differences in death rates. They often claim that a poor country whose population is growing rapidly will increase its per capita income faster if it lowers its birth rate rather than maintaining it at a high level.

How do demographers know these things? Many readers will be surprised to learn that in a science thought of as empirical and often criticized for its lack of theory the most important relations cannot be established by direct observation, which tends to provide enigmatic and inconsistent reports. Confrontation of data with theory is essential for correct interpretation of such relationships, even though on a particular issue it more often generates an agenda for further investigation than it yields useful knowledge. Much of this book is devoted to examining the ways in which demographers distill knowledge from observation and from theory. The present summing up shows a relatively heavy weight of evidence for theory, illustrated briefly with an application to economic demography. I am grateful to Paul Demeny for many improvements and clarifications in this account.

Let no one think that the questions of demography, and the issues of method for finding answers to them, are remote or purely abstract. The resolution of major policy issues of our time depends on the answers. How much of its development effort should a poor country put into birth control if it deems its rate of population growth excessive? Some would put nothing, in the expectation that rapid increase of income will by itself bring population under control. Once people have automobiles, once their countryside is paved over with roads, once enough air-conditioned houses are built, they will lower their fertility. But is this not a circuitous way of getting people to use pills and IUDs? Surely direct persuasion aimed at lowering fertility would help to reach desired developmental goals more quickly.

Any answer to such questions must take into account the degree to which a low rate of population increase promotes development and conversely. This is no simple matter. Figure 12.1 shows the relation between rates of population growth and increase of income per capita. Even the most imaginative viewer would hardly perceive the negative relationship that the dominant theory (later to be summarized) requires. In the pages ahead, the irregularity of empirical data as they appear in charts and tables will be repeatedly contrasted with the clear-cut mathematical relationships of the theory.

The theoretical approach can be described as "holding unmentioned variables constant"; the empirical, for example in the form of a regression between measured variables, as "allowing unmentioned variables to vary as they vary in actuality." The difference will be studied with an example

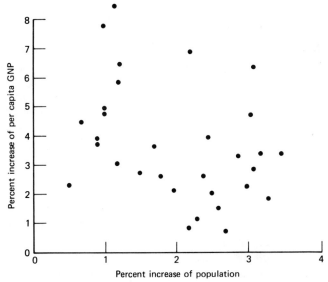

Fig. 12.1 Average annual increase of per capita gross national product and of population for countries with over 20 million population, 1960–72.

in which we think we know the true nature of the relationship between two variables.

12.1 GROWING POPULATIONS HAVE SMALLER PROPORTIONS OF OLD PEOPLE

The population of Mexico grows at 3.5 percent per year; its proportion of ages 65 and over is about 3 percent. The United States has been growing at less than 1 percent per year; its proportion 65 and over is about 10 percent. The relation can be expressed as a linear equation. For 1966 (Keyfitz and Flieger, 1971, pp. 344, 354) the four numbers are as follows:

Variable	Mexico	United States
Rate of natural increase (percent)	3.44	0.89
Percent aged 65 and over	3.31	9.42

Call the annual percentage rate of increase $100r$, and $100P_{65+}$ the percentage over age 65. Then the straight line from the 1966 information for the United States and Mexico is

$$P_{65+} = 0.116 - 2.40r,$$

which tells us that for each 1 percent by which the rate of increase is higher there is a decrease of 2.4 percent in the proportion aged 65 and over. With zero increase the percentage over 65 would be 11.6; with 3 percent increase it would be $11.6 - 7.2 = 4.4$ percent.

We should be able to obtain a more reliable result with a larger and more homogeneous group of countries, so let us try those of Latin America shown in Table 12.1. The regression is $P_{65+} = 0.0846 - 1.63r$. Apparently the more homogeneous group gives a less steep slope than do the United States and Mexico. Now each 1 percent increase in r is associated with a drop of 1.6 in P_{65+}—only two-thirds as much. A scatter diagram (Fig. 12.2) shows that we could have chosen two countries that would provide almost any given slope; if we wanted to show a positive rather than a negative relation, we could have taken Mexico and Brazil, or else Panama and Guatemala. Moreover, much of the overall negative correlation is due to three countries of the southern cap—Argentina, Uruguay, and Chile—that are culturally distinct from those farther north, along with Puerto Rico and Martinique. To exaggerate a little, it looks as though countries fall into two groups, those with low r and high P_{65+}, and those

Table 12.1   Proportion aged 65 and over and rate of natural increase, 18 Latin American countries

Country	Percent aged 65 and over $100P_{65+}$	Percent rate of natural increase $100r$
Argentina, 1964	6.05	1.40
Brazil, 1950	2.45	2.80
Chile, 1967	4.47	1.89
Colombia, 1964	3.00	2.85
Costa Rica, 1966	3.18	3.44
Dominican Republic, 1966	3.57	2.85
Ecuador, 1965	3.16	3.25
El Salvador, 1961	3.18	3.81
Guatemala, 1964	2.77	2.89
Honduras, 1966	1.76	3.55
Martinique, 1963	4.96	2.50
Mexico, 1966	3.31	3.44
Nicaragua, 1965	2.90	3.57
Panama, 1966	3.57	3.29
Peru, 1963	3.42	2.83
Puerto Rico, 1965	5.77	2.36
Uruguay, 1963	7.81	1.03
Venezuela, 1965	2.99	3.65

with high r and low P_{65+}. In short, much of the pertinent information was contained in the comparison of the United States and Mexico with which we started.

What about taking one country and following changes through time in the two variables? Sweden provides information over nearly 200 years, and also yields a very different regression from any obtained cross-sectionally.

The comparisons and regressions summarizing them are highly inconsistent in reporting how much difference in the proportion over 65 is to be associated with differences in the rate of increase. A large research project could be undertaken to see why they fail to agree; it might reveal that the changing mortality over 200 years in Sweden is confounded by the changing birth rate, or that the more homogeneous the group, the lower the correlation and the lower the slope of regression. It happens that in this instance no one will undertake such research because a simple theory is available that provides a better insight into the nature of the relationship between growth rate and age distribution. Let us use this theory to back off and take a fresh approach to the question.

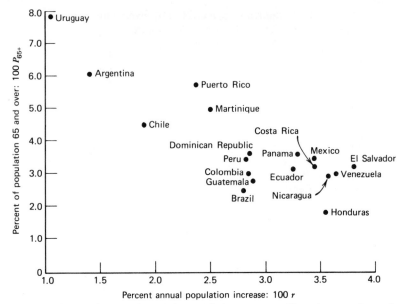

Fig. 12.2 Relation of proportion of the population over age 65 to the rate of population increase: 18 Latin American countries.

Older Population as a Function of Rate of Increase When All Else Is Constant

The approach is that of Chapter 4 above. Suppose that the fraction of births surviving to age x is given by a fixed survival function $l(x)$, and the annual rate of increase in births is r, so that compared with x years ago the number of births is now e^{rx} greater. Then for each present birth there were e^{-rx} births x years ago, and of these past births a fraction $l(x)$ have survived, the surviving persons being now aged x. Thus the number of present persons of age x must be $Be^{-rx}l(x)$, where B is the number of current births. This applies for all ages and suffices to specify the age distribution, as we saw in Chapter 4.

The expression for persons aged x will tell the relation between a fraction of the age distribution, on the one hand, and the rate of increase r on the other:

$$P_{65+} = \frac{\int_{65}^{\omega} e^{-rx} l(x)\, dx}{\int_{0}^{\omega} e^{-rx} l(x)\, dx}.$$

(12.1.1)

If $l(x)$ is fixed, (12.1.1) establishes P_{65+} as a function of r and of nothing else. The equation is not very instructive in this form, for we cannot easily see whether P_{65+} increases or decreases with r, let alone by how much.

Taking the logarithm and expanding the exponential provides a series of cumulants that are a good approximation to the full expression 12.1.1. Up to the first two terms we have, by the method of Chapter 4,

$$P_{65+} = \frac{\int_{65}^{\omega} l(x)\,dx}{\int_{0}^{\omega} l(x)\,dx}\exp\left[-(m_2 - m_1)r - (\sigma_1^2 - \sigma_2^2)\frac{r^2}{2}\right], \quad (12.1.2)$$

where m_2 is the mean and σ_2^2 the variance of those 65 and over, and m_1 the mean and σ_1^2 the variance of all, in the stationary population. With $m_2 - m_1 = 40$, and disregarding the square term, we have column 3 of Table 12.2; including the square term with $\sigma_1^2 = 400$ and $\sigma_2^2 = 130$, so that $(\sigma_1^2 - \sigma_2^2)/2 = 135$, gives column 4, which is a good fit, and it is based on little more data than a demographer carries in his head.

Table 12.2 Fraction over 65, P_{65+}, tabulated as a function of rate of increase r, and first and second approximations

r	P_{65+}	$0.1379e^{-40r}$	$0.1379e^{-40r-135r^2}$
(1)	(2)	(3)	(4)
0.000	0.1379	0.1379	0.1379
0.005	0.1140	0.1129	0.1125
0.010	0.0932	0.0924	0.0912
0.015	0.0753	0.0757	0.0734
0.020	0.0602	0.0620	0.0587
0.025	0.0477	0.0507	0.0466
0.030	0.0374	0.0415	0.0368
0.035	0.0291	0.0340	0.0288
0.040	0.0225	0.0278	0.0224

Based on mortality of Coale and Demeny (1966, p. 20) Model West Females, $\overset{o}{e}_0 = 65$

Such a theoretical relation largely escapes defects of the data. Another advantage of the theoretical approach is that we know exactly its assumptions. In this instance, our model specifies that the comparison be among populations closed to migration, with the same life table but different rates of increase, and that each of them have had births increasing exponentially during the lifetimes of persons now alive or, alternatively, have had fixed age-specific birth and death rates over a long past period. Consequently, this model does not tell anything about the change through time from one such condition to another; the trajectory from rapid increase to stationarity for a given population requires a more difficult kind of mathematics. That the theory here, like the comparative statics of economics, permits the comparison of stable conditions only is both a strength and a weakness.

Instead of supposing fixed rates in a closed population, the empirical regression takes into account migration, in whatever proportion it has been occurring in the populations whose data are included. Insofar as mortality has been falling, the influence of that fall is also incorporated. Thus it is a better description of the state of affairs covered by the data; it is a worse statement of the intrinsic relationship between the stated variables. If underlying conditions are the same in the future, the regression will predict more accurately; if they change substantially, the theory will be more dependable. If an underlying interference is caused by some known and measurable variable, the empirical regression can partial it out, and in this degree approach closer to theory.

In another aspect the regression inevitably depends on a data base, and that base is determined by what data are available. One can hardly apply sampling notions to it, since whether one takes countries or some other unit, the number of existing populations that are truly independent is small and predetermined for the observer, beyond any possibility of his arranging a randomized design. Moreover, data on many countries are lacking. Even if each entity describable as a nation could be thought of as providing independent evidence, and if all had good data, the collection of nations is not easy to conceptualize as a homogeneous universe.

This simple example shows how uncertain our knowledge would be if analytical tools like the stable model were not available. One can imagine methodological controversies, and schools of opinion, some perhaps taking the view that the relationships were really different for different races or different continents. One who has been through the theory would no sooner say that the underlying relationship between increase and age composition is different for different continents than he would say that the laws of thermodynamics so differ.

Are Births or Deaths Decisive?

The same stable model can help one to decide whether the age distribution of a population depends more on its births or on its deaths.

Venezuela in 1965 had a greater proportion of children plus old people than did Sweden in 1803–07. To compare a contemporary nonindustrialized country with one in the early nineteenth century reveals an aspect of the difference in the process of getting development launched then and now. A high dependency ratio (children under age 15 plus adults over 65 as a proportion of the number of working ages 15 to 65) is a disadvantage for development: Venezuela's dependency ratio in 1965 of 1.021 was 73 percent greater than Sweden's in 1803–07 of 0.589. One would like to know to what extent this was due to Venezuela's lower death rate and to what extent to its higher birth rate. No such decomposition is even conceivable, however, on the observed rates—they show what they show.

The stable model of Chapter 4, in which the number of persons aged x is proportional to $l(x)e^{-rx}$, allows one to synthesize dependency ratios from various combinations of birth and death rates:

Venezuelan births and Venezuelan deaths	1.021
Swedish births and Venezuelan deaths	0.703
Swedish births and Swedish deaths	0.589

as shown in Table 7.2. The effect of the birth rate when the death rate is constant is $1.021 - 0.703 = 0.318$; the effect of the death rate when the birth rate is constant is $0.703 - 0.589 = 0.114$; of the total difference of 0.432, the part due to births is about 74 percent, and that due to deaths about 26 percent.

We could alternatively have used as the intermediate term in the decomposition the dependency ratio with Swedish deaths and Venezuelan births, which is 0.856. The death effect would have been $1.021 - 0.856 = 0.165$, and the birth effect $0.856 - 0.589 = 0.267$. Now 62 percent of the difference is due to births, still the larger part. We can say that between 62 and 74 percent is due to births, the interval between these numbers being an interaction that cannot be allocated.

Any other feature of age can be similarly analyzed. Sweden's percentage under age 15 was 31.3, and Venezuela's 47.7; the combination of Swedish births and Venezuelan deaths would produce 34.2 percent. Hence, of the difference of 16.4 percentage points obtained as $47.7 - 31.3$ only 2.9 ($= 34.2 - 31.3$) is due to deaths and 13.5—over 4 times as much—to births.

12.2 PROMOTION IN ORGANIZATIONS

Everyone knows that in a fast-growing organization promotion is likely to be faster than in one growing slowly. Neither elaborate empirical data nor a model is required to demonstrate that bare fact. What one would like to know is the quantitative relation: in a fast-growing organization does one advance to a middle position a few months sooner than in a slow-growing one, or several years sooner?

We can imagine collecting a great volume of data to settle this point. The survey organizer would have to give attention to the universe of organizations from which he proposed to sample—perhaps he would settle on all commercial, transport, and manufacturing firms in the United States. He would have to define the boundaries of each organization, whether it included all establishments constituting a firm or whether each establishment was to be considered a separate organization. A lower limit would have to be set on the size of organization considered, say 100 employees. One would want to distinguish family-run enterprises, since the conditions for promotion in these would certainly be different. If a one-time survey was to be made, the information on promotion would have to be obtained retrospectively, with the errors of recollection that this entails. On the other hand, a succession of surveys that statistically followed careers of individuals would take time and be expensive. Many decisions would have to be made to establish the universe and to conduct the sampling operation within it.

Moreover, when the results were in we would notice that in some organizations there were many resignations, so that promotion was rapid for personnel that remained; indeed, this effect might be strong enough to hide the effect of growth. We would have to classify organizations into homogeneous groups according to their turnover, or else obtain an index of turnover for each and use regression analysis to partial it out. This is only one of many disturbing elements that could be expected to make the results, so painstakingly obtained, uncertain in interpretation in relation to the question to which an answer is being sought.

A simpler approach that avoids the errors to which a survey is subject is to compare the number of employees ahead of a representative individual —let us call him Ego—in a fast-growing and in a slow-growing organization, as if promotion depended only on age. Superimposed on individual ability, assiduity, influence, luck, and all the other elements that determine promotion in the real world is the pure effect of organizational growth on individual careers, and that is what we want to ascertain. That effect can be studied by use of a suitable model as we saw in Section 4.8.

First suppose a given schedule of survival—knowing that the deaths of his contemporaries help Ego's promotion, we do not want differences in mortality to cloud our analysis. Then suppose an age distribution that is a function only of this survival function and rate of increase, so that the stable model is applicable. Finally, take as the arbitrary benchmark for measurement the age at which individuals arrive at a level where one-half of their fellow-workers are below them and one-half above, say a junior supervisory position.

After that, the simple mathematics of Section 4.8 shows that, for given rates of death or resignation, the age x at which Ego reaches such a position is shortened by two-thirds of a product of three factors:

1.   The time from age x to retirement, discounted at the rate of population increase.
2.   The difference between the mean age of the group senior to the point of promotion considered, and the mean age of those junior to it. This difference cannot be far from half of the length of working life.
3.   Increase of the rate of increase of the population.

With an entry age of 20 and a retirement age of 65, comparison of two populations whose increase differs by Δr percent gives for the difference in ages

$$\Delta x = -\left(\tfrac{2}{3}\right)(15)(22.5)\Delta r = -225r.$$

Thus the time of promotion is delayed by 2.25 years for each 1 percent by which population growth is lower. This demographic factor is overlaid on all individual differences of ability, influence, and luck. Although the model is based on pure seniority, some such effect will apply if any element of seniority is present. Only if length of service in the organization is wholly disregarded in promotion will the model be irrelevant.

12.3   NO MODEL, NO UNDERSTANDING

A large volume of data is on hand regarding breast cancer. Despite stepped-up efforts to deal with it, expensive operations and other forms of treatment, and widespread publicity urging women to examine themselves and to see their doctors at once if there is any suspicion, the increase in deaths from breast cancer is considerable in North America and Western Europe, just where the most intensive therapeutic effort is being made. Breast cancer is the leading cause of death for women aged 35 to 54 and second only to heart disease for older ages. Some of the increase may be due to more awareness and hence more frequent diagnosis now than in the past, and to better diagnosis in America and Europe than in Asia and Latin America, but apparently this is not the whole cause. Women who bear children early seem to have a lower risk of breast cancer, but no one thinks that having children—early or late—can prevent the disease or account for the differences. Breast cancer is less common in warm climates and among poor populations, but that warm climate or poverty is a preventive seems unlikely.

Such statistical differentials will continue to be unsolved puzzles until someone comes along with a model that explains the differences. In the meantime, all that can be done is to continue gathering data to discriminate among proposed models.

The ratio of male to female births is a similar case, in that there is no obvious model, and no clear-cut result has so far emerged from differentials and correlations. We know that births to young mothers have a higher sex ratio (males to females) than births to older ones, that first births to mothers have a higher sex ratio than later births, and that children of young fathers have a higher sex ratio than children of older fathers. But among age of mother, parity of mother, and age of father, which is the effective cause. The high intercorrelations among the possible causes make it difficult to distinguish. Mechanisms have been suggested involving the relative activity and viability of sperm producing male and female babies, but until some such mechanism is shown to be the operative one, our knowledge is tentative and uncertain.

12.4 TOO MANY MODELS

India and some other countries have raised the legal age of marriage, partly with the aim of lowering the birth rate. Implicit in the thinking of legislators and others is a theory in which marital fertility age for age is relatively fixed, and a legal minimum age effectively eliminates the part of the fertility curve below the age specified. Given the curve, the amount of effect is easily calculated. Our sample survey data for India show that, of 18.14 million births in 1961, some 3.24 million or 18 percent were to mothers under age 20 years (Keyfitz and Flieger, 1968, p. 659).

This seems a potentially powerful argument for restriction of marriage, supposing it feasible to raise the age as high as 20 for women. But before one reaches a firm conclusion, it ought to be noted that on an opposite model raising age at marriage would be wholly ineffective.

Suppose that married couples are not reproducing to the maximum, but that they want a certain number of children, and will have later what the law forbids them to have sooner. After all, the birth rate of India is now under 40 per thousand, well below the physiologically possible maximum. Under these circumstances, the only gain from a legal minimum age for marriage would be a delay of a few years that would lengthen the time separating successive generations and hence lower the average annual increase, but by a small amount. Illegitimacy is also a problem; it is low in India, but one of the reasons parents want their daughters married early is to avoid their engaging in premarital sex. If the parents' fears are not altogether imaginary, there could be some increase in the number of children born outside of marriage.

Yet these arguments are in the end unconvincing; one has the impression that couples that lose time before they are 20 may make up some part of the lost ground but not all, and that extramarital fertility would remain low. To determine the net drop in overall fertility as a result of the restriction, behavioral data would be required. These alone can discriminate between the competing models and predict the quantitative effects of an induced change in age at marriage.

12.5 EFFECT OF DEVELOPMENT ON POPULATION INCREASE

This brief chapter is not the place to consider intricate issues of population economics, which is an entire academic discipline having scores of specialists, a literature running to many hundreds of articles and books, and its own lines of cleavage and of controversy. It is worth saying here only enough to show that both theoretical and empirical methods are applied in this field, and that, notwithstanding their extensive and skilled use, much remains to be done in disentangling the lines of causation. The literature speaks of "development" as the socioeconomic transformation into the modern condition, and of "income" as sufficiently correlated with development to be used as a proxy.

First, in regards to the effect of development on population, a quick look at cases suggests a familiar negative relationship, with which theory conforms. Development seems sooner or later to have brought a reduction in population growth in all the instances where it has occurred. All of the rich countries have low birth rates today, and the very richest are not replacing themselves. For example, West Germany had fewer births than deaths in 1973, and in 1974 it had fewer births plus net immigrants than deaths, so that its population actually declined. But the countries of Eastern Europe are much less rich, and they also have low birth rates, while in Britain the birth rate first started to fall almost a century after development was under way. Thus the correlation is not perfect, but still history seems to be saying that, with more or less lag, industrialization has led to reduced family size.

In theory this may be due to women finding jobs and sources of prestige outside the home, so that they do not need to rely on childbearing for their standing, and to children being, on the one hand, more expensive and, on the other, less directly useful to their parents as income increases, both effects being related to the decline of the family as a productive unit with the growth of industry. As contraception is made easier and more available, relatively weak motivation suffices to cut the birth rate. What we ought to believe in this matter, summed up in the concept of demographic transition, is relatively unambiguous because the dominant theories and the most conspicuous anecdotal evidence all point the same way.

Yet even here, the more closely and systematically scholars have looked at the data, the less clear they have found the effect of development on family size. Taking income as a proxy for development, Adelman (1963) made "an analysis of fertility and mortality patterns as they are affected by economic and social forces." Her materials, based mostly on national statistics for 1953, showed a decidedly *positive* relation between income and fertility. Friedlander and Silver (1967) partialed out more variables, and found that for developed nations fertility and income are positively related, but for less developed nations the relation is negative. Heer (1966) calculated correlations for 41 countries that suggested that the direct effect of economic development is to increase fertility, and the indirect effects (through education, and so on) are to reduce it. But it makes a difference when the data for the 24 less developed countries are separated from those for the 17 more developed and more than one point of time is introduced, so that changes rather than levels are correlated. Ekanem (1972) used two points of time, the 1950 decade and the 1960 decade, but the effect of his greater care seems to be a less clear-cut result than Heer's. Again, Janowitz (1971) followed five European countries and found that variables shifted enough through time so that the longitudinal relations, more likely to indicate causation, are decidedly different from the cross-sectional regressions.

It would be unkind to say that these efforts constitute raw empiricism. They are oriented by an economic theory: that increased affluence causes people to buy more of most things, the exceptions being labeled inferior goods. Since no one considers children inferior goods, many argue that children and income "really" are positively related, but the relation is concealed by the intervention of other factors. The better-off have access to contraceptives of which the poor are ignorant; the better-off have higher quality (i.e., more expensive) children and so can afford fewer of them (Becker, 1960; Leibenstein, 1974).

12.6 EFFECT OF POPULATION GROWTH ON DEVELOPMENT

The writers cited above were trying to find the impact of development on fertility, a situation where, despite some complications and contradictions, causation seems clearer than in the inverse problem: in which direction and to what extent does rapid population growth affect development? Among all the questions that demographers seek to answer, this last is the one that is truly important for policy.

In the classic theory rapid growth means many children—40 percent or more of the population under age 15. The children have to be fed, clothed, and educated, and however the cost is divided between parents and the state, it requires resources that compete with industrial and other investments. In addition, children grow up and want jobs, and hence growth requires that a larger labor force be provided with capital goods. Thus a fast-growing population is doubly handicapped.

So much for the static aspect of the demographic–economic relationship. In regards to dynamics, when fertility falls from an initially high level, the dependency ratio begins to shift immediately in an economically favorable direction. Thus investment can be greater than it was before. Lagging 15 or 20 years behind is a longer-run dynamic effect: a slackening of the growth of the population in the labor force ages. When relatively fewer children grow up to enter these ages, there is less competition for productive jobs and each entrant may have more capital to work with than if the birth rate had not been cut (Coale and Hoover, 1958).

All this is based on the view that development is capital-limited rather than resource-limited. But if it is resource-limited, population is an even more serious consideration, although now the absolute level of population is of concern rather than the birth rate; the more people, the less resources at the disposal of each, on a theory dating back to John Stuart Mill and ultimately to Malthus. In the most general statement, certain ratios of labor to the other factors of production—land and capital—are more favorable than others, and most developing countries are moving away from the optimum with present population sizes and birth rates.

How would matters stand if no theory had ever been presented? Let us try to wipe theory out of our minds, and look at the data with complete naiveté. Among developing countries, Pakistan is increasing at over 3 percent and India at less than 2.5 percent, yet Pakistan seems to be making more economic progress. Iran's rate of population increase is much greater than Nepal's, and so is its economic advance. Brazil and Venezuela are not increasing in population less rapidly than their economically stagnant neighbors; indeed, Argentina and Chile, with very low birth rates, may be becoming poorer absolutely. Mexico is advancing economically with an annual population increase of 3.5 percent per year, one of the highest in the world and higher than that in Paraguay or Bolivia, where economic dynamism is absent. On the other hand, sub-Saharan Africa has high rates of population increase and low income growth. Figure 12.1 depicts the broad array of relationships between population growth and increase in income for large countries in the contemporary world. As noted at the start of this chapter, the relation that theory predicts is not at all evident.

It makes a difference if we compare birth rates rather than natural increase, and for the theory, births less infant deaths might be the best indicator of the economic impact. But whatever measure is used, the inverse correlation with economic dynamism simply does not appear.

Of course individual countries can be analyzed, and by making allowance for such nonpopulation aspects as leadership, political conditions, the educational system, religion, and the dissolving of patrimonial social relations as expressed in landholding and other ways, along with resource endowment, we need not be at a loss to account for the observed national differences. This explanation a posteriori can be made to sustain the theory, but hardly answers a disturbing question: to what extent would naive examination of population and income data for the poor countries of the world have revealed any clear effect of population on development? Would the effect have been as blurred as the effect of population increase on age distribution?

It is just this incapacity of the raw data to speak for themselves that permits some to argue that population and its growth do not harm development and should be allowed to take care of themselves. One might expect the facts to silence anyone who could utter such opinions, but as presented either anecodotally as above or in simple correlations they do not. To make the facts speak clearly to this issue is not easy.

12.7   HOW NATURE COVERS HER TRACKS

The reason for bringing these very difficult matters into the present exposition is the hope that their investigation can be aided by going back to some simpler issues, like the relation between age distribution and the rate of increase of a population. In that case most would agree that theory gives the right answer: the rate of increase determines the proportion of old persons (as well as middle-aged and young) in the population. Where the relationship is obscured by migration or by changing birth and death rates, as it commonly is, these are seen as mere disturbances. Such "noise" could drown out the relationship in the observed data without weakening our conviction that the relationship is "really" as stable theory says it is. Up to this point stable theory has the immutability of the laws of logic: if over a sufficient period of time death rates are the same in two populations, the one with the higher birth rate will have the lower proportion at older ages. Belief in this is unshaken by the fact that El Salvador is higher than Honduras both in rate of population increase and in percentage over age 65. A supporter of the theory would convincingly argue that the official data must be wrong (perhaps registration of births is differentially incomplete), or there has been age-selective migration, or some other reason underlies the discrepancy between expected and observed relationships.

Although stable theory can never be disproved, it could be deprived of all interest if in the real world certain things that it assumes constant were in fact steadily changing. If death rates were always falling at a certain pace, the proportion of old people would everywhere be different from that given by stable theory, and a different theory would be required for interpreting reality. Any steady change that was universal would make us want to replace stable theory with its fixed rates by some other, inevitably more complicated, theory that would have equal force of logic but be more applicable. In fact, change is not so uniform under different real conditions, but is rather erratic, a means by which nature covers up her mechanisms, rendering their interpretation less amenable to a universal theory.

But change, whether steady or erratic, is not the means by which the mechanisms of nature are most effectively concealed. More deceiving is the clinging together of variables. Suppose all countries of natural growth were countries of emigration, so that they lost their young people to countries of slower growth; then the conclusion derived from the application of stable theory would be downright misleading. We would want some other theory, perhaps one on which populations tend to spread out evenly in relation to resources. Such a view is held regarding internal migration, where free movement occurs and people go to distant places unless they are attracted to intervening opportunities (Stouffer, 1940).

The Oblique Use of Data to Challenge Theory

How then can the classical theory that rapid population growth checks development be challenged? The matter is important because a theory that is immune to challenge has little value for science.

One way is by declaring that there is a trend toward development everywhere in the world, as well as a trend toward smaller families, and that the latter makes no difference to the former. Suppose that the trend to development occurs everywhere sooner or later and nothing can either stop it or hasten it. On this comfortable view of development as immanent in human history no detailed causal theory would be possible, and no policy measures would be sought or needed. Such a view is not entirely absent from contemporary discussion, although by its very nature little evidence can be summoned for or against it.

Another direction of attack is to adduce evidence that enterprising personalities are more often born into large families and to show quantitatively that this greater enterprise is sufficient to overcome the capital and land shortage caused by the large family's propensity to consume. Or else that couples with more children have a greater incentive to save and so increase investment funds. Or else that having many children indeed increases consumption but fathers of large families work correspondingly harder to offset this. All of these are statements on the individual level that there is a sticking together of the variables concerned with development—population growth, motivation to work, motivation to save. Nothing in logic proves that such sticking together does not occur, but it is the obligation of anyone who challenges the theory to adduce evidence.

On the national level, the countries that are developing may be the ones in which the authorities are development minded and persuade their people to make sacrifices that more than offset the disadvantages of population increase. Again, evidence bearing on this specific point would be required.

To take an example that, alas, may not be entirely unrealistic, if dictatorial technocratic regimes are effective in producing development, and if these are lukewarm about population control, the population effect might be dominated by the dictator effect. But one would give up the classical theory only if there were shown to be some necessary relationship between technocratic dictators and development, on the one hand, and dictators and large families, on the other. Otherwise one would still have to insist that the dictator was paying a price for population growth, and the price could be avoided.

Why, then, does the failure of a correlation-type approach to show that development follows a slowing of population growth present no challenge to the theory? Certainly a purely cross-sectional analysis can at best be suggestive of propositions concerning longitudinal changes, and proves nothing concerning them. Aside from this, the major difficulty is that many other factors affect the correlations. In principle, the disturbing factor of "motivation to work" or "making sacrifices" could be partialed out or held constant while the relation of population to development was examined. Yet, even if one or two disturbing factors could be identified and measured, many others would remain. And to partial out a number of variables simultaneously raises logical difficulties if any of them is correlated with the independent variable of interest.

Nonetheless, empirical data have to be applied to verify theory, and such application is the heart of demography, as of any other science, but data must be brought to bear in an oblique fashion. If we are going to detect nature's hidden mechanisms, we need a subtlety that approaches hers. An attack by directly correlating the variables of immediate interest is less promising than a search to determine what other subsidiary variables stick to them. This applies equally to the analysis of age distribution, the effects of age at marriage on the birth rate, and population and development.

12.8   THE PSYCHOLOGY OF RESEARCH

A footnote concerning the mental conditions in which research occurs may help to illuminate the way we get to know the facts of demography. Faced with a variety of data, the investigator listlessly surveys them, in the hope of somehow tying them together. He is swamped by the multiplicity of observations and tries to fit them into a scheme, if only to economize his own limited memory. He becomes more animated when he sees that some general connections do subsist in the data, and that a model, however crude, helps him to keep their relationships in mind. The model is much more than a mnemonic device, however; it is a machine with causal linkages. Insofar as it reflects the real world, it suggests how levers can be moved to alter direction in accord with policy requirements. The question is always how closely this constructed machine resembles the one operated by nature. As the investigator concentrates on its degree of realism, he more and more persuades himself that his model is a theory of how the world operates.

But now he is frustrated—he has just turned up an incontrovertible observation that is wholly inconsistent with his theory. Such an observation is a stubborn fact, an exception to the theory that cannot be avoided or disregarded. A struggle ensues as the investigator attempts to force the theory to embrace the exception. As his efforts prove vain, he questions the theory, and looks back again at the raw data whose complexity he thought he had put behind him. The intensity of the struggle that follows is one of the hallmarks of scientific activity and distinguishes it from mindless collecting of data, on the one hand, and complacent theorizing on the other.

The problem and its possible solutions have now taken possession of the investigator. In this phase of research his unconscious is enmeshed and is working on the question day and night. Sleep is difficult or impossible; eating and the daily round of life are petty diversions. He is irritable and distracted. Whatever he does, the contradiction he has uncovered comes into his mind, and stands between him and any normal kind of life.

During the struggle the investigator is like a person with high fever. Then with luck he comes on the answer, or his unconscious does. He finds a model that fits, perhaps nearly perfectly, perhaps only tolerably, but well enough to provide a handle on the varied data. His tension relaxes, and he proceeds with the normal and dull work of establishing the details of the fit and presenting his results. He must indeed revert to a calmer state before he can hope to communicate his finding to an audience that is perfectly normal. An immediate test of his result will be whether it makes sense to his contemporaries; an ultimate test is whether it can predict outcomes involving data not taken into account in the establishment of the model.

Only with exceptional good fortune will one cycle of feverish concern produce a final theory and permit immediate relaxation. More often a long series of false starts and disappointments will precede the resolution. Sometimes the problem turns out to be unsolvable in the existing state of knowledge or is beyond the capacity of the investigator, and then he has the unhappy task of winding himself down without the desired denouement.

None of the psychological accompaniment of scientific production is special to demography, but this field may show it in heightened form, at least in comparison with other social sciences. The abundant data of demography cause an inappropriate theory or an erroneous prediction to stand out more clearly than a corresponding failure in interpreting history or in the general analysis of society. When the possibility of a sharp rejection by hard data is lacking, the game of research loses its seriousness —it is like playing solitaire with rules that are adjustable to the cards that appear.

Mathematical demography has become too big a field to be covered in one book, or even to be effectively summarized. Many important themes are omitted altogether from the foregoing, and many others are treated much too summarily. More extensive theory is available than has been included, and (a much graver omission) only a minute fraction of the data bearing on the issues raised has been brought under examination. What points are made in the book had best be considered as examples of the ideas and methods of the subject. A full and systematic account remains to be written.

BIBLIOGRAPHY

Adelman, Irma. 1963. An econometric analysis of population growth. *American Economic Review* **53**: 314–339.

Agnew, Robert A. 1972. Crude confidence interval estimates for future U.S. population levels. Letter in *The American Statistician*, February, pp. 47–48.

Alonso, William. 1972. Problems, purposes, and implicit policies for a national strategy of urbanization. In *Population, Distribution, and Policy*, edited by S. M. Mazie, pp. 635–647. U.S. Commission on Population Growth and the American Future. Washington, D.C.: U.S. Government Printing Office.

Alonso, William. 1975. A general framework for migration. Unpublished manuscript.

Anderson, Henry. 1971. The sample period in economic prediction, *The American Statistician* **25**: 46–50.

Arriaga, Eduardo A. 1968. *New Life Tables for Latin American Populations in the Nineteenth and Twentieth Centuries*. Population Monograph Series No. 3. Berkeley, Calif.: Institute of International Studies.

Barlow, R. E., and Proschan, F. 1964. *Mathematical Theory of Reliability*. New York: John Wiley & Sons.

Barlow, R. E., and Saboia, J. L. M. 1973. The use of reliability notions to make predictions and establish bounds for population growth. In *Reliability and Biometry: Statistical Analysis of Lifelength*, edited by Frank Proschan and R. J. Serfling. Philadelphia: SIAM.

Barrett, J. D., and Marshall, J. 1969. The risk of conception on different days of the menstrual cycle. *Population Studies* **23**: 455–461.

Bartholomew, David J. 1967. *Stochastic Models for Social Processes*. New York: John Wiley & Sons.

Bartlett, M. S. 1960. *Stochastic Population Models in Ecology and Epidemiology*. London: Methuen.

Bartlett, M. S. 1962. *An Introduction to Stochastic Processes, with Special Reference to Methods and Applications*. Cambridge, England: University Press.

Beckenbach, Edwin, and Bellman, Richard. 1961. *An Introduction to Inequalities*. New York: Random House.

Becker, Gary S. 1960. An economic analysis of fertility. In *Demographic and Economic Change in Developed Countries*, edited by Ansley J. Coale. Princeton, N.J.: Princeton University Press.

Bernardelli, Harro. 1941. Population waves. *Journal of Burma Research Society* **31**: 1–18.

369

Berry, B. J. L. 1973. *Growth Centers in the American Urban System*, Vol. 1. Cambridge, Mass.: Ballinger.

Blumen, I., Kogan, M., and McCarthy, P. J. 1955. *The Industrial Mobility of Labor as a Probability Process*. Vol. VI of Cornell Studies of Industrial and Labor Relations. Ithaca, N.Y.: Cornell University Press.

Boldrini, Marcello. 1956. *Demografia*. Revised Edition. Milan: Dott. A. Giuffre.

Boldrini, M. 1928. *Lezioni di Demografia*. Milan: Tipografia Mariani.

Bourgeois-Pichat, Jean. 1958. Utilisation de la notion de population stable pour mesurer la mortalité et la fécondité des populations des pays sous-développés [Using the concept of a stable population for measuring mortality and fertility in underdeveloped countries]. *Bulletin de l'Institut International de Statistique* (Stockholm) **36**: 94–121.

Bortkiewicz, L. V. 1911. Die Sterbeziffer und der Frauenüberschuss in der stationären und in der progressiven Bevölkerung. *Bulletin de l'Institut International de Statistique* **19**: 63–183.

Bowley, A. L. 1924. Births and population of Great Britain. *Journal of the Royal Economic Society* **34**: 188–192.

Brass, William. 1953. The derivation of fertility and reproduction rates from restricted data on reproductive histories. *Population Studies* **7**: 137–166.

Brass, William. 1963. The construction of life tables from child survivorship ratios. In *International Population Conference (IUSSP) New York, 1961: Proceedings*, Vol. 1, pp. 294–301. London: International Union for the Study of Population.

Brass, William. 1971a. A critique of methods for estimating population growth in countries with limited data. *Bulletin of the International Statistical Institute* **44**: 397–412.

Brass, William. 1971b. On the scale of mortality. In *Biological Aspects of Demography*, edited by William Brass, pp. 69–110. London: Taylor and Francis.

Brass, William. 1974. Perspectives in population prediction, illustrated by the statistics of England and Wales. *Journal of the Royal Statistical Society*, Series A: General **137**: 532–583.

Brass, William. 1975. *Methods for Estimating Fertility and Mortality from Limited and Defective Data*. An Occasional Publication. Chapel Hill: The University of North Carolina at Chapel Hill, International Program of Laboratories for Population Statistics.

Brass, William, et al., Editors, 1968a. *The Demography of Tropical Africa*. Princeton, N.J.: Princeton University Press.

Brass, William, and Coale, Ansley J. 1968b. Methods of analysis and estimation. In *The Demography of Tropical Africa*, edited by William Brass et al., pp. 88–142. Princeton, N.J.: Princeton University Press.

Burch, T. K. 1970. Some demographic determinants of average household size: An analytic approach. *Demography* **7**: 61–70.

Burks, Barbara S. 1933. Statistical method for estimating the distribution of sizes of completed fraternities in a population represented by a random sampling of individuals. *Journal of the American Statistical Association* **28**: 388–394.

Cannan, E. 1895. The probability of cessation of the growth of population in England and Wales during the next century. *Economic Journal* **5**: 505–515.

Chiang, C. L. 1968. *Introduction to Stochastic Processes in Biostatistics*. New York: John Wiley & Sons.

Cho, Lee-Jay. 1972. On estimating annual birth rates from census data on children. In *Proceedings of the Social Statistics Section, 1971*, pp. 86–96. Washington, D.C.: American Statistical Association.

Clark, R. L., and Spengler, Joseph J. 1976. Changing demography and dependency costs. Unpublished manuscript.

Coale, Ansley. 1956. The effects of changes in mortality and fertility on age composition. *Milbank Memorial Fund Quarterly* **34**: 79–114.

Coale, Ansley J. 1957. A new method for calculating Lotka's *r*—the intrinsic rate of growth in a stable population. *Population Studies* **11**: 92–94.

Coale, Ansley J. 1963. Estimates of various demographic measures through the quasi-stable age distribution. In *Emerging Techniques in Population Research* (39th Annual Conference of the Milbank Memorial Fund, 1962), pp. 175–193. New York: Milbank Memorial Fund.

Coale, Ansley J. 1965. Appendix: Estimates of average size of household. In Ansley J. Coale et al., *Aspects of the Analysis of Family Structure*, pp. 64–69. Princeton, N.J.: Princeton University, Office of Population Research.

Coale, Ansley J. 1968. Convergence of a human population to a stable form. *Journal of the American Statistical Association*, **63**: 395–435.

Coale, Ansley J. 1971. Age patterns of marriage, *Population Studies* **25**: 193–214.

Coale, Ansley J. 1972. *The Growth and Structure of Human Populations: A Mathematical Investigation*. Princeton, N.J.: Princeton University Press.

Coale, Ansley J. 1973a. The demographic transition reconsidered. *International Population Conference, Liege*. International Union for the Scientific Study of Population.

Coale, Ansley J. 1973b. Age composition in the absence of mortality and in other odd circumstances. *Demography* **10**: 537–542.

Coale, Ansley J., and Demeny, Paul. 1966. *Regional Model Life Tables and Stable Populations*. Princeton, N.J.: Princeton University Press.

Coale, Ansley J., and Demeny, Paul. 1967. *Method of Estimating Basic Demographic Measures from Incomplete Data*. Manuals on Methods of Estimating Population, Manual 4. ST/SOA/Series A/42. New York: United Nations.

Coale, Ansley J., and Hoover, Edgar M. 1958. *Population Growth and Economic Development in Low-Income Countries: A Case Study of India's Prospects*. Princeton, N.J.: Princeton University Press.

Coale, Ansley J., and McNeil, D. R. 1972. Distribution by age of the frequency of first marriage in a female cohort. *Journal of the American Statistical Association* **67**: 743–749.

Coale, Ansley J., and Trussell, T. James. 1974. Model fertility schedules: Variations in the age structure of childbearing in human populations. *Population Index* **40**: 185–258.

Coale, Ansley J., and Zelnik, M. 1963. *New Estimates of Fertility and Population in the United States*. Princeton, N.J.: Princeton University Press.

Cohen, Joel E. 1973. Economic evaluation of small changes in the life table. Paper presented at Conference of International Union for the Scientific Study of Population, Liege.

Cole, Lamont. 1954. The population consequences of life history phenomena. *Quarterly Review of Biology* **19**: 103–137.

Coleman, James S. 1973. Loss of power. *American Sociological Review* **38**: 1–17.

Cook, Robert C., Editor. 1962. How many people have ever lived on earth? *Population Bulletin* **18**: 1–19.

Coombs, C. H., Coombs, L. C., and McClelland, G. H. 1975. Preference scales for number and sex of children. *Population Studies* **29**: 273–298.

Correa, Hector. 1967. A survey of mathematical models in educational planning. In *Mathe-*

matical Models in Educational Planning. Technical Report. Paris: Organization for Economic Co-operation and Development.

Cramer, James. 1972. Personal communication.

Das Gupta, Prithwis. 1976. Age–parity–nuptiality-specific stable population model that recognizes births to single women. *Journal of the American Statistical Association* **71**: 308–314.

David, P. A. 1974. Fortune, risk, and the microeconomics of migration. In *Nations and Households in Economic Growth*, edited by P. A. David and M. W. Reder, pp. 21–88. New York: Academic Press.

Deevey, Edward S., Jr. 1950. (1974) The probability of death. *Scientific American.* Reprinted in *Readings from Scientific American*, edited by Edward O. Wilson, pp. 106–108. San Francisco: W. H. Freeman, 1973.

Demeny, Paul. 1965. Estimation of vital rates for populations in process of destabilization. *Demography* **2**: 516–530.

Demetrius, Lloyd. 1971. Primitivity conditions for growth matrices. *Mathematical Biosciences* **12**: 53–58.

Demetrius, Lloyd. 1976. Measures of variability in age-structured populations, *Journal of Theoretical Biology* **61**: (To appear).

Dobbernack, W., and G. Tietz. 1940. Die Entwicklung von Personengesamtheiten vom Standpunkt der Sozialversicherungstechnik, *Twelfth International Congress of Actuaries* **4**: 233–253.

Dorn, Harold F. 1950. Pitfalls in population forecasts and projections. *Journal of the American Statistical Association* **45**: 311–334.

Easterlin, Richard A. 1961. The baby boom in perspective. *American Economic Review* **51**: 869–911.

Easterlin, Richard A. 1966. On the relation of economic factors to recent and projected fertility changes. *Demography* **3**: 131–153.

Easterlin, Richard A. 1968. The current fertility decline and projected fertility changes. Chapter 5 in *Population, Labor Force, and Long Swings in Economic Growth: The American Experience.* New York: Columbia University Press.

Ehrlich, Paul R., and Ehrlich, Anne H. 1972. *Population, Resources, Environment: Issues in Human Ecology.* Second Edition. San Francisco: W. H. Freeman.

Ekanem, Ita. 1972. A further note on the relation between economic development and fertility. *Demography* **9**: 383–398.

Espenshade, Thomas J. 1975. The stable decomposition of the rate of natural increase. *Theoretical Population Biology* **8**: 97–115.

Euler, L. 1760. Recherches générales sur la mortalité et la multiplication [General researches on mortality and multiplication]. *Mémoires de l'Académie Royale des Sciences et Belles Lettres* **16**: 144–164. Translated by Nathan and Beatrice Keyfitz. *Theoretical Population Biology* **1**: 307–314, 1970.

Feeney, Griffith. 1970. Stable age by region distributions. *Demography* **7**: 341–348.

Feeney, Griffith. 1973. Two models for multiregional population dynamics. *Environment and Planning* **5**: 31–43.

Feichtinger, G. 1971. Stochastische Modelle demographischer Prozesse. In *Lecture Notes in Operations Research and Mathematical Systems*, Vol. 44, edited by M. Beckmann and H. P. Künzi). Berlin: Springer.

Bibliography

Feichtinger, G. 1972. Markoff-Modelle zur sozialen Mobilität, *Jahrbuch für Sozialwissenschaft.*

Feldstein, Martin. 1976. The social security fund and national capital accumulation. Paper presented at the Federal Reserve Bank of Boston conference on "Funding Pensions: The Issues and Implications for Financial Markets."

Feller, W. 1941. On the integral equation of renewal theory. *Annals of Mathematical Statistics* **12**: 243–267.

Feller, W. 1957. *An Introduction to Probability Theory and Its Applications*, Vol. 1. Second Edition. New York: John Wiley & Sons. Vol. 2 1971.

Fisher, R. A. 1930 (republished 1958). *The Genetical Theory of Natural Selection.* New York: Dover Publications.

Flieger, Wilhelm. 1967. A re-examination of the demographic transition in the light of newly collected data. PhD. dissertation, Department of Sociology, University of Chicago.

Foerster, H. v., Mora, P. M., and Amiot, L. W. 1960. Doomsday: Friday, 13 November, A.D. 2026. *Science* **132**: 1291–1295.

Foerster, H. v. 1959. In *The Kinetics of Cellular Proliferation*, F. Stohlman, Jr., Ed. New York: Grune and Stratton.

Fredrickson, A. G. 1971. A mathematical theory of age-structure in sexual populations. *Mathematical Biosciences* **10**: 117–143.

Freeman, Harry. 1962. *Finite Differences for Actuarial Students.* Cambridge, England: University Press.

Frejka, Tomas. 1973. *The Future of Population Growth: Alternative Paths to Equilibrium.* New York: John Wiley & Sons.

Friedlander, Stanley, and Silver, Morris. 1967. A quantitative study of the determinants of fertility behavior. *Demography* **4**: 30–70.

Frisch, Rose E. 1972. Weight at menarche: Similarity for well-nourished and undernourished girls at differing ages, and evidence for historical constancy. *Pediatrics* **50**: 445–450.

Frobenius, G. 1912. Uber Matrizen aus nicht negativen Elementen. *Sitzungsberichte Preussischer Akademie*, 456–477.

Fuchs, Wilhelm. 1951. Über die Zahl der Menschen die bisher gelebt haben. *Zeitschrift für die gesamte Staatswissenschaft* **107**: 440–450.

Galton, F., and Watson, H. W. 1874. On the probability of extinction of families. *Journal of the Anthropological Institute* **6**: 138–144.

Gilbert, John P., and Hammel, E. A. 1966. Computer simulation and analysis of problems in kinship and social structure. *American Anthropologist* **68**: 71–93.

Gini, C. 1924. Premières recherches sur la fécondabilité de la femme [Preliminary research on female fertility]. In *Proceedings of the International Mathematics Congress*, Vol. 2, pp. 889–892.

Glass, David V., and Grebenik, E. 1954. *The Trend and Pattern of Fertility in Great Britain: A Report on the Family Census of 1946.* Vol. 6 of Papers of the Royal Commission on Population. London: H. M. Stationery Office.

Glick, Paul C. 1955. The life cycle of the family. *Marriage and Family Living* **17**: 3–9.

Goldstein, S. 1976. Facets of redistribution: research challenges and opportunities. Presidential address presented at the Annual Meeting of the Population Association of America, Montreal, Canada.

Golini, Antonio. 1967. L'Influenza delle variazioni di mortalità sulla struttura per sesso della popolazione. Società Italiana di Statistica, *Atti della XXV Riunione Scientifica*, pp. 865–898.

Goodman, Leo A. 1953. Population growth of the sexes. *Biometrics* **9**: 212–225.

Goodman, Leo A. 1961a. Some possible effects of birth control on the human sex ratio. *Annals of Human Genetics* **25**: 75–81.

Goodman, Leo A. 1961b. Statistical methods for the mover-stayer model, *Journal of the American Statistical Association* **56**: 841–868.

Goodman, Leo A. 1969. The analysis of population growth when the birth and death rates depend upon several factors. *Biometrics* **25**: 659–681.

Goodman, Leo A., Keyfitz, Nathan, and Pullum, Thomas W. 1974. Family formation and the frequency of various kinship relationships. *Theoretical Population Biology* **5**: 1–27.

Goodman, Leo A., Keyfitz, Nathan, and Pullum, Thomas W. 1975. Addendum to "Family formation and the frequency of various kinship relationships." *Theoretical Population Biology* **8**: 376–381.

Greville, Thomas N. E. 1943. Some methods of constructing abridged life tables. *Record of the American Institute of Actuaries* **32**, Part 1 29–43.

Greville, T. N. E. 1968. Some new generalized inverses with spectral properties. In *Theory and Application of Generalized Inverses of Matrices*. Texas Technological College Mathematics Series No. 4, pp. 26–46. Lubbock: Texas Technological Press.

Greville, T. N. E., and Keyfitz, Nathan. 1974. Backward population projection by a generalized inverse, *Theoretical Population Biology* **6**: 135–142.

Hadwiger, Hugo. 1940. Eine analytische Reproduktionsfunktion für biologische Gesamtheiten [An analytic reproduction function for biological groups]. *Skandinavisk Aktuarietidskrift* (Stockholm) **23**: 101–113.

Hajnal, J. 1955. The prospects for population forecasts. *Journal of the American Statistical Association* **50**: 309–322.

Hammel, Eugene A. 1972. The matrilateral implications of structural cross-cousin marriage. In *Proceedings of the Advanced Seminar in Anthropology and Demography* edited by Ezra Zubrow. Santa Fe, Calif.: School of American Research.

Hammel, E. A., et al. (1976) *The Socsim Demographic-Sociological Microsimulation Program*. Institute of International Studies. Berkeley: University of California.

Harris, Theodore E. 1963. *The Theory of Branching Processes*. Englewood Cliffs, N. J.: Prentice-Hall.

Hatzold, Otfried. 1974. "Possibilities of a pre-conceptional sex-determination and their effects on sex ratio at birth." Program summary of the research project. University of Munich, Germany. (Mimeographed)

Heer, David M. 1966. Economic development and fertility. *Demography* **3**: 423–444.

Henry, Louis. 1960. Mesure indirecte de la mortalité des adultes. *Population* **15**: 457–465.

Henry, Louis. 1969. Schémas de nuptialité: déséquilibre des sexes et célibat, *Population* **24**: 457–486.

Henry, Louis. 1972. *On the Measurement of Human Fertility: Selected Writings of Louis Henry*. Translated and edited by Mindel C. Sheps and Evelyne Lapierre-Adamcyk. Amsterdam: Elsevier.

Herglotz, G. 1908. Über die Integralgleichungen der Elektronentheorie [Concerning the integral equations of the electron theory]. *Mathematische Annalen* **65**: 87–106.

Hernes, Gudmund. 1972. The process of entry into first marriage. *American Sociological Review* **27**: 173–182.

Hertz, P. 1908. Die Bewegung eines Elektrons unter dem Einflusse einer stets gleich gerichteten Kraft [The movement of an electron under the influence of a force of constant unchanging direction]. *Mathematische Annalen* **65**: 1–86.

Hirschman, C., and Matras, J. 1971. A new look at the marriage market and nuptiality rates, 1915–1958. *Demography* **8**: 549–569.

Hoem, J. M. 1971. On the interpretation of the maternity function as a probability density. *Theoretical Population Biology* **2**: 319–327.

Jain, A. K. 1969. Fecundability and its relation to age in a sample of Taiwanese women. *Population Studies* **23**: 69–85.

Janowitz, Barbara S. 1971. An empirical study of the effects of socioeconomic development on fertility rates. *Demography* **8**: 319–330.

Jordan, C. W. 1952. *Life Contingencies.* Chicago: Society of Actuaries.

Karmel, P. H. 1948a. The relations between male and female nuptiality in a stable population. *Population Studies* **1**: 352–387.

Karmel, P. H. 1948b. An analysis of the sources and magnitudes of inconsistencies between male and female net reproduction rates in actual populations. *Population Studies* **2**: 240–273.

Karmel, P. H. 1950. A note on P. K. Whelpton's calculation of parity-adjusted reproduction rates. *Journal of the American Statistical Association* **45**: 119–124.

Kemeny, J. G. Snell, J. L., and Thompson, G. L., 1974. *Introduction to Finite Mathematics.* New York: Prentice-Hall.

Kendall, David. 1949. Stochastic processes and population growth. *Journal of the Royal Statistical Society*, Series B **11**: 230–264.

Kendall, Maurice G., and Stuart, Alan. 1958. *The Advanced Theory of Statistics.* 3 vols. New York: Hafner.

Keyfitz, Nathan. 1968. *Introduction to the Mathematics of Population.* Reading, Mass.: Addison-Wesley.

Keyfitz, Nathan. 1969. Age distribution and the stable equivalent. *Demography* **6**: 261–269.

Keyfitz, Nathan. 1972. Population waves. In *Population Dynamics*, edited by T. N. E. Greville, pp. 1–38. New York: Academic Press.

Keyfitz, Nathan. 1973. Individual mobility in a stationary population. *Population Studies* **27**: 335–352.

Keyfitz, Nathan, and Flieger, Wilhelm. 1968. *World Population: An Analysis of Vital Data.* Chicago: University of Chicago Press.

Keyfitz, Nathan, and Flieger, Wilhelm. 1971. *Population: Facts and Methods of Demography.* San Francisco: W. H. Freeman.

Keyfitz, Nathan, Nagnur, Dhruva, and Sharma, Divakar. 1967. On the interpretation of age distributions. *Journal of the American Statistical Association* **62**: 862–874.

Kitagawa, Evelyn M. 1964. Standardized comparisons in population research. *Demography* **1**: 296–315.

Krakowski, Martin. 1972. Lacunology, entropy, and keeping up with the Joneses. In *The Mathematics of Large-Scale Simulation*, edited by Paul Brock, pp. 55–59. Simulation Councils Proceedings Series, Vol. 2, No. 1.

Kunstadter, Peter, et al. 1963. Demographic variability and preferential marriage patterns. *American Journal of Physical Anthropology*, New Series **21**: 511–519.

Lachenbruch, Peter A. 1967. Frequency and timing of intercourse: its relation to the probability of conception. *Population Studies* **21**: 23–31.

Lachenbruch, P. A., Sheps, M. C., and Sorant, A. M. 1973. Applications of POPREP, a modification of POPSIM. In *Computer Simulation in Human Population Studies*, edited by Bennett Dyke and Jean W. MacCluer, pp. 305–328. New York: Academic Press.

Le Bras, Hervé. 1973. Parents, grandparents, diaeresis bisaïeux. *Population* **28**: 9–37 (English translation Kenneth Wachter, Ed., *Quantative Studies in Historical Social Structure*, Academic Press 1977. In press.)

Le Bras, Hervé, and Chesnais, Jean-Claude. 1976. Cycle de l'habitat et âge des habitants. *Population* **31**: 269–298.

Lee, Byung Moo, and Isbister, John. 1966. The impact of birth control programs on fertility. In *Family Planning and Population Programs*, edited by B. Berelson. Chicago: University of Chicago Press pp. 737–758.

Lee, Ronald D. 1968. Population cycles. Unpublished manuscript. Department of Economics, Harvard University.

Lee, Ronald D. 1974. The formal dynamics of controlled populations and the echo, the boom and the bust. *Demography* **11**: 563–585.

Leibenstein, Harvey. 1974. An interpretation of the economic theory of fertility: Promising path or blind alley? *Journal of Economic Literature* **12**: 467–479.

Leslie, P. H. 1945. On the use of matrices in certain population mathematics. *Biometrika* (London) **33**: 183–212.

Leslie, P. H. 1948. Some further notes on the use of matrices in population mathematics. *Biometrika* (London) **35**: 213–245.

Lewis, E. G. 1942. On the generation and growth of a population. *Sankhya, Indian Journal of Statistics* (Calcutta) **6**: 93–96.

Lexis, W. 1875. *Einleitung in die Theorie der Bevölkerungs-Statistik* [*Introduction to the Theory of Population Statistics*]. Strasbourg: Trubner.

Liu, P. T., Chow, L. P., and Abbey, H. 1972. A study of IUD retention by curve fitting. *Demography* **9**: 1–11.

Livi, Livio. 1974. *Trattato di Demografia*. 2 volumes. Padova: Cedam.

Lopez, Alvaro. 1961. *Problems in Stable Population Theory*. Princeton, N. J.: Princeton University, Office of Population Research.

Lotka, Alfred J. 1922. The stability of the normal age distribution. *Proceedings of the National Academy of Sciences* **5**: 339–345.

Lotka, Alfred J. 1931. Orphanhood in relation to demographic factors. *Metron* (Rome) **9**: 37–109.

Lotka, Alfred J. 1939. *Théorie analytique des associations biologiques*. Part II. *Analyse démographique avec application particulière à l'espèce humaine*. Actualités Scientifiques et Industrielles, No. 780. Paris: Hermann et Cie.

Lotka, Alfred J. 1948. *Application of recurrent series in renewal theory*. Annals of Mathematical Statistics **19**: 190–206.

Lowry, I. S. 1964. *A Model of Metropolis*. Santa Monica, Calif.: Rand Corporation.

Macdonald, George. 1965. The dynamics of helminth infections, with special reference to schistosomes. *Transactions of the Royal Society of Tropical Medicine and Hygiene* **59**: 489–506.

Majumdar, H., and Sheps, Mindel C. 1970. Estimators of a Type I geometric distribution from observations on conception times. *Demography* **7**: 349–360.

March, James G. 1975. Comments at Conference on the Demography of Education, Harvard University, April.

Marks, Eli S., Seltzer, William, and Krotki, Karol J. 1974. *Population Growth Estimation: A Handbook of Vital Statistics Measurement*. New York: Population Council.

Martin, M. D. P. 1967. Une application des fonctions de Gompertz à l'étude de la fécondité d'une cohorte. *Population* **22**: 1085–1096.

Masnick, George S., and McFalls, Joseph A., Jr. 1976. The twentieth century American fertility swing: A challenge to theories of fertility. Paper presented at the Annual Meeting of the Population Association of America.

May, Robert M. 1973a. *Model Ecosystems*. Princeton, N.J.: Princeton University Press.

May, Robert M. 1973b. Time-delay versus stability in population models with two and three trophic levels. *Ecology* **54**: 316–325.

McDonald, John. 1973. Sex predetermination: Demographic effects. *Mathematical Biosciences* **17**: 137–146.

McFarland, David D. 1969. On the theory of stable populations: A new and elementary proof of the theorems under weaker assumptions. *Demography* **6**: 301–322.

McFarland, David D. 1970. Effects of group size on the availability of marriage partners. *Demography* **7**: 411–415.

McFarland, David D. 1975a. Some mathematical models of marriage formation and their relevance to fertility models. *Social Forces* **54**: 66–83.

McFarland, David D. 1975b. Models of marriage formation and fertility. *Social Forces* **54**: 66–83.

McGinnis, Robert. 1968. A stochastic model of migration. *American Sociological Review* **33**: 712–722.

McNeil, Donald R. 1973. *Pearl-Reed Type Stochastic Models for Population Growth*. Technical Report 35, Series 2. Princeton, N.J.: Princeton University, Office of Population Research.

McNicoll, Geoffrey. 1972. Optimal policies in economic–demographic growth models. Ph.D. dissertation, Graduate Division, University of California, Berkeley.

Menken, Jane. 1975. Biometric models of fertility. *Social Forces* **54**: 52–65.

Mode, Charles J. 1975. Perspectives in stochastic models of human reproduction: A review and analysis. *Theoretical Population Biology* **8**: 247–291.

Morrison, P. A. 1971. Chronic movers and the future redistribution of population. *Demography* **8**: 171–184.

Mosteller, Frederick, et al. 1949. *The Pre-election Polls of 1948: Report to the Committee on Analysis of Pre-election Polls and Forecasts*. New York: Social Science Research Council.

Muhsam, H. V. 1956. The utilization of alternative population forecasts in planning. *Bulletin of the Research Council of Israel* **5**: 133–146.

Murphy, Edmund M., and Nagnur, Dhruva N. 1972. A Gompertz fit that fits: applications to Canadian fertility patterns. *Demography* **9**: 35–50.

Nortman, Dorothy, and Bongaarts, John. 1975. Contraceptive practice required to meet a prescribed crude birth rate target: A proposed macro-model (TABRAP) and hypothetical illustrations. *Demography* **12**: 471–489.

Notestein, Frank W. 1945. Population—the long view. In *Food for the World*, edited by Theodore W. Schultz. Chicago: University of Chicago Press.

Oechsli, Frank W. 1971. The parity and nuptiality problem in demography. Ph.D. dissertation, Graduate Division, University of California, Berkeley.

Orcutt, Guy H., et al. 1961. *Microanalysis of Socioeconomic Systems: A Simulation Study*. New York: Harper and Brothers.

Orcutt, Guy H., et al. 1976. *Population Exploration through Microsimulation*. Washington, D. C.: Urban Institute.

Parlett, B. 1970. Ergodic properties of populations, I: The one sex model. *Theoretical Population Biology* **1**: 191–207.

Pearl, Raymond. 1939. *The Natural History of Population*. New York: Oxford University Press.

Pearl, Raymond, and Reed, L. J. 1920. On the rate of growth of the population of the United States since 1790 and its mathematical representation. *Proceedings of the National Academy of Science* **6**: 275–288.

Perron, Oskar. 1907. Zur Theorie der Matrizen. *Mathematische Annalen* **64**: 248–263.

Pollard, J. H. 1973. *Mathematical Models for the Growth of Human Populations*. New York/London: Cambridge University Press.

Potter, Robert G. 1967. The multiple decrement life table as an approach to the measurement of use effectiveness and demographic effectiveness of contraception. In *Contributed Papers*, Sydney Conference, pp. 871–883. Sydney, Australia: International Union for the Scientific Study of Population.

Potter, R. G. 1970. Births averted by contraception: An approach through renewal theory. *Theoretical Population Biology* **1**: 251–272.

Potter, R. G. 1972. Births averted by induced abortion: An application of renewal theory. *Theoretical Population Biology* **3**: 69–86.

Potter, R. G., and Parker, M. P. 1964. Predicting the time required to conceive. *Population Studies* **18**: 99–116.

Pressat, Roland. 1961. *L'Analyse Démographique: Méthodes, Résultats, Applications* [*Demographic Analysis: Methods, Findings, Applications*]. Paris: Presses Universitaires de France, for L'Institut National d'Etudes Démographiques.

Preston, Samuel H. 1969. Mortality differentials by social class and smoking habit. *Social Biology* **16**: 280–289.

Preston, Samuel H. 1970. The age-incidence of death from smoking. *Journal of the American Statistical Association* **65**: 1125–1130.

Preston, Samuel H. 1974. Effect of mortality change on stable population parameters. *Demography* **11**: 119–130.

Preston, Samuel H., for Committee for International Coordination of National Research in Demography. 1975a. *Seminar on Infant Mortality in Relation to the Level of Fertility*. Paris: Committee for the International Coordination of National Research in Demography. (CICRED).

Preston, Samuel H. 1975b. Estimating proportion of marriages that end in divorce. *Sociological Methods and Research* **3**: 435–459.

Preston, Samuel H., Keyfitz, Nathan, and Schoen, Robert. 1972. *Causes of Death: Life Tables for National Populations*. Studies in Population Series. New York: Seminar Press.

Price, D. O., and M. M. Sikes. 1975. *Rural-Urban Migration Research in the United States: Annotated Bibliography and Synthesis*. Washington, D.C.: U.S. Government Printing Office.

Ralston, A. 1965. *A First Course in Numerical Analysis*. New York: McGraw-Hill.

Rao, C. R., and Mitra, S. K. 1971. *Generalized Inverse of Matrices and Its Applications*. New York: John Wiley & Sons.

Reed, Lowell J., and Merrell, Margaret. 1939. A short method for constructing an abridged life table. *American Journal of Hygiene* **30**: 33–62.

Repetto, Robert. 1972. Son preference and fertility behavior in developing countries. *Studies in Family Panning* **3**: 70–76.

Rhodes, E. C. 1940. Population mathematics, I, II, and III. *Journal of the Royal Statistical Society* (London) **103**: 61–89, 218–245, 362–387.

Ridker, Ronald G., Editor. 1976. *Population and Development: The Search for Selective Intervention*. Baltimore: Johns Hopkins University Press.

Ridley, Jeanne C., et al. 1975. *Technical Manual—Reproductive Simulation Model: REPSIM-B*. Washington, D.C.: Georgetown University, Kennedy Institute Center for Population Research.

Rogers, Andrei. 1968. *Matrix Analysis of Interregional Population Growth and Distribution*. Berkeley: University of California Press.

Rogers, Andrei. 1975. *Introduction to Multiregional Mathematical Demography*. New York: John Wiley & Sons.

Rogers, A., and Willekens, F. 1975. Spatial population dynamics. RR-75-24. Laxenburg, Austria: International Institute for Applied Systems Analysis.

Rogers, A., and Willekens, F. 1976. Spatial zero population growth. RM-76-25. Laxenburg, Austria: International Institute for Applied Systems Analysis.

Ryder, Norman B. 1963. The translation model of demographic change. In *Emerging Techniques in Population Research* (39th Annual Conference of the Milbank Memorial Fund, 1962), pp. 65–81. New York: Milbank Memorial Fund.

Ryder, Norman B. 1964. The process of demographic translation. *Demography* **1**: 74–82.

Ryder, Norman B. 1974. The family in developed countries. In *The Human Population*, pp. 81–88. A Scientific American Book. San Francisco: W. H. Freeman.

Ryder, Norman B., and Westoff, Charles. 1967. The trend of expected parity in the United States. *Population Index* **33**: 153–168.

Samuelson, Paul A. 1976. Resolving a historical confusion in population analysis. *Human Biology* **48**: 559–580.

Savage, I. Richard. 1973. *Sociology Wants Mathematics*. FSU Statistics Report M-247. Tallahassee, Fla: Florida State University.

Scarborough, James B. 1958. *Numerical Mathematical Analysis*. Fourth Edition. Baltimore: Johns Hopkins Press.

Schoen, Robert. 1970. The geometric mean of the age-specific death rates as a summary index of mortality. *Demography* **7**: 317–324.

Schoen, R. 1975. Constructing increment-decrement life tables. *Demography* **12**: 313–324.

Schultz, T. Paul. 1973. A preliminary survey of economic analysis of fertility. *American Economic Review* **63**: 71–78.

Schultz, T. Paul. 1974. *Fertility Determinants: A Theory, Evidence, and an Application to Policy Evaluation*. Prepared for Rockefeller Foundation and Agency for International Development. Rand Corporation.

Schultz, T. Paul. 1976. Interrelationships between mortality and fertility. To appear as Chapter 8 in *Population and Development: The Search for Selective Interventions*, edited by R. G. Ridker. Baltimore: Johns Hopkins Press.

Schultz, T. W., Editor. 1974. *Economics of the Family: Marriage, Children, and Human*

Capital. Chicago: University of Chicago Press. (Also appeared as supplements to *Journal of Political Economy*, March/April 1973 and March/April 1974.)

Sharpe, F. R., and Lotka, A. J. 1911. A problem in age-distribution. *Philosophical Magazine*, Ser. 6, **21**: 435–438.

Shepard, Donald S. 1976. Prediction and incentives in health care policy. Ph.D. dissertation, Kennedy School of Government, Harvard University.

Shepard, Donald, and Zeckhauser, Richard. 1975. The assessment of programs to prolong life, recognizing their interaction with risk factors. Discussion Paper 32D. Cambridge, Mass.: Kennedy School of Government, Harvard University.

Sheps, Mindel C. 1959. An examination of some methods of comparing several rates or proportions. *Biometrics* **15**: 87–97.

Sheps, Mindel C. 1963. Effects on family size and sex ratio of preferences regarding the sex of children. *Population Studies* **17**: 66–72.

Sheps, Mindel C. 1964. On the time required for conception. *Population Studies* **18**: 85–97.

Sheps, Mindel C., and Menken, Jane A. 1973. *Mathematical Models of Conception and Birth*. Chicago: University of Chicago Press.

Sheps, Mindel C., and Perrin, E. B. 1963. Changes in birth rates as a function of contraceptive effectiveness: some applications of a stochastic model. *American Journal of Public Health* **53**: 1031–1046.

Sheps, Mindel C., and Ridley, Jeanne C., Editors. 1966. *Public Health and Population Change: Current Research Issues*. Pittsburgh, Pa.: University of Pittsburgh Press.

Shryock, Henry S., and Siegel, Jacob S. 1971. *The Methods and Materials of Demography*. 2 vols. U.S. Bureau of the Census. Washington, D.C.: Government Printing Office.

Siegel, J. S., and Akers, D. S. 1969. Some aspects of the use of birth expectations data from sample surveys for population projections. *Demography* **6**: 101–115.

Sivamurthy, Matada. 1971. Convergence of age–sex distributions and population change in the presence of migration. Doctoral thesis, Institute of Advanced Studies, Australian National University, Canberra.

Smith, David. 1974. Generating functions for partial sex control problems. *Demography* **11**: 683–689.

Smith, David, and Keyfitz, Nathan, Editors. 1977. *Mathematical Demography: Selected Readings* New York: Springer-Verlag.

Spiegelman, Mortimer. 1968. *Introduction to Demography*. Revised Edition. Cambridge, Mass.: Harvard University Press.

Spurgeon, E. F. 1932. *Life Contingencies*. Cambridge, England: University Press.

Stone, L. O. 1971. On the correlation between metropolitan area in- and out-migration by occupation. *Journal of the American Statistical Association* **66**: 693–701.

Stone, L. O. 1973. Personal communication.

Stone, Richard. 1972. A Markovian education model and other examples linking social behavior to the economy. *Journal of the Royal Statistical Society*, Series A (London) **135**: 511–543.

Stone, Richard. 1975. *Towards a System of Social and Demographic Statistics*. United Nations Statistical Office, Studies in Methods, Series F, No. 18. Sales No. E. 74. XVII. 8. New York: United Nations.

Stouffer, Samuel A. 1940. Intervening opportunities: A theory relating mobility and distance. *American Sociological Review* **5**: 845–867.

Süssmilch, Johann Peter. 1788 (1941). *Die göttliche Ordnung in den Veränderungen des menschilichen Geschlechts, aus der Geburt, dem Tode und der Fortpflanzung desselben erwiesen.* 3 volumes. Berlin: Verlag der Buchhandlung der Realschule.

Sykes, Zenas M. 1969. Some stochastic versions of the matrix model for population dynamics. *Journal of the American Statistical Association* **64**: 111–130.

Tabah, Léon. 1968. Représentations matricielles de perspectives de population active [Matrix representations of projections of active population]. *Population* (Paris) **23**: 437–476.

Thompson, W. R. 1931. On the reproduction of organisms with overlapping generatioᴉ *Bulletin of Entomological Research* **22**: 147–172.

Thonstad, Tore. 1967. A mathematical model of the Norwegian educational system. In *Mathematical Models in Educational Planning.* Technical Report. Paris: Organization for Economic Co-operation and Development. 125–158.

Tietze, C. 1962. Pregnancy rates and birth rates. *Population Studies* **16**: 31–37.

Trussell, James T. 1975. The determinants of the complex roots of Lotka's integral equation. Unpublished manuscript.

Todaro, M. P. 1969. A model of labor migration and urban unemployment in less developed countries. *American Economic Review* **59**: 138–148.

United Nations. 1955. *Age and Sex Patterns of Mortality: Model Life Tables for Underdeveloped Countries.* New York: United Nations.

Verhulst, P. F. 1838. Notice sur la loi que la population suit dans son accroissement. *Correspondence Mathématique et Physique Publiée par A. Quételet* (Brussels) **10**:113–121.

Vincent, P. 1945. Potential d'accroissement d'une population stable. *Journal de la Société de Statistique de Paris* **86**: 16–29.

Waugh, W. A. O'N. 1971. Career prospects in stochastic social models with time-varying rates. *Fourth Conference on the Mathematics of Population.* East–West Population Institute, Honolulu.

Weck, Frank A. 1947. The mortality rate and its derivation from actual experience. *Record of the American Institute of Actuaries* **36**: 23–54.

Westoff, Charles, Potter, Robert G., Jr., and Sagi, Philip C. 1963. *The Third Child: A Study in the Prediction of Fertility.* Princeton, N.J.: Princeton University, Office of Population Research.

Westoff, Charles F., and Rindfuss, Ronald R. 1974. Sex preselection in the United States: Some implications. *Science* **184**: 633–636.

Whelpton, Pascal K. 1936. An empirical method of calculating future population. *Journal of the American Statistical Association* **31**: 457–473.

Whelpton, Pascal K. 1946. Reproduction rates adjusted for age, parity, fecundity, and marriage. *Journal of the American Statistical Association* **41**: 501–516.

Wicksell, S. D. 1931. Nuptiality, fertility, and reproductivity. *Skandinavisk Aktuarietidskrift* (Stockholm), pp. 125–157.

Widjojo Nitisastro. 1970. *Population Trends in Indonesia.* Ithaca, N.Y.: Cornell University Press.

Wilson, Edward O. 1975. *Sociobiology: The New Synthesis.* Cambridge, Mass.: Harvard University Press.

Wilson, Edwin B., and Puffer, Ruth R. 1933. Least squares and population growth. *Proceedings of the American Academy of Arts and Sciences* **68**: 285–382.

Winkler, Wilhelm. 1959. Wieviele Menschen haben bisher auf der Erde gelebt? *International*

Population Conference, Vienna, 1959, pp. 73–76. International Union for the Scientific Study of Population.

Winsor, Charles P. 1932. A comparison of certain symmetrical growth curves. *Journal of the Washington Academy of Sciences* **22**: 73–84.

Wolfenden, Hugh H. 1925 (rev. ed. 1954). *Population Statistics and Their Compilation.* Chicago: University of Chicago Press.

Wunsch, G. 1966. Courbes de Gompertz et perspectives de fécondité. *Recherches Economiques* (Louvain) **32**: 457–468.

Yellin, Joel, and Samuelson, Paul A. 1974a. A dynamical model for human population. *Proceedings of the National Academy of Sciences* **71**: 2813–2817.

Yellin, Joel, and Samuelson, Paul A. 1974b. Non-linear population analysis. Unpublished manuscript.

Yule, G. Udney. 1906. Changes in the marriage and birth rates in England and Wales during the past half century. *Journal of the Royal Statistical Society* **68**: 18–132.

Zelinsky, W. 1971. The hypothesis of the mobility transition. *Geographical Review* **46**: 219–249.

INDEX